Quality

Second edition

John Beckford

London *and* New York

First published 1998
by Routledge
11 New Fetter Lane, London EC4P 4EE

Simultaneously published in the USA and Canada
by Routledge
29 West 35th Street, New York, NY 10001

Reprinted 2000, 2001
Second edition 2002

Routledge is an imprint of the Taylor and Francis Group

© 1998, 2002 John Beckford

Typeset in Perpetua and Bell Gothic by Florence Production Ltd, Stoodleigh, Devon
Printed and bound in Great Britain by
TJ International Ltd, Padstow, Cornwall

British Library Cataloguing in Publication Data
A catalogue record for this book is available from the British Library

Library of Congress Cataloging in Publication Data
A catalog record for this book has been requested

ISBN 0–415–25918–5 (hbk)
ISBN 0–415–25919–3 (pbk)

Contents

CONTENTS

Quality

The second edition of this best-selling textbook provides a complete knowledge platform for all those wishing to study the development of the theory and practice of quality.

This enhanced and updated edition sets the study of the quality movement within the context of management thinking over the course of the twentieth century, and its wide-ranging approach encompasses both traditional approaches to quality and contemporary approaches based on systems thinking.

Quality, Second Edition, retains the structure and substantial content of the first edition with minor revisions where necessary to reflect contemporary developments in quality thinking. Particular differences are:

■ revised and updated chapters which explore the notion of quality in greater depth and relate quality directly to organizational effectiveness;
■ a look at the substantial changes brought about by the introduction of ISO 9000:2000 and an exploration of the links to ISO 14000, ISO 19000 and the Business Excellence Model;
■ a revised examination of BPR which points towards the application of chaos and complexity theories;
■ a completely rewritten approach to statistical methods;
■ a wholly new section on Skills-Based Quality Management – an approach to quality in the professional sector developed by the author and his colleagues;
■ a new section dealing with the Business Excellence Model;
■ new chapters dealing with Sustainable Organization and Skills-Based Quality Management.

The value of the book is further enhanced by:

■ a detailed 'handbook' of methods, tools and techniques;
■ in-depth reviews of the contributions of 'quality gurus';
■ a discussion of contemporary developments in theory and practice;
■ international case studies drawn from both public and private sectors;
■ equal emphasis on the manufacturing and service sectors.

Taken together, these features significantly increase the established appeal of the book to students and tutors of quality programmes, as well as to managers requiring a comprehensive introduction to the subject.

John Beckford lectures extensively at masters and doctoral level and has researched, written and developed a wide variety of management education courses for universities and commercial organizations. He established and is Director of Integra Management Systems Limited, and has worked world-wide in both the public and private sectors with a variety of organizations including Great North Eastern Railway, Hoverspeed, Doncaster and South Humber Healthcare NHS Trust, Parcelforce Worldwide, Fletcher Challenge, Honda (UK) Ltd and Rank Hovis McDougall.

CONTENTS

 viii

Figures

Boxes

Vignettes

Preface to the second edition

INTRODUCTION

In preparing this second edition of *Quality*, I have retained the structure and substantial content of the first edition. While many minor revisions have been made for the sake of clarity, substantial changes have been introduced to reflect the developments in my knowledge in the four years since the first edition was written, and especially to reflect recent changes in the quality arena such as the launch of ISO 9000:2000 and increased use of the Business Excellence Model.

The aims of this book, its target readership, use and structure remain as explained in the preface to the first edition.

THE CHANGES

Chapter 1, 'The Quality Imperative', has been extended to explore the notion of quality in greater depth and relate quality directly to its justification, which rests in increasing organizational effectiveness. The development and application of Skills-Based Quality Management, which takes advantage of the changes to ISO 9000, is discussed in Chapter 27, 'Sustainable Organization', and provides a wholly new Chapter 28.

Following the introduction of ISO 9000:2000, Chapter 21, 'Quality Management Systems', has been completely revised to address the very substantial changes introduced to this standard. The links between these changes and the development of Skills-Based Quality Management are explored. The chapter also examines ISO 14000 and the Business Excellence Model.

Chapter 22, 'Statistical Methods', was the subject of particular criticism from readers of the first edition. It has been rewritten to focus on problems surrounding the use of statistics, while the gurus' methods are explored in the individual chapters of Part two of the book.

I am grateful to readers and critics for the many complimentary comments and observations on the first edition, but where the comments were critical, I have attempted to improve the book to address them. If I have failed to do so, it is not the fault of my critics.

THE AUTHOR

John Beckford was awarded a Ph.D. in organizational cybernetics by the University of Hull and is a corporate member of the Institute of Management Services. He has published numerous refereed journal and conference papers and is regularly invited to deliver seminars and workshops to organizations internationally in both the public and the private sectors.

Commencing his career in the Royal Bank of Scotland, John worked as an internal consultant on organizational effectiveness before leaving the bank to pursue his doctorate. He established Integra Management Systems Limited (previously Beckford Consulting) in 1990 and has worked in the United Kingdom, the Middle and Far East, Australia and New Zealand with organizations in a variety of sectors including finance, steel, public and private healthcare, public education, food, property, retail, manufacturing and transport. These companies include GNER, Fletcher Steel, Hoverspeed, Diethelm Healthcare, Doncaster and South Humber NHS Trust, Honda (UK), Hong Kong Quality Assurance Agency and Sunbase (Hong Kong).

John has researched, written and presented numerous management education courses for universities and commercial organizations. He regularly works with researchers and teams from the Universities of Hull and Manchester, Liverpool John Moores University and Dublin Business School.

Preface to the first edition

INTRODUCTION

The pursuit of organizational effectiveness and success – however that may be defined – through higher quality in products and services is a dominant theme for organizations throughout the world. However, many quality initiatives fail to achieve their objectives or only partially succeed, contributing to improvement but not leading to the higher levels of organizational performance expected. This failure perhaps results from the narrow focus of many quality programmes and a consequent lack of breadth in the understanding of the true role and meaning of quality in organizational effectiveness. Contributing to this lack of success is the apparent desire of many organizations and managers to adopt a relatively simple pre-packaged programme based upon a single approach to achievement of quality.

Drawing on case studies from around the world in organizations such as McDonald's, Cathay Pacific, the Hong Kong Police and Fletcher Challenge Steel, China, and many other private and public sector organizations, this book enables the reader to develop a unique and broad understanding of quality – one which will work for him or her in a particular organization. The book shows the full breadth of approaches and tools available to support a quality initiative and considers the importance of the socio-cultural context in selecting and using these approaches.

THE AIM OF THIS BOOK

There is a substantial body of literature already published in the field of quality – so why yet another book? The principal established texts in the field are those produced by the 'quality gurus' themselves. Each of these takes only the particular author's view of the subject, while books by other writers reflect a bias towards one aspect of the subject or one narrow view of it. None of these provides either the breadth of information or the critical stance adopted in this book. The 'discipline' of quality is now mature; the time is right to develop a non-partisan, complete approach to the subject.

WHO SHOULD USE THIS BOOK?

This book provides a complete and coherent knowledge platform for all those (whether students or managers) wishing to fully understand the theory and practice of quality. It does *not* offer the latest quality-focused 'miracle' cure for all organizational ills. Instead, the book brings together in a single text the plethora of ideas, approaches and methods espoused in the pursuit of quality in recent years. It draws on the published writings of many quality experts and incorporates the practical experience of the author and his associates in using these ideas throughout the world.

It features:

- a complete introduction to quality in the context of management thinking;
- in-depth reviews of the contributions of the 'quality gurus' and contemporary management authors to quality theory and practice;
- international case studies drawing on the public and private sectors;
- particular emphasis on the neglected service sector as well as manufacturing industry.

STRUCTURE

The book is divided into four parts. Part one provides a foundation for the book by considering the arguments surrounding the pursuit of quality, the role of quality in the organization, barriers to its implementation and the developments in management thinking which appear to underpin the quality movement.

Part two provides a critical review of the works of those writers who have made a distinct and valuable contribution to the achievement of quality. These are Philip Crosby, W. Edwards Deming, Armand Feigenbaum, Kaoru Ishikawa, Joseph Juran, John Oakland, Shigeo Shingo and Genichi Taguchi.

Part three moves beyond these traditionally based approaches to consider the value to be derived from contemporary management thinking. This part relates to the quality theme ideas ranging from the emergence of contingency theory to the more radical notions of critical systems thinking, re-engineering and organizational learning.

Part four shifts the focus away from quality theory to quality practice by introducing the methods, tools and techniques used for achieving quality. This section works from basic and common techniques such as process analysis through to current strategies for engaging all of the organization's stakeholders in the quality process and concludes with guidance on implementing quality programmes.

HOW TO USE THIS BOOK

This book, as with all textbooks, provides a simplified perspective of its topic and of the daily realities of pursuing quality in organizations. The information is presented in what seems to the author a logical, systematic order, teasing apart topics which are necessarily closely interrelated.

The clue to successful reading is to recognize the connections which exist between the various parts and topics (these connections are regularly made within the text). The chapters, then, while presented in one particular order, need not be read in that way. Equally, the chapters can be read in a fully sequential manner, although each is intended to be able to stand alone, offering a perspective on a particular topic. Hence, some chapters are short, some long.

Each part of the book commences with a user guide to the content and makes suggestions about how to maximize learning from it. These introductions each summarize the major points made in the contained chapters.

Practical illustrations and short vignettes will be found in each chapter. These are intended to help consolidate learning as well as being informative and entertaining. Many readers will find that remembering the story helps them to remember the key points of the associated chapter. These illustrations arise from the author's own knowledge and practice, or have been contributed by friends and colleagues drawing on their working experience in positions of responsibility for quality.

Each chapter concludes with a question. This may be used either as a formal assignment, or as a discussion topic for classroom or study group work. Attempting to answer these questions will help to reinforce and consolidate learning. If you cannot adequately answer the question, you should revisit the chapter to enhance your knowledge. Working through the book in this way will help you to develop your knowledge in a systematic and critical way.

Acknowledgements

I am extremely grateful to all those who have helped in the development and production of this book. First, to the many managers and students who have debated quality ideas with me and contributed ideas to the book, especially Bing Zeat Mah, John Cox, Tony Fletcher, Mike Gooddie, Sonal Kumar and Mike Smith; their theoretical and practical contributions have altered and shaped my views. Second, are Dr Peter Dudley, with whom I have enjoyed many robust discussions and who developed with me the Skills-Based Quality Management System, Sarah Beadell, Wanda Szeto and Peter Hoyer, who work with me in Integra and who shape and influence the work we do. Third, are the reviewers of the first edition, who have supported the work of preparing this edition and guided my thinking. I have attempted to address the issues they have raised but I remain responsible for any errors, oversights or omissions. Fourth, are the many organizations that have allowed the sharing of their quality experiences – specifically Cathay Pacific; Chesswood Produce Limited; Derwentside District Council; Fletcher Challenge Steel, China; the Hong Kong Police Force (formerly the Royal Hong Kong Police Force); Kennet School, Thatcham, Berkshire, the United Kingdom; McDonald's, Hong Kong; and West Berkshire Music Centre in the United Kingdom. Fifth are Catriona King and the editorial team at Routledge for accepting the idea of the book and supporting its production. Special thanks are due to Sara, who, as well as reading, reviewing and editing the draft text, continues, along with Paul and Matthew, to show amazing tolerance, support and friendship.

Quality:

n. the essential attribute of anything
(Collins, *New English Dictionary*, 1968)

Introducing quality

USER GUIDE

This part of the book provides an introduction to the whole quality debate. Chapter 1, which has been substantially revised from the first edition, looks at the arguments for and against the pursuit of quality, examining economic, social and environmental imperatives. Chapter 2 considers the role of quality in the organization with particular reference to the ongoing debate as to whether it should be considered a strategic or an operational issue. Chapter 3 focuses on barriers to the pursuit of quality, highlighting how the established cultures, systems and processes of organizations inhibit quality initiatives. In Chapter 4, the 'classical' and 'human relations' schools of management thinking are introduced and their apparent influence on the thinking of the quality gurus is elaborated.

This part of the book provides the necessary foundation for a study of quality by examining the four key dimensions:

■   the need for quality;
■   the role of quality;
■   the barriers to its achievement;
■   the thinking which underpins the dominant approaches to management.

Chapter 1

The quality imperative

There is a surplus of everything.
(Tom Peters, 1992)

KEY LEARNING POINTS

Five arguments about quality: economic, social, environmental, service challenge, the problem of quality.

- *Economic*: mature markets, saturation coverage; work follows (relatively) cheap labour; manufacturing drives services income – economies must be balanced; the public sector must deliver better services at the same or lower cost to meet public expectations; the ultimate demand is economic survival;
- *Social*: non-quality goods and services are wasteful of human capabilities and talent; working in a non-quality environment is ultimately demoralizing for the individual; the imperative is to minimize waste of talent and maximize satisfaction;
- *Environmental*: the world has finite material resources; we have a responsibility to minimize waste and environmental damage;
- *Service challenge*: services represent 70 per cent of post-industrial economies, and industrial quality control models do not work in the service context; key to quality in services is skilled people;
- *The problem of quality*: two problems – neo-Taylorist management approach, and isolation of quality to the productive part of the organization; resolution through systemic approach to quality based on doing the right things right in every part and level of the organization.

INTRODUCTION

Quality has emerged as and remained a dominant theme in management thinking over the past fifty years. While the initial approaches arose from American theorists and practitioners, it was predominantly Japanese companies that undertook the early commercial applications. The need for enhanced quality was initially largely ignored or rejected in the West. More recently, organizations throughout the world have begun to embrace the theories and practices of quality, and quality initiatives in the public sector are being actively pursued by many national governments. For example, in the United Kingdom the government has introduced a national plan for modernizing the National Health Service and is supporting this with the National Standards Frameworks, which constitute explicit service standards that must be achieved. Other UK government initiatives include the Best Practice and Best Value programmes, and active support of the Business Excellence Model as a framework for service quality improvement. This chapter is concerned with *why* quality has achieved this pre-eminence among the concerns of so many managers. It presents three arguments for the pursuit of quality – the economic, the social and the environmental – before considering the specific challenge for service organizations. Finally, the chapter considers the problems generated in organizations by the use of the word 'quality' itself. Each of these is pursued through the author's own perspective on the management and achievement of quality.

1.1 THE ECONOMIC IMPERATIVE

During the years immediately following the Second World War, consumer demand grew to such an extent that the manufacturing focus in the Western world was on productivity. Effectively, growing markets were starved of products, and with increasing economic prosperity, everything that could be produced could be sold. Simply, with unfulfilled demand, organizations were under no pressure to focus on the quality of their product and perhaps perceived that they had already achieved the ultimate standards. Coupled to this, consumer expectations of product longevity and reliability were relatively low compared with those of today, as was the technology level of both the products and the manufacturing processes.

As markets matured and growth consequently stabilized, organizations, faced with increasing costs of production – particularly the cost of labour and, in the 1970s, the cost of power – began to challenge their established ways of working. Some organizations further increased the pressure on workers for more productivity gains while pursuing cost reductions in raw materials and through research and development; others relied on the emerging technologies of automation, robotics and electronic data processing. Most adopted a mix of these approaches. Where technologically and financially feasible, other organizations followed the more conventional approach of exporting jobs to lower-cost manufacturing centres, especially in South-East Asia. Rather than reducing costs through improving their processes, they relocated manufacturing plants to take advantage of lower-cost labour.

This phenomenon of chasing cheap labour can be traced from the late nineteenth century, when manufacturing emerged in the United States with its ready supply of cheap land and labour. At that time, European organizations began to establish overseas operations. From the mid-1960s, Western organizations have developed operations in the so-called 'Tiger Economies' of Asia. The first of these to emerge, Singapore, Hong Kong and Taiwan, are now maturing economies (GDP per capita is at or approaching Western levels) and have been losing jobs to their newly emergent and lower-cost neighbours such as Cambodia, Indonesia, Korea and Vietnam.

Following changes in the United Kingdom's economy over recent years, it can be observed that there is a trend by certain Asian companies to relocate manufacturing operations there as labour is relatively cheaper than before, the workforce has the skills required for high-quality manufacturing operations, and the costs of transporting goods are substantially reduced. Notable organizations following this trend include Sony, Nissan, Toyota and Honda from Japan and Lucky Goldstar from Korea. Cathay Pacific Airlines has relocated much of its paper-processing and accounting work to Australia from Hong Kong and a UK airline operates its customer call-centre from the Middle East.

It seems relatively clear that where technology and total costs enable such a move, jobs are attracted to sources of cheap labour. The economic consequences for the originating economies are currently uncertain. However, it is easy to observe relative growth in the wealth of emerging economies and decline in those which are mature. While there may be profits for the 'home' economy to repatriate (after tax!), the jobs and much of the wealth remain in the host manufacturing economy — as this is where the workers spend their wages.

It would seem to be the case that work continues to follow low total production costs. If the observed cycle continues, it should be apparent that the long-term decline of the mature economies is guaranteed as emergent economies develop the skills and abilities necessary to absorb a greater proportion of both manufacturing and service-sector jobs.

In parallel with this phenomenon, and notwithstanding the substantial apparent progress in products, services and information technology in recent years, it also appears to be the case that for many products, with the exception of certain emerging products and services such as computer games and leisure facilities, demand is in effect satisfied.

Consumers are operating in a replacement cycle for a large proportion of established products, for example cars, domestic appliances, home entertainment equipment, even personal computers, although new features and changes in functionality do ensure a degree of obsolescence in some products. In this replacement phase of the product life cycle, consumers are demanding greater reliability and longevity from their purchases, and these characteristics are significant in their decision making. It also appears that for many products, diversity and choice are expanding, with competitive products from emergent economies challenging those of the established players. The number of emergent, relatively low-cost economies has also increased substantially in recent years, not just with the Far East countries but also those of Eastern Europe. Each of these new producers and economies adds to the level of competition in the established markets. A good example of this is in the motor industry, where not only are the products from European, Japanese and US manufacturers available but also those such as Proton, Kia, Hyundai and Daewoo — all with Asian origins. All these are relatively new competitors in the United Kingdom and are attempting to establish themselves throughout Europe at the lower end of the market.

MANUFACTURING ACTIVITY DRIVES THE SERVICE SECTOR

It can be argued that it is largely the wages of manufacturing workers which drive prosperity in the service sector of an economy. Observation of any community which has lost its manufacturing base will tend to confirm this view. For example, south Wales in the United Kingdom, which has largely lost its mining, steel and shipping industries, continues to suffer high unemployment. It has a depressed retail sector, low house prices compared to those in other areas and relatively lower costs/incomes for professional services such as legal and accountancy services. Signs of recovery which were apparent in the late 1990s with the planned establishment of high-technology manufacturing plants in the area have in several cases simply vanished with the apparent over-supply of products and the effective conversion of what were once specialized high-cost items to commodities. It was anticipated that, as in the north-east of England, these high-technology-based jobs would provide the impetus for overall economic recovery in the area, extending to the service sector. This has not yet proven to be the case.

Since 1997 and the so-called 'Asian economic crisis', several of the emerging economies have been struggling to maintain employment and have seen sharp reversals in the previous patterns of economic growth. The impact of this crisis has been severe. Some countries, such as Indonesia, saw massive collapse of their currency values; major industrial combines have seen large falls in business volumes and looming bankruptcy. Hong Kong and Singapore have seen substantial reductions in the numbers of both business visitors and tourists, with consequent impacts on the service sector: reduced hotel bookings and under-utilized airport facilities, knocking on to both service and manufacturing sector employment. This apparent reversal in the fortunes of these countries may not have been a crisis at all, simply a reflection of the fact that the sustained growth over many years had changed such that the economic advantage of lower relative total costs for the provision of goods and services no longer applied. Certainly this would be the case for Japan, Hong Kong and Singapore, the living standards of which are now often at least as high as those in most Western economies.

So much for private industry, but what of the public sector – does the same economic imperative apply? The pursuit of quality is equally important to this sector of every economy. From their behaviour and actions throughout the world, governments can be observed to be dissatisfied with the cost and effectiveness of many public services. There has been for some years a trend towards privatization, commercialization or agency status of many public sector bodies. Such changes impose on them many of the same commercial constraints faced by private sector, profit-oriented institutions. It seems to be the case that the share of GDP absorbed by governments is unacceptable to many voters and potentially damaging to economies, given, for example, the tendency for organizations to relocate from economies with high employment costs to lower-cost ones. An example of this can be seen in the acquisition by BMW of Rover (now largely sold off as MG Rover and seeking survival as an independent manufacturer of sporting cars). Mercedes is believed to be exploring a similar move and has already established assembly plants outside Europe, while other companies have made further substantial investments in the United Kingdom. The current mantra for many is that low taxation equals greater wealth creation, which in turn implies job creation and a satisfied society.

At the same time, in those relatively wealthy established economies such as the United Kingdom, there is a drift of public service consumers away from the public offerings towards private services. This occurs where the public service is perceived to be failing to meet the needs of its consumers. Examples include the apparent trend in the United Kingdom towards private healthcare, or the preference among some parents for grant-maintained schools. If these public services do not address the problems which their users observe, then they must eventually fall into disrepair, either collapsing altogether through lack of public support or offering a second-rate service to the less well off members of the society which supports them, thereby increasing the unit cost of such provision. The pursuit of quality in their products and services offers these institutions the opportunity to provide services comparable to those available in the private sector. There is nothing inherently 'better' about a privately owned and offered service than a public one. It is merely that the economic imperative for survival has traditionally been greater in the private sector.

The economic imperative for quality is, then, essentially quite simple. The imperative is survival for the individual organization and ultimately the total economy. The 'gurus' promise that achieving quality will reduce costs and improve productivity, and certainly many of the tools will lead towards these things. As consumers become more selective in their choices, quality has ceased to be an optional extra and become essential for any organization in a saturated marketplace. From the perspective of the total economy of a nation, it is more cost-effective to cure quality problems than it is to export jobs or lose them to alternative or overseas suppliers.

1.2   THE SOCIAL IMPERATIVE

In parallel with the developments in technology over the past fifty years or so has been massive development in our understanding of humankind. Through the works of management writers and practitioners such as Barnard (executive functions), Mayo, Herzberg and McGregor (human psychology), Beer (organizational cybernetics), Ackoff and Checkland (soft systems), management theorists and scientists have become aware of many alternative ways of designing and managing jobs and organizations. However, clinging to the homespun philosophical and short-term arrogance of 'If it ain't broke, don't fix it', managers and academics have collectively failed to embrace the many possibilities that these developments in thinking make available to us. Many academics (though by no means all) at universities and colleges continue to teach classical methods either because these are all they know or because they reject the 'new' ideas. Expansion of higher education opportunities has led to a situation where not all lecturers can be active researchers in the disciplines which they teach, and with increasing teaching loads they struggle to keep up to date with emerging ideas. Those who are active researchers tend to be engaged in those relatively few institutions which are well established and well funded. Practically, for managers it is often easier in the short term to keep things as they are – particularly when the focus is forced onto the short-term financial performance measures by higher management and external demands.

To bring about change in the established order of anything always involves the expenditure of energy – to overcome the initial resistance, to persist with the change programme through the 'painful' times, to provide the changed infrastructure to support the new order. Similarly, the impact of the change programme may, at least in the short term, reduce the ability of the organization to acquire fresh supplies of energy. This energy, for most organizations, is expressed in the form of money. Where the money is not made available, for example in the public sector or in low-margin industries (commodity manufacturing and distribution), or where the demand for high investment returns restricts the available cash, then the change programmes will fail.

An equivalent energy is required from the most senior management in terms of their commitment to supporting the change. Although it is most frequently expressed in financial terms, the failure of support very often rests in the very human desire of managers to work with what they understand, deliver what has worked in the past and seek to preserve their power and position within the organization. It is a rare manager who will voluntarily relinquish his or her own power base for the good of the organization. Observing change programmes is a little like watching a corrupt game of musical chairs at the senior level: when the music stops, everybody is sitting in a different place, but there are the same number of chairs as at the outset! Consequently, the ways in which we run organizations and manage people are often extremely wasteful of the human capabilities and talent of the majority.

What is perhaps worse is that many of the people affected by inefficient, ineffective systems know both that the system is ineffective and, importantly, how to fix it. Such systems are not only wasteful but demoralizing and destructive to the talents of their members and users. It is staggering how often those responsible for a job can identify a short cut which enables the job to be completed on time and within specification, whereas the organization of the system itself would drive towards at least one and often both of these important parameters being missed.

One effect of the failure of organizations fully to exploit the talents they employ is that they lose them! Recent years have seen a huge rise in the number of new professional service organizations whose proprietors and directors have become disenchanted with the limitations of life in large organizations and who have the confidence and ability to build their own, independent organizations. The joke on the large organizations is that they then, very often, hire back at much greater expense the very set of talents and skills which they had previously failed to exploit! The large organization loses in two ways: it has to compete actively to obtain the particular skills it needs at higher cost, and the career model provided to young employees features the organization as victim rather than predator. The underlying message to talented young staff is that they will not be able to exploit their talents within the organization.

At the operational level, organizations have in many cases failed to respond to improvements in our understanding of human behaviour and in levels of education. They continue to manage their staff through a Taylorist mental model, imposing bureaucracy and regulation and insisting on mindless adherence to 'the procedure'. While there are many circumstances in which adherence to the procedure is essential for safety or consistency, there are similarly many circumstances where 'the procedure' inhibits rather than enhances quality. This particularly applies to the service sector and will be explored in section 1.4. Even in manufacturing, the regulatory and policing burden imposed by a heavily proceduralized organization could be substantially reduced by a higher initial investment in training. The benefit obtained from this would at least outweigh the cost of providing it. A well-trained member of staff who understands *why* something should be done in a particular way will do so willingly, reducing the cost of supervision. Perhaps more importantly, he or she will be able to appreciate when the procedure has become inappropriate and, if not free to change it, will at least be able to bring it to the attention of those who have that authority. 'I was only following orders' is not a guarantee of success in manufacturing any more than in any other walk of life. Relatively well-educated staff in a relatively wealthy, high-employment economy have choices. If they are not treated appropriately, they will exercise them!

If, as can be shown to be the case, individuals have the capacity to perform more complex tasks to higher standards or in greater volume than the system permits, then managers are wasting resources. This is in itself sufficient evidence of the need for change, quite apart from the potential benefit to the human spirit that change could offer. From the perspective of social cohesion, it must be the responsibility of every manager to maximize the opportunity for development for each of his or her fellow workers. This will surely lead to a more satisfied workforce, a commitment to the organization and a society more at ease with itself.

The negative risk of minimizing apparent waste of human resources is that if quality is achieved, and markets do not grow to absorb increased higher volume outputs, there may be a substantial increase in levels of unemployment. This will arise because organizations will find it unnecessary (and costly – since there are indirect additional costs involved in employing extra staff) to retain current numbers of employees. Such pressures led in the 1980s to the fashion for 'down-sizing' in organizations, reducing staff numbers to the minimum level.

As has been seen in many conurbations in developed countries over the past twenty years, high levels of unemployment tend to create conditions of social isolation, a sense of hopelessness and unease, often leading to unrest and what we call anti-social behaviour such as drug and alcohol abuse or increasing crime rates. Examples of this were riots in Liverpool, Birmingham and other UK cities, an increase in drug abuse reported in crime statistics, increased levels of shoplifting, and a rise in illegitimate births, particularly among teenagers. It cannot be regarded as acceptable that by achieving quality we also achieve social destruction. Neither can it be regarded as sustainable to produce poor-quality outputs in order to maintain employment in the short term – above all else, consumer markets will not allow this. A substantial debate is required to address this issue. After all, it may be argued that by succeeding in the pursuit of quality, any particular country will act as an attractor of industries, leading to economic success for that country. Inevitably this will have international consequences which are beyond the capacity of any individual or normal organization to address. In the meanwhile, the markets will not wait, and action must be taken to preserve, maintain and develop all industries.

The second imperative for quality, then, stems from the responsibility of all managers to minimize waste of costly human resources and maximize satisfaction through work for their colleagues in order to support social cohesion within their own sphere of influence.

1.3 THE ENVIRONMENTAL IMPERATIVE

The third imperative for quality is environmental. As a result of the experiments and perspectives of writers such as Lovelock (1979, 1988, 1991) and the emergence of the environmental movement, it is now widely recognized that the world has only finite supplies of natural resources, particularly fossil fuels, and that the use of these appears damaging to the total ecology of the planet. Renewable energy sources, such as solar power, wind energy or wave energy, are not yet readily available, nor as cheap as may be possible in the future. While Lovelock in *Homage to Gaia* (2001) has presented an argument for the adoption of nuclear power as an available alternative to fossil fuels, this is unlikely to prove any more acceptable to the established power groups than his arguments against fossil fuels did in the 1970s.

The need for change has, however, been recognized. International accords are being actively pursued to reduce fossil fuel emissions, and the Kyoto Agreement, which demands substantial reductions in harmful emissions, also heralds the emergence of a market in which the right to produce emissions can be bought and sold. This provides an economic incentive for organizations to pursue the environmental imperative.

At a national level a number of initiatives are being pursued in this area. In the United Kingdom, the SIGMA Project (Sustainability: Integrated Guidelines for Management), sponsored by the British Standards Institution, the Department for Trade and Industry and an increasing number of private and public sector organizations, is developing guidelines for the creation of environmentally sustainable organizations. It might be argued that the narrow focus on environmental sustainability detracts from the broader arguments about the overall sustainability of organizations, but nonetheless, the project indicates that organizations cannot any longer afford to ignore this subject. It is to be expected that the guidelines, even if they do not gain the force of law, will in due course certainly become recognized as the principles for best practice and there will be a societal expectation that they will be adhered to. Perhaps, as with certification to ISO 9000 in certain countries, adherence to the principles of SIGMA will become a qualifying factor for government contracts.

Operating our organizations without a sharp focus on quality is to be wasteful of limited resources. It is argued that quality products, processes and systems minimize the use of all the factors of production (human, material, land and money) and thereby minimize damage to the environment. For example, a process which achieves Crosby's 'Zero Defects' or Shingo's 'Poka-Yoke' standard involves no rework or rectification. A process such as this makes minimum use of money, materials and labour in obtaining its output and consequently reduces damage to the environment compared with a process producing any number of defective outputs.

Clearly, with the exception of fictional characters such as Superman, it is too much to expect any one individual or organization to 'save the world'. Each individual or organization can, however, be expected to make a contribution to saving the world at the appropriate level – that is, their own level and the ones above and below. The levels could be thought of as the individual, the organization, the stakeholders, the local community, the national community and the international community.

All individuals have a responsibility to themselves and their employers to minimize use of resources in the completion of their duties. The organization must support this by creating the conditions which enable the individual's work to be carried out with minimum waste, for example by ensuring that tools are properly functional (sharp, accurate), that sufficient time is permitted for the task to be carried out with appropriate care and that the individual worker holds the necessary skill set to complete competently the given task.

The management have the additional responsibility of considering the total effectiveness of the organization in terms of its use of all resources and the environmental implications of their actions. This may mean undertaking additional investments to reduce environmental damage. This approach must of course be supported by the other stakeholders in the enterprise, in particular the shareholders, who must accept responsibility for the actions of the organization and be prepared to accept the returns generated by an organization which fully accepts its responsibilities – even if these are less in the short term than those offered by competing investments.

A substantial conflict may arise for some companies when it comes to additional investment. In the chemicals industry, economic reality is that simply to keep pace with their competitors, organizations in this sector must reduce costs, year on year, by around 3 per cent. In an industry dominated by high-volume manufacturers of predominantly low-margin commodity products, this is a challenging target, especially for smaller companies. When coupled to increases in the regulatory load governing the behaviour of the organization and the testing, storage and use of its products, the target becomes harder. To achieve sustainable improvements in quality (however that may be defined in the circumstances), to enhance the skill set of the employees and to ensure the long-term viability of the organization against this background of, in effect, falling margins is harder still. It may well be that the only truly sustainable business strategy (as far as the capital held by the organization is concerned) is to leave the industry! The ultimate challenge is not simply to improve quality and reduce costs to remain competitive but to achieve a position which satisfies competing ethical demands: the imperatives to preserve jobs for society, to improve the quality of the product, to minimize damage to the environment, to avoid imperilling the local (or wider) community and to satisfy shareholder demands.

The community in which the organization exists must hold and impose expectations concerning the behaviour of the organization as regards environmental matters while at the same time accepting its own responsibilities. For example, if it wishes to continue purchasing the relevant product, the community must impose expectations as regards the dumping of waste, but must also provide an appropriate mechanism for such dumping to take place. Economically, certain resources can be provided only at the community level, for example incinerators and recycling plants. The responsibility of the community is to ensure that these are available.

At a national level, the same considerations apply. The nation has a responsibility to itself, its constituents and the international community. This responsibility includes setting, maintaining and enforcing environmental standards and expectations, and creating conditions (perhaps through the use of taxes and duties) which reinforce those expectations.

At the international level, the responsibilities are much the same. Creation and enforcement of environmental standards must be undertaken by the international community. While other aspects of organizational life may be very different, for example wage rates, organizational culture and so on, the international community must demand common environmental standards from all those wishing to be part of that community.

At every level, there is a need and a responsibility to educate and inform on environmental matters and to understand the needs from a total rather than a partial perspective. Thus the third imperative for quality is to address the rising desire for reductions in environmental damage, helping to ensure the survival of all species – a responsibility which pertains at every level of the world community.

1.4 THE CHALLENGE FOR SERVICE ORGANIZATIONS

The origins of the quality movement and the philosophies, tools and techniques reviewed in this book rest in the manufacturing sector. It was manufacturing that addressed the contemporary issue of quality and it might be argued has, at least at one level, 'solved' the specific problem of manufacturing quality. The organizational and economic world has, however, changed. In the 1960s, manufacturing was the dominant economic force in every advanced economy; the service sector was relatively small in relation to it, employing small numbers of highly qualified professionals. This situation has substantially changed. In the 'post-industrial' or 'knowledge' economy, manufacturing is generally high-volume, highly automated, highly specialized, highly important, as already stated, but represents a relatively small proportion of total economic activity and employs a similarly small proportion of the workforce. The service sector is now the dominant employer and generator of economic growth. For example in Hong Kong, since the 1960s a strong manufacturing economy, around 70 per cent (depending on the basis of measurement) of economic activity is derived from the service sector. Similar proportions pertain in the Western economies.

The challenge for the service sector is to develop ways of addressing the 'quality problem' which are appropriate to the needs of a sector whose principal asset is people and where the application of the skills and knowledge of those people it employs is the key differentiator between 'good' and 'bad' service. To date, the signs are not encouraging. Many organizations are simply adapting the manufacturing models of quality to the service sector to no great effect.

Manufacturing models of quality, as will be seen in Part two, rely on an outmoded understanding of notions of quality, organization, people and consumers. They tend to be incremental in their impact and create bureaucracy, ultimately falling into disrepute and disuse. The focus of manufacturing-based quality systems is often on doing that which is required to secure the necessary 'badge', not on delivering quality. Applied to the provision of services, these models are mechanistic and alienating, lead to deskilling of the workforce and devalue the notion of professionalism. They generate situations where the words used – 'Have a nice day' – are considered more important than the emotion conveyed. Words without meaning, without sincerity, without commitment, will not suffice for quality in a service organization – particularly one where, however long the procedure chart, it never quite reaches the specific needs of the individual consumer (Beckford and Dudley, 1998; Dudley, 2000). Where the words are insincere, or the customer's problem or need does not fit the organization's procedures, the relationship has no future!

Whereas addressing quality in manufacturing rested on the resolution of tangible, visible, persistent issues, quality in services is totally different. Service quality is directly measurable only in relation to the tangible aspects of the transaction – did the teller cash the cheque and pass over the right amount of money? This is measurable, verifiable, auditable. Did the teller handle this customer in the way that she or he wanted to be handled? Opinions might vary; the teller may well have used the 'right' words, but did he or she employ the 'right' manner? The teller may think so, the customer may not – neither can irrefutably prove their viewpoint.

Service quality is, then, intangible and instantaneous. It perishes with the completion of the transaction and cannot subsequently be verified or audited. It depends not on what actually happened but on how the parties to the transaction feel about what happened. The manufacturing models of quality cannot deal with the problem of service quality because they focus on the tangible, not the intangible, and because the means by which they verify and audit quality are *post hoc*. Service quality cannot be verified after the event; it must be assured beforehand.

The key to quality in service provision is not standardization and verification but skills, knowledge and education. To paraphrase UK prime minister the Right Honourable Tony Blair MP, the key to quality in service provision is people, people, people! The challenge for service organizations is to embrace those notions of process control which can be usefully applied to the service environment and couple them to management of the skills of the staff to assure quality.

1.5 A PROBLEM WITH 'QUALITY'

Inevitably there is more than one 'problem with quality'. The first problem, a precursor to the second, is the way in which organizations pursue quality programmes, very often adopting a neo-Taylorist or neo-managerialist philosophy (Taylor's work is briefly explored in Chapter 4) and driving quality through the traditional models espoused by the gurus (Part two). The second problem is the understanding of precisely what is meant by quality and what is its role in generating effective organizations.

Section 1.2 of this chapter explores the social imperative for quality. It is this imperative which must be recognized in order for organizations to address the first problem of quality. Simply, the traditional, industrial model of quality focuses on control, conformance and standardization. This approach treats the human actors in the situation as expensive, unreliable, unthinking parts and is, in many cases, actively distrustful of them. This leads to expensive, and often ineffective, inspection and audit routines, and on occasion to the generation of products and services which the organization wishes to make rather more than the consumer wishes to buy. In the manufacturing context, consumers simply purchase elsewhere; in the service context, it leads to disuse of the service by the consumers, or to revolt. It has been observed, for example, that the methodology adopted by certain government agencies in the United Kingdom rests on this industrial model and there has, in more than one instance, been vociferous protest from the affected professionals – the nearest they will get to revolution, although potential breakaway groups have emerged in some sections.

Those working within such organizations will, in general, not give their best work to the organization because the organization does not want it. It simply requires them to follow the laid-down procedure. They will act to produce those aspects of performance which the organization measures (normally productivity and some narrow measure of quality such as reject rate) and do the job with the minimum of positive engagement. Given the opportunity, they will seek work elsewhere. The organization, in adopting this model, will simply drive away over time those staff most capable of genuinely adding value to its functioning.

The problem rests in a massive schism between the managers and the managed. The first core assumption underpinning the neo-Taylorist approach is that the managers know best. More often than not, this is simply not the case (Townsend, 1985). The second core assumption is that when things go wrong, as they will in any organization from time to time, it is somebody's fault – and that somebody is not a manager (or at least not a manager at the level of the person identifying the fault!). Thus we create organizations in which the managers instruct the workers in what to do and then blame them when it doesn't work. The key change required is the acceptance of real responsibility and accountability by those who give the instructions and a new generation of

13

organizations where genuine communication occurs between the managers and the managed and there is real collaboration between these participants to solve the problems of the organization.

The first problem is driven by the second problem, and that is the understanding of what quality really means in the context of creating an effective organization. Typically, the focus of quality action has been very narrow, looking only at that part of the organization which makes a physical product or, in the service sector, directly interacts with the customer. The balance of the organization – very often the greater part of it – is uninvolved.

The narrow focus of quality programmes and initiatives followed the early development of the quality movement, which was focused on standardisation and improving manufacturing performance. Such a focus can no longer be considered acceptable when what it often means is that the organization focuses on doing the wrong thing better rather than on doing the right thing! Quality improvement in a product no longer suited to its market for whatever reason will not solve the problems of the organization; it is futile. The organization will simply lose money at a slightly lower rate. Quality in this interpretation means doing the right thing right! By implication, the organization must have a shared understanding of its present and future market or environment; it must have products positioned to meet the known and anticipated expectations of its customers or users; and it must have strategies in place to enable it to respond at an appropriate rate to the changes as they occur. For many managers, this means that their own ego must be subsumed into the organizational interest. Nobody can win unless the organization wins.

An effective organization is capable both of dealing with its current market or environment and of anticipating and responding to emergent changes in that market to ensure its own survival. Quality thought of in that way is not an operational, single-function issue but an organization-wide systemic issue. In such an organization, the impact, either direct or indirect, on every other part is explicitly recognized. Quality will then be embedded in every part and every level of the organization rather than isolated and handed over to the production or customer service director, who cannot possibly deliver it in isolation.

SUMMARY

This chapter has identified and elaborated three imperatives for the contemporary pursuit of quality – economic, social and environmental – and then moved to examine the difficulties and challenges faced by the service sector. From these different perspectives, brief arguments have been developed which not only justify, but collectively demand, that the idea of quality be pursued in every aspect of every organization.

QUESTION

To what extent do the five arguments about quality set out in the Key Learning Points at the start of the chapter apply in your own organization or country?

Chapter 2

Quality: a strategic decision?

Focus on quality, not quantity.
(Jiang Zemin, President,
People's Republic of China, 1996)

KEY LEARNING POINTS

Four levels of management decision: operational; administrative; strategic; normative.

- ■ *Operational*: immediate impacts, day-to-day activity.
- ■ *Administrative*: allocation of resources to achieve objectives.
- ■ *Strategic*: activity scope, development directions.
- ■ *Normative*: the nature of the organization, values, beliefs and expectations.

Quality must be inherent at every level.

INTRODUCTION

The successful pursuit of a quality programme requires the dedication of substantial organizational resources, and it is vital to understand whether and how the programme generates value for the organization. It is evident from the quotation above that China, the world's largest emerging economy, consisting of 1.2 billion potential consumers, is treating quality not just as an organizational issue but as a national one. Such a position reinforces the message that all organizations which want to survive and succeed must take quality seriously.

In this chapter, the role and implications of quality in the organization will be explored through consideration of the conventionally recognized different levels of management decision making (operations, administration and strategy). The idea of 'normative' decision making (Beer, 1979) will be introduced to enhance understanding. The implications for an organization of pursuing quality will be assessed, starting with operational management.

2.1 OPERATIONS

Operational management is concerned with the day-to-day activities which ensure that the organization fulfils its present purposes and objectives. These may include short-run profitability and achievement of particular levels of output, yield or productivity. Operational decisions are generally more or less immediate in their impact on the organization, affecting what happens during a particular day, shift or even part-shift – for example, where there are product changes during the course of a shift. In the service sector, immediate operational decisions are often about the short-term allocation of staff resources to meet continuously varying customer volumes.

The chapters in Part four of this book will show how the traditional tools of quality are predominantly aimed at this operational level. They are intended to assist the manager and staff in the production of quality goods and services on a daily basis, focusing on prevention of error and minimization of rework or rectification, aiming to minimize inspection and to achieve continuous improvement. These things are achieved through the use of measurement system outputs at the shop-floor level to inform devices such as quality circles and work improvement teams. These engage workers in reflection on the difficulties and problems experienced with a product or service and through their joint efforts seek to reduce them.

In terms of the needs of the organization an analogy can be suggested with the ideas of Herzberg *et al.* (1959) on motivation theory (Figure 2.1). Herzberg *et al.* suggested that working conditions affecting motivation fall into two broad bands, hygiene factors and motivating factors. Hygiene factors are those characteristics of the working environment which, if absent, will lead to dissatisfaction. Their presence will not motivate workers but will create conditions in which motivation becomes possible. Motivating factors are those characteristics of the work which will inspire those involved to greater efforts.

For the purposes of this analogy, we can equate the hygiene factors to the need for operational quality. The absence of an operational quality focus will mean higher levels of error and failure. Its presence will not guarantee greater quality since so many aspects are driven by other parts of the organization – for example, planning, design and marketing.

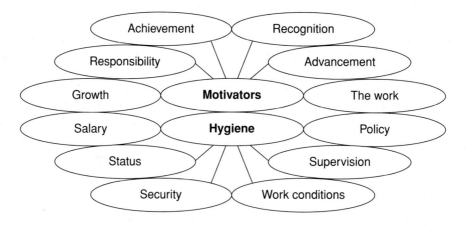

Figure 2.1 *Herzberg's two-factor theory of motivation*

The role of operational management is to achieve the quality expectations of the organiza-tion – but this can be done only within the constraints imposed by higher-order decision making. Clearly, if quality is not an inherent part of the thinking at higher levels in the orga-nization, it will be difficult, if not impossible, to achieve quality at the operational level.

2.2 ADMINISTRATION

Administrative management is concerned with the allocation, use and control of the current operational resources of an organization to achieve its present purposes and objectives. It is the control function for operational management. Administrative managers acting within the constraints imposed on them from higher management seek to maximize the use of resources in the pursuit of organizational goals.

At this level, the first serious constraint upon the achievement of quality comes into focus. The administrative manager, for example a factory or production manager, may find her- or himself in a position of conflict between meeting the customer expectations in terms of volume of product delivered and meeting those customers' expectations concerning quality of product or service. At this point, the priorities imposed upon this manager from above will determine the outcome of any conflict. The question is simply – 'Which does the organization regard as more important to deliver, volume or quality?' In addition to observation of the behaviour of the manager, clues to the answer can be discerned in an examination of the performance measurement system of the organization. If this emphasizes volume, then delivery of volume will prevail at the expense of quality and vice versa.

The quality management system (whether or not certified to ISO 9000:1994, ISO 9000:2000 or other standard systems) will, or should, form a significant part of the perfor-mance management system employed by the administrative manager. However, if quality is not perceived as a priority within the overall management system, then it will probably not be perceived as a priority at this level.

It is also important to realize at this stage that the pursuit of quality does not apply solely to the operational aspects of the organization, but also to all the support and administrative processes which enable it to function. For example, a personnel recruiting system should be thought of as a productive process delivering to the operational system (its customer) staff who meet the skill and personality criteria necessary to perform the tasks required. If it fails to do this, then it is unreasonable to expect the operational processes to function to appropriate quality standards. The same thinking applies to training, to reward systems, to equipment and materials procurement, and so on.

The administrative manager, then, has a dual responsibility for the delivery of quality, neither of which is more important than the other; they are equally necessary. One is to create the operational conditions which make it possible for the product or service to meet customer expectations. The other is to ensure that his or her own systems and processes deliver outputs to the operational 'customers' which meet their needs and expectations.

2.3 STRATEGY

Strategic management is concerned with the scope of the organization's activities: its markets, products or services and market stance. It deals with the questions of how the organization should develop and adapt itself for the future. The strategic process necessarily leads to outcomes with a degree of uncertainty. Strategic decisions are, then, best thought of in terms of probable results rather than the short-term absolutes which may be associated with operational or administrative decisions. Despite or rather perhaps because of this, and as with administrative management, quality must be inherent in the strategic process itself to maximize the probability of success and reduce the chances of failed strategic decisions. The classic and often-quoted example of such a failure is that of IBM, which determined for itself that the future of computing rested in mainframe systems. This decision led to the organization falling behind competitors in the development of personal computers with associated failure, at least initially, to gain market share. The strategic process itself must be subjected to the same rigorous approach to quality as the operational processes. However, it must be considered whether the decision to pursue a quality programme or become a quality organization is itself strategic.

Michael Porter in a *Harvard Business Review* article (1996), in common with this author's thoughts in section 2.1, suggests that 'operational effectiveness and strategy are both essential to superior performance', but also makes the point that 'many companies have been frustrated by their inability to translate those gains [achieved from improved organizational effectiveness] into sustainable profitability'. He suggests that practices such as benchmarking and technology transfers between organizations create conditions where performance gains achieved by one organization are rapidly replicated in others, potentially leading to a sustained stalemate with no long-term winners and no long-term losers, merely an increasing homogeneity of product and service characteristics. If strategic management is about creating and sustaining competitive advantage for an organization, then this suggests that the pursuit of quality, particularly in a collaborative environment, may be the very opposite of strategic. If it acts to reduce competitive advantage rather than increase it, and to increase similarities between organizations, there is potential for all to pursue the same quality goal – which may not represent the true potential of the product or service.

However, that is not to say that the pursuit of quality has no strategic implications. Porter's work implies that every organization in a particular market will seek to emulate the behaviour of the one perceived as 'best'. That is not inevitably the case. Some organizations will not willingly collaborate. They may regard process knowledge (one key to organizational effectiveness) in the same proprietary manner as they regard a particular brand or item of intellectual property – for example, in the petrochemical industry, where the aphorism 'the product is the process' is used. In the United States, for example, it is not unknown for a process to be subject to patent. Equally, because of contextual differences, a working practice which delivers benefits for one organization in a particular cultural or social setting will not necessarily deliver the same benefits for another in a different one. Developing quality programmes internationally has highlighted the extent to which the success of any change or innovation and the business benefit it delivers are a function not simply of its apparent appropriateness to the process but also, to a very great extent, of the knowledge, skills, attitudes and behaviours of both the management and the workforce involved. An innovation which works in London or New York may well not work in Tokyo or Hong Kong and vice versa. Even where cultures are more closely aligned, such as in South-East Asia, what works in Singapore will not necessarily work in Hong Kong. Hofstede (1980) has examined this aspect in some depth.

Thus the apparent loss of competitive advantage will not spread uniformly and universally across any industry.

Meanwhile, the leading organizations – that is, the ones against which others benchmark themselves – will seek continually to further improve their products and processes to sustain their perceived advantage – always provided that they do not become complacent. It is possible to discern, then, that for any industry there will be leaders and followers, with an inevitable time lag between the introduction of an improvement by the leader and its dissemination to others within the industry – through either benchmarking or creative imitation. This time lag will serve to sustain competition within the industry and hence support either price or cost advantage for the leading organizations. It is improbable that any innovation will bring benefits to an entire industry at the same instant except where it is externally driven, such as by governmental or regulatory authority involvement, or where the structure of the industry demands it. Innovation in the banking system, such as a new method of clearing payments between banks, would necessarily have to be adopted by a number of organizations at the same time to actually function. An improvement in operational effectiveness will, then, in most circumstances generate a gain for the innovating organization until that improvement is emulated by others. A focus on constant innovation and improvement fits quite neatly into Porter's (1980) strategy of 'differentiation': the creation of a market perception of value advantage.

However, the strategic implications go much further than this. The comments on strategic management have, so far, been essentially inward-looking – to the organization and the industry. If we now look outwards at the environment, the effect of improved quality on customer behaviour can be examined. For perishable or consumption goods, there is little perceived impact. Improvement in the quality of a loaf of bread or a mushroom may affect customer choice but, if anything, is likely to lead to advantage for one player against others and a slight overall increase in volume, assuming a relatively mature market. It is when we examine consumer durables that the full impact becomes clear.

Any established consumer durable – that is, one in the mature phase of its life cycle – will be subject to constraints of growth in volume. There is only a finite market for items such as cars, washing machines, microwaves or dishwashers. Buying activity in these circumstances is determined by the need to replace, or possibly upgrade, existing equipment. The products have entered the buyer's replacement cycle. The quality of these items, in the consumer's mind, is perhaps determined by a number of factors. Inevitably these will include reliability and longevity, as well as other factors such as price, appearance, noise level in operation, and brand. If, as a manufacturer of consumer durables, we focus on improving reliability and longevity, then the effect is to stretch the replacement cycle (the period of time between purchases), which has a direct impact on apparent market size. Thus improved quality will act to reduce the overall level of sales of a particular item and, if the market is mature, then the growth opportunity for any one supplier is determined by the number of consumers who can be taken from the competitors. In addition to this, the implications loop back into the organization to affect the volume of output necessary for the manufacturer to meet demand. This directly affects every strategic decision made by the organization because those strategic decisions imply the commitment of substantial resources towards a desired outcome. Thinking which follows the pattern:

19

improving quality =
increased sales =
increased manufacturing volume =
requirement for additional capacity

may be fundamentally flawed. First, because quality improvement should lead to greater volume output from existing facilities. Second, because improvements in quality may substantially extend the replacement cycle, leading to a loss of total market volume. The motor industry exemplifies this potential (Vignette 2.1).

It can be concluded, then, that the pursuit of quality must be considered as strategic. First, the process for formulating strategy must exhibit quality characteristics – that is, the process itself must be correctly designed and implemented. Second, the impact of the choice to pursue quality fits with the generic strategy of differentiation. Third, the pursuit of quality has an impact on strategic decisions because it may generate changes in consumer behaviour. This in turn may obviate the need to establish additional facilities or new distribution channels.

2.4 NORMATIVE DECISIONS

The conventionally recognized levels of decision making in organizations have been considered. However, the changing nature of the world of organizations and the increasing concern with ethical issues such as morality, environmentalism, and so on demand that we go further. Normative management decisions are concerned with these aspects, helping to define the nature of the organization itself, that is, the values, expectations and beliefs espoused by its members. The norms so derived should ensure that the organization makes a good ethical fit with all its stakeholders and with society in general.

An organization which does not generate this 'fit' with its stakeholders will either lose customers – because it does not reflect their expectations – or fall into disregard, as have branches of the civil service in many countries. While customer loyalty to organizations, and particularly brands, does exist, to the extent that some brands become synonymous with the product – the Hoover, Sellotape, Post-it notes – and is encouraged through various loyalty schemes (such as air miles or supermarket bonus cards), these will not retain customers who are genuinely unhappy with products or services. Political parties are particularly prone to failure of fit when they do not listen to an electorate that holds them in power. When the norms of a particular political grouping no longer reflect the wishes of their society, they will be deposed, either through democratic process or by revolution. Similar observations can be made of commercial organizations. When the characteristics of the products or services do not meet the expectations of consumers, or the behaviour of the organization is considered unacceptable, the customers will 'vote with their feet' and buy elsewhere. One example of this is those organizations which traded with South Africa during the apartheid era. When sales and profit targets are not met, the shareholders in the organization, increasingly the large financial institutions, will depose the chief executive and appoint a new one in an attempt to correct the situation. Thus it is imperative for organizational survival (and for the self-preservation of those in power) that they listen to the demands of customers and formulate organizational norms which will meet those demands.

VIGNETTE 2.1 **THE MOTOR INDUSTRY**

During the 1950s, 1960s and 1970s, the products of the motor industry, whether American, British or European, were in general (with a few honourable exceptions), regarded as unreliable and expensive. These factors, coupled to the then enormous labour cost difference across the East–West divide, enabled the very rapid growth of the Japanese motor industry and its substantial penetration of the established markets. Cars were generally considered to have a relatively short life of five or six years, and after three years (or around 40,000 miles) to have become so unreliable and prone to breakdown that they needed to be replaced. The ancillary components, for example clutches, steering systems, brake systems and electrical generators, were likely to need replacement at around this mileage.

Faced with the threat of extinction by the rapidly improving quality of imported vehicles, the industry eventually, and with much financial and personal pain, addressed its product quality. It is now a normal expectation that a car will generally be reliable for perhaps five or six years and that components, such as those specified above, have much longer lifespans than before. Mileage has also become a much less important factor in determining the reliability of a vehicle. Service history (that is, a good maintenance record) has become more important. The collaboration of manufacturers and their suppliers has so dramatically improved the quality of the outputs that, almost without exception, manufacturers are struggling to utilize the capacity of their assembly plants. Although the market for new cars is substantially larger than in the 1950s and 1960s, it has not grown to meet the potential numbers of vehicles now available. Consumers are able to rely on second-user vehicles, and with improvements in the longevity of bodywork as well as other components, these maintain a greater proportion of their value. The cost of new vehicles, particularly in the fleet purchaser-dominated UK market, has reached levels where the private consumer is often unwilling or unable to pay the manufacturer's price. What constitutes value for money for those consumers can adequately be met through the used car market or, with advances in communications technology and the increased openness of European markets, by buying abroad at a lower price.

These changes in buyer behaviour, driven by the quality improvements made by manufacturers, have in effect impacted adversely on the strategic decisions to build new factories, launch new products, expand capacity, and so on.

The pursuit of quality by so many organizations in recent years is precisely this kind of response. Consumers in mature markets are seeking the reassurance of reliable, high-quality goods and services (as defined by themselves), with a number and variety of choices available to them. Organizations which do not respond will fail.

The gurus of quality, as will be seen in Part two, all stress the need for senior management commitment to the idea of quality in order to ensure its achievement. Normative management is where this commitment arises. The feedback of consumer expectations to senior management closes the loop for the organization in determining behaviour. This loop explains why senior management must adhere to and believe in this commitment.

Normative decisions determine what questions and decisions are acceptable to the organization at the strategic level. They therefore pre-control (Espejo and Schwaninger, 1993) strategic decision making. Strategic decisions create potential new value for the organization – how profits will be made tomorrow. This in turn pre-controls the potential decisions at the administrative and operational levels – today's profits. At this point, and notwithstanding the potential for marketing activity to influence consumer behaviour, the organization largely loses control to the market. If the normative decisions are incorrect, the consumers will not buy.

In many organizations, the normative decisions are expressed through devices such as mission statements or publicized 'visions' which attempt to express the values for which the organization stands. It is often considered that once this statement has been made, the job is complete. However, if the values so expressed are not enacted in the behaviour of the senior management and in the performance measurement and reward systems of the organization, then the junior management and operational staff will not respond to them. They will rather respond to the actual behaviour and expectations of the senior management measured by what they do and how they act, not by what they say. It is vital, as Professor Charles Handy so eloquently puts it, that the senior management 'walk the talk'.

SUMMARY

This chapter has reviewed the role and positioning of quality in the context of the four levels of management decision making; operational, administrative, strategic and normative. It has made clear that quality must be inherent throughout the organization in order for it to survive. While the principal traditional tools of quality focus on the operational and administrative aspects, this chapter has shown that it must extend well beyond this. If the senior management are not absolutely committed to quality in everything that they say and do, then the organization will not 'care' about quality. If this caring is absent, it is impossible to build a quality organization.

QUESTION

What are the 'norms' of your own organization (either a business or a university/college)? How do you know?

Chapter 3

Barriers to quality

Passive resistance is the most potent weapon ever wielded by man.
(Benjamin Tucker)

KEY LEARNING POINTS

Four principal barriers to quality: systems and procedures, culture, organization design, management perspectives.

- *Systems and procedures*: supporting or inhibiting the pursuit of quality?
- *Culture*: attitudes, values and beliefs. Is the culture supportive of quality?
- *Organization design*: does the organization design support or inhibit quality achievement?
- *Management perspectives*: is quality recognized as a problem? Is the focus right for achieving quality? Is the mindset holistic or reductionist?

Two categories of quality cost: direct, invisible

- *Direct costs*: rework, rectification, defective inputs, inspection.
- *Invisible Costs include*: lost customers, in-process errors, high staff turnover, unnecessary capital costs, reduced availability of working capital.

INTRODUCTION

This chapter aims to introduce readers to some of the many barriers which prevent the achievement of quality. It will identify what those barriers are, how they arise and how they can be identified or recognized. The barriers have been grouped under four main headings:

- systems and procedures;
- culture;
- organization design;
- management perspectives.

These headings encompass a variety of other factors which are considered as symptoms rather than fundamental issues. The final part of the chapter will look at identifying the costs of quality (or the costs of a non-quality process or product).

3.1 SYSTEMS AND PROCEDURES

Many organizations, in particular those which are medium to large in size and long established, operate through a more or less bureaucratic process. That is to say, they are organized through a hierarchical system of offices or 'bureaux' (Weber, 1924) and maintain that organization through formal reports, documents and record keeping. This is not in itself a bad thing; indeed, it is essential to the delivery of a standardized product – particularly in service organizations or those operating through a distributed delivery network such as retail chains or banks. In the absence of a standardized approach, the customer might easily be confused and the organization itself would spiral out of control.

However, problems can arise with such a system. First, the systems and procedures can become fixed – that is, they become 'frozen' into the organization such that pressure for change and adaptation meets with high resistance. In this instance, when change is necessary to meet a new level of customer expectations, it can be difficult to achieve. This is a barrier to the achievement of quality. It can be recognized when staff use expressions such as 'We've always done it like that.' This approach of using precedent as the basis of current decisions is common in many aspects of life, in particular in the practice of law, which relies heavily on past cases and in civil administration. Readers may recall Lynn and Jay's *Yes Minister* (1982), when the fictional Sir Humphrey and the minister James Hacker were discussing the United Kingdom's honours system:

> 'I told him not to be silly. This infuriated him even more.
> "There is *no reason*," he said, stabbing the air with his finger, "to change a system which
>   has worked well in the past."
> "But it hasn't," I said.'

In the contemporary organizational climate, the reliance on precedent must be open to question if emergent threats are to be neutralized and advantage taken of opportunities, even if such precedents were at one time reliable.

A particular problem arises from the use of procedures in service organizations. While, as mentioned in the previous paragraph, procedures help to ensure standardization and repeatability, they can, as suggested in Chapter 1, miss the customer. Every service transaction is unique. They may follow a common pattern – each successive customer at a supermarket checkout goes through an identical process – but the human interaction taking place is specific only to that particular customer. If customers, as they often do, have a problem or issue which does not fit the procedure, then the transaction may *fail* – not in the process itself (though that is possible), but in the human interaction. The customer may walk away dissatisfied with the service.

It is often neither practical nor reasonable in a service transaction to attempt to create a procedure which covers every conceivable circumstance. It is the attempt to do so that leads to bureaucratic management systems of the kind which, so often, fall into disuse and disrepute.

Public and personal safety demand that before an aircraft departs, the cockpit crew work through extremely rigorous pre-flight checklists. These are designed to evaluate every control and safety system to ensure that the aircraft is fit for the flight and that it will not endanger its crew, its passengers or the public at large. This routine is essential and possible. The aircraft, a machine, has a defined and limited number of systems, each of which has two essential conditions, working or not working. Failure or uncertainty in relation to any control or safety critical system means that the aircraft cannot depart.

Compare this with a visit to the dentist. While there is a set of procedural or process steps through which the dentist and patient must pass, neither the dentist nor the patient is a machine. The number of variables in the transaction is incalculable: the mental and physical condition of the dentist, the mental and physical condition of the patient, the moods of both, their past experiences of each other (and of other patients and other dentists), the extent to which the patient is currently suffering pain, the events they experienced on the way to the clinic. Each and every one of these factors will influence the transaction. Now, try to write the procedure chart for this! During the course of a quality project, a dentist was asked to do this. He had written seven pages before he got the patient's mouth open!

Variety, the number of possible states of the system, proliferates enormously in service transactions. Every possible question or requirement from a customer demands a specific response and a route for getting to that response. In a financial services organization, it was calculated that for only six 'core' transactions with clients, variety had proliferated such that they had nearly 3,000 individual procedures, each an adaptation or derivation from another and each designed to meet the specific requirement of a customer or small group of customers. Even with this number of possibilities, there were numerous individual customers who fell through the gaps between the procedures. Such a system has a number of drawbacks. Quite apart from the fact that it continues to fail in meeting customer expectations, the cost of maintaining, policing and auditing it far outweighs its benefit – to either business or customer. A better solution, especially given the highly qualified professional staff employed, would have been to focus on the six core processes, develop and rely on the skills, knowledge and experience of the staff, and then allow them to exercise judgement in closing the gap between the high-order process outcome and the specific requirements of the individual customer. Human beings make excellent variety managers.

The second problem, the perception of what is important, is probably as great a barrier to quality, particularly in the context of a Crosby (1979) style quality programme. Such a programme relies heavily on an exhortative, evangelical approach. In most cases, managers and staff focus on achieving those aspects of performance which are explicitly measured. The systems and procedures of the organization, especially those involving performance measurement, tend to determine which characteristics of the organization receive most attention. For example, Beckford (1993) reports a case of a cake factory where the performance of the production department was monitored against two simple measures: volume throughput and labour utilization. The production managers sought to maximize these two characteristics in their daily work with considerable success. Complaints about quality, arising from either the internal quality control function or from the customers, were acknowledged but ignored in pursuit of productivity. A business issue arising from this case was that the production managers were, in effect, manufacturing for reject. The demand to increase

25

throughput and labour utilization was not capped by the simple expression 'to the extent of customer orders'. In order to keep the plant occupied, the production managers were generating volumes significantly higher than customer demand. The excess production was sold off (at materials cost only) to a local secondary market trader. While outside the direct scope of Beckford's work, it was necessary for the subject organization to redesign its measurement system before any sustainable improvement could be achieved.

The barrier to quality revealed here is that of workforce perception – including all managers. Staff in an organization will seek to achieve the targets which are established through reported measurement – those things which the organization instructs them through its measurement system to regard as important. Discovering such a barrier in an organization is easy. It is simply necessary to look at the way in which performance is measured; this tells you what the organization regards as important. Even where quality performance is formally measured – and often it is not – its importance can be judged against the priority it is given when compared to productivity or other measures.

How to overcome these barriers will be dealt with in later chapters of this book. For now, it is sufficient to say that systems and procedures must be (re)designed to support the achievement of quality, with particular attention paid to the selection of performance criteria. If quality is a desired characteristic of the outputs of the organization, it will somehow, and to some degree, have to be measured and must take account of the expectations of customers – whether internal or external.

3.2 CULTURE

The development of a quality culture is a critical area of the achievement of quality, but what is culture? Clutterbuck and Crainer (1990: 195) describe it as

> a set of behavioural and attitudinal norms, to which most or all members of an organisation subscribe, either consciously or unconsciously, and which exert a strong influence on the way people resolve problems, make decisions and carry out their everyday tasks.

Schein, cited by Clutterbuck and Crainer (1990: 196), suggests that culture describes the 'artefacts, values and underlying assumptions' that govern behaviour within the organization. For the purposes of this book, it is 'values' and 'beliefs' that are the key cultural drivers, although these may be expressed in a variety of ways. They often emerge from the measurement systems and procedures which are seen to communicate to staff and workers what senior management consider important about performance. Eventually, such aspects become culturally embedded – that is, they become a part of the value system of the organization.

Beliefs and values are also often expressed through the rituals, stories and myths of the organization. These are exchanged through both formal and informal processes and may be seen as guiding new entrants towards particular forms of behaviour and attitudes. Those who do not conform may be seen as radicals and remain outside the 'cultural web' (Johnson and Scholes, 1993: 60) of the organization.

Entrenched norms of behaviour are some of the most difficult aspects of an organization to change. Where achievement of quality has previously not been considered important in comparison to achievement of some other target, it requires considerable determination and effort to change the established values. Again, a case history can perhaps explain the point. Many companies are currently abandoning the formal dress codes which grew up in the post-Second World War period, even enjoying 'Dress-Down Friday', when smart casual clothes are expected. Perhaps the most famous example of this is IBM, which adopted a 'uniform' style of dress for its male employees: grey suit, white shirt, boring tie. Adoption of this dress standard was seen as acceptance by the individual of his subordination to the organization – of his becoming a 'company' man. IBM, along with many other organizations, have recently formally abolished the requirement to wear standard office clothes, but how long will it be before the staff themselves accept the change? Fletcher Challenge, one of New Zealand's largest companies, formally abandoned its dress code in the 1980s, yet the majority of staff still adhere to it. The then chief executive of Fletcher Challenge Steel, who had been in the post for over six years, adopted a very informal style: short sleeves, sometimes an open-necked shirt. This was remarked upon by others within the organization, but did not succeed in changing their approach. Relative to changing attitudes to achieving quality, changing the dress code can be considered as easy. Contrarily, in some, but by no means all, Japanese companies, all employees – up to and including the chief executive – wear common corporate workwear. They argue that this approach helps to reduce or even eradicate differences between grades and enhances communication, and that the sense of uniformity increases the common bond between employees.

It has been shown that culture is often a very strong determinant of behaviour. In the next few pages, some specific aspects of organizational culture will be considered.

'Politics' in the organizational context does not usually refer to overt competition between groups with differing ideologies, although this is possible. Normally, it refers to covert competition between various sub-groups in the organization for power – that is, for positions of influence and authority from which they can manage the organization to reflect their own preferences. These groupings may have their roots in a particular technical or functional ability, for example marketing, finance or production, or in common backgrounds, such as among groups of people who joined the organization at the same time and whose careers developed together, or who share the same school or university background, the same religion, the same home town or the same club tie. Working as a subcultural group within the organization's total culture, such groups often exercise immense, frequently tacit influence. When such groupings are strong in an organization, they may place their interests before those of the organization itself. This presents another barrier to quality. From the perspective of such sub-groups, achievement of quality must come to be seen as a meta-cultural requirement. The interests of the particular group must become aligned with, or subordinated to, the interest of the organization in pursuing quality.

A question that links with some of the points already made about measurement systems and about politics is: do the employees of the organization care about the work, and in particular about the quality of the product or service? If they do not, for whatever reason, then quality will probably not be achieved. Such attitudes are often driven by management through the priorities that they set and the results through which they manage the organization. For example, if those who are rewarded well by the organization are those who produce most, regardless of quality, then productivity (output) will be the focus of everyone's attention. If, on the other hand, quality is rewarded in preference to volume, then quality will be dominant.

Achievement of quality, particularly in the *kaizen* (continuous improvement) sense, depends upon an appropriate level of innovation. Creativity (the origination and implementation of new ideas or innovations) is often suppressed in organizations in pursuit of the status quo. This is revealed through the use of such expressions as 'Don't rock the boat' or 'Yes, you're right, but in the interests of your career/overtime/colleagues . . .'. A lack of creativity in the organization is not a sign that the people are not creative, since creativity is inherent in all of us. More frequently it is a sign that their creativity is stifled within the organization and thus has become expressed outside the workplace.

Large or successful organizations often emit a hum of satisfaction. They have an air of complacency and contentment with the way things are which can be almost tangible. Such a situation imposes an immense barrier to quality since there is no apparent compulsion or impetus for change. Frequently such satisfaction is present in organizations which have a short-term focus – perhaps a lack of foresight. They assume that if everything is all right at present, then everything will surely continue to be all right. Disasters and near-disasters frequently overtake such organizations.

VIGNETTE 3.1 **COMPAQ COMPUTERS**

It has been widely reported that in 1990, Compaq, then one of the world's top 400 companies, achieved sales of US$3.6 billion and profits of US$455 million. In the second quarter of the following year, profits fell by 80 per cent. The third quarter produced a loss! The business had been built on an unrivalled reputation for quality; price was seventh on its list of procurement criteria. Thus, while its products enjoyed high quality, its prices to consumers were higher than its rivals'. When market conditions changed so that price became a priority issue for customers, the drone of satisfaction from the company drowned out the warning signals from the marketplace. Compaq subsequently went through a major reappraisal of its strategy in its efforts to return to profit.

This may appear a somewhat perverse story in a book about quality, but it usefully emphasizes the point that quality is not only about quality!

Perhaps the best illustration of lack of foresight is given by Handy (1990a: 7–8):

I like the story of the Peruvian Indians who,
seeing the sails of their Spanish invaders on
the horizon, put it down to a freak of the
weather and went on about their business,
having no concept of sailing ships in
their limited experience. Assuming continuity,

they screened out what did not fit and let
disaster in. I like less the story that a frog if
put in cold water will not bestir itself if
that water is heated up slowly and gradually
and will in the end let itself be boiled
alive, too comfortable with continuity to
realize that continuous change at some
point becomes discontinuous and demands
a change in behaviour.

In the prevailing turbulent business environment, an assumption of continuity is highly dangerous. While the organization is pursuing quality, with its implications of continuous improvement, standardization and regularity, it is equally vital for it to be alert to the potential for discontinuous change, especially since strategic advantage may rest in such discontinuities.

The last barrier to quality which will be briefly explored under the general heading of culture is that of accountability. Achievement of quality requires that errors be acknowledged, that sources of error be tracked down and rectified, and that both curative and preventive action be taken by those involved.

In many organizations, this process is inhibited by a subculture which adopts a penal attitude. The realization of error is followed by a process of detection, prosecution – sometimes persecution – and punishment. This book is not the place for a debate on the societal value of such an approach, but it can be suggested that it is likely to be essentially negative in its effects. This may in turn lead to a situation where, as Deming (1982: 107) suggests, 'fear grips everyone'. In such a situation, errors may be suppressed or hidden. Where this is not possible, for example in manufacturing organizations, there will be a tendency to avoid punishment by blaming others and by a refusal to accept responsibility.

This barrier can be overcome by recognizing that errors are normally opportunities for learning, the basis for modifying a process, system, skill or behaviour to inhibit or prevent future occurrences. Naturally there must be a limiting case, when the error is consciously or deliberately provoked, in which those responsible must be found and appropriate action taken. However, in most organizations, and in many circumstances, the cause of error can be traced to some failure in the design or execution of a process, in the training of the employee or in the equipment provided for the completion of the task. These aspects should be the first focus of attention and, in a quality organization, will inhibit the use of disciplinary action. In many cases, though, they are the last. Managers often prefer to find someone to blame, perhaps because it is easier to do that than to accept responsibility for their own failure. From this approach arises the blame culture. For example, one organization employed a group of administrative staff to operate a post office and administration system servicing the needs of an off-site sales force. The salespeople rarely visited the office and relied heavily on the administrators to maintain diaries and timetable customer visits. An activity-based reward system meant that the sales force were absolutely reliant on the administrative system to ensure that they were paid the correct amount for the work done. Time lags in the system caused regular delays in payment. Work done was not paid for, and adventurous salespeople submitted claims for work which was incomplete, relying on the time lags to beat the system. Inevitably, problems arose in this operation. Members of the sales force began to fall behind with commitments; others received no pay at the end of certain months. After some delay, an administrator and two of the sales force left the organization; their temporary contracts were not renewed as a result of their poor performance. Today, no member of the workforce will take any action without at least one management signature. This ensures that they have to take no responsibility. The system, the driver of the problems, is unchanged.

3.3 ORGANIZATION DESIGN

When discussing organization design, it is not simply the organization structure – the classic pyramidal hierarchy or, more recently, the very flat organization chart – which is to be considered. It must also incorporate the interactions between units, the information and management systems and their total interrelatedness. As Beer (1985: i) suggests, the organization chart may be seen as 'frozen out of history', revealing whom to blame when things go wrong but not showing how the organization actually works. A number of barriers to achievement of quality can be found in this area.

The first, and most frequent, error is what can be called institutionalized conflict. This means that an organization has been designed in such a way that conflict between quality and some other characteristic, such as productivity, is inherent. Such a conflict is commonly found where the quality control or quality assurance manager reports to the production manager. In such a case, the need to meet customer orders will often override the need to achieve quality standards. The quality manager is, in effect, redundant since no value is added to the operation of the organization by his or her presence. Flood (1993: 210–221) reports how when production fell short of customer orders at 'Tarty Bakeries', the production manager would pass as acceptable output which had already been rejected by the quality inspectors.

This situation, replicated in many organizations, presents a major barrier to quality. A structure must be created in which the quality function is independent of the production function, and, as shall be seen, where quality is inherent in the product, the process and, importantly, the culture. This leads to a situation where rather than rejects and errors being 'inspected out', quality can be 'baked into' the product.

The second barrier to quality in this context is the design of the organization's information systems. This does not simply mean the computerized management or executive information system, but the whole of the information generating and processing activity of the organization, both formal and informal. These activities must generate the right information, in the right format, at the right time and deliver it to the right decision maker(s) if it is to be of any benefit. Most frequently, users of information spend much time analysing and discussing yesterday's or last week's errors while paying no attention to today or to the future. While they may be criticized for this, it is as much a function of the design of the information system as a matter of managerial desire. Hindsight is always twenty-twenty, and a common requirement in organizations is for managers to explain what went wrong, to justify mistakes and failures. Such organizations are attempting to manage their past and not their future, perhaps because they find this easier to do – a little like driving a car by looking in the rear view mirror to see where you have been!

The informal system refers to communication through devices such as trade unions and other staff bodies and the grapevine. Beer (1985: 58–59) encourages such informal communication between functions, which may be concerned with immediate operational matters such as the timing of the next batch of a product, or with longer-term issues such as competition for capital. However, he specifically sees informal communication as supplementary to and not a replacement for the formal systems. Beckford (1993: 300–323) shows how the union and the grapevine were perceived by both management and staff as the most reliable information sources in an organization. It is worth making the point at this stage that managers cannot stop communication within an organization. Data will find a means of transmission whatever barriers are placed in the way, but the organization will be effective only if the communication channels are properly designed.

Another aspect of this information system is performance measurement. To recap briefly, performance measurement tends to determine which aspects of the organization will be perceived as important. Those characteristics or outputs which are measured will be the focus of work; that which is not measured may well be ignored. Thus the design of the measurement system, its prime content and the way its outputs are responded to by managers may be expected to drive the performance of the organization.

Similarly, many organizations operate with no formal measurement system at all; everything is done by 'gut feel' and rule of thumb. In these circumstances, quality simply cannot be known to have been achieved since, even if it has been defined, it is not being measured. As the conversation goes in *Alice's Adventures in Wonderland* (Carroll, 1866):

> 'Would you tell me, please, which way I ought to walk from here?' [said Alice]
> 'That depends a good deal on where you want to get to.' [said the Cheshire Cat]
> 'I don't much care where.' [said Alice]
> 'Then it doesn't matter which way you walk.' [said the Cheshire Cat]
> 'So long as I get *somewhere*.' [said Alice]

An appropriate form and degree of measurement is vital. That is enough for managers to know what is happening but not so much that the 'measured' feel burdened or oppressed by the system, since in such a case they may seek to pervert the results. Perhaps, as Beer (1985: 102) proposes in the context of autonomy, we should have as much measurement 'as guarantees cohesion'.

The next barrier to quality is one of role understanding and articulation within the organization, particularly among the staff involved in the control and development functions: general management, marketing, human resource management, accounting, strategic planning, and so on. There is a tendency among many such staff to delve down into the operations of the organization, perhaps taking direct control when errors occur or the unexpected happens. While doing so they may be neglecting their own roles within the organization. This 'fire-fighting' or 'crisis' style of management is seen in many organizations as heroic, with plaudits and awards handed to those who perform in this way. However, as the apocryphal saying goes, 'When you are up to your armpits in alligators, it's easy to forget that the original objective was to drain the swamp.' Solving today's crisis is extremely important, but, as suggested by Senge (1990: 15), to manage a crisis is to deal with 'symptoms not underlying causes'. A low-level intervention by senior management will rarely address the root, or fundamental, cause of the problem, and *that* is their proper role, not to deal with operational matters. The operational managers must be allowed the freedom and given the support to solve their own problems. If senior management continually intervene in a junior manager's daily problem-solving activity, two things will occur. First, the junior manager will never learn to solve his or her own problems, thus reducing organizational effectiveness and increasing costs. Second, the senior manager's work will never get done, and consequently the organization will hurtle out of control into the nearest obstacle because nobody is watching where it is going.

The final barrier which will be explored in this section is that of irrelevant, or inappropriate, activities. This section is titled 'Organization design', but frequently the truth is that an organization has not been designed; it has grown and undergone metamorphoses almost of its own accord. Many features of an established organization, whether they be structural such as the set-up of departments or units, organizational, that is, activities and procedures or cultural and attitudinal, have not been not intentionally and deliberately created. Often they just grow. They develop, perhaps to support some long-forgotten or superseded purpose of the organization, and are simply never stopped. Cases are common where procedures have become institutionalized and carried on for years. To take one example, a manager had once requested a particular report, which had to be produced by hand at set intervals. That the manager concerned had long since moved on (and retired) and no further request had ever been received for the report was not seen as a reason for stopping – 'after all, you never know'! Equally, that a computerized version of the same report was available had not been noticed, and 'anyway, the technology is unreliable'.

A similar process occurs with what, in Business Process Re-engineering (BPR), are known as cowpaths. These are the routes through an organization which develop naturally without the purposeful intervention of the staff. A procedure in use may never have been the subject of deliberate design, it may have simply developed and its users become accustomed to it, complete with all its unique peculiarities and foibles. Such processes are often inefficient; sometimes ineffective, everybody complains about them, but they are seen as nobody's responsibility.

These cowpaths and inappropriate processes may well present barriers to the achievement of quality, since they are an 'unconscious' part of the organization and their quality-inhibiting properties may not be recognized.

3.4 MANAGEMENT PERSPECTIVES

'Management perspectives' refers not simply to the attitude to quality, but to the whole management ethos of the organization as it impacts on quality – a subject which was touched on in the previous chapter. The issue of corporate politics has already been raised in section 3.1, so will not be covered again here.

In order for an appropriate attitude to be developed to quality, it must be recognized as an issue – that is, the lack of quality in a product or service must be acknowledged. Frequently, companies adopt an ostrich-like attitude to quality, finding it easier to blame poor performance on a host of other reasons. For example, when a previously successful sales performance declines, a common reaction is to focus on market changes, the sales team or activity by competitors rather than on the product or service itself. Issues such as pricing and margins are often raised, perhaps leading to a focus on manufacturing performance in terms of productivity. Rarely is quality of product or service considered as a potentially primary issue at the outset.

It is essential that quality be treated as a potential part of the problem and be considered as a possible cause of decline. Even where a company is performing well, a positive attitude to quality needs to be developed and maintained. A product which is considered 'good enough' probably isn't so in today's competitive markets. There is no room for such complacency.

A further barrier to achievement of quality is a focus on short-term results only – that is, the result in a particular shift, day, week, quarter or even year. Often, salary or wage packages and performance bonuses are related directly to current-period performance. Therefore, currently acceptable performance parameters are used as a reason (or excuse) for not addressing the issue of quality. It is often, though not necessarily, the case that a focus on quality, or any other major change programme, will lead to a short-term decline in performance (particularly of productivity) while staff and management adjust to changes. This is known as the 'hockey stick' effect. It may be related to a complete change of emphasis, where achieving quality of output needs to override, perhaps for the first time, the achieving of quantity of output. The change required in management attitudes is fundamental, away from pure productivity to productivity with quality. After all, output which is rejected, either internally or by the customer, cannot really be considered output at all – it is waste.

Thus a major barrier to quality may be built into the reward system of the organization. This barrier can be overcome only by changing that system; it cannot be overcome through exhortations, evangelism, penal action or statistical measurement. Effective change may mean negotiating fresh terms with a variety of stakeholders in the enterprise, from the workforce and their bonus system to the shareholders or providers of equity and loan capital, whose short-term interests may be affected and will need to be addressed.

Management often focuses on 'output today at all costs'. No real concern with or interest in quality is evident. In order to boost performance, a focus is maintained exclusively on current output. In the event of an apparent or expected shortfall in output, the rate of production is increased in an attempt to compensate. Such increases are usually doomed to failure unless the system of production itself is addressed.

A food factory case study highlights the problem. The production lines had an established level of throughput for each of their various product lines, an optimal rate at which the equipment and operators could cope, and a 'satisfactory compromise' had been reached between productivity and quality. The established or recorded reject rate, with which the management were quite content, was 10 per cent.

In the event that production was likely to fall short of customer orders, the throughput rate across the product range would be increased from an average of 12 units per minute to an average of 16 units per minute. It was assumed by the factory management that over the running time this would give a net increase of around 33 per cent in output compared to optimal-rate running. In practice, an increase of only about 10 per cent was achieved, the balance of additional throughput being rejected for failing to achieve the required quality standard. Naturally, the management's reaction was to speed up the process even further, seeking to gain the elusive extra output. Figure 3.1 shows the effect of *slipping clutch syndrome* diagrammatically.

Although it is portrayed for the sake of simplicity as a step change, in practice, the quality gap widened on a progressive basis with every small increase in output. The greater the throughput, the greater the reject rate, every increase in running speed generating an

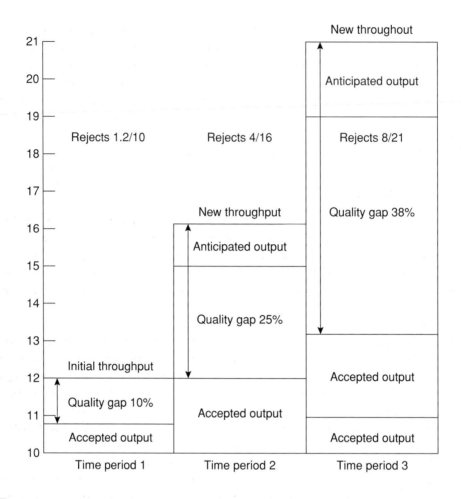

Figure 3.1 *Slipping clutch syndrome*

ever-reducing increase in acceptable output. One other major factor in this case was that the necessary work rate of the individual members of staff had to increase in line with the speed of the production belt – something which would not generally be sustainable regardless of the quality issue. The major solution applied in this particular case was to reduce throughput and thereby reduce the quality gap, ensuring that operators had sufficient time with each unit to reach the appropriate quality standard. A series of other measures were also taken; simply changing production rates was not the entire solution to the subject company's quality problems.

Each of the barriers highlighted in this section reflects a common mindset on the part of management. That mindset is called reductionism, the belief that anything can be understood by continually breaking it down into parts, breaking the parts down into further parts, and so on, in what is often called an analytical approach. The reductionist mindset seeks singular causes for singular effects and reflects the mechanistic thinking which has dominated science.

Contemporary thinking suggests that a holistic approach to problem solving is more effective – that is, one which deals with systems as wholes, which recognizes the interrelationships and interdependencies between parts of a system and which acknowledges that fixing one part of a system will not necessarily improve the whole. Such an approach broadens the attack on a problem by widening the scope of inquiry to study also those factors which influence it – its inputs – as well as considering the consequences of any changes – the effect on outputs. For example, simply replacing the tyres on a car, while it will potentially improve grip, will do little or nothing to improve the car's overall performance.

3.5 COSTS OF QUALITY

The last issue to be briefly explored in this chapter is the costs of quality. This means the direct and invisible costs unnecessarily incurred by any organization which does not have an effective quality system in place. Direct costs in this context means those costs arising as a result of the non-achievement of quality and visibly attributable to that fact. Invisible costs in this context means those costs arising in the organization as a result of not achieving quality but not visibly attributable to that fact – those where the relationship between non-quality and the cost may not have been discerned by the organization.

Any production system for a product or service which is not designed to achieve the quality standard 'first time, every time' will incur rework and rectification costs. These are the costs of putting right errors, performing again a particular task or disassembling and reassembling (or scrapping) a product. Traditionally, such costs have been treated by organizations as part of the overall cost of production, and a percentage is included in the price of every item sold for the ones that go wrong. Thus acceptance of error is both institutionalized and carefully hidden!

In the era of quality, with lean production systems and just-in-time delivery, these costs need to be uncovered, and attention paid to their reduction and eradication. They must be challenged, not accepted. All processes receive inputs in the form of either materials or information from prior steps in the chain. That is to say, each process is the customer of either an internal or an external supplier. If the inputs received are defective, then costs may be incurred in a number of ways.

The first way, and potentially the most damaging, is that entire consignments have to be returned, holding up or stopping production and leading to unfilled orders and lost revenue. A commonly used answer to this is to increase holding stocks (ensuring that there is sufficient to cover a break in supply). Such an approach simply increases stocking costs, reducing the supply of working capital available to the organization and inhibiting its overall performance; it does nothing to solve the quality problem.

The second way is that costs are incurred in validating the quality of goods or information received before it is processed, inspecting out failures from suppliers and, in effect, absorbing part of the suppliers' operating cost. Costs can also be incurred by not inspecting goods received, leading to the use of defective parts or information at the next stage of production. This ensures that the final product will also fail, leading back to rework and rectification.

A third way is that goods received are inspected and defective parts rectified before use. This again generates cost which should have been incurred by the supplier. Strategies to address some of these issues are incorporated in Chapter 24, 'Supplier development'.

Inspection, as an auditing activity, can never be completely eradicated. Reports generated by inspection provide higher-level management with information necessary for them to control and develop the operation. However, inspection is most commonly used as *the* quality mechanism, the one procedure which attempts to ensure that products and services are being provided at the agreed level. For such an approach to quality to work, it requires at least a statistically valid sampling approach, and 100 per cent confidence requires 100 per cent inspection – an impossible task in nearly all industries. Although frequently attempted, this is rarely successful and always inordinately expensive. It is often impracticable. Beckford (1993: 308) refers to an inspection system with a notional target of 100 per cent – in practice, 5 per cent was supposedly achieved. The target figure was not practical given throughput, and was in any case irrelevant, since the product to be inspected was sealed into a plastic bag, inside a cardboard box – the only inspection was of the box, provided by an independent external supplier, not of the product!

The level of inspection can be significantly reduced where quality is inherent in both the product and the process. Effective auditing can be substituted. This has a direct impact on both the cost of the activity and its utility.

Invisible costs are much harder to identify and specify, but are nonetheless incurred when quality has not been addressed properly. They may include:

- dissatisfied customers, who fulfil future needs with an alternative supplier;
- customer site service and maintenance costs, often operated as a separate business division. The costs of customer service are very often driven by the inadequacies and failures of the design and manufacturing process;
- in-process rework costs (costs incurred by reworking unfinished products within a process). Beckford (1993: 300–323) reports a case where the reported reject figure of 10 per cent ignored in-process rectification, which amounted to a further 25 per cent of throughput;
- high staff turnover leading to increased recruitment and training costs as a result of dissatisfied staff leaving;
- capital costs for equipment and warehousing to provide for rectification of defective parts and storage of additional materials;
- reduced availability of internal working capital, leading to unnecessary reliance on loan/overdraft capital (i.e. increased gearing).

Such costs are rarely attributed directly to the quality issue. However, they are in an interdependent relationship with all the other factors of the business and so to a large extent they are related to and driven by quality.

SUMMARY

This chapter has reviewed a number of the barriers to quality, looking particularly at the issues of systems and procedures, culture, organization design and management approach. The chapter concluded with a brief look at some of the costs of quality.

QUESTION

Identify the barriers to quality in your own organization (or one which is well known to you). Justify your choices and outline ways in which they might be overcome.

The emergence of management

'These all look like "Whats". It's the "Hows" that I have trouble with.'
Winnie-the-Pooh (A. A. Milne, 1926)

KEY LEARNING POINTS

The study of managing has emerged in parallel with the emergence of large organizations.

Principal dominant models of organization: classical – 'machine' model; human relations – 'organic' model.

Classical management theorists: Frederick Taylor – Scientific Management; Henri Fayol – Administrative Management; Max Weber – Bureaucracy Theory.

Human relations theorists: Elton Mayo – the Hawthorne studies; Abraham Maslow – the hierarchy of human needs; Frederick Herzberg – two-factor theory of motivation.

Each model is considered responsible for some aspects of contemporary quality problems.

INTRODUCTION

The purpose of this chapter is to introduce the principal models that still appear to govern much management behaviour. The formal study of management has emerged as a discipline in its own right only over the past hundred or so years. Indeed, it is still considered by many (particularly practising managers) as being at least as much 'black art' as science.

Theoretical and practical development of the discipline have more or less paralleled the emergence of the major corporations. Prior to the industrial revolution, the only permanent large-scale organizations (other than states which were then extremely volatile) were the various churches and the standing armies and navies of the wealthier nations. The majority of the workforce were either agricultural labourers living at not much better than a subsistence standard of living; land-owning farmers; craftsmen; or professionals such as doctors and lawyers.

Following the industrial revolution, many agricultural workers moved from the country to the towns and cities to improve their standard of living, often becoming factory workers. The increasing size of such organizations (and the increasing wealth and desire to pursue other interests of the factory owners) created the opportunity for the emergence of professional managers – those whose job it was to oversee and supervise the activities of the workers on behalf of owners. The need to manage these large-scale organizations and the drive for additional profitability can be interpreted as having given impetus to the study of management. The development of early management theories is the topic of the next sections.

The principal early models in organization (or management) theory are the Classical, also known as the Traditional or Rational, and the Human Relations. These two approaches have their own particular strengths and weaknesses and these will be explored. These theories are to some extent the causes of many quality problems, and have been reflected in the dominant quality models which will be considered in the next part of the book.

4.1 CLASSICAL THEORY

The classical or 'machine' (Morgan, 1986: 20) model of organization reflects the scientific management approach developed by Frederick Taylor, the classical theory of Henri Fayol and Max Weber's Bureaucracy Theory. These collectively still dominate mainstream management thinking. Each of these approaches regards the design of organizations as a technical exercise and depends upon fragmenting or dissecting an organization into its component parts for analysis and efficient operation.

The 'machine' approaches to organization arose, as suggested, in the late nineteenth and early twentieth centuries and may be considered logical extensions of the advances then being made in machine technology. Machines are, in general, designed to perform specified tasks at known input/output rates and within specified tolerances; these management approaches assume that organizations can be similarly designed.

Frederick Taylor's Scientific Management (Taylor, 1911) is based on four key principles (see Box 4.1): scientific task design, scientific selection, management–worker co-operation and equal division of work. Huczynski and Buchanan (1991: 282–283) see Taylor's objectives as being first, to improve efficiency by increasing output and reducing 'underworking' – what Taylor described as 'natural soldiering' and 'systematic soldiering'. Second, to achieve 'standardisation of job performance, by dividing tasks up into small and closely specified sub tasks'. Finally, to instil discipline, 'by establishing hierarchical authority and introducing a system whereby all management's policy decisions could be implemented'.

While Taylor recognized that the worker in a given situation had a 'mass of rule of thumb or traditional knowledge', which constituted his 'principal asset or possession', he had a poor view of the capabilities and intelligence of the worker. For example, he believed that

> the science of handling pig iron is so great and amounts to so much that it is impossible for the man who is best suited to this type of work to understand the principles of this science, or even to work in accordance with these principles without the aid of a man better educated than he is.

> **Box 4.1** *Principles of Frederick Taylor's Scientific Management*
>
> 'Develop a science for each element of a man's work, which replaces the old rule of thumb method.'
>
> 'Scientifically select and then train, teach and develop the workman, whereas in the past he chose his own work and trained himself as best he could.'
>
> 'Heartily co-operate with the men so as to insure all of the work being done in accordance with the principles of the science which has been developed.'
>
> Ensure that 'There is an almost equal division of the work and the responsibility between the management and the workmen. The management take over all the work for which they are better fitted than the workmen, while in the past almost all of the work and the greater part of the responsibility were thrown upon the men.'

Taylor saw the organization as a machine capable of being specified, designed and controlled by management to achieve a given purpose. The workmen were viewed as standardized machine parts, interchangeable with every other of like design and to be used at the discretion of management. His approach was later followed by Gilbreth and Gantt, who both attempted to humanize Scientific Management, recognizing the need for rest (Gilbreth) and human needs and dignity (Gantt). Taylor's key assumption that the worker was principally motivated by money was retained, and this is still the case in many organizations.

Henri Fayol (1916) used the 'machine' metaphor in writing that

> The body corporate of a concern is often compared with a machine or plant or animal. The expressions, 'administrative machine,' 'administrative gearing,' suggest an organism obeying the drive of its head and having all of its effectively interrelated parts move in unison towards the same end, and that is excellent.

This perception of the excellence of the 'machine' view is evident in his proposals for organizing and managing. He proposed that 'to organise a business is to provide it with everything useful to its functioning: raw materials, tools, capital, personnel' and saw the organization as comprising six sets of activities; technical, commercial, financial, security, accounting and managerial. Fayol's proposed duties of managers reinforce this view (Box 4.2) and reflect Fayol's fourteen principles of management (Box 4.3).

Some of these managerial duties and principles of management appear to conflict with the machine view and with each other. For example, take 'Define duties clearly' and 'Encourage a liking for initiative and responsibility', or 'specialization' and 'initiative'. The first of these in each case would appear to preclude, or at least make difficult, the second. The admonition to managers to 'fight against excess of regulation, red tape and paper control' stands in sharp contrast to his view that the work should be 'clearly divided', 'judiciously planned and strictly carried out', aspects which carry with them an implication of machine-like precision and heavy reliance on record keeping.

The overall impression remains that Fayol, like Taylor, viewed the organization as a machine. The management were responsible for forecasting, planning, organizing, commanding, co-ordinating and controlling, while the 'workers', distinguished by 'technical ability

Box 4.2 *Duties of managers, according to Henri Fayol*

Ensure that the plan is judiciously prepared and strictly carried out

See that the human and material organization is consistent with the objectives, resources and requirements of the concern

Set up a single, competent, energetic guiding authority

Harmonize activities and co-ordinate efforts

Formulate clear, distinct, precise decisions

Arrange for efficient selection: each department must be headed by a competent, energetic man; each employee must be in that place where he can render greatest service

Define duties clearly

Encourage a liking for initiative and responsibility

Have fair and suitable recompense for services rendered

Make use of sanctions against faults and errors

See to the maintenance of discipline

Ensure that individual interests are subordinated to the general interest

Pay special attention to unity of command

Supervise both human and material order

Have everything under control

Fight against excess of regulation, red tape and paper control

Box 4.3 *Principles of management, according to Henri Fayol*

Division of work (specialization)

Authority

Discipline

Unity of command

Unity of direction

Subordination (the interest of the organization is more important than that of the individual)

Remuneration

Centralization (a question of continuously varying proportion)

Scalar chain

Order

Equity

Stability of tenure

Initiative

Esprit de corps

characteristic of the business', were component parts to be fitted into the machine at the most appropriate place, with 'a place for everyone and everyone in his place'.

Max Weber's Bureaucracy Theory developed from his view that there are three types of legitimate authority in organizations: rational, traditional and charismatic. Traditional authority rests on established acceptance of a natural order of society: the rulers and the ruled – perhaps reflecting the idea of monarchy. Charismatic authority rests on the personal devotion of individuals to a particular leader. Both these styles of management exist in organizations today. For example, traditional authority is found in many of the patriarchal family-owned businesses of Asia, while charismatic authority may be considered to be the style of organizations such as easyJet, Virgin Atlantic and many of the, now failing, 'dotcom' businesses. Rational authority is the principal interest of this text, as it has come to dominate many large organizations.

Rational authority was seen by Weber (cited by Pugh 1990: 3–13) as representing legal authority, with 'obedience owed to the legally established impersonal order'. He considered that the 'purest type of exercise of legal authority is that which employs a bureaucratic administrative staff', and that bureaucracy was not simply desirable but indispensable to cope with the complexities of the organizations of his time. He considered that the increase in general technical knowledge had as a consequence a need for an increase in the particular technical knowledge of individuals, in order for them to administer an organization effectively.

A bureaucracy was seen by Weber as being composed of a hierarchical organization of 'offices', each acting according to the rules and norms of the organization within a specified area of competence. Individuals within this structure were appointed on rational grounds to perform a specified function, without gaining rights to that appointment or having ownership of the organization. All decisions, rules and acts were to be recorded in writing, in order, together with the 'continuous organization of official functions', to 'constitute the office'. Weber saw a clear choice in organizations between 'bureaucracy and dilettantism' and proposed that bureaucracy was an inevitable requirement to support large organizations.

The machine view is evident again in this case, Weber proposing that every function, and every act of every office is capable of being specified to an exact degree. People were clearly viewed as functionaries within the bureaucracy, bringing no human element to the conduct of the affairs of the organization.

Box 4.4 *Principles of bureaucracy, according to Max Weber*

Specialization	Each office (or 'bureau') has a defined area of expertise
Hierarchy	Supervision and control or lower offices by higher ones
Rules	Exhaustive, stable rules, learned by all
Impersonality	Equality of treatment for all according to the rules
Appointment	Selection according to competence not election
Work to be full-time	Occupation of office as the primary task of the individual
Career	Promotion, tenure and seniority within the system
Segregation	The official activity is distinct from the private individual

4.2 CRITICAL REVIEW

Several assumptions about the world and organizational life seem to underlie these three rational views of organization. These need to be stated before considering their strengths and weaknesses.

The first assumption is that an organization can be regarded as isolated from the influence of its environment. While this may have been an acceptable view in a fast-growing producer-led economy, it clearly cannot be considered appropriate in consumer-led, low-growth and highly competitive markets. Despite the observations of Galbraith (1974) concerning producer dominance, organizations must respond to the needs and demands of external stakeholders if they are to survive. In the mature, post-industrial economies, enabled by instant communications, the informed consumer genuinely does have the potential to determine the fate of organizations. A good example of this is the perception in the United Kingdom that cars cost too much relative to their value. Numerous consumers, taking advantage of the open European market and reliable communications, are simply choosing to purchase their cars in cheaper countries – saving 25 per cent or more of the UK purchase price. It is clear that the manufacturers and dealers must respond to this threat if they are to survive. An internally focused organization does not have the capability to do this.

The second assumption is that an improvement in the performance of a part of the organization will necessarily improve the performance of the whole. There appears to be some merit in this idea at the purely mechanical level: the repair or replacement of a defective part will possibly generate some improvement. However, the approach ignores interdependence within the organization, which means that the whole will perform only at the level of the weakest or slowest part. Similarly, the idea of 'emergent properties' – the conception that the whole may be more than the sum of the parts – is ignored. The ideas of systemic thinking will be pursued explicitly in Part three of this book. Meanwhile, it is sufficient to suggest that organizations often have characteristics or properties which belong only to their entirety and not to any of their individual parts. These characteristics cannot be addressed except by considering the capacity for interaction. It was suggested in Chapter 1 that quality is not an issue which can be isolated but must be pursued systemically, organization-wide. The classical model of organization cannot cope with this need.

The third assumption is that the organization must be studied only from the perspective of the goals of management. Later studies have shown that organizational effectiveness depends on the co-operation of many parties to the organization. Commonly called 'stakeholders', these parties include owners, employees, customers, suppliers, and those outside the organization who are affected by its activities and behaviour. The contemporary concept of 'good corporate citizenship' recognizes the need for organizations to take account of the wishes of the community in which they exist. This assumption is further challenged by the change in the ISO 9000 standard, which now sees the customer as the focus of organizational performance and, as mentioned above, capable of sophisticated, informed behaviour.

The final assumption is that an organization can be designed and understood in 'machine' terms. It can be created to perform a given task and, once designed, need not be adapted. Operating in a global economy which is best characterised as turbulent and dynamic and subject to rapid changes in technology and customer expectations, any organization which cannot adapt reasonably readily cannot expect to survive.

43

Apart from the foregoing comments, each of these assumptions has been challenged through developments in thinking about organizations and in ideas about human well-being during the past century. Practical experience of using the model in organizations has also shown that the assumptions are flawed.

4.3 REITERATION

Flood and Jackson (1991: 8–9) provide a useful summary of the 'machine' view which forms the basis of this section. They consider that it is useful in practice when the organization operates in a stable environment, performing a straightforward task, such as repetitive production of a single product, and when the 'human parts' are prepared to follow 'machine-like' commands. They suggest that its usefulness is limited since it reduces the adaptability of organizations, and the 'mindless contribution' is difficult to maintain with 'mindful parts', leading to dehumanization or conflict.

The strengths of the model are:

- It enables, systematic, methodical analysis of specific tasks.
- It provides assistance in establishing order in organizations.
- It is a useful guide to creating organizations where demands on individuals need to be precise or exact, for example in the nuclear industry or multiple-outlet operations such as banks.

It has the following weaknesses:

- Its fails to recognize environmental interaction.
- It fails to acknowledge the interdependence of parts.
- It provides no inherent capacity for adaptation.
- The model is static, not dynamic.
- People are 'dehumanized'.
- Goals are inherent in the design.
- The focus on control may encourage inefficiency.
- It cannot help with informal or virtual organizations such as network arrangements, which are increasingly common.
- It is diagnostic but not prescriptive.

It can be seen, then, that while the machine view offers some assistance, its weaknesses are such that it must be considered an inadequate approach for managers today. The impact of this thinking on quality will be considered in section 4.7.

4.4 HUMAN RELATIONS THEORY

While benefits could, and may still, be obtained from the rational approaches, their lack of humanity is demonstrated by the difficulties which emerge during their application with the people involved. The Human Relations Model of organization emerged as a means of addressing these difficulties and was the first significant challenge to the 'machine' view.

The 'organic' or 'organism' (Morgan, 1986: 39–76) analogy stems from the origins of modern systems thinking in the biological sciences and attempts to deal with the attainment of survival of the system or organization rather than the achievement of particular goals. While survival may be seen as a legitimate goal, it may not sufficiently represent the purpose of the organization. This organic view first found expression in organizations through what has become known as the Human Relations Model. This considers that attention must be paid to the human aspects of organization and gives primacy to the roles, needs and expectations of the human participants. Particular emphasis is given to issues of motivation, management style and participation as critical success factors.

The 'Hawthorne' studies of Roethlisberger and Dickson with Elton Mayo (Mayo, 1949) may be interpreted as an early systems approach to management (Flood and Carson, 1988). Although they were originally focused on the application of scientific management principles, their findings led away from this perspective, and they subsequently recognized the need to capture and understand the relatedness of all the parts involved. Later work in this field by Maslow and Herzberg did not adopt the systemic perspective. These later developments still adopt a reductionist and 'closed system' view of the organization, concentrating on improving the performance of parts, not wholes, and emphasizing internal rather than external influences on the organization.

Mayo (1949) argued that:

In modern large-scale industry the three persistent problems of management are:—

- The application of science and technical skill to some material good or product.
- The systematic ordering of operations.
- The organisation of teamwork – that is, of sustained co-operation.

Following Chester Barnard, Mayo saw that the first two of these would operate to make an industry effective, the third to make it efficient. He considered that the application of science and technical skill and the systematic ordering of operations were attended to, the first by continuous experiment, the second being already well developed in practice. He saw the third element as neglected but necessary if the organization as a whole was to be successful.

Mayo became involved in the 'Hawthorne' studies after they had examined the effects on workers of changes in the physical environment. Experiments had shown that social and psychological factors were present, and the studies became focused on these human issues. Records were kept of every aspect of changes made and their impact, to establish a 'systemic' view. Further experiments were conducted and followed by formal interviews, which revealed that many of the particular organization's difficulties related to emotional rather than rational conditions. Further experiment showed that informal group pressures had more influence on output and performance than the economic pressures of the formal organization.

The 'Hawthorne' studies are credited with having discovered the importance of groups in organizations, the influence of the observer on the observed, and the need to ensure that the goals and objectives of staff are not in conflict with those of the organization. Notwithstanding subsequent criticisms of the research methodology and interpretation of the findings, the studies are generally seen as the foundations of the human relations approach.

45

Maslow (1970), while seeing that the 'individual is an integrated, organised whole', proposed a hierarchy of human needs (Figure 4.1). These needs were: physiological (food and health), safety (security), belongingness and love (the need to belong to a group), esteem (the need to be valued by oneself and others), and self-actualization (the need to be all that one can be). He suggested that the needs were all contained within each other such that 'if one need is satisfied then another emerges', although the satisfied need remains present. That means that each need is ever-present even when not 'prepotent'.

Frederick Herzberg (Herzberg *et al.*, 1959), in his studies of motivation in the industrial and commercial context, built upon the foundation laid by Maslow. Through a series of observations and interviews with samples of people at work, he found that two sets of factors influenced the level of motivation. These were the 'hygiene' and 'motivating' factors discussed in Chapter 2. Briefly, 'hygiene' factors concerned the maintenance of conditions that were conducive to satisfaction. If satisfactory conditions did not pertain, then the worker would be dissatisfied with his or her job position; conversely, achievement of a satisfactory standard would not positively motivate. Positive motivation would be derived from 'motivators', factors which were seen as actively encouraging an increased contribution. These factors were illustrated diagrammatically in Figure 2.1.

Summarizing, Herzberg concluded that in order for organizations to achieve improved levels of performance, they must address both types of factor. He considered that 'good hygiene will prevent many of the negative results of low morale', but this on its own was not enough, suggesting 'our emphasis should be on the strengthening of motivators'. This he saw as being achieved by restructuring jobs; providing workers with some degree of control over their achievement; meaningful job rotation; selection of staff to match the needs of the task; effective supervision through planning, organizing and support (a link with Taylor's work) and appropriate participation.

Finally, Herzberg recognized that 'there are large segments of our society to which these prescriptions cannot possibly apply'. He considered that these people could obtain a good life from 'fruitful hobbies and improved lives outside the job', and that 'the greatest fulfilment of man is to be found in activities related to his own needs as well as those of society'.

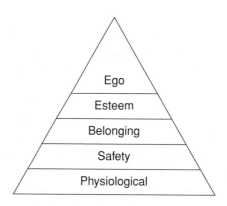

Figure 4.1 *Maslow's hierarchy of needs*

4.5   CRITICAL REVIEW

Again, several assumptions about the world and people seem to underpin the human relations approaches to organization, some of which represent a major shift in thinking from the machine view. From the organization design perspective, the influence of the environment is still largely neglected and there continues to be a focus on improving the performance of parts rather than the whole.

The first major shift, and perhaps the most significant, is the assumption that people may be motivated by rewards from work other than money. This assumption is of great significance in mature economies, where ever-rising salaries and wages are not a realistic prospect. If motivation is to be maintained in such circumstances, it is vital that managers recognize this assumption and discover what characteristics of the work and its environment are likely to stimulate staff.

The second assumption is concerned with the abilities of people. Whereas the machine view largely assumes limited ability and finite competence, the human relations view assumes much greater, albeit variable, competence and encourages a greater degree of autonomy and flexibility. It stresses delegation of decision making and enrichment of jobs, in direct contrast to the simplification associated with classical theory.

4.6   REITERATION

The Human Relations Model gives primacy to the role of the people in the organization and suggests ways of increasing their satisfaction. However, it does nothing for the achievement of the objectives of the organization and says little about how the complex tasks of the organization could be structured.

Flood and Jackson (1991: 10) consider that the 'organic' view is of practical value when there is an open relationship with the environment, when survival or adaptation needs are predominant and when the environment is complex. They believe that the human relations view fails. First, because it does not recognize that organizations are socially constructed phenomena which, it can be argued, need to be understood from the perspective of the participants. Second, because the emphasis is on harmonious relations, whereas conflict and coercion are often present. Third, because change is often environmentally driven, rather than driven by the organization itself.

The principal strength of the 'organic' model is the emphasis that it places on the human element of organizations, recognizing that people are not 'machine' parts but individuals who have needs and desires. There are, though, a number of weaknesses in this approach that make it inadequate for the needs of contemporary managers. First, notwithstanding the warning from Herzberg that human needs can be, and for some people need to be, met outside the workplace, the assumption underlying many applications of the human relations approach is that these needs must be met at work. Second, the Human Relations Model does not allow for the supremacy of organizational goals and objectives, needs driven by technology, or the operating environment, over human goals and needs. Such supremacy may be necessary to ensure the survival of the organization. Finally, the model does not assist with the specifics of designing and structuring organizations to cope with the complex tasks faced by contemporary managers nor with the interface between the organization and its environment.

47

This 'organic' view, while offering some significant advantages over the 'machine' view, still appears inadequate.

4.7 RELEVANCE TO QUALITY

The classical and human relations theories of management have relevance to quality for a number of reasons. First, they remain the dominant approaches to management in many cultures and contexts. They retain this dominance because they do have considerable value and appear to offer simple, fast solutions to management problems while serving to support the currently powerful groups in organizations. The second reason is that many management schools and training organizations do not teach many of the more contemporary and, arguably, radical ideas, rejecting them in favour of the traditional approaches. It must be acknowledged that in a newly developing country where the workforce are perhaps unfamiliar with the concept of having a job, the highly disciplined and autocratic styles which fit with the traditional view or organization may offer advantages in the short term. In more sophisticated contexts, this is unlikely to be the case, and may indeed be directly damaging to the organization.

A further point which needs to be recognized is the loss of skill and status associated with the introduction of modern highly productive and factory-based methods of working. For example, when agricultural or craft workers left the land or traditional occupations to work in factories, their accumulated store of knowledge became redundant. The progressive deskilling of the workforce particularly associated with increased specialization and mechanization in factories has served to reinforce this situation. Previously, a worker would have exercised a large share of his or her skill, knowledge and abilities in the completion of a task. However, a factory-style operation requires much less of these qualities, and for this reason much of the pride of the worker in the job has been lost. This may reasonably be considered to be a primary driver of quality problems in organizations. Trist and Bamforth (1966, cited by Pugh, 1990: 393–416,) make this point in relation to the sociological idea of 'responsible autonomy' in a three-man coal-getting team.

While the human relations approach, which emerged in response to the problems associated with the classical school, may appear to offer the solution, this is not the case. The human relations view gives priority to the needs of the individuals over those of the organization. In this case, the potential exists for the needs of the customers to be completely ignored in the pursuit of employee satisfaction. Thus it may be considered more important for employees to go home on time, or take a tea break, than to meet a customer's expectations. Similarly, the organization may develop products and services which exercise the skills, knowledge and aspirations of its workers rather than fulfilling a customer's needs.

Clearly, both these schools of thought offer advantages to the organization. All too often these advantages are pursued internally (because they are internally focused) and the needs of the customer are neglected.

Part two of the book considers the work of those called the 'quality gurus'. The influence of the classical and human relations schools of management thinking on these writers will be apparent. While all stress the importance of the customer, perhaps in response to the internally focused approaches just outlined, they place emphasis on tools and techniques which seem to sit most comfortably with the traditional approaches, and suffer from many of the same problems in the contemporary context.

SUMMARY

This chapter has, through a critical review, shown the inadequacy of the dominant classical and human relations theories used by managers to deal with the complexity of contemporary organizations. In the final section, a comment was offered on the relevance of these theories to quality.

QUESTION

Compare and contrast the machine view of organizations with the organic view. Suggest other metaphors which might be appropriate for these styles of management.

The quality gurus

USER GUIDE

This part of the book provides a comprehensive introduction to the eight writers whose individual ideas continue to dominate the quality movement. In every field of human thought and endeavour, there is continual change and development. Many ideas and approaches to addressing specific issues are considered and tried, but very few withstand the rigours of testing to become established in the mainstream of theory and practice and to become part of the accepted wisdom in the field. Those writers and practitioners whose ideas come to form this body of accepted knowledge, who lead and advise a movement, become known as 'gurus'. It is notable that although, as will be seen in Part four of this book, there has been substantial change in quality management systems, no new individuals have emerged to lead the field.

This part of the book focuses on the theory and practice espoused by eight writers and practitioners of quality management. They are those whose philosophies, methods and tools have survived and become embedded in best practice. Collectively they are 'the quality gurus'.

The aim of this part is to assist readers in the development of a critical appreciation of the contributions to the quality movement of Philip Crosby, W. Edwards Deming, Armand V. Feigenbaum, Kaoru Ishikawa, Joseph Juran, John Oakland, Shigeo Shingo and Genichi Taguchi. Seven of them have been selected as having made the most significant and enduring early contributions to quality management; the eighth, John Oakland, is chosen as being the dominant European current practitioner of quality management. The work of each is explored through a five-point critical framework:

- philosophy;
- assumptions;
- methods;
- successes and failures;
- critical review.

Through this approach, the reader should develop a platform for understanding the strengths, weaknesses and different perspective of each writer. While each of those featured has much in common with the others, there are significant differences in their views of the quality problem. None of these views is 'right' or 'wrong'; they are simply different, formed from the differing backgrounds, knowledge and experiences of the various writers. Each is based on the particular guru's view of the world and is valid from his theoretical and practical perspective. While being critical of these perspectives in our own contemporary contexts, it is important to respect the contexts in which the approaches were developed.

Philip B. Crosby

Quality is not only right, it is free. And it is not only free,
it is the most profitable product we have.
Harold S. Geneen (cited by Crosby, 1979)

KEY LEARNING POINTS

Philip B. Crosby's definition of quality: conformance to requirements.

Five absolutes of quality management:

- quality as conformance;
- no such thing as a quality problem;
- always cheaper first time;
- the only measurement of performance is the cost of quality;
- zero defects.

Three key beliefs: quantification; management leadership; prevention.

Principal methods: fourteen-step quality programme; the 'quality vaccine'

INTRODUCTION

Philip Crosby is a graduate of the Western Reserve University and has a professional background in quality. Following military service, he went into quality control in manufacturing,
where he worked his way from line inspector to quality director and subsequently corporate
vice-president of ITT. Based on many years of practical experience, his first book became a
best-seller and led him to establish the consulting organization Philip Crosby Associates
Incorporated and the Quality College based in Florida. He is described by Bendell (1989) as
'particularly well marketed and charismatic', by the *Financial Times* (26 November 1986)
as having 'the look of a sunbelt Senator rather than a man from the quality department' and

by Bank (1992) as delivering his message with 'almost religious fervour'. Clearly, he is a man who acts as he speaks, or 'walks the talk'. His approach has been well received: over 60,000 managers have been trained at the Quality College and his quality books, particularly *Quality Is Free* and *Quality without Tears*, continue to sell well.

5.1 PHILOSOPHY

Crosby's philosophy is seen by many, for example Gilbert (1992), to be encapsulated in his five 'absolutes of quality management' (Box 5.1). Each of these absolutes will be examined in turn to consider its meaning.

First is Crosby's definition of quality. It suggests that when he talks about a quality product or service he is referring to one which meets the requirements of the customer or user. This means in turn that those requirements must be defined, in advance, and that 'measures must be taken continually to determine conformance' (Flood, 1993: 22). The requirements may, of course, include both quantitative and qualitative aspects, although as shall be shown, Crosby's target emphasis is towards the quantitative – that is, 'Zero Defects'. The first fundamental beliefs, then, are that quality is an essentially measurable aspect of a product or service and that quality is achieved when expectations or requirements are met.

Crosby's second absolute is that 'There is no such thing as a quality problem.' He is implying that poor management creates the quality problems; they do not create themselves or exist as matters separate from the management process. In other words, the product and product quality do not exist in a vacuum; they are a result of the management process, and if that process has inherent quality, then a quality product will emerge. The second belief, then, is that management must lead the workers towards a quality outcome.

Third, 'It is always cheaper to do it right first time.' Logothetis (1992) suggests that 'A company which relies on mass inspection of the final output to improve quality is doomed to stagnation.' It is possible to go further than this and suggest that a company focused on inspection will be achieving more than it deserves if it stagnates. It is more likely, in the long run, to fail altogether. Here, Crosby is making clear his belief that inspection is a cost and that quality needs to be *designed into* a product, rather than flaws being *inspected out*. This can be taken as a belief in the potential to achieve quality – that is, conformance to requirements – by developing a quality process and product from the outset with no expectation of failure. Prevention of error is better than rectification.

Fourth, 'The only performance measurement is the cost of quality.' Crosby clearly believes that the cost of quality is always a measurable item – for example, the cost of rework, warranty

---

Box 5.1 *Philip Crosby's five absolutes of quality management*

Quality is defined as conformance to requirements, not as 'goodness' or 'elegance'

There is no such thing as a quality problem

It is always cheaper to do it right first time

The only performance measurement is the cost of quality

The only performance standard is Zero Defects

---

costs, rejects – and that this is the only basis on which to measure performance. It is, as suggested by Logothetis (1992: 85), the 'price of non conformance'. As a practical measurement of quality, this might generally be considered to be useful, although it cannot be seen as the only measure. Rather, it is a direct monetary measure of quality within the overall performance of the organization. Crosby's belief in a quantitative approach is evident.

Finally, 'The only performance standard is zero defects.' The idea here is that perfection is the standard to aim for, through sound initial process and product design, continuous improvement, and underpinning that 'Zero Defects' is an achievable and measurable objective. Here again, Crosby's fundamental belief in the quantitative approach to quality is made clear, with perfection, 'Zero Defects', proposed as the target.

To summarize Crosby's perspective on quality, there appear to be three essential strands:

- a belief in quantification;
- leadership by management;
- prevention rather than cure.

Quality, then, is suggested by Crosby to be an inherent characteristic of the product, not an added extra. He believes, for example, that 20 per cent of manufacturing cost relates to failure, while for service companies this is around 35 per cent. He considers that the workers must not be blamed for error, but rather, that management should take the lead and that the workers will then follow. Crosby suggests that 85 per cent of quality problems are within the control of management.

5.2 ASSUMPTIONS

The assumptions about the world that seem to underpin Crosby's approach will now be considered.

First, it can be clearly seen that Crosby focuses attention on the management process as the key driver of quality. That is to say, if the management process is not functioning to achieve quality, then a quality product or service will not arise. If a causal chain view of the development of a product or service is adopted, it is easy to see value in this assumption. For example, if quality is defined as 'conformance to requirements', then it is absolutely essential that requirements are defined and communicated among all stakeholders. If this first step is not taken – for example, if the company manufactures what it can, rather than what the consumers demand – then there will be an eternal quality problem since the customers' requirements can never be met. This constraint, to define conformance requirements, must be met for every aspect of the product: design, function, colour, delivery, price, and so on.

The second assumption is that 'zero defects' is an achievable objective. The implication here is that any product can reliably be made, in relevant volumes, entirely free of defects. This raises the question of exactly what constitutes a defect. Work in this respect must start from Crosby's quality definition – conformance to requirements – and say that any product which conforms to requirements is defect-free. This again highlights the importance of the product specification in determining what constitutes quality.

The third assumption is that it is possible to establish a company that 'does not start out expecting mistakes', where errors are not expected or inevitable. While this is an admirable ideal, it must be considered exceedingly difficult to achieve in practice. Culture, staff, levels of training and skill, and aptitude for the particular task are all aspects that move over time. In any large manufacturing facility, for example, labour turnover at the shop floor level is likely to run at a level of around 8–10 per cent simply from natural causes such as ill health and retirement. To achieve and maintain a consistency of expectation of zero defects in these circumstances may be seen as unreasonable – unless the management is sufficiently determined in its resolve to achieve quality. Operationally, and particularly where some qualitative or subjective judgement element applies to a product, managers are often faced with a dilemma between delivering volume or achieving conformance to requirements.

This problem was frequently met by management at 'Tarty Bakeries' (Flood, 1993: 209–221), makers of hand-decorated cakes, where the production manager could fulfil one or the other requirement exactly. More often he would make a subjective decision that cakes rejected at inspection actually conformed to requirements! This again leads back to the basic issue of 'requirements': what are they, how are they defined, who decides them?

Crosby is not particularly illuminating on this issue, which, as can be seen, has critical impact. In the context of a physically hard and readily definable product, specifying requirements is essentially straightforward. In the context of natural products such as foods, whether processed or not, and services, certain characteristics of the product are less tangible, or even intangible, except at the point of consumption. Consequently, it is very difficult to specify requirements and even more difficult to know whether these have been met. The Chesswood Produce story (Vignette 5.1) illustrates this point. Since you cannot have your cake and eat it, it is difficult to know whether it matched the requirements unless these requirements are so loosely specified as to be almost meaningless.

5.3 METHODS

Crosby's principal method is his fourteen-step programme for quality improvement (Box 5.2). It is essentially very straightforward and relies on a combination of both quantitative and qualitative aspects.

The first two steps may be seen as addressing cultural aspects of the organization. The first is about management commitment; this means the management accepting responsibility for, or an obligation to, achieving quality. Such a commitment then constrains management to consistently behave in a manner oriented towards quality achievement. This may proscribe or inhibit many of the traditional ways in which they have managed – however effective or ineffective these may have been.

When linked to the second step – the formation of quality improvement teams – a further traditional boundary is broken. Organizations are still structured predominantly on functional lines. Crosby specifically requires multidisciplinary teams. This means that managers and other staff must break out of their 'comfort zones' and, inevitably, relinquish some of the 'expert' and 'position' power (Handy, 1985: 124–126) that goes with the functional organization. A wholehearted embrace by management of these two steps alone may be considered a major achievement!

CHESSWOOD PRODUCE LTD

Chesswood Produce is a long-established and successful mushroom-growing business. Operating from two sites in the United Kingdom, it supplies mushrooms to the major supermarket chains and the wholesale market. Mushroom growing is a 24 hour per day, all year round business.

As with other production businesses, the keys to success in a highly competitive market are productivity, yield and quality. To ensure that quality standards are maintained, the staff at Chesswood adhere to rigorous controls in the entire process of growing, cropping and packing the mushrooms – over 400,000 lb (180,000 kg) of them per week – around 200 tons!

The eight-week growing process starts with the preparation of compost, which is mixed and matured to a standard 'recipe' consisting of straw, different kinds of manure, water and various trace ingredients. Once pasteurized, the compost is run with spawn, placed in trays and cased with a protective layer of peat. The mushroom spawns are sourced from a single supplier and, once again, adhere to rigorous quality and performance standards. The cased trays are then moved to climate-controlled growing sheds, where they are monitored during the growth period. The monitoring system controls the air temperature, moisture content of the trays and air movement, with the aim of maximizing yield and minimizing damage to the very delicate crop. To meet the demands of the supermarket customers, careful planning is required to enable sufficient quantities of mushrooms to be available on the correct day of each week; mushrooms have a very short shelf life.

Despite these efforts, and the considerable skill and expertise of the mushroom growers, the crop matures at slightly different rates so that the mushrooms do not all appear at the same time or are not all the same size; each one doubles in size every 24 hours in the final stage of growth. Some are early, being ready to pick ahead of the others, some late.

This presents a problem. The mushrooms will not grow to meet accurately the exacting specifications laid down by the supermarkets. Each quality specification fills a binder covering around eight product categories from buttons, through closed cups and open cups to flats (open field-type mushrooms). The specification covers the size, shape and colour of the mushrooms as well as the packaging and labelling standards. While these latter standards can be specified and met exactly, when it comes to the mushrooms themselves Chesswood and their customers are relying on the judgement of individuals. This natural product just cannot be 'made' to a standard specification.

Chesswood is continually under pressure from its customers to improve quality – whatever that may mean in the circumstances. Eight lorry-loads a day leave Cheswood's sites, and very few mushrooms are returned as out of specification!

Consider how Crosby's approach could be applied to any other business in which natural variation in the product is inherent.

Box 5.2 *Philip Crosby's fourteen-step quality programme*

Step 1   Establish management commitment – it is vital that the whole management team participate in the programme; a half-hearted effort will fail.

Step 2   Form quality improvement teams – the emphasis here is on multidisciplinary team effort. An initiative from the quality department will not be successful. It is essential to build team working across arbitrary, and often artificial, organizational boundaries.

Step 3   Establish quality measurements – these must apply to every activity throughout the company. A way must be found to capture every aspect, design, manufacturing, delivery, and so on. These measurements provide a platform for the next step.

Step 4   Evaluate the cost of quality – this evaluation must highlight, using the measures established in the previous step, where quality improvement will be profitable.

Step 5   Raise quality awareness – this is normally undertaken through the training of managers and supervisors, through communications such as videos and books, and by displays or posters.

Step 6   Take action to correct problems – this involves encouraging staff to identify and rectify defects, or pass them on to higher supervisory levels where they can be addressed.

Step 7   Undertake zero defects planning. This is done by establishing a committee or working group to develop ways to initiate and implement a Zero Defects programme.

Step 8   Train supervisors and managers. This step is focused on achieving understanding by all managers and supervisors of the steps in the quality improvement programme in order that they can explain it in turn.

Step 9   Hold a 'Zero Defects' day to establish the attitude and expectation within the company. Crosby sees this as being achieved in a celebratory atmosphere accompanied by badges, buttons and balloons.

Step 10   Encourage the setting of goals for improvement. Goals are of course of no value unless they are related to appropriate timescales for their achievement.

Step 11   Encourage obstacle reporting, whereby employees advise management of the factors which prevent them achieving error-free work. Such factors might include defective or inadequate equipment, poor-quality components, etc.

Step 12   Provide recognition for contributors. Crosby considers that those who contribute to the programme should be rewarded through a formal, although non-monetary, reward scheme. Readers may be aware of the 'Gold Banana' award given by Foxboro for scientific achievement (Peters and Waterman, 1982).

Step 13   Establish quality councils. These are essentially forums composed of quality professionals and team leaders allowing them to communicate and determine action plans for further quality improvement.

Step 14   Do it all over again. The message here is very simple: achievement of quality is an ongoing process. However far you have got, there is always further to go!

The third and fourth steps are quantitative and directly linked again – the fourth is simply not possible without the third. Measurement is a necessary precursor to evaluation.

These steps in turn provide a platform for the fifth step: raising quality awareness, a more qualitative issue. To make the quality training relevant for supervisors and managers, it needs to be set firmly in the context of the quality status of the firm as evidenced by the measurements.

This step also may be seen to act as reaffirmation of the first two steps: gaining commitment and the multifunctional approach. Through measurement and evaluation, the interrelatedness of quality issues across internal boundaries can be highlighted.

Step 6 is to take action. The other steps are worthless unless they lead to preventive and corrective action. At this point, staff really must 'walk the talk'. It has both qualitative and quantitative aspects. If the numbers generated through the measurement system are simply used as clubs with which to beat the heads of the staff, they are unlikely to prove very helpful. The numbers must be used to provide guidance and support to the action taken and the actions taken must be in harmony with the words spoken.

Once step 6 has commenced, the organization can be seen to have established a sound platform for quality improvement: staff and management are committed and action is being taken. It could be argued at this stage that provided the momentum of improvement is maintained, quality will continuously improve. Crosby's process, however, sees this as insufficient; with the process firmly established he proposes an increased effort and impetus towards 'zero defects'. This is the thrust of step 7 – zero defects planning – which strives to establish a zero defects programme, an essentially quantitative target but achieved through both soft and hard approaches. Step 8 involves training of supervisors and managers so that they can pass on the programme to their subordinates. This tactic of 'train the trainer' is a powerful mechanism for culturally embedding the behaviour changes that are required – provided always that the more senior managers similarly embrace the changes.

Step 9, Zero Defects Day, may be seen as both a celebration of achievements to date and a new beginning to the quality improvement programme. This takes Zero Defects as a very precise, quantifiable and achievable objective. Following the previous steps, it should be accepted by the whole organization as possible and necessary. Step 10 is a natural consequence of step 9 and requires commitment to achieving goals for improvement tied to defined and relatively short-term timescales. Again it is quantitative in nature, the results being directly measurable.

Step 11 – obstacle reporting – is a communication device which recognizes that failure to achieve quality in one area may be related to failure in another, or to local factors which inhibit quality achievement. This process enables those facing problems to report them, and, importantly, it places obligations on management to address those issues. Time-frames for response and action are built into this step, which requires both a change in culture – the acceptance by management of criticism from the workers – and a change in the nature of managers' roles. Particularly for problems which cross functional boundaries, it will be insufficient for managers to concentrate on their own direct areas of responsibility; they will have to work with managers of other areas to achieve the targets.

Step 12 requires acknowledgement of the contribution of staff to the process – a direct reward for the efforts made. Crosby is very specific that these rewards should be formal but non-monetary. This step is largely cultural in its impact. Recognizing and rewarding the contributors to the programme is a device for reinforcing among the whole staff a particular kind of behaviour, further embedding the quality culture.

The establishment of quality councils at step 13 is seen as 'institutionalizing' the quality programme – making it a part of the embedded culture. It becomes at this stage an integral part of the way in which the company is managed and controlled. Mainly qualitative in nature, it will affect many aspects of the way in which the staff of the company behave in the future.

The final step – 'Do it all over again' – should be seen as a reminder that quality improvement never stops. Any programme such as this will, over time, lose impetus and thrust simply because the original, perhaps revolutionary, leaders will achieve the objectives which they set themselves. They may find it difficult to maintain the initial enthusiasm and drive. In order to sustain and develop the programme, it will be necessary to pump new energy into it by the appointment of fresh people and the establishment of new objectives.

Crosby's 'quality vaccine' (Logothetis, 1992: 82–83) is an essential part of his process. It is based on three principal ingredients:

- integrity;
- dedication to communication and customer satisfaction;
- company-wide policies and operations which support the quality thrust.

Logothetis proposes a triangle (Figure 5.1) of interaction between these three ingredients which must be supported by Crosby's belief in how the vaccine is administered. This again has three strands:

- determination – awareness that management must lead;
- education – for management and staff;
- implementation – creating an organizational environment where achievement of quality is regarded as the norm, not the exception.

This chapter is not intended to provide an exhaustive account of methods, tools and techniques; that is for Part four, where aspects of Crosby's approach will be returned to in more detail. The 'how' rather than the 'what' will be dealt with in the appropriate chapters. This section has, however, provided an introduction to the principal strands of Crosby's method, which can be seen as based largely in quantitative outcomes and to rely heavily on an evangelical attitude among both the management and the staff.

5.4 SUCCESSES AND FAILURES

Quality gurus, like doctors, are prone to advertising their successes and burying their failures. Companies act similarly: a successful quality programme will be advertised in order to attract

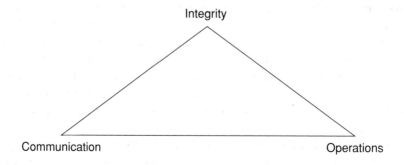

Figure 5.1 *Philip Crosby's triangle of interactions*

customers, whereas a failure will be swept under the carpet, with executives pretending that it never happened. It thus becomes impossible to find reported empirical evidence of failure.

Success, on the other hand, is shared. The guru proclaims the success of his method, while the company proclaims the success of its strategy and acknowledges the contribution made by its interpretation of the particular guru's approach. Chrysler's Lee Iacocca, for example, cited by Bank (1992: 75), says, 'we established our own Chrysler Quality Institute in Michigan, modelled after his [Crosby's] operation – our company's put about twenty thousand of our people through it . . . and I admit they do return with QUALITY stamped on their foreheads.' Thus Crosby's contribution has been explicitly acknowledged here, but Chrysler has used his work as a model. What we cannot see is how closely the model follows the original!

With his consulting company, Quality College and overseas operations firmly established, Crosby must be acknowledged as having been successful. It is also the case that sufficient client organizations must have found the approach useful to have sustained the development and growth of that organization over a lengthy period of time. It must be concluded that there is some real value to be found in his approach.

Flood (1993: 27–28) acknowledges this in identifying five strengths to Crosby's work. Summarizing, he sees these as:

- clarity;
- recognition of worker participation;
- rejection of a tangible quality problem, acceptance of the idea of solutions;
- Crosby's metaphors – 'vaccine' and 'maturity';
- Crosby's motivational style.

Flood also criticizes perceived weaknesses, however. He sees:

- a danger of misdirected effort from 'blaming' workers;
- emphasis on marketing more than recognition of barriers;
- failure of the management and goal orientation of the fourteen-step programme to 'free workers from externally generated goals';
- the potential for 'zero defects' to be interpreted as zero risk;
- ineffectiveness in coercive power structures.

Looking at the strengths, it could be argued that clarity and simplicity of approach are not necessarily beneficial in dealing with increasingly complex problems. It must be the case that the adequacy of any problem-solving tool must be measured in terms of its suitability for the problem being addressed. This must be considered when selecting an approach.

The value of the second strength, worker participation, cannot be denied. First, the people who do the work may be the only people who can recognize the roots of a particular problem. Second, their involvement implies easier acceptance of ownership of the programme and the solutions.

The conception that all quality issues can be resolved is very useful in provoking ideal goal seeking behaviour among the participants in the situation. Bank (1992: 23) compares this to the British ice-skaters Jayne Torvill and Christopher Dean aiming for perfect scores even though

61

these may not be attainable. He cites Thomas J. Watson, founder of IBM, as saying, 'It's better to aim at perfection and miss than it is to aim at imperfection and hit it.' Acceptance that certain problems cannot be solved could be seen as reinforcing behaviour and attitudes which ensure that they never will be.

Creativity and leadership must be seen as essential strands in quality improvement. However, while some writers see great strength in Crosby's approach to this, there is also, perhaps, inherent danger. The 'charismatic' or 'evangelical' style adopted by Crosby has been criticized by Juran, the subject of Chapter 9. Crosby, cited by Bank (1992: 76), says, 'Dr. Juran seems to think I am a charlatan and hasn't missed many opportunities to say that over the years.' The founding charge here seems really to be one of a lack of substantial underpinning to Crosby's approach, perhaps reflecting other comments about promotion 'through slogans and too often full of platitudes'.

There can be no doubt that many of the most sustained management theories and approaches through the years have been well marketed, yet when examined by others have been demonstrated to have either theoretical or methodological weaknesses. This is almost inevitably true. Theories validated within one paradigm can probably always be disputed from within another. Similarly, it is often said that there is no such thing as bad publicity, and that, to quote Oscar Wilde in *The Picture of Dorian Gray*, 'There is only one thing in the world worse than being talked about, and that is not being talked about.'

That Crosby is an effective self-publicist cannot be denied. However, this does not necessarily detract from the value of what he is saying. Perhaps the comments of another great self-publicist, Winston Churchill, Britain's Second World War prime minister, should be noted. Churchill is known to have annotated his speeches with what might be seen as 'stage directions'. One of his most well known is the reported admonition in the margin of a speech, 'Weak point – SHOUT!'

Regarding the weaknesses, it is arguable whether the interpretation of Crosby as blaming the workers is reasonable. Bendell (1989), for example, states that Crosby 'does not believe that workers should take prime responsibility for poor quality; the reality, he says, is that you have to get management straight first'. Bendell further suggests that in the Crosby approach, 'management sets the tone on quality and workers follow . . . the initiative comes from the top'. Thus it could be argued that rather than creating a 'blame the workers' culture, the Crosby approach is a form of empowerment, led by the management. The difficulty rests in how the messages are translated by the managers in the middle – and that to a large extent depends upon how they receive them and how competent they are to retransmit them.

The issue of platitudes and lack of substance has already been largely addressed and goal orientation comes into focus. It is clear that Crosby considers only one goal for the organization, and that is 'zero defects'. Flood's criticism here is much better founded. The external setting of goals by the management is far from empowering or emancipatory and neglects to address workers' perception of their own values and needs. It must be recognized, however, that the requirement for quality is being driven from the environment of the organization. If survival of the organization is to be achieved, then quality products which 'conform to requirements' are an essential feature.

Misinterpretation of 'zero defects' as meaning the avoidance of risk is another reasonable point. There will always be an element of risk involved in a change of behaviour or process. To overcome the danger of risk aversion, management must develop a cultural environment where risks can be calculated and minimized, and where learning from mistakes is encouraged, perhaps incorporating ideas of the 'learning organization' (Senge, 1990; see Chapter 19 of this book).

Flood's strongest criticism is of the assumption that people will work in an open and conciliatory manner. He makes it clear that in a political or coercive context, this will not apply. Many management writers agree that an element of politics and coercion is present in most organizations, whether or not this is explicit. There will always be a dominant group or sub-group, and it is suggested that having a fully open and conciliatory atmosphere is an ideal rather than an easily achievable objective.

5.5 CRITICAL REVIEW

Overall, the foundation of Crosby's approach can be seen in two elements. First, his extensive professional background in quality will have provided the quantitative bias to his method; second, his reportedly charismatic personality will have provided the qualitative aspects.

The general value of measurement in establishing standards and objectives for quality is readily recognizable, while the principles are transferable between organizations and people. The value of the qualitative issues are much harder to evaluate and transfer. The majority of managers would not perhaps consider themselves to be 'charismatic' leaders, an epithet more readily used in respect of others than it is of ourselves. A wholehearted commitment to quality achievement throughout the organization is undoubtedly required; what is questionable is whether the exhortative, inspirational slogans and platitudes will work in all circumstances and for all managers.

It has to be concluded that the process and quantitative aspects of Crosby's programme – a word which in itself implies a discrete activity rather than ongoing management behaviour – may be readily transferable. However, the management style adopted will have to reflect the needs, values and personalities of those involved in the programme.

Similar comments can be applied to other aspects of the approach. For example, while encouraging reward, Crosby suggests that this should not be monetary. It is perhaps the case that the reward, to be truly meaningful to the recipient, should reflect his or her needs and aspirations. For an individual whose focus is professional achievement, then public recognition of his or her contribution may be all the reward that is required. For an individual on low wages, perhaps seeking to reduce personal indebtedness or, in an extreme case, to pay for life-preserving medical treatment, a monetary reward may be precisely right.

Reflection is also necessary on the suitability of the approach for different industries. With his manufacturing background Crosby has developed an approach which reflects that it is essentially possible, in the manufacturing environment, to know when a defect-free product has been achieved. This is far more difficult in the service sector where definitions of the product are harder to generate and delivery is almost impossible to control. Certain aspects of service are relatively straightforward to quantify – for example, how many times the telephone rings before it is answered, or precisely what words of greeting are used (although there have been cases reported where the telephone was being answered too promptly, frightening the customers!). Other aspects are less susceptible to measurement and control – for example, tone of voice. The nature of many of these transactions is that the service is provided and consumed instantly. While they can, to some extent, be designed and planned, their production is uncontrollable. They also depend on factors which are perhaps outside the ability of the organization to influence effectively. These factors include the expectations of the customer, his or her mood, the sort of day the customer has already experienced and the level of service he or she has received before. These factors cannot be known until after service has commenced.

Therefore Crosby's approach has to be marked with some cautions about its general applicability across a range of industries and cultures. What works very well for Philip Crosby at ITT, or for Lee Iacocca at Chrysler, may not work in a bank in Hong Kong, or on a North Sea oil production platform.

SUMMARY

This chapter has presented the work of Philip Crosby through a five-point critical framework. It has described his philosophy and its underpinning assumptions, outlined his principal methods, examined the successes and failures of the approach, and summarized these in a brief critical review. Readers may refer to Crosby's own works, particularly *Quality Is Free* (1979), to enhance and develop their own knowledge and understanding.

QUESTION

Discuss Crosby's assertion that 'There is no such thing as a quality problem.'

W. Edwards Deming

A prophet is not without honour, save in his own country.
(Matthew 13:57)

KEY LEARNING POINTS

W. Edwards Deming's definition of quality: a function of continuous improvement based on reduction in variation around the desired output.

Seven Deadly Sins and Diseases:

- lack of constancy;
- short-term profit focus;
- performance appraisal;
- job-hopping;
- use of visible figures only;
- excessive medical costs;
- excessive liability costs.

Five key beliefs: quantification; recognition of failure causes; systematic approach; continuous improvement; constancy.

Principal methods: fourteen principles for transformation; the seven-point plan

INTRODUCTION

W. Edwards Deming, who died in 1994, is considered by many to be the founding father of the quality movement. He is perhaps the most widely known of the gurus, both within and outside the quality field. Deming held a doctorate in physics from Yale and was a keen statistician, working in the US government for many years in the Department of Agriculture and the Bureau of Census. According to Bendell (1989: 4), Deming rose to prominence in Japan,

65

where he was closely involved in (and, Bendell suggests, largely responsible for) the post-war development of quality there. Heller (1989) sees Deming as having a 'passionate belief in man's ability to improve on the poor and the mediocre, and even on the good', a belief which, as we shall see, is evident in both his theory and his practice. Logothetis (1992: xii) sees Deming as advocating 'widespread use of statistical ideas, with management taking a strong initiative in building quality in'. Bank (1992: 62) cites Hutchins's belief that a major contribution made by Deming to the Japanese quality movement was in helping them 'to cut through the academic theory, to present the ideas in a simple way which could be meaningful right down to production worker levels'.

Summarizing, Deming's approach can be seen as founded in the traditional scientific method (arising from his physics and statistics background). He was also a very capable communicator. Although, as Bendell (1989: 5) suggests, it is 'difficult to delimit his [Deming's] concepts', owing to the constant refinement and improvement of his ideas, his successful and widely read book *Out of the Crisis* (1986) presents his approach to both management and quality in its most succinct, coherent form.

6.1 PHILOSOPHY

Deming's initial approach, largely rejected by US industry at the outset, was based on his background in statistical methods. His quantitative method provided a 'systematic, rigorous approach to quality' (Bendell, 1989: 4). Drawing on the work of the statistician Walter Shewhart, his tutor, Deming urged a management focus on causes of variability in manufacturing processes.

Deming's first belief can be seen here, that there are 'common' and 'special' causes of quality problems. 'Special' causes are those relating to particular operators or machines and requiring attention to the individual cause. 'Common' causes are those which arise from the operation of the system itself and are one of the responsibilities of management.

Deming believed in the use of statistical process control (SPC) charts as the key method for identifying special and common causes and assisting diagnosis of quality problems. His aim was to remove 'outliers' – that is, quality problems relating to the special causes of failure. This was achieved through training, improved machinery and equipment, and so on. SPC enabled the production process to be brought 'under control'. Remaining quality problems were considered to be related to common causes – that is, they were inherent in the design of the production process. Eradication of special causes enabled a shift in focus to common causes to improve quality further.

Deming's second belief is apparent here, a quantitative approach to identifying and solving problems. It is suggested by Bendell (1989: 4) that this statistically based approach brings its own problems. He reports lack of technical standards and limitations of data, and, perhaps more importantly, 'human difficulties in the form of employee resistance and management lack of understanding as to their roles in quality improvement', particularly in the US applications. Bendell considers that perhaps 'too much emphasis was being given towards the statistical aspects'. It can be suggested that Deming's approach reflects to a significant degree the 'machine' view of organizations outlined in Chapter 4. It is also fair to make two further observations. First, the normal level of learning about statistics for most of us does not proceed beyond the age of 16; our grasp of the subject is usually tenuous and we often find it hard to understand fully what the results achieved really mean. Second, given contemporary information technology, the results which Deming's methods reveal could be presented more meaningfully. As is also true of other experts in their respective fields, the value of Deming's work could be obscured by our ability to interpret it.

Notwithstanding these problems, Deming became a national hero in Japan and his methods were widely taken up. In 1951, the Deming Prize for contributions to quality and dependability was launched, and in 1960 he was awarded the Second Order of the Sacred Treasure, Japan's premier Imperial honour.

A third strand to Deming's work was the formulation of his systematic approach to problem solving, an approach which is now commonplace and frequently reinterpreted in other methodologies – for example, the EPDCA cycle in Oakland's work (see Chapter 10) – and is central to the application of the ISO 9001:2000 standard. This has become known as the Deming, Shewhart or PDCA cycle – Plan, Do, Check, Action – which is illustrated in Figure 6.1. The cycle is continuous. Once it has been systematically completed, it recommences without ceasing. This is in agreement with Crosby's admonition, already considered, to 'Do it all over again.' The approach is seen as re-emphasizing the responsibility of management to be actively involved in the organization's quality programme, while Logothetis (1992: 55) considers that it provides the basis for a 'self-sustaining quality programme'.

Two further beliefs can be derived here. First, Deming believes in a systematic, methodical approach contrasting sharply with the *ad hoc* and random approach found in many quality initiatives. The second belief is in the need for continuous quality improvement action. This contrasts sharply with the overtones in Crosby's approach, which suggest a discrete set of activities.

Deming's later work focused on Western, and particularly US, management. Here Deming (1986: 97–148) elaborated seven fundamental beliefs (the 'Seven Deadly Sins' – Box 6.1) about bad management practices which he considered must be eliminated before Western styles of management could be transformed to support the implementation of a successful quality initiative.

Sin 1, 'lack of constancy', is seen by Logothetis (1992: 46) as urging 'an absolute and constant commitment on the part of senior management to quality, productivity and innovation'. Inherent in this is a continuing drive towards better quality and reliability of product in

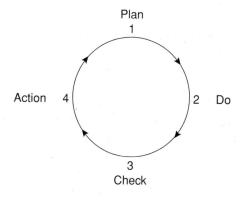

Figure 6.1 *W. Edwards Deming's Plan, Do, Check, Action cycle*

Box 6.1 *The 'Seven Deadly Sins', according to W. Edwards Deming*

Sin 1	Lack of constancy
Sin 2	Short-term profit focus
Sin 3	Performance appraisals
Sin 4	Job-hopping
Sin 5	Use of visible figures only
Sin 6	Excessive medical costs
Sin 7	Excessive costs of liability

---

order to drive down costs, protect investment and employment, create and enlarge markets, and hence generate more jobs. It is seen as providing a positive and achievement-oriented focus for the organization. Deming (1986: 98) criticizes management, particularly in US industry, for being 'run on the quarterly dividend'. It is certainly true that today ever more organizations throughout the world are managed according to the 'flavour of the month', with senior managers flitting from miracle solution to miracle solution while more junior managers keep their heads down and wait for the passion to pass.

Sin 2, 'short-term profit focus', is seen as challenging and potentially defeating the 'constancy of purpose' previously urged. Deming (1986: 99) suggests that

> Anyone can boost the dividend at the end of the quarter. Ship everything on hand, regardless of quality: mark it shipped, and show it all as accounts receivable. Defer till next quarter, so far as possible, orders for material and equipment. Cut down on research, education, training.

Here, Deming is making clear his belief in a management approach with a long-term orientation. He gives explicit recognition to the need to satisfy shareholder expectations, but points out that these expectations must go beyond the immediate return on capital to consider the long-term future of the organization. Much criticism has been levied in recent years at what is now known as 'short-termism' in the City of London, on Wall Street, in Exchange Square or Raffles Place. The underlying reasons and causes are not the subject of this book, but readers may wish to consider issues such as the increasing ownership of shares by financial institutions and the difficulties of making money by making products in a harsh business environment. Pension and investment companies are frequently the largest stockholders in public companies; it is worth thinking about their requirements and the reward packages of their employees, which are often tied to short-term performance measures.

Sin 3, performance appraisal, is considered by Deming (1986: 102) to 'nourish short-term performance' and 'leave people bitter, crushed, bruised, battered, desolate, despondent, dejected, feeling inferior' – a somewhat damning indictment. Logothetis (1992: 47) sees appraisal as encouraging 'rivalry and isolation' and demolishing teamwork, again leading back to a focus on individual and short-term results, noting that 'people who attempt to change the system (for the better) have no chance of recognition'.

While acknowledging Deming's belief in the potential damage that a poor appraisal system can cause, this is rather more a function of a badly designed system than a necessary outcome of performance review. As with the quality of a manufactured product, the quality and impact of an appraisal system will depend upon the quality of its design. Most of us need and enjoy recognition of our achievements and can benefit from the guidance delivered through a constructive and effective appraisal system. This benefit perhaps partly reflects the esteem element in Maslow's hierarchy of needs.

Job-hopping – regular movement of management between jobs either within or between organizations – is the fourth sin. Originally seen as a particular attribute of Western management, this has been increasingly common in Far East locations such as Singapore and Hong Kong, although recent economic reversals in those and other Asian economies have challenged the trend. Job-hopping is considered to lead to instability and further reinforce the short-term orientation of the organization. Logothetis (1992: 39) suggests that it destroys teamwork and commitment, and ensures that many decisions are taken in whole or partial ignorance of the circumstances surrounding them. The belief this time is in the need for commitment on the part of management to the long-term future of the organization.

Sin 5 is 'the use of visible figures only'. Here Deming criticizes failure to recognize and evaluate the intangible aspects of the organization – for example, the additional sales generated through satisfied customers, the benefits to productivity and quality derived from people feeling part of a success story and the negative impact of performance appraisal or barriers to achieving quality. Deming (1986: 123) considers that managers who believe that everything can be measured are deluding themselves and suggests that they should know before they start that they will be able to quantify only 'a trivial part of the gain'. This should be seen as a belief in intangible, invisible benefits arising from good management practice. It does, however, conflict with his espousal of statistical methods, since the reliable measurement of intangibles is notoriously difficult. Lessons could perhaps be drawn here from organizational psychology, which can help to measure some of the aspects that Deming considered intangible, and by re-examining the organizational and financial structure of the organization, which often obscures where the true profits and costs arise.

The sixth and seventh sins revealed by Deming are given little attention by other writers on his work. His points are simply made. The sixth sin, medical costs, both direct in lost labour costs and indirect in the sense of medical insurance premiums, are met largely by the employer. Thus they are an additional cost to be recovered in the price of the product. According to Deming (1986: 98), William Hoglund of the Pontiac Motor Division informed him that the direct cost of medical care to the company exceeded the amount spent on steel for every vehicle produced!

The cost of insurance is driven by claims experience and actuarial expectation, and it is arguable whether Deming is making a fair point here. Medical costs are currently covered in every developed nation. If they are not supported by private insurance schemes such as prevail in the United States, France, Singapore and many other nations, they may be met by a national scheme such as the National Health Service in the United Kingdom. Either way, the company may be considered to bear the cost, through direct contribution, or by increased basic wages which enable the employees to meet the cost themselves. For example, in the United Kingdom, employees receiving an appropriate level of income pay between 7 per cent and 10 per cent of their wages into a National Insurance scheme intended to cover the costs of primary health care and provision of a state pension. In addition, employers pay a contribution of around 10 per cent of total salary costs into the same scheme on behalf of the employees. It is doubtful whether there is any real difference in the cost related to this between employers in the United States and those in the United Kingdom.

The seventh and final sin is one that now seems to be gaining further ground – that is, 'liability costs'. There is evidence throughout the developed world of an increasingly litigious public, perhaps encouraged by lawyers working on a 'no win, no fee' basis. While many potential liability issues are insurable, many others are not. The costs of these must be borne by the organization. Whether management and manufacturers can reasonably be blamed for this issue is certainly arguable and it is questionable whether it is within their power to control it effectively. It is suspected that it relates to broader societary changes such as an increasing trend towards individual rather than collective values and the hunt, whenever things go wrong, for the often elusive 'someone to blame'.

Summarizing Deming's philosophy, we can identify a number of clear strands. There are evident beliefs in:

- quantitative, statistically valid, control systems;
- clear definition of those aspects under the direct control of staff – that is, the 'special causes' – and those which are the responsibility of management – 'the common causes'. Deming suggests that these are as high as 94 per cent!;
- a systematic, methodical approach;
- continuous improvement;
- constancy and determination.

Taken together, these cover the first five of his 'Deadly Sins'. The other two are highly arguable.

Along with Crosby, Deming (1986: ix) considers that quality should be designed into both the product and the process. He believes that 'transformation of the style of American [sic] management' is necessary, requiring a 'whole new structure, from foundation upward'.

6.2 ASSUMPTIONS

The assumptions about the world that Deming seems to make in order to underpin his approach will now be explored.

First, it can be seen that while the approach initially focuses attention on existing processes to derive immediate improvement – the eradication of 'special causes' of failure – it is rapidly refocused to the management process and attitudes. Deming seems to believe that these must be, in his own words, 'transformed' in order for sustained improvement to be achieved. The management is seen to be responsible and, significantly, to be capable of undertaking the proposed transformation. He does not suggest, in organization design terms, how this should be achieved.

Second is the assumption that statistical methods, properly used, will provide quantitative evidence to support changes. At the same time, he recognizes that some aspects cannot be easily measured, and suggests that managements frequently fail to take seriously those aspects which they consider unmeasurable.

The third key assumption is that continuous improvement is both possible and desirable. Taking his definition of quality as 'meeting the needs of the customer, both present and future' (1986: 5), this has to be questioned. If the needs of the customer are fully understood and fully met, where is the benefit in further improvement?

A further aspect to this is perhaps more significant in the new millennium. The assumption is that continuous improvement supported by an orientation towards the long term will enable the organization to meet customers' 'future needs'. If, however, the contemporary world is characterized, as Handy (1990a) suggests, by 'discontinuous change', then a long-term view and continuous improvement may no longer be enough. Perhaps organizations must be built which can anticipate and prepare for sudden, maybe catastrophic, change. The Compaq example in Chapter 3 illustrates the point: continuous improvement and incremental change may not be sound recipes in a discontinuous world. The 'boom and bust' of the supposed new economy dotcom businesses is another example. While many of these businesses were undoubtedly built on weak foundations, many others should have been capable of survival. The inevitable collapse of the weak brought down many of the strong.

Deming's final assumption, as with Crosby, is about the service sector. Simply, he sees that the prime role of the service sector, in the context of a national economy, rests in enabling manufacturing to do its job. He suggests (1986: 188), for example, that

> A better plan for freight carriers would be to improve service and thus to decrease costs. These cost savings, passed on to manufacturers and to other service industries, would help American industry to improve the market for American products, and would in time bring new business to carriers of freight.

While offering specific advice in the same text about quality improvement in the service sector, Deming, unlike Crosby, does explicitly recognize the difficulty of measuring certain aspects of it. He seems also to assume an initially altruistic effort which contrasts sharply with his accusations of short-termism. To some extent, he is possibly correct: cost savings should be passed back down the chain, and in a systemically developed solution this could occur. Such a move, though, is probably more a function of truly competitive and open markets rather than an altruistic or collaborative gesture.

The implications of his assumption about the role of services should also be considered. As suggested in Chapter 1 (Vignette 1.1), it can be observed that few local communities thrive when their manufacturing base is lost. For example, the shipbuilding and coal-mining communities in the United Kingdom suffer from major economic difficulties, social fragmentation and mass unemployment. Notably, many service sector jobs and organizations can now be clearly seen to have depended upon local manufacturers through the direct purchase of services by the major organizations and the expenditure of wages by the employees. The wealth generated by the employer was in large part expended in the same community. As the manufacturing sector has declined, so too has the service sector.

Those sectors where services have continued to thrive are in areas of specialist technical expertise such as banking, insurance, finance and other knowledge-based industries. These industries have a less dependent relationship on the manufacturing sector than, say, retailing and real estate. Notwithstanding these particular aspects, there is perhaps a warning at a national and multinational level. If individual communities cannot be adequately sustained when manufacturing is lost to them, then is there any future for nations if their manufacturing base as a whole is lost?

6.3 METHODS

Deming has four principal methods:

- the PDCA cycle;
- statistical process control;
- the fourteen principles for transformation;
- the seven-point action plan.

The first of these has been introduced already and will not be dealt with further here. The second, statistical process control (SPC), is briefly explained below. The fourteen principles for transformation and seven-point action plan will provide the major content of this section.

SPC is a quantitative approach based on measurement of process performance. Essentially a process is considered to be under control – that is, stable – when its random variations fall within determined upper and lower limits. That is seen by Deming as the process having achieved a position where the special causes of failure have been eradicated.

A control chart, a sample of which is provided in Figure 6.2, is used to record the value of a measurement associated with an event in a process. Statistical analysis of the values recorded will reveal the mean value. Normal variation from this mean value for the particular process in its established state is conventionally taken as any value within ± 3 standard deviations of the mean. Events which fall outside that normal variation are considered 'special' and should prove tractable to individual diagnosis and treatment. Events falling within the norms are considered to have 'common' causes – that is, they are a product of the organization of the system and require treatment at the system level. Here we can refer directly to Deming (1986: 315) and re-emphasize the role of management in the development of quality:

> I should estimate that in my experience most troubles and most possibilities for improvement add up to proportions something like this:
>   94% belong to the system (responsibility of management)
>   6% special.

It has to be acknowledged here that Deming's split of special and common causes, and consequently his allocation of responsibility for error, relates directly to the product of SPC. At ± 3 standard deviations in a stable system, it is inevitable that 95 per cent of errors will belong to the system – 95 per cent is only 2 standard deviations in a normal distribution. Three standard deviations (approximately 99.7 per cent of results) are recognized through SPC as representing stability – the system is under control. The standard (± 3 sigma) was originally devised by Shewhart to minimize net economic loss from rectifying mistakes, the objective of Taguchi's 'quadratic loss function', to be elaborated in Chapter 12.

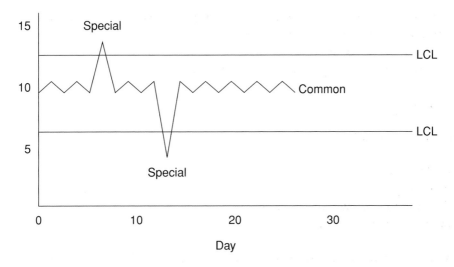

Figure 6.2 *Sample control chart. LCL and HCL are the lower and upper confidence limits, respectively*

Box 6.2 *W. Edwards Deming's fourteen principles for transformation*

Principle 1	Create constancy of purpose to improve product and service
Principle 2	Adopt a new philosophy for the new economic age, with management learning what their responsibilities are and assuming leadership for change
Principle 3	Cease dependence on mass inspection to achieve quality, by building quality into the product
Principle 4	End the awarding of business on price; award business on total cost and move towards single suppliers
Principle 5	Aim for continuous improvement of the system of production and service to improve productivity and quality and to decrease costs
Principle 6	Institute training on the job
Principle 7	Institute leadership with the aim of supervising people to help them to do a better job
Principle 8	Drive out fear so that everyone can work effectively together for the organization
Principle 9	Break down barriers between departments. Encourage research, design, sales and production to work together to foresee difficulties in production and use
Principle 10	Eliminate slogans, exhortations and numerical targets for the workforce since they are divisory, and anyway difficulties belong to the whole system
Principle 11	Eliminate quotas or work standards and management by objectives or numerical goals; leadership should be substituted instead
Principle 12	Remove barriers that rob people of their right to pride in their work
Principle 13	Institute a vigorous education and self-improvement programme
Principle 14	Put everyone in the company to work to accomplish the transformation

We can now turn to the first main focus of this section, Deming's fourteen Principles for Transformation (Box 6.2). These, like Crosby's fourteen steps, are essentially straightforward and rely on a combination of statistical and human, or cultural, aspects. The principles will be reviewed in turn.

The first three principles – creating constancy of purpose, adoption of a new philosophy and ceasing dependence on mass inspection – may all be seen as focused on the cultural aspects of the organization. The first principle is aimed at creating a 'team' type of environment where all are working together towards a common goal. It requires the management to commit themselves to achieving ever-improving quality as a primary objective of the organization. The story of the regeneration of Kennet School (Vignette 6.1) illustrates this point.

The second principle, that of embracing management learning and a leadership-based style of management, concerns acceptance by the management that the responsibility for developing and achieving the changes is theirs. It requires explicit recognition by management that the workers are not necessarily to blame for quality deficiencies. This may well require a dramatic change in both words and actions on the part of management, particularly if they have been accustomed, as so many are, to pushing the blame down through the hierarchy.

The third principle, ceasing dependence on mass inspection by building quality into the product, requires a further dramatic change in management approach and has major implications for issues such as organization structure and information management. A simple abandonment of mass inspection not supported by changes in other aspects will potentially be disastrous. A successful example of such a change is the introduction in recent years of

VIGNETTE 6.1 **KENNET SCHOOL: A TALE OF CONSTANCY AND DETERMINATION**

Until January 1989, Kennet School presented a disappointing picture. The lack of coherence and consistency in support to the teachers constrained them from exploiting their talents and abilities. While some pupils performed exceptionally well, certain parents perceived the school as a 'glorified youth club' – somewhere to send the children to keep them occupied while they, the parents, were out at work. Limited leadership was in evidence: there was little communication between members of staff, parental complaints were ignored and the buildings were neglected. The school was suffering a falling pupil roll, threatening the sixth form of only 90 pupils with closure. In measured performance terms, only 28 per cent of pupils obtained five or more passes at grades A–C in the General Certificate of Secondary Education (GCSE) examinations – a dismal record.

In 2001, despite the provision of extra buildings, the school is practically at capacity in pupil numbers and the sixth form is thriving. The 2000 examination results show 63 per cent of pupils obtaining five or more GCSE passes at grades A–C. The standards attained by the school led to it being listed in early 1997 as outstanding in examination results and inspection. Kennet School is one of only 63 secondary schools in England and Wales recognized in this way, and the only school in West Berkshire.

The achievement of this turnaround has been through 'constancy and determination' rather than the use of a 'miracle cure', or the adoption of any particular guru's methodology. The new headmaster appointed in 1989 adopted a 'classical' approach to management in the early days. He imposed discipline on both the children and the staff, letting 'nothing go by that [he] didn't like'. Development and imposition of rules and standards for staff and children was immediate. These covered issues such as movement, behaviour, uniform and homework, and were supported by action on his part. The smooth functioning of the school now rests on these rules, which received high visibility at the outset. A staff handbook is in use which sets out the aims of the school and is supported by clarity of responsibility, with everyone now knowing 'who is responsible for what'.

The priority of the school is academic excellence. Sporting success (a regular achievement) and pastoral issues are regarded as important in supporting the academic objectives, the means to achieve educational ends, rather than ends in themselves. The creation of an 'inner cabinet' chaired by the headmaster emphasizes this priority. The cabinet consists of the heads of the eleven academic faculties within the school, together with one head of house. This unbalanced representation confirms in action the words of the headmaster – 'walking the talk'!

The headmaster recognized that some 'early wins' were required to ensure that his different way of running the school would be perceived as correct. Ten members of staff left in the first three years, some voluntarily, some less so. Two children were expelled. There was necessarily some conflict during those early days, and while there was much discussion with the people affected, the head held, and still holds, an absolute veto on all matters – although he exercises extreme caution in using it. He recognizes the need to achieve a balance between making things happen and doing everything himself – a possible outcome of an autocratic approach.

With a system of rules in place and acceptance by the staff of the new way of working, much of the decision-making power has been passed to the heads of departments (notwithstanding the headmaster's veto). Their decisions (as well as those referred to the headmaster) rest on one simple question: 'What is the benefit in the classroom?' If there is no benefit, then the proposal will fail. The criterion for the introduction of new ideas or approaches is simply educational benefit.

Creation of a three-year rolling development plan for the school is undertaken by the heads of departments and their staff and subjected to a 'round robin' process of modification and refinement. Every member of staff receives a copy of the completed plan. The final column of the plan shows who is responsible for which aspects – making accountability open and public. The senior staff undertake a review and refocusing of the plan at termly intervals.

The school, now managed in a much more decentralized manner, with trust given to staff and pupils wherever possible, still adheres to three global targets:

- continuous improvement in academic standards;
- staff development;
- improved behavioural standards and sustained improvement in the environment of the school.

In the words of the headmaster, 'There is so much more to do.'

multidisciplinary product development teams in organizations such as John Deere Tractors. These teams include both design and production engineers so that products are now designed with production requirements in mind rather than having to be re-engineered for production. This speeds up the development of new products, reduces manufacturing complexity and leads to improved quality. Other major manufacturing companies are following the same route.

The fourth principle, that of no longer awarding business on the basis of price rather than total cost, is a recognition that the invoiced unit price of a sub-assembly or part is only a fraction of its total potential cost (or value) to the organization. For example, a part which has the lowest unit cost may carry with it a high level of rejects. This leads to either high inspection costs to identify poor-quality parts or a poor quality of finished product, leading in turn to high inspection and rework costs, and potential for product failure in the hands of the customer.

A number of aspects need to be considered in the identification of the total cost of a purchased item. These may include unit cost, quality (failure and reject rate), inspection costs, inventory costs (for example, the potential for implementing a 'just-in-time' or kanban system) and ease of use in the manufacturing environment – that is, the impact of the supplied item on labour and other costs. The other aspect which must be considered is the purchase of items which support the manufacturing process such as machine tools, conveyor systems and control systems. Particularly with these latter items, the ongoing running costs are often a far greater part of the total lifetime cost than the initial purchase price. Significant benefits can be obtained by bearing a higher initial cost in order to generate longer-term savings. A prime example of this is with Mercedes cars. While the initial capital cost of buying a Mercedes is significantly greater than for competitors' equivalent models, the Mercedes is reputed to depreciate at a far lower rate (under 40 per cent over the first three years life compared to more than 60 per cent) than vehicles made by those competitors, and with greater component reliability and longevity also has lower running costs (although many other manufacturers are now achieving comparable levels of performance).

Deming also recommends a move towards single suppliers. As with so many things, this approach has both advantages and drawbacks. The principal advantages are that it provides the purchaser with significant leverage in negotiating improvements in product quality and price, it enables long-term relationships based on trust and mutual support, and it provides a more secure financial platform for the provider. Conversely, reliance on a single source of parts supply makes the purchaser vulnerable to any failure on the part of the supplier, either financially or in quality. Such exposure may give cause for concern to bankers and other financiers. A worthwhile approach here would be to consider the use of a single supplier based on Porter's (1980) model for competitive rivalry. Where supplier power is weak (there are many suppliers and the product is undifferentiated or non-critical), a single-supplier strategy may bring significant benefits to the company, enabling it to take effective control of its supplier. Where supplier power is strong (there are few suppliers, the product is differentiated or critical), the organization may maximize its position by supporting more than one supplier.

The fifth principle, aim for continuous improvement, if considered appropriate to the customer's needs and industry circumstances, gives greater substance and focus to the first two by focusing attention on productivity, quality and decreasing costs. Objectives at this stage can be made more quantifiable, moving from the ideals of the first principles to a more practical, achievement orientation.

The sixth principle, on-the-job training, emphasizes the need to improve competencies and skills in the practical context. While not excluding classroom-based training, this principle suggests that the objective of continuous improvement applies at least as much to people as it does to processes.

The seventh principle, leadership, is again qualitative and cultural, and is closely associated with the eighth, 'drive out fear'. These principles are connected with the management style of the organization. The objective here can usefully be seen as a requirement to move away from an adversarial style of management towards a collaborative style. Effective management in this way, supported by the SPC techniques, will focus attention on how to improve the individual (special causes) or the system (common causes), rather than on who to blame. The approach will again target curing the diseases rather than convicting the victims.

The ninth principle, that of breaking down barriers, can be seen as linked to the fourth. The suggestion here is, in effect, for the creation of multidisciplinary teams for product and service development, aiming to enhance the development, production and delivery of new products or services. Deming does not discuss how this can be achieved or specifically recognize the difficulties that can be associated with it. There are a number of cultural and professional issues which often emerge in the creation of multidisciplinary teams, and any reorganization into either a matrix form of management or project teams needs to be associated with commensurate changes in salary and bonus packages to enable congruence of individual and organizational goals.

The tenth principle, 'eliminate slogans, exhortations and numerical quotas', is again more a cultural than a quantitative statement. Here Deming is suggesting that these features act more to vex the staff than to encourage them. His argument is simple. If through the use of SPC the 'special causes' of failure related to individual machines and workers have been removed, then all other causes of failure relate to the system itself. These are seen as the responsibility of management, so no amount of slogans, exhortations and quotas will have any positive effect. Instead, Deming (1986: 67) suggests, they will 'generate frustration and resentment'. This principle clearly links to the second, which required management to accept their responsibilities.

The eleventh principle, 'eliminate quotas, work standards and management by objectives or numerical goals and substitute leadership', seems to be something of a contradiction. Improvement targets must be an inherent part of measuring and monitoring achievement, and statistical process control provides one form of measurement of achievement. However, Deming's point here is that if the system is stable, as will be revealed by the control charts, then its performance cannot be improved by the setting of targets, only by changes to the system. As with slogans and exhortations, Deming sees the setting of targets and quotas as potentially both meaningless and divisive unless accompanied by a specific action plan to improve the process. This may well mean reappraising what the system is designed to achieve.

Removal of barriers that rob people of their right to pride in their work is the twelfth principle. Deming distinguishes management and workers from each other here. He sees that annual appraisal or merit review focuses the attention of management on the matters that will be covered in the appraisal or merit system. He implies that they will strive to achieve those things regardless of the impact on quality or productivity – that is, they will do the right thing by the appraisal system, not by the customer!

77

The workers he sees as being constrained by uncertainty of employment, by lack of definition as to what constitutes acceptable workmanship, by poor-quality materials, tools and machines, and by ineffective supervision and management. He suggests that if these aspects are corrected, then quality products will follow. Deming (1986: 85) suggests, 'Give the work force a chance to work with pride, and the 3 per cent that apparently don't care will erode itself by peer pressure.' He seems to ignore the idea that the whole organization of many factories, based on the principles of classical management theory, is established (whether or not intentionally) to remove pride in achievement from the workers by fragmenting tasks.

Principle 13 is to institute a vigorous education and self-improvement programme. This is Deming's recognition that if the organization is to continuously improve, then the people must continuously improve. He suggests that future competitive advantage will be achieved through knowledge, a conclusion that there can be little argument with.

The fourteenth and final principle is to put everyone to work to achieve the transformation. This suggests that the whole programme can be successful only if a 'total' approach is taken. This will require a strong, unified and cohesive culture within the organization with commitment from top to bottom. Such a culture can be achieved only when the behaviour of management is consistent with their words – that is, when they 'walk the talk'.

Taken together, these principles can be summarized as proposing wholesale attitudinal change throughout the organization (a qualitative approach), supported where appropriate by reliance on validated statistical analysis (quantitative).

To enable the principles to be implemented, Deming proposed a seven-point action plan (Box 6.3). This action plan is perhaps best interpreted as a series of statements about what to do, rather than the more important question of how to do it. Its first three points clearly focus attention on the top management group and are based on attitudes and communication. They suggest that this group must understand what they are trying to achieve, commit themselves to a successful outcome and then communicate to subordinates throughout the organization

---

Box 6.3 *W. Edwards Deming's seven-point action plan*

Point 1	Management must agree on the meaning of the quality programme, its implications and the direction to take
Point 2	Top management must accept and adopt the new philosophy
Point 3	Top management must communicate the plan and the necessity for it to the people in the organization
Point 4	Every activity must be recognized as a step in a process and the customers of that process identified; the customers are responsible for the next stage of the process.
Point 5	Each stage must adopt the 'Deming' or 'Shewhart' cycle – Plan, Do, Check, Action – as the basis of quality improvement
Point 6	Team working must be engendered and encouraged to improve inputs and outputs; everyone must be enabled to contribute to this process
Point 7	An organization for quality must be constructed with the support of knowledgeable statisticians

why it is necessary. This has distinct overtones of Crosby's more directly evangelical approach and reflects what can be thought of as the ethical aspect of the programme – that is, the need for quality to be embraced in the values and beliefs of *all* members of the organization. It can surely be agreed that if the management are not wholly committed to the programme, and are unable or unwilling to communicate it effectively to the workforce, who must similarly accept it, then it will not work.

The fourth point recognizes the process-based work flow of most organizations and calls for the processes to be divided into stages. Each stage becomes a clear task, with the recipients of its outputs being treated as its customers. Thus at every stage there are customers whose needs must be identified and satisfied. This can be seen as an attempt to overcome the problem of workers in many processes, for example in the manufacture of sub-assemblies. These staff are often unaware of customers and do not recognize the sub-assembly as a product in its own right, but rather see it as a part of a larger product which perhaps they never see. It is suggested that this shift of emphasis enables workers to take a pride in their work that is otherwise absent.

The fifth point is simply to implement continuous improvement at every stage through the PDCA cycle. Achievement of implementation in this way implies acceptance, by both management and workers within each process, of responsibility for the process. This in turn implies that higher management must allow them authority to develop and implement the changes.

The next point, participation in team work to improve all inputs and outputs, can be seen to operate at several levels. First, a team culture must be developed within each process to improve it internally. Second, since changes in one area may have implications in another, a team culture must be engendered between process owners (the management) to enable effective communication between them. Third, to be truly effective, a means of sharing and developing improvements across processes must be developed. This links the whole programme back to top management.

The seventh point, construction of an organization for quality, is perhaps a further development of the third part of stage 6, improvement across processes. The requirement is to build an organization which reflects and nurtures the achievement of quality. Perhaps reflecting his own background, Deming suggests the use of knowledgeable statisticians to support this aspect. It is useful to go well beyond this and propose the support of a multidisciplined team of management scientists and experts such as cyberneticians, psychologists, statisticians and accountants to work with the management team in the pursuit of the programme, thereby emphasizing the collaborative nature of achieving quality. It is not suggested that the management scientists develop and impose a programme of change; such a course of action would be almost certainly doomed to failure. It is suggested rather that the management and workers should be responsible for the whole programme, having both control and ownership. The role of the management scientists is to use their expertise in a supportive, guiding manner, as experts within the team.

The introduction to Deming's approach is now complete. SPC and methodologies for implementing quality will be addressed in the appropriate chapters. This section is concluded by reaffirming that while initially Deming's approach was rooted in quantitative methods, it later came to be supported by more qualitative techniques.

6.4 SUCCESSES AND FAILURES

While overall Deming can be said to have been very successful in his achievements, there have been both successes and failures. His movement into Japan, for example, was to some extent a result of the early rejection of his ideas by American managements. This perhaps reflects the maxim that 'a prophet is not without honour, save in his own country'. It was only after his substantial successes with Japanese industry that Deming was able to turn his attention again to the problems of industrial America.

Here, what Flood (1993: 14) calls Deming's fundamentally 'mechanistic' approach ran into 'strong workforce resistance, from both the managers and the workers'. Deming, taking account of these issues, together with matters of reliance on technology, standards of practice and the cultural issues, substantially revised his methods. The change is reflected in the shift in emphasis from quantitative to qualitative approaches and in the codification of the 'Seven Deadly Sins'.

According to Flood (1993), the principal strengths of Deming's approach are:

■ the systemic logic, particularly the idea of internal customer–supplier relationships;
■ management before technology;
■ emphasis on management leadership;
■ the sound statistical approach;
■ awareness of different socio-cultural contexts.

Significant weaknesses are also recognized:

■ lack of a well-defined methodology;
■ the work is not adequately grounded in human relations theory;
■ as with that of Crosby, the approach will not help in an organization with a biased power structure.

Reviewing the strengths, the value of the systemic and logical approach cannot be denied. Put simply, it is an organized and systematic rather than chaotic approach. The 'Plan, Do, Check, Action' cycle as a mechanism for organizational learning is recognized in other areas of management as a 'learning cycle'. Handy (1985), for example, refers to a process of:

■ questioning and conceptualization – fundamental parts of effective planning;
■ experimentation – trying out ideas, the testing and evaluation of hypotheses;
■ consolidation – the alteration of habits, the basis for future action.

Handy sees this as the basis of human learning – that is, continuous personal improvement. It is unsurprising that a similar process works for organizations, which, after all, have people as their fundamental organizational units. This cycle will be seen echoed in Chapter 19 on organizational learning.

Deming's prioritization of management before technology represents a reversal of the attitudes of many managers. The British adage that 'a bad workman always blames his tools' recognizes that the tendency for most managers is to look at external rather than internal factors as responsible for failure. If, as Deming suggests, 94 per cent of problems belong to the management, then acceptance by them of responsibility is a primary step in enabling change. Equally, even the worst tools can be made to perform better in the hands of a good workman, but a bad workman will not achieve good performance however good the tools.

The recognition of the importance of leadership and motivation can be seen to reflect the development of human relations theory as a major strand of management thinking, although Deming does not draw heavily on the body of knowledge that became established in that area during his productive years.

Regarding the strong quantitative base, perhaps Flood does not go far enough, and it could be suggested that some form of measurement system, whether relying on hard, physical measures or on softer aspects using techniques from organizational psychology, is fundamental to achievement of quality. A simple attempt to 'do better' will always be followed by questions such as 'how much' or 'when'. Vagueness on these issues would be expected to have a dispiriting effect on the participants, while a form of achievement target orientation would be motivational. Success is said to breed success, but first of all it must be known that success is being achieved!

The recognition by Deming of different cultural contexts is a vital strength. His failure to draw heavily on the literature of human relations theory for this aspect suggests that his embrace of it was driven by pragmatism rather than desire, perhaps a reluctant recognition that it was necessary to allow the other ideas to work. Nonetheless, the recognition of different cultures, and adaptation to them, are essential in achieving success. Hofstede (1980) produced theprincipal work in this area. In the context of quality, the recognition needs to go well beyond the country differences highlighted by Hofstede to recognize the particular culture of organizations themselves, and even sections, functions and departments within organizations. These frequently have unique, perhaps very strong, cultural contexts.

Flood's criticism of a lack of a clear 'Deming method' can be seen as reasonably well justified. Like many gurus and experts, Deming suggests what to do without indicating very precisely how to do it. While perhaps constraining on the one hand, this lack of precision can be seen as potentially disemprisoning and empowering. It encourages experimentation and debate within each individual context to find an approach which will work there rather than using an approach which was developed in another time and context. Perhaps the most important issue is reliance on Deming's principles.

The second weakness having been covered within the strengths, the third can be examined. Deming is criticized for saying nothing about intervention in political and coercive situations. Perhaps, following the previous point, nothing needs to be said. The second principle and the first three points of the action plan all call on management to accept their responsibility for quality and productivity and to embrace a new philosophy. These remarks are targeted directly at the most senior members of the management team – that is, those who hold power in a political or coercive context. If they do not accept responsibility at the outset, they are ignoring the principles, and, by default, not following the Deming method. If they seek to impose a quality approach on others, failure will certainly follow. Deming's whole approach rests on the attitude of management.

81

6.5 CRITICAL REVIEW

The foundation of Deming's approach can be seen in his statistical background and his training in the science of physics. These essentially 'hard' sciences based in scientific method will have informed the development of his early approaches. It must be acknowledged that they continue to make a major contribution to work in the field of quality.

The principles and practice of SPC have been demonstrated over time to have considerable value to organizations in both the service and manufacturing sectors. They also have value for the workers who use them, providing rapid and personal performance feedback information, enabling them to recognize their own successes and failures and to take corrective action where appropriate, provided always that the outputs are expressed in a language which they can understand.

Deming's work in relation to the softer issues is considered to be narrow and underdeveloped, failing to take account of much of the thinking in that area over the period of his career. It must, though, be acknowledged that Deming did not claim to be an expert in this area. Nevertheless, the value of his approach could have been further enhanced by a clearer focus on that aspect.

The Plan, Do, Check, Action cycle is a clear directive to both management and workers that achieving continuous improvement is the purpose of the quality activity. This contrasts directly with the hints of a discrete programme suggested in Crosby's work.

Deming makes quite clear reference to the service sector in his work, but again places much emphasis on quantitative aspects of this area. For example, he refers to aspects such as how long a telephone is out of action before it is repaired. While this is of great importance, of equal importance is the tone of voice which a person uses in answering the telephone when it rings. This may be a stronger determinant of how the customer perceives the level of service quality than the number of times that it rings, or even the words that are said – readers will recall the comment on this issue in the Chapter 5.

It is often the case that managers take measurements of the things which are easy to measure, rather than the things which, while difficult to measure, are of greater importance. In a world which relies ever more heavily on telecommunications devices, these aspects, which are more difficult to quantify, will have increasing importance. The reliability and clarity of modern digital telecommunications systems are such that these are no longer significant issues, and many businesses are run entirely through them – for example, telephone-based banking and insurance services. Of increasing importance, then, is tone of voice, since technical issues are less problematic and digital technology makes tone of voice transparent to the listener. The more recent development of videophone technology and Internet telephony, which are not yet widespread, will have further impacts on this area of service.

It is accepted that Deming has probably made the most substantial contribution to quality management. However, enthusiasm must be tempered with the knowledge that if he had provided a clearer method, a more explicit and developed recognition of the human aspects, and a precise focus on what constitutes quality of service in the contemporary world, the value of his work would have been enhanced.

SUMMARY

This chapter has presented the main strands of the work of W. Edwards Deming through the five-point critical framework. Readers wishing to develop their knowledge further should read the relevant chapters in Part four of this book and refer to Deming's own work, in particular *Out of the Crisis* (1986).

QUESTION

Deming suggests that 94 per cent of quality problems are the responsibility of management. Review this statement.

Armand V. Feigenbaum

Quality is simply a way of managing a business organisation.
(Logothetis, *Managing for Total Quality*, 1992)

KEY LEARNING POINTS

Armand V. Feigenbaum's definition of quality: a way of running a business organization.

Key beliefs: systems thinking, relevant measurement, participation.

Principal methods: the four steps to quality, operating quality costs.

INTRODUCTION

Armand Feigenbaum originated the approach to quality known as Total Quality Control (TQC), which has a clear industrial focus. After completing a doctorate at MIT (the Massachusetts Institute of Technology), Feigenbaum joined the General Electric Company, where he was manager of world-wide manufacturing operations and quality control, before becoming president of General Systems Company. His book *Total Quality Control* (1986), completed while he was still a doctoral student, and his other works were discovered by the Japanese in the early 1950s. He was also involved with them through his business contacts with Hitachi and Toshiba.

Bendell (1989: 15) states that Feigenbaum presented a case for a 'systematic, or Total approach to quality', and it is argued by Bank (1992: xv) that he was the first to do so. Logothetis (1992: 94) suggests that to Feigenbaum, 'quality is simply a way of managing a business organisation', while Gilbert (1992: 22) concurs with that and adds that Feigenbaum sees 'quality improvement as the single most important force leading to organisational success and growth'.

Feigenbaum's contribution has been widely recognized. He was founding chairman of the International Academy for Quality and is a past president of the American Society for Quality Control, which awarded him the Edwards Medal and Lancaster Award for his international contribution to quality and productivity (Bendell, 1989: 15).

7.1 PHILOSOPHY

Feigenbaum's philosophy is clearly founded in his early idea of the 'total' approach, reflecting a systemic attitude of mind. He saw it as fundamental to quality improvement that all functions in an organization should be involved in the quality process and that quality should be built into the product rather than failure being inspected out. He defines quality as 'best for the customer use and selling price' and quality control as 'an effective method for co-ordinating the quality maintenance and quality improvement efforts of the various groups in an organization so as to enable production at the most economical levels which allow for full customer satisfaction'.

There is no difficulty in accepting the systemic nature of Feigenbaum's philosophy. While the work of both Deming (see Chapter 6) and Juran (see Chapter 9) can be interpreted in a systemic manner, Feigenbaum is explicit from the outset that such an approach is vital. In the contemporary, complex world of organizations, there is every need to manage from a systemic perspective – recognizing and dealing with interactions across internal and external organizational boundaries and at all levels within them, as well as with the suppliers, customers and other stakeholders in the enterprise.

The issue of building quality in can also be addressed here. This recognizes that organizations do not simply manufacture products; they also design and develop them. Feigenbaum appears to be suggesting that many quality problems can be eradicated from both the products and the manufacturing process by paying attention to the quality issue from the conception of the idea, right through to delivery of the first and subsequent items. Basic design techniques here might include colour-coding wires so that electronic products cannot be incorrectly wired, or varying bolt positions in otherwise apparently symmetrical pieces of metal so that they can only be mounted correctly.

Looking at Feigenbaum's definition of quality, two constraints are discovered which have not previously been seen: 'customer use' and 'selling price'. The first of these is perhaps no different from Deming's 'needs of the consumer' or Crosby's 'conformance to requirements', but it suggests a constraint, rather than an ideal to aim for. It seems to imply that there are, perhaps, limits to useful quality. The issue of selling price clearly indicates that for any given price, Feigenbaum perceives limitations to the expectations of quality. This can perhaps be interpreted as saying that a quality differential, in terms perhaps of longevity, performance or reliability, between, say, a car costing US$10,000 and one costing US$100,000 is to be expected and is acceptable. This also implies developing an understanding of the real use to which a customer will put the product.

His definition of quality control emphasizes the integral nature of the quality process, stressing 'co-ordination' of maintenance and improvement efforts across 'groups'. It is notable that he does not say 'functions' or 'departments'. This should be interpreted as a recognition of the human relations aspects of organizations.

To summarize Feigenbaum's philosophy, a commitment to a systemic, 'total' approach and an emphasis on designing for quality and involving all departments are evident. Supporting this is recognition of, and reliance on, the human aspects of the organization. Statistical methods are used as necessary, which contrasts quite sharply with the greater statistical emphasis in the work of Deming.

7.2 ASSUMPTIONS

Feigenbaum's apparent assumptions about the world reveal a different understanding from that of Deming of Crosby.

First is his explicit assumption of a world composed of systems. He works with the inter-relationships that he perceives to exist between all aspects within the organization, and, importantly, in its environment or market. He recognizes the contribution made by suppliers, and the constraints, particularly on performance expectations and price, imposed by customers.

The systemic view is clear again in his second assumption, that human relationships are a basic issue in quality achievement. This concurs with the developments in management thinking being made by the human relations school that were occurring at the time of his early work.

In these assumptions, he clearly focuses attention on the whole enterprise, from suppliers to users, through every function and to all the groups who are involved in it. The development in more recent times of global businesses serving global markets, of ever more complex and interdependent relationships between organizational, social and individual well-being and the emergence of many more virtual organizations based on strategic partnerships, leads to the conclusion that this systemic view must be sustained.

An organization can today be more clearly seen to exist within an eco-system comprising economic and social relationships, in which it will ultimately either thrive or become extinct. Although not explicitly referring to adaptation of the organization, Feigenbaum's commitment to 'full customer satisfaction' implies constant awareness of customer needs and expectations within the organization, and the need for change to satisfy them.

Feigenbaum further assumes that continuous improvement is both desirable and achievable. Referring again to his definition of quality, we can see the potential for conflict and contradiction. For example, if customer expectations on performance and price are met, then quality, by his definition, has been achieved. However, unless the process of TQC ends, then further improvement will arise. This in turn implies a need for the organization to interact with its customers, aiming to alter their expectations of quality, perhaps as suggested by Galbraith (1974). There is a danger, therefore, that as with that of Crosby, Feigenbaum's approach can be interpreted as a finite, ends-oriented and discrete programme, whereas his intent appears to have been for continuous improvement.

7.3 METHODS

Flood (1993: 35) has reduced Feigenbaum's philosophy to a four-step approach, but these steps (Box 7.1) should be viewed as a simplification of his overall method. Nevertheless, the steps may certainly be seen as capturing the fundamental essence of Feigenbaum's approach, which is intended to lead to a 'Total Quality System'. This is defined by Bendell (1989: 16) as

> the agreed companywide and plantwide operating work structure, documented in effective, integrated technical and managerial procedures, for guiding the co-ordinated actions of the people, the machines and the information of the company and plant in the best and most practical ways to assure customer quality satisfaction and economical costs of quality.

86

VIGNETTE 7.1 **MCDONALD'S, HONG KONG: FULL CUSTOMER SATISFACTION**

McDonald's, Hong Kong, which has built its business on the three characteristics of food quality, convenience and price, has clearly developed a unique approach to the idea of full customer satisfaction. The two letters reprinted below show that McDonald's has recognized that customer satisfaction in its case goes well beyond simply serving the right food at the right time and price. The first letter demonstrates its commitment to the total McDonald's experience. The customer does not mention food but is impressed by the quality of overall service and the hygiene standards of the washrooms.

January 19, 1996

The Managing Director
McDonald's Restaurant (HK) Ltd.
Upper G/F, Park Vale
1060 King's Road
Quarry Bay, H.K.

Dear Sir:

I would like to draw your attention to the outstanding performance and good job done by your staff of the Sai Kung Court outlet.

I live in Sai Kung, occasionally I pay visits to your Sai Kung Court outlet for afternoon coffee. In each of the visits, I am so impressed by the cleanliness and tidiness of the shop. Your staff work hard to do the cleaning work in turns, while the staff at the counters handling customers efficiently. In addition, the lady's room is not big though, it is always filled with paper rolls and smells pleasant. The excellent quality of hygiene standard and customer service should be considered as a model among the McDonald's shops.

Congratulations for hiring such a team of good staff in providing comfortable environment. I'll certain keep visiting this shop with my family.

Best regards,

Christine Chan

Christine Chan
A Fan of the McDonald's

cc: Shop Manager, Sai Kung Court

The second letter shows how far McDonald's has gone in becoming a part of the community in which it thrives as a business. Again, food is not the issue; it is service which counts.

March 19, 1996

Miss Doctor Law
First Assistant
McDonald's Restaurants (H.K.) Ltd.
Upper G/Fl., Park Vale
1060 King's Road
Quarry Bay
Hong Kong

Dear Miss Law,

I wanted to write to you to express my deep thanks for looking after my daughter Erin yesterday. The first aid assistance and the very helpful and concerned attitude you showed greatly helped her. It took me 2 hours to drive from my office to your restaurant due to heavy traffic and your understanding was much appreciated.

McDonald's is an amazing part of the community. When Erin was looking for somewhere safe and friendly to shelter she headed straight for the familiar "Golden Arches".

She has had her leg stitched and is resting comfortably now. Thank you again for your help and I hope you enjoy the chocolates.

Kind regards,

Mark I. McCallum

cc: Mr. Don Dempsey (McDonald H.K.)

These examples emphasize the 'total' understanding expressed in Feigenbaum's work. Customer service for McDonald's Hong Kong goes well beyond the standard products and services offered, to include the broader aspects of the McDonald's experience and interaction with the community.

Box 7.1 *Armand V. Feigenbaum's four steps to quality*

Step 1	Set quality standards
Step 2	Appraise conformance to standards
Step 3	Act when standards are not met
Step 4	Plan to make improvements

The Weberian, bureaucratic overtones and dangers inherent in this definition are quite clear. A heavy reliance on documentation and integration of procedures and on co-ordinating the people, machines and information certainly presents an opportunity to those 'keener on talking about work than doing any' (Beckford, 1993). The recent standard ISO 9000:2000 challenges this notion of documentation, with its shift from compliance with documented procedures to a focus on customer satisfaction and continuous improvement and with particular attention paid to active management of skills – a change which Feigenbaum would surely have welcomed. It is fair to say that contemporary information technology makes possible far greater availability of information than was the case when Feigenbaum formulated his approach.

To counter the danger, Feigenbaum used in the first sentence the word 'agreed'. This stresses that everyone must be committed to the design of the organization through effective communication. However, while proposing that gradual development of the programme is preferred, little is said about how agreement is achieved, which permits scope for either autocratic or democratic processes to be employed. While Feigenbaum proposes participation as a means of harnessing the contribution of people and encouraging a sense of belonging, it remains the case that the approach need not be used in this participative manner.

A further tool is the measurement of what Feigenbaum calls 'operating quality costs'. These are divided into four self-explanatory categories and have been met before, in Chapter 3:

- prevention costs, including quality planning;
- appraisal costs, including inspection costs;
- internal failure costs, including costs arising from scrap and rework;
- external failure costs, including warranty costs and complaints.

It can be seen again how Feigenbaum's concept of total quality extends from product development right through to product use – that is, product quality in the hands of the consumer. Bendell (1989:16) states that

reductions in operating quality costs result from setting up a total quality system for two reasons:

1. Lack of existing effective customer-orientated customer standards may mean current quality of products is not optimal given use.
2. Expenditure on prevention costs can lead to a several fold reduction in internal and external failure costs.

The proposal overall is that by measuring quality at every critical stage, the total costs of running the organization will be reduced. A similar concept is met in the food manufacturing industry, which uses a system called HACCP – Hazard Analysis Critical Control Points to evaluate and ensure food product quality and safety at points of risk. This would include such aspects as temperature. If, for example, a product must be boiled, then the HACCP system would test it to ensure that boiling point is actually reached. The emphasis on design again stresses the importance to Feigenbaum of designing quality in to the product.

Overall, Feigenbaum's approach is best seen as part of the kaizen management practices, which are oriented towards management responsibility and involve effective team working across the organization. These tools will be examined in more depth in the appropriate chapters.

7.4 SUCCESSES AND FAILURES

Feigenbaum's approach has undoubtedly been successful and has been adopted in whole or in part by a number of organizations. There is little doubt that his recognition of quality as a way of running an organization, rather than as a secondary activity, was a major breakthrough in thinking in this area, yet even today, many organizations continue to consider quality as an added extra rather than a fundamental of organizational effectiveness. Recent experience with a number of organizations internationally has shown that many continue to focus on 'badge-hunting' through a quality management system rather than on organizational survival through quality products or services. Finally, his systemic concept of 'total' – that is, quality running throughout the organization, from its inputs to its outputs – has immense value.

Flood (1993: 36) again provides a summary of the principal strengths and weaknesses of Feigenbaum's approach, from which the following is adapted. He sees its main strengths as being the following:

- It stresses a total or whole approach to quality control.
- It places emphasis on the importance of management.
- Socio-technical systems thinking is taken into account.
- Participation is promoted.

The principal weaknesses he identifies are as follows:

- The work is systemic but not complementarist.
- The breadth of management theory is recognized but not unified.
- The political or coercive context is not addressed.

It can be added to this critique that the industrial orientation of the approach provides little of real value for service-based organizations. Similarly, it could be said that, as with Deming, there is a lack of clarity of method: ample instruction in what to do is not supported by guidance on how to do it.

The necessity and contribution of the systemic view proposed has already been acknowledged. Similarly, the focus on the importance of management to the process is supported, although as Bendell (1989: 16) suggests, 'modern quality control is seen by Feigenbaum as stimulating and building up *operator responsibility* and interest in quality'. While this is to be achieved through management commitment to the programme, the need for management to *sell* the ideas is stressed, suggesting a certain resistance by employees to accepting the concepts of quality. Although Feigenbaum fully accepts the value of a participative approach, the question has again to be raised – how is such participation to be achieved? Even Flood's choice of the word 'harnessing' in respect of individual contributions is suggestive of a less than wholehearted commitment, having overtones of compulsion.

Looking at the weaknesses, Feigenbaum's work says nothing about the identification and selection of tools, whether management theories or systems approaches, which are most appropriate for a particular organizational or national context. For contemporary managers, this issue is of great importance. Many organizations are globally based, and to achieve agreement, which Feigenbaum requires among the top management, account must be taken of the varying cultures and expectations of the participants. An approach which works well in Hong Kong may fail completely in Tokyo, Los Angeles or London.

Finally, Flood's comment that nothing is said about political or coercive contexts is valid. Feigenbaum's assumption that people can and will work together for the improvement of the organization and its outputs is clear in his work. However, his recognition of the need to *sell* the total quality concept perhaps suggests that a degree of political or coercive pressure may, for him legitimately, be brought to bear to achieve the end result. That said, it is perhaps a little unfair to criticize someone for not offering a solution to a problem he did not set out to address.

7.5 CRITICAL REVIEW

There appear to be three founding ideas to Feigenbaum's work: his acceptance of the systems paradigm; a belief in appropriate measurement; and the recognition of participation as a means of developing and encouraging support for change and enabling creativity. Feigenbaum's strong academic background in issues of quality control, supported by his extensive practical managerial experience, undoubtedly provided a substantial platform for the further development and successful application of his ideas.

The apparent lack of a well-developed, clear methodology telling managers how to proceed with his approach is a major drawback. It is suspected that personal and management styles are much greater factors in the success or failure of a Total Quality Control initiative than is normally recognized. Adoption by the most senior management of a collaborative, team-based working pattern is not easily achieved or maintained – especially in organizations where rewards are calculated on the basis of personal rather than team achievement.

Functionally structured companies, for example, normally have power bases within each function. If these power bases are strong, then they may resist the perceived loss of individual or function power that arises from any other orientation. Companies are often heard of which are 'production led', 'marketing led' or 'accounting led'. These are companies which are dominated by a particular power group within a professional specialization. They appear to perceive the world from a particular professional standpoint, and in so doing, perhaps undervalue the contribution of other professions. Adoption of a team-based approach where each profession is valued for its contribution to the whole, perhaps in the form of a project or matrix management system, is unlikely in such companies. Similar comments can be made about issues such as sexual orientation, gender and race – take for example, the privileged positions of WASPs (White Anglo-Saxon Protestants) in the United States, Oxbridge graduates in the United Kingdom, or Bumiputras (indigenous Malaysians) in Malaysia. Professional and other biases must be overcome in the creation of organizations based on expertise, but Feigenbaum says nothing of how to achieve this.

The quantitative aspects of Feigenbaum's approach are welcome. Reliance on statistics 'where appropriate' is a useful guide, encouraging managers to use discretion in their choice of measurements. This contrasts quite sharply with the strong emphasis on measurement proposed by Deming. Feigenbaum is quite selective about what it is useful to measure and when. Like Deming, he proposes, through the four-way division of operating quality costs, a form of customer chain analysis which can be seen to be helpful in identifying not simply the costs of quality but, very importantly, where they arise.

Feigenbaum has undoubtedly made a substantial contribution to work in the field of quality, and certain current developments in quality management carry powerful influences from his work. However, enthusiasm for his approach must be tempered by recognizing some weaknesses with respect to methodology and cultural context, and the important understanding that his work does not go beyond the industrial sector.

SUMMARY

This chapter has introduced the principal strands of the work of Armand Feigenbaum, presenting and reviewing his philosophy, assumptions, methods, and successes and failures. Readers may wish to refer to Feigenbaum's own *Total Quality Control* (1986) to enhance and further develop their understanding.

QUESTION

The chapter suggests that difficulties might arise from Feigenbaum's definition of a 'Total Quality System' with its 'Weberian, bureaucratic overtones'. Critically review Feigenbaum's work in the context of this suggestion.

Kaoru Ishikawa

'At last,' he said, '*el pueblo*'.
(Salvador Allende, President of Chile,
cited by Beer, 1981: 258)

KEY LEARNING POINTS

Kaoru Ishikawa's definition of quality: quality of product, service, management, the company itself and the human being.

Key beliefs: systemic approach; participation; communication.

Principal methods: seven tools of quality control; the fishbone diagram; quality circles.

INTRODUCTION

Kaoru Ishikawa, who died in 1989, commenced his career as a chemist, held a doctorate in engineering and was an emeritus professor at Tokyo University. Bank (1992: 74) describes him as the 'Father of Quality Circles' and as a founder of the Japanese quality movement. He became involved in quality issues in 1949 through the Union of Japanese Scientists and Engineers (JUSE) and subsequently became a world-wide lecturer and consultant on quality. Gilbert (1992: 23) suggests that Ishikawa was the first guru to 'recognise that quality improvement is too important to be left in the hands of specialists'. Ishikawa's writings explaining his approach include the *Guide to Quality Control* (1986) and *What Is Total Quality Control? The Japanese Way* (1985), which have both been translated into English. Ishikawa was widely honoured for his work, receiving the Deming, Nihon Keizai Press and Industrial Standardization prizes and the Grant Award from the American Society for Quality Control.

8.1 PHILOSOPHY

Gilbert (1992: 23) and Logothetis (1992: 95) see the philosophical roots of Ishikawa's work in the concept of Company-Wide Quality. Ishikawa himself, cited by Bendell (1989: 18), said, 'The results of these company-wide Quality Control activities are remarkable, not only in ensuring the quality of industrial products but also in their great contribution to the company's overall business'. Bendell (ibid.) proposes that Ishikawa defines quality as meaning 'not only the quality of the product, but also of after sales service, quality of management, the company itself and the human being'.

Flood (1993: 33) interprets Ishikawa's approach as involving 'vertical and horizontal co-operation'. Thus the approach takes account of communication and co-operation between different levels of managers, supervisors and workers, and from suppliers to customers. Ishikawa's first belief, then, is that everyone involved in or affected by the company and its operations should be involved in the quality programme. This is similar to the 'total' approach advocated by Feigenbaum (see Chapter 7).

The level of involvement proposed is also significant. Ishikawa asks that the programme not just be company-wide (and beyond) but that it involve active participation. His approach to participation emphasizes greater worker involvement and motivation, which Bendell (1989: 19) sees as being created through:

- an atmosphere where employees are continuously looking to resolve problems;
- greater commercial awareness;
- a change of shop floor attitude in aiming for ever increasing goals.

These strands stress three words, all of them qualitative rather than quantitative: atmosphere, awareness and attitude. They are cultural requirements which have direct implications for the behaviour of management.

An 'atmosphere where employees are continuously looking to resolve problems' implies acceptance by management that:

- Workers have the ability to recognize both problems and solutions.
- Management will either accept the need for change and implement proposals, or explain why a proposed change is not possible or desirable in a way which maintains the employees' enthusiasm.

A 'greater commercial awareness' imposes two responsibilities on management. First is to provide or enable training and education for the workforce in this area. Second is to provide to the workforce accurate, meaningful and timely data in respect of the company's performance, as well as that of its competitors. Although commercial awareness is stressed in this regard, these matters should be considered equally important in a public sector or not-for-profit organization, which, rather than focusing on profit, should be focused on delivering the maximum level of service within a constrained resource – that is, value for money.

The third strand, 'a change of shop floor attitude' towards a focus on ever-increasing goals – the culture of continuous improvement – again implies management responsibility. Management must adopt this attitude in their behaviour as well as their words to make its achievement possible. Deming's concern about 'exhortations' is important here, as well as Crosby's promotion through slogans and platitudes.

Clearly, Ishikawa believed that effective participation, like effective communication, is a two-way street, and as suggested by Hagima Karatsu, managing director of Matsushita Communication (cited by Bendell, 1989: 19), 'creative co-operation' between people is an absolute requirement for a quality organization.

Another element of Ishikawa's work is its emphasis on direct, simple communication. According to Bendell (1989: 17), Ishikawa saw 'open group communication' as critical, particularly in the use of his tools for problem solving. A fundamental part of communication for Ishikawa seems to have been an emphasis on simplicity in his methods. For example, his book *Guide to Quality Control* (1986) was deliberately written as a 'non-sophisticated' text, and Bank (1992: 75) suggests that Ishikawa worked in a 'straightforward manner'. Logothetis (1992: 95) stresses that Ishikawa concentrated on 'simple statistical techniques for data collection and presentation'. The requirement for simplicity covers both the qualitative and quantitative issues.

The emphasis on simplicity and using what might be called the language of the shop floor is considered to have an empowering effect. The workers, having been trained in the appropriate methods, are not obliged to use obscure or arcane terminology. Management are unable to hide behind complex approaches and sophisticated language, which in many cases betray a lack of real understanding. Since training is given to all levels of employee, a common quality language is spoken by all, which in turn aids and enhances communication.

Three principal strands can be identified in Ishikawa's philosophy. First, in company with Feigenbaum, is the systemic or holistic approach advocated by 'Company-Wide Quality', an all-embracing view. Second is participation, active and creative co-operation between those affected. The third element is the emphasis on communication through two strands of thinking: simplicity of analysis and method, and commonality of language.

8.2 ASSUMPTIONS

Ishikawa's apparent assumptions about the world will now be explored.

It can be seen that his first assumption is concerned with interrelatedness, a 'total' or systems view. He explicitly recognizes that every aspect of the organization and the relevant parts of the environment must be considered. As with Feigenbaum, it is difficult to argue with that approach, although whether Ishikawa's techniques and methods may be thought of as systemic will be considered in the next section, since some of them seem to rely heavily on a reductionist perspective.

Ishikawa's second assumption is that a fully participative approach can be adopted. This implies a belief that every individual within the organization can, and will, commit themselves to addressing the quality issue. This suggests that a quality 'religion' or creed must become established, and the achievement of higher quality become a superordinate goal, overriding all others as a requirement for organizational success. The primacy of this goal, while perhaps accommodating the requirements of the management or even the owners or shareholders, seems to assume that the primary goals of the workforce will be congruent with those of the organization. However, little is said about how such a state can be achieved, and for example

Bendell (1989: 19) says that '[quality] circle members receive no direct financial reward for their improvements'. Commitment to quality, then, very like religious belief, is considered to be its own reward! This can be contrasted with Crosby's dictum to reward those who contribute to the quality programme.

A further assumption implied is that the quality activity takes place in an organizational environment which is free from political or power relations between participants. While this may be an admirable ideal, it must be perceived as being unrealistic. Both Eastern and Western organizations are subject to internal issues of power and, potentially, coercion. These may be dominant or subordinate issues in the management of the organization but they nonetheless exist. Ishikawa is silent on this aspect and how it may be addressed, perhaps reflecting the strength of his own position, or a lack of awareness of the problems faced by others who are less educated or in less privileged positions. Alternatively, it may simply reflect the strongly collective nature of the Japanese value system.

The third assumption, effective communication, is to some extent associated with the second. Participation relies on effective communication for its success. While the development of a common 'language' for discussing quality issues throughout the company is considered to be a substantial benefit in this regard, it is still possible that communication will be inhibited by cultural or political issues which prevent viewpoints from being expressed. For example, respect for age or status, or fear of loss of face, may prevent an open exchange of views, without which no real communication takes place. The 'loser' in the transaction, who may have a valid viewpoint, is not heard.

Finally, we can turn to the assumption that 'simplicity' in technique and method is useful. While acknowledging that the sophistication of tools must match that of the people who work with them, Ishikawa's work to some extent may be seen as undervaluing or underestimating the people in the organization in assuming that they can cope only with simple concepts and methods. If the complexity of life for an individual is considered, in either the West or the East, it must be recognized that the majority of people deal extremely well with a highly complex existence. For example, coping with accommodation requirements, raising children and managing families (surely the ultimate management challenges), organising pensions and health matters, dealing with state bureaucracies, even driving a car, require complex problem-solving and organizational skills. These skills are rarely articulated and acknowledged, but nonetheless they exist and are used for the most part very well. To assume, as Ishikawa appears to, that everything must be simplified is perhaps arrogant. To forget that, starting from simple skills that we all acquire as children, we can develop through education and experience the ability to handle greater complexity is to underestimate the potential of the workforce and perhaps sow the seeds of future discontent.

A second assumption Ishikawa apparently makes is that problems of quality will be tractable when examined using simple methods and approaches. Products and services are considered by many to be becoming more complex, as are the environments in which organizations exist and the organizations themselves. There are increasing numbers of interrelationships between factors; at the same time, there are perhaps more factors to be considered. The complexity of any situation may be suggested to be increasing through these two prime driving forces. Experience suggests that simple problem-solving approaches are unlikely to be adequate in these circumstances. Other, more sophisticated but not necessarily less accessible tools must be used. Despite their increasing availability and prominence, especially in Western nations during Ishikawa's time, he does not appear to have taken account of them. Some, as will be seen in Part four of this book, reflect values in relation to the workforce which accord well with those of Ishikawa and would have, perhaps, enhanced his approach.

8.3 METHODS

Ishikawa's overarching method is Company-Wide Quality Control. This he sees as being supported by the quality circles technique, and the 'seven tools of quality control'. These will be dealt with in turn.

Company-Wide Quality Control has already largely been addressed as the founding philosophy of Ishikawa's approach, and deals with organizational aspects. It is seen as embracing all departments and functions and uses the tools which will be described in the following pages. Bendell (1989) suggests that fifteen effects arise from this approach (Box 8.1). While acknowledging that these are benefits which may arise from the approach, it cannot be agreed that they are necessarily consequent upon adopting the Company-Wide Quality Control approach. Perhaps, as Logothetis (1992: 96) suggests, 'kaizen consciousness [implied within Ishikawa's work] can only be established when management changes the corporate culture', an area which is not discussed by Ishikawa.

The use of quality circles is Ishikawa's principal method for achieving participation. They are composed of between four and twelve workers from the same area of activity and led

Box 8.1 *Fifteen effects of company-wide quality control, according to Kaoru Ishikawa (Gilbert 1992)*

Effect 1	Product quality is improved and becomes uniform; defects are reduced
Effect 2	Reliability of goods is improved
Effect 3	Cost is reduced
Effect 4	Quantity of production is increased, and it becomes possible to make rational production schedules
Effect 5	Wasteful work and rework are reduced
Effect 6	Technique is established and improved
Effect 7	Expenses for inspection and testing are reduced
Effect 8	Contracts between vendor and vendee are rationalized
Effect 9	The sales market is enlarged
Effect 10	Better relationships are established between departments
Effect 11	False data and false reports are reduced
Effect 12	Discussions are carried out more freely and democratically
Effect 13	Meetings are operated more smoothly
Effect 14	Repairs and installations of equipment and facilities are done more rationally
Effect 15	Human relations are improved

by a worker or supervisor. Their function is to 'identify local problems and recommend solutions' (Gilbert 1992: 92). Bendell (1989: 18) identifies three aims:

- To contribute to the improvement and development of the enterprise;
- To respect human relations and build a happy workshop offering job satisfaction;
- To deploy human capabilities fully and draw out infinite potential.

Gilbert (1992: 92) suggests that there are a number of 'cornerstones' to successful quality circles (Box 8.2). The first four of these factors apply to every successful quality programme: management at all levels must be committed and workers must be trained and willing participants. The 'shared work background' has some limitations, as it may fail to address cross-functional or interdepartmental needs. Solution orientation is a means of ensuring that quality circles do not simply descend into complaint sessions where the focus is on what the management, or adjacent processes, could do or not do. Considerable benefit could be gained in using Ishikawa's approach if the notion of the willing participant and how to encourage willingness had been addressed. In adversarial cultures, or where loyalty between the organization and its employees is limited, as is often the case in Western organizations, such participation is often provided very unwillingly.

Recognition of efforts is a difficult area. If there is only effort and no achievement, then should this be recognized? To maintain efforts and encourage further attempts, it is probably valuable to recognize the work done. However, the difference between effort and substantial achievement should also be acknowledged.

Minutes and an agenda provide, in essence, control devices for the circle. They enable the circle to consider what has or has not been achieved since the last meeting, to keep track of implementation of solutions and to maintain a focus within the circle on innovation rather than reiterating old points. The agenda provides the opportunity both to control the discussion once

---

Box 8.2 Gilbert's 'cornerstones' to successful quality circles (Gilbert 1992)

Top management support

Operational management support and involvement

Voluntary participation of the members

Effective training of the leader and members

Shared work background

Solution-oriented approach

Recognition of the quality circle's efforts

Having an agenda, minutes and rotating chairmanship

Keeping to the time allowed for the meeting

Informing bosses of meeting times

Making sure that quality circles are not hierarchical; if seniority plays any sort of part, you'll find the MD's [CEO's] secretary thinks he or she's too good to attend the regular secretaries' quality forum a meeting has started and, if issued in advance, to give thinking time to the participants before the meeting to consider the issues to be raised. Keeping to time is a matter of good discipline which will be supported by the previous two items.

Informing bosses of meeting times is both courteous and good communication practice. A boss may wish to attend or to provide some input to the meeting, in the form of either ideas or implementation progress, or to support the effort in other ways.

Ensuring a non-hierarchical approach will very much depend on the culture and political issues within the organization. If an ethos of equality in problem solving has genuinely been achieved, there will be little difficulty with this aspect. However, experience of working within quality circles and other team-type environments suggests that hierarchy, of some sort, will very often emerge (Vignette 8.1).

Ishikawa suggests that quality circles should be an integral part of the quality effort, not an isolated approach. They have met with success and failure both in the West and in Japan. Bendell (1989: 19) comments that 'Even in Japan, many Quality Circles have collapsed, usually because of management's lack of interest or excessive intervention.' Both Crosby and Juran are stated to have questioned their effectiveness in the West and the experience outlined in Vignette 8.1 demonstrates some of the scope for failure. Crosby is reported to consider that quality circles are abused as a cure for poor employee motivation, productivity and quality, while Juran suggests that if an organization's management are not trained in quality, then quality circles will have limited effectiveness.

The quantitative techniques of Ishikawa's approach are referred to by Bendell as the 'seven tools of quality control' (Box 8.3). Taken together, they are a set of pictures of quality, representing in diagrammatic or chart form the quality status of the operation of the process being reviewed. Ishikawa considered that all staff should be trained in these techniques.

This chapter will examine only the Ishikawa or fishbone diagram, since this is the only technique that originated with Ishikawa. He developed the approach while at the University of Tokyo to explain relationships between factors. It subsequently became part of his quality tools portfolio and has been widely adopted throughout industry.

The Ishikawa diagram (Figure 8.1) is essentially an end- or goal-oriented picture of a problem situation. The goal or objective is placed at the head of the fish and contributing factors categorized. Gilbert (1992: 111) suggests that major categories such as 'Men, Machines, Materials and Methods' may provide a useful first set of factors. Each of these categories is then subdivided again, the 'fishbones' gaining further ribs and sub-ribs as the whole issue of concern is explored. Other forms of categorization such as processes, technology, knowledge or information systems may also be appropriate. Moreover, the approach is useful in enabling and encouraging participants to express their views.

The approach does not carry with it any automatic means of prioritization of issues, and ideas emerging are not constrained by any limitations. The pragmatic world of management, however, does impose constraints of issues such as time, technology and capital, and these may affect the value of the approach. Issues emerging which are not responded to adequately by those responsible will cause discontent, and perhaps fragmentation of the quality effort. The diagram can easily be used as a device for apportioning blame instead of one for enabling improvement.

Equally, the diagram assumes a linear, 'cause–effect' chain of events. Such an understanding of any problem is limited in that it does not address the potential for interrelationships between

99

VIGNETTE 8.1 **QUALITY CIRCLES INACTION**

In the late 1970s, a retail distributor with several hundred outlets decided to launch a service quality initiative to improve its performance in an increasingly competitive and over-supplied market. The organization, apparently committed to this initiative at its head office, selected 'quality circles' as the driving mechanism to be used at the outlet level.

The senior management of the organization at head office attended training sessions to learn the rules for quality circles, and this training was then extended to the outlet managers themselves. After some time had elapsed, all the training events had been completed and the programme was ready to be launched. Staff were informed by a letter to each outlet from the head office that the organization was to adopt quality circles as a device for improving service quality. The letter further informed them that the local manager would be arranging these events. Other than the outlet managers, no one at the local level was provided with any training whatsoever.

The local managers then called the staff together – at the end of the working day – and informed them that the first meeting of the quality circle would take place at 5 p.m. the following Wednesday. Overtime would not be paid and all staff were expected to volunteer to join the circle. At the first meeting, the rules would be explained and roles allocated within the circle.

The first meetings took place, at which the managers naturally took the role of chair and explained the purpose of the circles. The meetings were then thrown open to suggestions from the staff to improve service quality. Discussion in one outlet focused on the number of ashtrays in the customer-facing areas – were there enough, not enough, too many? Another focused, perhaps quite usefully, on the issue of opening hours, until the manager ruled the discussion 'out of order' since opening hours fell beyond the scope of the outlet to change – a constraint applied in many outlets and to many suggested discussion topics. In most cases, the manager's secretary recorded the discussion and produced minutes. The managers edited these and dispatched the edited version to head office as evidence of the meetings having taken place.

The organization persisted with these events for around twelve months, but no significant or useful ideas emerged and were implemented across the organization. No major changes took place in the organization's systems and procedures which would improve service quality to either internal or external customers. The whole exercise was essentially a waste of time although it could be argued that awareness of quality of customer service was raised among the staff, perhaps bringing some intangible benefit.

There were perhaps four major mistakes made by the organization in pursuing this quality circles initiative. First was the absolute lack of training for the staff involved. Second was the structure of the circles, with managers being appointed (or appointing themselves) as quality circle leaders, thus maintaining the hierarchy of decision. Third, the attempt to achieve participation was by unilateral dictat or coercion, quite apart from the staff not being persuaded that there was a problem to solve. Fourth was the failure by the senior management to understand the structure of the enterprise which they managed, a structure which, in effect, determined where problems could be solved. Any large retail organization adopts standardized systems and procedures to ensure continuity and accuracy of service delivery across its outlets. Even in the 1970s, these were increasingly tied to the capabilities of centralized computer networks. The operation of these networks and their interaction with those of other organizations in the same industry controlled large parts of the customer-facing activity, dictating what it was, or was not, possible to deliver. Changes proposed to these systems were ruled 'out of order' by managers, thereby closing off any possible communication to those running the organization of the customer needs as perceived by the staff who actually dealt with those customers. What it was possible to change locally was the way in which individual staff members dealt with customers – a change which could not be created through the chosen mechanism, but only through individually focused training effort.

This was a classic case of the senior management of the organization appearing to 'blame' the staff for poor customer service, while blinding (or perhaps deafening) themselves to the potential for improvement which lay only within their own power.

Box 8.3 *Kaoru Ishikawa's seven tools of quality control*

Tool 1	Pareto charts	used to identify the principal causes of problems.
Tool 2	Ishikawa (fishbone) diagrams	Charts of cause and effect in processes.
Tool 3	Stratification	Layer charts which place each set of data successively on top of the previous one
Tool 4	Checksheets	To provide a record of quality
Tool 5	Histograms	Graphs used to display frequency of various ranges of values of a quantity.
Tool 6	Scattergraphs	Used to help determine whether there is a correlation between two factors
Tool 7	Control charts	Used as a device in statistical process control

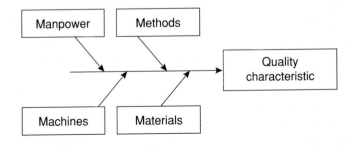

Figure 8.1 *The Ishikawa or 'fishbone' diagram*

causes, or the possibility of dynamic or time-related effects. For example, the interrelationship between workers and machines, called ergonomics, can have a substantial impact on the ability to produce a quality product or service, whereas looking at either in isolation may produce no clue as to the cause of any lack of quality. A successful 'cure' to any problem may mean making adjustments or changes in a number of places both to fix the specific problem and to ensure that the whole system remains in balance. Often, changing only one aspect can push other aspects to a point where they may fail.

To summarize Ishikawa's approach, it can be seen to contain both quantitative and qualitative aspects which, taken together, focus on achieving 'Company-Wide Quality'.

8.4 SUCCESSES AND FAILURES

Ishikawa's world-wide reputation and the widespread acceptance of his ideas suggest that his approach has met with considerable success. That he is best known for the fishbone diagram should not inhibit appreciation of the value of his other work. Similarly, that quality circles have been successful cannot be doubted, notwithstanding the level of failure that has been seen in some organizations. An organizational idea such as quality circles which has been adopted to the extent that Bendell (1989: 19) reports – 'more than 10 million circle members' in Japan alone – has undoubtedly been a successful, useful idea.

According to Flood (1993: 34–35), the strengths of Ishikawa's approach are:

- its emphasis on participation;
- the variety of quantitative and qualitative methods employed;
- its whole-system view;
- the relevance of quality control circles (QCCs) to all sectors of the economy.

Its main weaknesses can be viewed as the following:

- Fishbone diagrams are systematic but not systemic.
- QCCs depend upon management support.
- It fails to address coercive contexts.

To look first at the strengths, participation and the development of tools usable by the stakeholders are of undeniable value. They enable people at all levels in the organization to make a meaningful contribution, in their own terms, to the process of achieving quality. Promoting creativity and increasing motivation have value for both the organization and the individual.

The choice of a mixture of methods and tools which are both qualitative and quantitative encourages a broader understanding of the organization than would be achieved with a simple focus on either a single tool, or a purely qualitative or quantitative approach. The holistic perspective proposed is again supported by the current view that a systemic approach is vital in the contemporary organizational context.

While agreeing that QCCs are relevant to all economic sectors, there remain considerable reservations as to their practical value. It is rare in the West to discover an organization where more than lip-service is paid to the QCC movement. It is very often used as a device for allowing workers to feel that they are involved but with little real commitment from managers. That is to say, the theory in practice is rarely as successful as the theory in theory!

Turning to the weaknesses, it is easy to concur with Flood's view that the 'causal chain' or linear view of problems proposed by the fishbone diagram is limited in its use. It would perhaps be better to recognize that problems are often interacting and far more complex than the fishbone approach will reveal.

The second weakness identified by Flood is the failure faced when management is not prepared to listen to the ideas emerging from quality circles, an aspect which has already been covered. In this case, the organization is probably facing the third weakness, that the approach struggles in a political or coercive context. The view that any human system is to some extent political and/or coercive has already been espoused, and a particular tendency currently prevalent in the West is that of seeking 'someone to blame'. In such a culture, genuine commitment and participation in the quality issue is unlikely to emerge since it implies acceptance of responsibility for both successes and failures. In a 'blame' culture, wholehearted participation will not easily occur since failure is met with some form of disciplinary action or punishment rather than being treated as an opportunity to learn.

8.5 CRITICAL REVIEW

There seem to be three founding elements to Ishikawa's work: an attempt at a holistic view; participation and communication through a common language; and simplicity of approach.

The first of these should be valued highly, as with the work of the other gurus. However, its use is limited by two failures. First, it does not take full account of interrelationships (the fishbone diagram tends to promote a linear view). Second, it fails to break down and work across organizational boundaries in any systemic sense, for example, QCCs are focused on a single area, or workshop, rather than being formed along interacting processes. These represent severe limitations of the approach in the contemporary context.

Participation is again highly valued, and the idea of training everybody in the same tools, language and techniques is a sound method to encourage this. However, the approach again relies rather too heavily on a willingness to participate which is often not easily found. The third strand, simplicity, is to be criticized for ignoring the complexity of and interrelationships within organizations.

The roots of Ishikawa's approach can be found in his early training and development as a chemist. Chemistry is a science which has traditionally been associated with a reductionist 'scientific method', heavily reliant on analysis and fragmentation of problems. The reductionist approach is clearly carried across into the quality sphere with the use of simple analytical tools and the 'breaking down' of processes into manageable parts.

Similarly, and as with Feigenbaum, there does not emerge from Ishikawa's work an overarching methodology which binds together and integrates all the different strands of his thinking. Thus, while many of the tools and techniques are useful in isolation, there is no clear means of implementing an 'Ishikawa' programme.

This element may itself explain, to some degree, the failure of quality circles in so many organizations. They appear to stand alone as a device for quality improvement rather than being seen as one part of a complete process of management leading towards quality improvement.

Taken in isolation, they are almost certainly doomed to failure since the changes in management attitudes and the development of a common language and a common set of problem-solving tools have not been developed to go with them.

Ishikawa appears to have taken account of developments in management thinking relating to people, what has been called the 'human relations' school, emerging in the West from the works of writers such as Mayo, Maslow and Herzberg. However, he does not seem to have given recognition to other developments, such as the emergence of the systems approaches, for example organizational cybernetics, soft systems thinking and a variety of other tools. Recognition of these approaches would have enhanced and further enriched his already substantial contribution.

Finally, recognition must again be given to the multi-dimensional approach espoused by Ishikawa. Unlike those of Deming, his methods are not predominantly quantitative (although he does use these methods widely) but incorporate a substantial qualitative element. Aspects such as attitudinal change, participation and communication are seen as vital elements in the management process.

Ishikawa's substantial contribution to the quality movement must be recognized, although the lack of a clear methodology is an obvious weakness.

SUMMARY

This chapter has outlined the principal work of Kaoru Ishikawa through the five-point critical review. Interested readers should refer to Ishikawa's own works to further develop their knowledge and understanding.

QUESTION

Quality circles are Ishikawa's principal method for achieving participation. Consider how they might function in your own organizational context.

Joseph M. Juran

... the vital few, the useful many ...
(Joseph M. Juran)

KEY LEARNING POINTS

Joseph Juran's definition of quality: fitness for use or purpose.

Key beliefs: management responsibility; planning; measurability; training, process.

Principal methods: company-wide quality control; the quality planning road map; the ten steps to quality improvement.

INTRODUCTION

Joseph Juran is a naturalized American. He commenced his initial career as an engineer in 1924, subsequently working as an executive, civil servant, academic, arbitrator, director and management consultant. This strong professional background supported his first work in the quality field, the *Quality Control Handbook*, which is seen by some, for example Bendell (1989: 8), as having led to his international pre-eminence in the field of quality. Like Deming, Juran worked extensively with the Japanese in the 1950s, where the focus of his work was with middle- and high-ranking executives since he considers that 'quality control should be conducted as an integral part of management control' (Juran, 1974).

He has received numerous awards for his work, including, again like Deming, the Second Order of the Sacred Treasure by the emperor of Japan in recognition of his contribution to Japanese quality control and friendship with the United States.

Juran is described by Bendell (1989) as charismatic, by Bank (1992: 70) as 'perhaps the top quality guru', and by Logothetis (1992: 62) as having made 'the greatest contribution to the management literature of any quality professional'. Juran has published twelve

105

books, which have been translated into thirteen languages. Perhaps the most relevant of these is *Juran on Planning for Quality* (1988). This may be seen as the definitive guide to his thinking on company-wide quality planning.

9.1 PHILOSOPHY

Juran's philosophy is perhaps best summed up in the saying, quoted by Logothetis (1992: 62), 'Quality does not happen by accident, it has to be planned.' This is reflected in his structured approach to company-wide quality planning, an aspect already met in the work of other gurus, for example Ishikawa and Feigenbaum. He is considered by Logothetis (1992) and Bendell (1989: 8) to emphasize management's responsibility for quality, with Bendell (ibid.: 10) quoting him as saying that 'management controllable defects account for over 80 per cent of the total quality problems'. The emphasis of his work is on 'planning, organizational issues, management's responsibility for quality and the need to set goals and targets for improvement' (ibid.: 8). Juran's first two beliefs can be derived from this: first that management are largely responsible for quality; second, that quality cannot be consistently improved unless the improvement is planned.

Logothetis (1992: 64) considers another aspect to Juran's work: the avoidance of slogans and exhortations. He cites Juran's view that 'the recipe for action should consist of 90% substance and 10% exhortation, not the reverse!'. Here can be seen Juran's third belief, that planned improvement must be specific and measurable. Logothetis sees in this aspect a 'formula for results' which consists of four elements:

- Establish specific goals to be reached – identify what needs to be done, the specific projects that need to be tackled.
- Establish plans for reaching the goals; provide a structured process for going from here to there.
- Assign clear responsibility for meeting the goals.
- Base the rewards on results achieved – feed back the information and utilize the lessons learned and the experience gained.

This approach indicates a clear reliance on quantitative methods, rather than any mere vague or woolly-minded aspirations to higher quality – what Flood (1993: 19) refers to as Juran's concern that 'Quality has become too gimmicky, full of platitudes and supposed good intentions, but short on real substance.'

Juran's definition of quality constitutes another strand of his philosophy. He defines quality as 'fitness for use or purpose' (Bank, 1992: 71). Bank suggests that this is a more useful definition than 'conformance to specification', since a dangerous product could conform to all specifications but still be unfit for use. It may be compared with Crosby's definition of 'conformance to requirements'. It would probably be reasonable to assume that safety in use would be a requirement for Crosby – although he does not say so!

The final important strand to Juran's thinking is in his 'trilogy' of quality planning, quality control and quality improvement (Box 9.1). This essentially simple formulation encapsulates the demand for substantial action inherent in all Juran's work. Juran's emphasis in this respect

Box 9.1 *Joseph Juran's 'quality trilogy'*

Quality planning	Determine quality goals
	Institute implementation planning
	Institute resource planning
	Express goals in quality terms
	Create the quality plan
Quality control	Monitor performance
	Compare objectives with achievements
	Act to reduce the gap
Quality improvement	Reduce waste
	Enhance logistics
	Improve employee morale
	Improve profitability
	Satisfy customers

is in three areas: changing management behaviour through quality awareness; training; and then spilling down new attitudes to supporting management levels. This top-down approach reflects Juran's belief that management is largely responsible for quality problems.

To summarize Juran's philosophy, five key beliefs can be identified:

■ Management are largely responsible for quality.
■ Quality can be only improved through planning.
■ Plans and objectives must be specific and measurable.
■ Training is essential and starts at the top.
■ A three-step process of planning, control and action is needed.

9.2 ASSUMPTIONS

The assumptions about the world which seem to underpin Juran's approach are discussed below.

The first point to be examined is the assumption by Juran, along with Deming, that there is a quality crisis. It is certainly the case that consumers' expectations of products and services have increased and there is a lower tolerance of faults than was once the case. We all expect our watches to keep time, our cars to start every day and that services will be provided reliably and consistently.

There are at least three potential views of the quality problem. First, it could be argued that the quality gurus 'created' the quality crisis by raising awareness of the quality issue, focusing attention on the negative aspects and driving up consumer expectations, which in turn has forced producers and providers to improve. A second argument is that awareness of the costs of poor quality among providers and producers increased, leading managements to focus their attention on improving quality, which then became a virtue for their product (and bottom line!). A third view is that consumers have driven the quality movement through increasing expectations and an unwillingness to tolerate defective or shoddy goods and services.

107

FLETCHER CHALLENGE STEEL, CHINA: PLANNING AND POLITICS

In 1995, Fletcher Challenge Steel formed a joint venture with Datong City Government in China – Fletcher Challenge Steel, China – to upgrade the Datong iron-making plant and build a new melt shop to melt and cast steel billets. The team from Fletcher Challenge had created a plan for the venture involving increases in both volume and quality of output and reductions in manning levels, together with a significant investment in new equipment. The overall aim was to achieve levels of performance comparable to those of Western mills. Fletcher Challenge had previously undertaken best practice studies and was successfully implementing performance improvements in its domestic steel operations in New Zealand.

Following the formation of the joint venture company, a management team was appointed, composed of some of the established local Chinese managers, the project team from New Zealand, and selected new appointees with Chinese origins but Western technical education and knowledge. It was recognized right from the outset that cultural barriers to success would exist and that effective communication would be vital. In part, this communication was seen to rest on common language and shared cultural background.

In 1997, well behind the planned timescale, the plant began to approach the levels of output performance necessary to be self-supporting in the long run and to justify the substantial investment made in it by Fletcher Challenge. The initial financial investment consisted of US$25 million, but this was supported by a substantial investment of personal credibility by the Fletcher Steel chief executive, Mike Smith. Smith, an Englishman, had persuaded the group board of Fletcher Challenge to make the investment, and despite his success in the New Zealand plants, could not afford to have this venture fail.

The delays in achieving the planned performance improvements did not result from poor technical planning but from an inadequate appreciation of the political difficulties and resistance that would be met from the Chinese partners. The local managers were suddenly faced with both technical and managerial challenges to the ways in which they had been accustomed to run their business. Such challenges alone are often sufficient to inhibit any change programme. When those challenges are reinforced by cultural and language differences between the parties, then significant problems are almost inevitable. Equally, the plans were externally derived. The local established management were not involved in the planning process; rather, the results of that process were presented to them, a factor which would further inhibit their acceptance – particularly when the standards of performance proposed were considered unachievable as they were outside the scope of local experience. These factors combined to generate significant internal resistance to the implementation of the plans and, without the commitment of the local senior management, workforce acceptance was also inhibited.

This story emphasizes that quality is not just a technical issue and that success in designing and implementing a quality programme really does depend on the whole-hearted commitment and active participation of all those involved in or affected by the programme. It can never be enough to cajole and persuade either managers or workers to support the programme. A mechanism must be found which enables genuine participation and genuine commitment from all parties.

The truth probably lies in a combination of all of these arguments, with interrelationships between the factors being the driving force. This moves the quality argument away from the linear view of the world, seen in the work of Crosby and Ishikawa, towards a more holistic approach.

Looking at wider issues, it can certainly be argued that in the world of relatively mature consumer markets, which is clearly evident not just in Europe and North America but also in parts of the Pacific region, and further industrialization in less economically developed nations, the substantial growth in availability of goods and services must lead to a focus on performance. Thus poor quality represents a major threat to organizational survival. Achievement of quality becomes not an ideal to aim for but, like profit, a fundamental requirement for staying in business.

To argue that there was a 'quality crisis' implies a decline in quality. It is more likely that there was an increase in expectations. As has often been said, 'If we can put a man on the moon, why can't we make a toaster that works?'

A second assumption is that management of the organization and of quality are both processes. This idea has considerable appeal. Management is often thought of as a set of discrete activities, but this view is rather narrow and simplistic. To recognize that management is a process, with all actions and decisions interacting with all others, is a much broader and perhaps more realistic view. There can be little argument with Juran in this respect, especially as much current thinking in management revolves around the ideas of organizing ventures on process lines and on 're-engineering' those processes.

A third assumption is of the potential for continuous improvement. This has already been addressed in the chapters on Deming and Ishikawa. To reiterate briefly, continuous improvement is a reasonable aspiration in a continuous world. However, when change outside the organization becomes discontinuous, then continuous improvement may lose its value. Discontinuity in the environment probably demands discontinuity in the organization.

The fourth and final assumption to be examined is that relating to quantification. Juran's work focuses very clearly on measurement and specific objectives. Again, as with other gurus, the validity of this approach must be questioned. Many aspects of quality, particularly in the service sector, are difficult to quantify accurately and reliably. Significantly, some aspects are outside the control of the organization providing the service. This leads to two problems. The first is the tendency to measure those aspects which are easily accessible, rather than those which are most important. The second is how to measure individual customer expectations, expectations which may vary each time the service is purchased. The normal route here is to provide a standard service and educate customers to understand what they can expect. A different, and rather more difficult route, is to adapt the service to meet individual expectations.

There is a clear bias in the use of quantitative methods, which can be considered to arise for Juran in the industrial/manufacturing basis of the greater part of his work. This perhaps limits to some extent the application of his ideas in the service sector.

9.3 METHODS

While Juran's 'quality trilogy' of planning, control, improvement offers the guideline to his approach, his overarching methodology for achieving quality is the 'quality planning road map'

(Bendell, 1989: 9). Recognizing both external and internal customers, the 'road map' (Box 9.2) offers a nine-step guide. These steps will be briefly reviewed in turn.

The first two steps refer not just to external customers but also to the customers of processes within the organization. The process of identifying the customers and determining their needs is normally seen as identifying the single next step in the process, although it might be thought that a more useful view is to identify the whole chain and all the interrelationships. It could be the case that a particular feature of a product is of no significance to the immediate customer but has enormous impact for one at a later stage of the process. It is therefore important to recognize and take account of the requirements of all possible customers in the chain.

The third step is really about effective communication. A package of requirements that is expressed in a language unknown or unfamiliar to the people in the organization will be of no help. Obvious examples of this are converting words in general or common usage – the customer's language – into the specific technical jargon of the organization. Less obvious are internal requirements. Here it is important that the requirements are expressed in terms meaningful to the working group involved. For example, a condition expressed in the language of accounting to meet a particular budget in terms of profit and loss may be meaningless to a group of engineers. It is essential that their 'budget' be expressed in relevant terms such as required throughput, machine utilization or levels of waste.

Developing a product that responds to customer needs takes the quality issue back to its most fundamental aspect: building quality in rather than inspecting defects out. This is one aspect where other gurus agree. It is better and cheaper to establish quality from the outset than to engage in rectification. Optimizing the product to meet the organization's or department's needs as well as those of the customer should ideally be seen as a constraint on the development process of the previous step rather than as a separate issue. It is, or should be, a design constraint that the product meets these requirements simultaneously.

The development, optimization and testing of a production process, making it operational, is an area that historically has received little attention. Consulting experience has shown that often, products have been developed by the research and development staff of a company, then

Box 9.2 *Joseph Juran's quality planning road map*

Step 1	Identify who are the customers
Step 2	Determine the needs of those customers
Step 3	Translate those needs into our language [the language of the organization]
Step 4	Develop a product that can respond to those needs
Step 5	Optimize the product features so as to meet our [the company's] needs as well as customers' needs
Step 6	Develop a process which is able to produce the product
Step 7	Optimize the process
Step 8	Prove that the process can produce the product under operating conditions
Step 9	Transfer the process to operations

simply handed over to the production staff with the instruction to make them. More recently, many companies are taking account of manufacturing requirements in the development process. Ease of manufacture is becoming accepted as a design constraint.

The final point is to transfer the process to operations. Again, historically this has been done very badly, and there is no argument with Juran's proposal. A useful device to assist with this aspect, and something which is being adopted by many companies, is to create teams for product development which include operational staff and managers. If the idea of designing for manufacture is adopted, then this step becomes very straightforward.

Supporting this fundamental approach to designing quality into the systems and processes is what Bank (1992: 70) refers to as Juran's 'ten steps' to continuous quality improvement (Box 9.3). Here it can be seen how Juran's philosophy is carried across into practice. The first step begins to establish a quality-oriented culture in the organization through the process of raising awareness of the need and scope – a qualitative approach. The second is quantitative: establishing objectives – goals – for improvement. The third step is an attempt to institutionalize quality, to embed the quality process in the management process so that it becomes an ingrained part of the organization.

The fourth step takes the organization forward to train the entire staff. This is seen as helping to make quality an integral part of everyone's thinking.

The fifth and sixth steps, 'carry out projects' and 'report progress', recognize that while continuous improvement is the objective, it must be achieved within visible and measurable elements. The reporting process is seen as enabling experience and learning to be shared and to allow those involved to share their sense of achievement. This also allows the seventh step, 'show recognition', to be actioned. The sixth and eighth steps are linked, 'communicate results' being a call to share the successes (and failures) throughout the organization.

The ninth step, keeping a record, is again an aid to organizational learning. A record may be thought of as an organizational 'memory' to which reference can be made in the future. While Juran suggests that this record should be of successes, it is arguably just as important

Box 9.3 *Joseph Juran's ten steps to continuous quality improvement*

Step 1	Create awareness of the need and opportunity for quality improvement
Step 2	Set goals for continuous improvement
Step 3	Build an organization to achieve goals by establishing a quality council, identifying problems, selecting a project, appointing teams and choosing facilitators
Step 4	Give everyone training
Step 5	Carry out projects to solve problems
Step 6	Report progress
Step 7	Show recognition
Step 8	Communicate results
Step 9	Keep a record of successes
Step 10	Incorporate annual improvements into the company's regular systems and processes and thereby maintain momentum

to memorize strategies and schemes that do not work as to remember those that do. This may enable the organization to avoid or encourage those forms of behaviour in the future. Most important of all – for both success and failure – is to understand why changes have succeeded or failed. To be able to distil the general principles of success from a specific instance or series of instances is to create a true basis for organizational learning, After all, the specific instance will never arise again, but the principles underpinning the solved problem will almost certainly recur many times, and the practice of problem solving is enhanced by understanding at the general rather than the particular level.

The tenth step is a corporate-level and public commitment to the achievement of higher quality. This should be seen as reaffirming the quality process in the minds of both employees and customers.

Juran shows awareness of the phenomenon of resistance to change, which is so common in organizations. Logothetis (1992: 75) reports Juran's belief that 'resistance to a technological change is due to social and cultural factors'. Juran proposes two principal methods for dealing with this. First, he considers that all those affected by the change should be 'allowed to participate'(ibid.). Second, he specifies that 'adequate time should be allowed for the change to be accepted'. These approaches are seen as providing an opportunity for evaluation and experimentation, promoting ownership of the changes and helping to overcome resistance.

To underpin the two processes outlined above – 'the road map' and the 'ten steps' – Juran uses a variety of statistical methods. Like Deming, Juran studied under Shewhart and so relies on many of the same approaches, for example control charts. Perhaps one of the best known of his approaches is using Pareto analysis to help separate the 'vital few' problems from the 'useful many'.

9.4 SUCCESSES AND FAILURES

It must be accepted that Juran, like the other gurus, has been hugely successful in developing and promoting his ideas. That his books have been translated into thirteen languages and his ideas accepted and exploited by so many organizations and in so many different countries is a measure of the perceived value of his contribution. However, his work has not been applied universally and can be seen to be less effective in the service sector than in manufacturing.

According to Flood (1993: 21–22), the strengths of Juran's approach are:

- its concentration on genuine issues of management practice;
- the new understanding of the customer that it offers, referring to both internal and external customers.
- its stress on management involvement and commitment.

The main weaknesses are perceived as the following:

- The literature on motivation and leadership is not addressed.
- Workers' contributions are underrated.
- Methods are traditional, failing to address culture and politics.

Another criticism is that the body of systems knowledge, and in particular managerial and organizational cybernetics, which could have enhanced and enriched Juran's approach, has, like human relations theory, been largely ignored.

The first strength that Flood identified, concentration on genuine management issues, is one with which most people would agree, although a programme which fails to motivate and develop the majority of the workforce is one which may well be seen as consisting merely of hype.

The second strength, that of recognizing other parts of the organization as customers, is again welcome. Readers will recall that this can also be found in the work of Deming and is now embedded in the ISO 9000:2000 standard as well as in other quality management system standards.

The third strength is management commitment and involvement. This is not simply because, by Juran's measure, 80 per cent of the total quality problem resides there, but also because the power, control and leadership reside there. A management which is seen by the workforce to be committed to quality will 'breed' a quality ethos for the organization. Workers wishing to progress and be content within a quality-oriented environment will probably emulate the behaviour and attitudes of their managers. If this occurs, then the quality ethos will tend to spill down through the organization over time.

Turning to the weaknesses, Flood's understanding that Juran fails adequately to incorporate theories of motivation and leadership is generally accepted. However, Juran is a practitioner; he deals best with the practice of quality, rather than the theory. It might be suggested that the second statement of weakness, that Juran undervalues the contribution of the worker, is countered to some extent by the explicit incorporation of participation.

Flood further suggests that Juran emphasizes a somewhat 'mechanistic' view of the organization, although acknowledging that he does take account of the organization's environment – that is, of its markets. The view is largely evident in the unstated assumption that what is good for the organization – higher quality – is also good for the individual. This perhaps reflects the thinking of the early management theorists such as Taylor, Weber and Fayol. In the contemporary world of 'knowledge workers', high-technology equipment and increasing emphasis on human rights, quite often what is good for the organization may appear to be bad for the workers. This applies to both the short- and long-term views. A company operating in the face of maturing or mature markets and not positioned to exploit emerging markets, with fresh, lower-cost-base competitors from newly industrializing countries, may be unable to absorb spare capacity through growth. This leads to the need, to use the politically correct terminology, to 'retrench' workers.

The interests of the organization and the individual worker may come into direct conflict. The organization wishes to improve quality to preserve and protect its customer base, to reduce its costs and ensure its survival. The workers may recognize that these same attributes can have different consequences for them – for example, job losses, pay freezes, reductions in overtime, or loss of other benefits. Often they can lead to the deskilling of jobs and the loss of craft skills in which individuals take great, and justifiable, pride. There is little incentive for the workforce to contribute to the quality programme if a successful outcome for the company threatens their own – short-term – sense of security. They may well seek to preserve their position in the short term while accepting the inevitable longer-term threat. Events in France and Germany during 1997 perhaps give this point extra emphasis. Compared with the United Kingdom, organizations in those nations had undertaken little by way of radical change and restructuring. Despite the emergent threat to jobs in those economies arising from high costs, questionable productivity and overseas competition, the workers, as represented by the unions, were strongly resisting change. The appeal for participation must deal with issues of this type if it is to have any hope of success. Juran offers little in this regard.

9.5   CRITICAL REVIEW

The founding idea of Juran's work might almost be called 'design and build'. His approach stresses planning as the fundamental requirement for quality, followed by action. This orientation towards the setting and achievement of objectives perhaps reflects Juran's engineering and statistical background.

The 'quality trilogy', the 'quality road map' and the 'ten steps to quality' (Boxes 9.1, 9.2 and 9.3 respectively) may all be considered systematic, somewhat mechanistic, approaches. While Juran established a new understanding of customers (the internal and external), he does not explicitly recognize the importance of the interdependence of processes and the interactions between people within the organization. This prevents his systematic approach from becoming systemic. Juran seems to be making the assumption that improvement in the individual parts will necessarily improve the whole organization, a view which is challenged by the systems thinking community.

With regard to management, two issues should be stressed. First, Juran views management as a process. Second, he sees management as responsible for quality, having control of 80 per cent of the problems. As regards the first of these, Juran's view is to be welcomed. An organization which recognizes that every action and decision is inextricably linked with every other in a continuous process of management must be considered to be on the verge of a breakthrough in its behaviour. Even today, management in many organizations is fragmented into pseudo-independent functions: marketing is separate from finance, which is in turn separate from production, and so on. Each of these units attempts to maximize its own function independently from the others. Similarly, even within departments, tasks are often seen as independent, rather than interdependent. For example, recruitment is often seen as a separate function, to be kept within the personnel or human resource function and having no relationship with training and development – and, crucially, no relationship with the units where those recruited will work. In this sort of organization, it is not surprising that there are conflicts, disputes and difficulties in matching people to tasks. A more holistic, integrated and interdependent 'process' view is essential. While Juran moves towards this approach, he perhaps does not go far enough.

Concerning the second issue, management responsibility, perhaps the question that should be asked is, why 80 per cent? Deming, for example, has provided statistics suggesting that the figure is 94 per cent, while Crosby's work may be interpreted as suggesting that the bulk of the responsibility lies with the workers. An argument can be proposed whereby management take complete responsibility for quality. If, as Fayol (1916) suggests, it is the responsibility of management to 'Plan, Organise, Command, Control and Co-ordinate', then responsibility should lie with them. The argument is this: management is expected to have control of every aspect of the organization:

- what is done;
- how it is done;
- when it is done;
- where it is done;
- who does it;
- why it is done.

This suggests that there should be no matter internal to the organization which is beyond the scope of management to address. Random errors in production, for example, might be eradicable through changes in design or process so that it becomes impossible to assemble a part incorrectly. Human error might be eradicable through training, adjustment of work rates, increases (or reductions!) in relaxation time or a range of other variables which could be altered to enable improved performance.

It is suggested that the ultimate responsibility for quality should rest with all those who are involved in the production of a good or a service – that is, every employee within every part and function of the organization. However, the power to achieve higher quality rests in the hands of those who have authority (power) to change things. If that power is in the hands of the management alone, then they have full responsibility. If, on the other hand, the power is shared throughout the organization, perhaps through empowerment initiatives, quality circles and other participative approaches, then everyone who shares in that power is responsible.

The strong emphasis by Juran on management responsibility fails to address adequately the needs and aspirations of workers. He does not properly take into account the contribution that they can make to the achievement of quality, nor does he provide mechanisms through which they can contribute.

Finally, the issue must again be raised of the applicability of Juran's work. It seems to be most suitable for the industrial and manufacturing sectors. It is suggested that it has limited application in service organizations since it does not adequately deal with human issues.

SUMMARY

This chapter has reviewed the major contribution made to the quality movement by Juran. Students should refer to Joseph M. Juran's (1988) own work to further inform and develop their views.

QUESTION

Juran defines quality as 'fitness for use or purpose'. Define 'fitness for use or purpose' in the context of the products or services of your organization. Consider your answer in terms of customers, owners, workers, suppliers and the surrounding community.

115

John S. Oakland

TQM starts at the top.
(John S. Oakland, 1993)

KEY LEARNING POINTS

John S. Oakland's definition of quality: quality is meeting the customer's requirements.

Key beliefs: quality is the only issue; quality from the top; errors can be prevented; quality is an organization-wide issue, quality involves everybody.

Principal methods: ten points for senior management; EPDCA cycle; TQM model; quality function deployment.

INTRODUCTION

John Oakland is executive chairman of Oakland Consulting plc and was previously Professor of Total Quality Management and head of the European Centre for Total Quality Management at the University of Bradford Management Centre in the United Kingdom. Oakland is considered by many to be the British guru of quality. His practice is internationally based and he has provided substantial support to the development of quality in the United Kingdom, particularly to the quality initiatives of the government there.

Oakland's early industrial career focused on research and development and production management. He holds a doctorate, is a Chartered Chemist, a Member of the Royal Society of Chemistry, a Fellow of the Royal Statistical Society, a Fellow of the Association of Quality Management Consultants, a Fellow of the Institute of Quality Assurance and a Member of the American Society of Quality Control.

The approaches used by Oakland and his colleagues in Oakland Consulting plc are essentially pragmatic and have apparently been used in thousands of organizations.

10.1 PHILOSOPHY

The philosophy underpinning Oakland's view of quality is perhaps best shown in the emphasis he places on its importance, saying, 'We cannot avoid seeing how quality has developed into the most important competitive weapon, and many organisations have realised that TQM is *the* [sic] way of managing for the future' (Oakland, 1993: preface). Through this statement, Oakland gives absolute primacy to the pursuit of quality as the cornerstone of organizational success. While it can be agreed that organizations which do not achieve quality in the contemporary environment will probably fail in the long term, it is more difficult to accept the concept of its absolute primacy. Although quality has strategic implications (as discussed in Chapter 2) and is a strategic issue, it cannot be accepted that it is the *only* strategic issue.

The concept of Total Quality Management (TQM) as the way of managing for the future does, on the other hand, have considerable value. If TQM is thought of as a way of managing (as seen with Feigenbaum's work), rather than an added extra, then other management philosophies, methods and tools must be subsumed within it. This idea reinforces Oakland's view that 'quality starts at the top', with quality parameters inherent in every organizational decision. He emphasizes seven key characteristics of pursuing TQM (Box 10.1).

First is Oakland's definition of quality: *quality is meeting the customer's requirements*. This definition is simple and very hard to disagree with as it emphasizes that quality is a characteristic or attribute defined by the customer, not the supplier. Oakland also stresses the importance of the quality chain. He emphasizes the internal supplier–customer relationships, stressing in the second characteristic that most problems are interdepartmental – that is, they occur in the interaction between process steps.

The third and fourth characteristics emphasize the purposes of quality control (QC) and quality assurance (QA). These definitions move the focus away from criticism and blame often associated with these mechanisms and towards the reason they need to be carried out, which is quite simply to improve quality performance. All too often, the QC and QA functions in organizations become self-serving activities, focusing on apportioning blame and identifying guilty parties rather than on improving the performance of the organization. Because of this, they frequently fall into disrepute and become disregarded by the operational personnel – who focus in turn on not getting caught rather than on not failing. A recent example of this could be found in an organization in which the managers, every month, had a quality day, the day

Box 10.1 *Seven key characteristics of Total Quality Management, according to John S. Oakland*

1	Quality is meeting the customers' requirements
2	Most quality problems are interdepartmental
3	Quality control is monitoring, finding and eliminating causes of quality problems
4	Quality assurance rests on prevention, management systems, effective audit and review
5	Quality must be managed; it does not just happen
6	Focus on prevention, not cure
7	Reliability is an extension of quality and enables us to 'delight the customer'

on which they ensured that all the non-conformance reports were resolved – which mainly involved lengthy explanations of why the non-conformance was not their fault. Little or no attention was paid to improvement in product or service quality.

The fifth and sixth characteristics focus on the proactive nature of the quality drive. The statement that 'quality must be managed, it does not just happen', reflecting Juran's suggestion that 'quality must be planned', sharpens the recognition that quality is not accidental, or achieved through reactive measures. Quality for Oakland – that is, meeting customer requirements – must be a parameter of every decision made within the organization, whether operational, administrative or strategic. Quality must, then, be inherent in management thinking, which in turn means that it must be part of the norms of the organization. This view is supported by the sixth characteristic, prevention not cure. Oakland suggests that one-third of all organizational efforts are wasted in error-based activity – for example, rework, rectification, inspection, and so on – and with an even higher proportion in service-based organizations. Working from experience, these proportions are difficult to argue with, and in some cases represent a significant underestimate. If quality can be achieved at the outset, rather than through detection and rectification, the total costs of the organization will always be reduced. The limitation on doing so arises very often from the functionally based budgeting common in organizations, where each manager seeks to reduce his or her own current-period costs with no regard for the effect on other parts of the organization.

The final characteristic deals with quality as more than a momentary attribute. Reliability has two dimensions which are related to the nature of the product itself. The first is reliability in use, and relates to durable products such as cars, domestic appliances, watches, and so on. In this case, what 'delights the customer' is enjoying the uninterrupted use of the product, other than for routine service-based maintenance. A car which breaks down will not delight the customer, regardless of how well it met the quality criteria on delivery. The customer requirement is to be able to turn the key and make a journey without fear of non-completion. In other words, each time the service is delivered, it must meet the customer requirements. In this context, reliability means consistency, and to achieve consistency of service means that there must be a consistent and reliable delivery process.

Quality is considered by Oakland, then, to be an organization-wide and fundamental requirement, driven by top management commitment and created through reliable, consistent organizational processes.

10.2 ASSUMPTIONS

The assumptions about the world that seem to underpin Oakland's approach will now be considered.

The first assumption which Oakland makes is that quality is the only issue for organizational survival. While this may be largely true of some organizations in fully developed, highly competitive and mature economies (those in which Oakland predominantly operates), it is certainly not true of all. Some organizations will succeed (a least in the short to medium term) because they have established such market dominance (and perhaps customer reliance) that the issue of quality simply does not arise. Customers buy the products or services through lack of an alternative rather than through choice. For example, the majority of personal computer users purchase Microsoft operating system compatible software, not necessarily because it does exactly what they require, but because it is what is readily available – and works with their computer's operating system. Interestingly, this tendency has been challenged in recent months following a significant change in the way Microsoft seeks to charge for its products, with some customers challenging the basis of the new charges and testing alternative systems. To take another example, with banking and other financial services providers, until very recently the issue of customer choice did not arise: the products, services and costs were all substantially undifferentiated. When one supplier is as good or as bad as every other, the product or service becomes a commodity and choice ceases to be a meaningful word. In other contexts, the sophistication of consumers and state of development of the market still means that providers of goods or services can predominantly focus on their own requirements, not those of the customers. Other suppliers enjoy state-sponsored or state-supported supply positions, and for them, quality is not a concern – the consumer again has no choice. Oakland's first assumption can be challenged, then, on the grounds that while perhaps correct as a matter of value, the constraint does not apply across the whole of the world's markets.

The second assumption, that quality must be driven from the top, carries complete support. Unless this commitment is achieved at the outset of a quality programme and maintained at a high level of enthusiasm, the initiative will fail. The revised ISO 9000:2000 standard focuses heavily on management commitment as a major issue – although many managements can be seen to be struggling to convert the concept into action.

The third assumption is that errors can always be prevented, through planning, design and effective processes. This is probably true, but requires a substantial shift in the traditional mindset of those in the organization, and a full appreciation of the softer, human issues, particularly in service-based organizations. As has been mentioned, while the process operation can be designed to operate in an error-free way, the actual minute-by-minute delivery of service depends very largely on the personal interaction between customer and supplier. However robust the technical process may be, there is always scope for error to arise in this context. No standard form of words can cater for the vagaries of mood, sense and interpretation which influence the outcome of such transactions and determine whether customer requirements are met – Oakland's measure of quality.

The fourth assumption is that quality is an organization-wide issue. This is in common with Flood's call for quality 'across all functions and all levels' and again cannot be argued with; quality must pervade the whole organizational atmosphere. This assumption suggests that Oakland's approach is systemic. While he makes no direct reference in his work to the systemic approaches to management, there is a systemic as well as systematic attitude reflected in his approach.

Finally, Oakland assumes the involvement of all people through communication, teamwork and participation – in other words, through redeveloping the culture of the organization. This view is again supported and reflects again the systemic nature of his approach.

10.3 METHODS

While Oakland quite rightly capitalizes on the many well-established methods, tools and techniques for achieving quality, he does offer his own overarching approach for TQM and some new insight. The overarching method is his 'ten points for senior management' (Box 10.2). Oakland represents the major features of this in his 'Total Quality Management Model' (Figure 10.1).

119

Box 10.2 *John S. Oakland's ten points for senior management*

Point 1	Long-term commitment
Point 2	Change the culture to 'right first time'
Point 3	Train the people to understand the customer–supplier relationship
Point 4	Buy products and services on the basis of total cost
Point 5	Recognize that systems improvement must be managed
Point 6	Adopt modern methods of supervision and training and eliminate fear
Point 7	Eliminate barriers, manage processes, improve communications and teamwork
Point 8	Eliminate arbitrary goals, standards based only on numbers, barriers to pride of workmanship, fiction (use the correct tools to establish facts)
Point 9	Constantly educate and retrain the in-house experts
Point 10	Utilize a systematic approach to TQM implementation

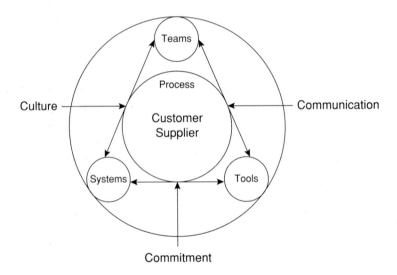

Figure 10.1 *John S. Oakland's Total Quality Management model*

Unlike some of the other gurus, Oakland focuses on the total process of achieving a TQM organization without relying inordinately on either qualitative or quantitative aspects. He recognizes that both are necessary and, if anything, is slightly biased towards softer aspects as the initial drivers of quality.

The ten-point process begins with the absolute commitment of senior and middle management to constant improvement. Oakland suggests that the quality process must start in the boardroom. Adoption of quality at that level is fundamental to its achievement since it is then a normative decision – a decision about the sort of behaviour that is desired. Unfortunately, this is rather more difficult to achieve in practice than is recognized. The senior management may say that they are committed to quality, but unless they change their behaviour – that is, the decisions they make, the things they say and do, the ways in which they measure and reward performance – then the commitment is not genuine. This will soon be detected at other levels within the organization.

The second point, arising from the first, is to change the culture of the organization at all levels to focus on 'right first time'. Oakland sees this focus as based on awareness of customer needs and teamwork, enabled by participation and use of the 'EPDCA helix'. This is a more dynamic representation of the Deming cycle already seen, with explicit recognition of the need for evaluation before planning. There is much else required in a cultural change, as is implied in the ideas of teamwork, participation and customer needs.

The third point represents the orientation of the organization, through training, towards customer–supplier relationships – both externally and internally. Oakland suggests this orientation must be achieved for everyone. This is an especially difficult area, and will meet with much resistance in many organizations. There will be particular difficulties where the staff of a particular process or function are traditionally poorly regarded, where there is functional organization design or a major difference of perceived relative expertise, with the customer being regarded by the supplier as of a 'lower order'. This is a particular concern in organizations which employ highly qualified professional staff for certain processes and these interact with 'customers' whose perceived level of professionalism is much lower – for example, medical doctors *vis-à-vis* nursing assistants or porters; chefs *vis-à-vis* kitchen assistants or waiters/waitresses.

Point 4 moves away from the culturally oriented changes to examine cost. Oakland calls for continuous improvement in everything to reduce the total cost of doing business. Here he recognizes, like Deming, that purchase price is not the sole determinant of the cost of any input. That is, the higher initial cost of a purchase may be more than outweighed by its reduced lifetime cost to the organization – its cost including running costs, depreciation and even, with increasing environmental concerns, disposal costs. For example, a stainless steel machine may be initially more expensive than its mild steel equivalent, but if the maintenance and running cost is significantly lower and the longevity greater, the total cost may be less over time.

Point 5 examines the systems used to manage the organization and calls for them to be actively managed to achieve improvement. While this may seem like common sense, it is an often neglected area. A key to success here is to step back and reconsider the utility and effectiveness of the systems employed. Many organizations suffer from what the IT industry calls 'legacy systems', those which have been purchased and developed over many years and which perhaps would require substantial investment to replace. Often, such systems, like the budget, are functionally owned – that is, they reside within a single department which makes effective use of them in its own terms – but the system is not configured in such a way that it can contribute to the whole organization. Often such systems are poorly understood in the wider organization, jealously guarded by their departmental 'owners' – but, through lack of integration with the rest of the organization, are at best failing to add value, at worst causing damage. Like any other capital investment, IT systems must be recognized as having a useful life and must be replaced at the due time. In choosing the replacement, managers should have regard to the integration of information needs of the whole organization.

Point 6 calls for modern methods of supervision and training. This recognizes that many traditional supervision and training approaches no longer have great value in organizations.

121

VIGNETTE 10.1 **THE HONG KONG POLICE FORCE**

In March 1995, the commissioner of the Royal Hong Kong Police Force, (now the Hong Kong Police Force), an organization consisting of some 40,000 personnel, publicly announced his strategy for the introduction of a service quality approach to meet the need for change in the culture and work attitudes within the force. At that time, there was no clear driver for change, but the force recognized the need for this initiative to meet the challenges ahead, and before it was forced on it. The programme gives equal focus to internal customers and external customer relationships.

The envisaged change is being implemented in a 'step-by-step' approach, and it is anticipated that the development and implementation of the strategy will take at least five years, probably longer. This process has been nominally structured into five phases:

- awareness;
- understanding;
- favour;
- involvement;
- commitment.

Early work focused on generating an understanding of the kinds of changes that were planned. Activities included a road-show for middle- to senior-level management; a video presentation for viewing by all personnel; publication of the strategy in various internal communications media; development of performance pledges (for the public) and internal service-level agreements (for internal customer interactions); the encouragement of voluntary work improvement teams in the work environment; and the commissioning of the first of a series of regular public opinion surveys.

However, although the project team assigned to undertake all these activities was reasonably clear as to its objectives, there was a perceived lack of expertise in knowing exactly how to achieve them. The team was also driving these changes from too far down the organizational 'food chain', and the lack of commitment from senior management was seen as a threat to this success. It was at this stage, in November 1995, that assistance was sought from a management consultancy.

After an initial scoping study, the consultants recommended refocusing the project team's efforts away from the customer interface towards a more holistic approach. This entailed a more detailed examination of the overall purpose of the organization and how it was going to set about achieving this, and an emphasis that this process needed to commence at the very top of the organization.

Until the advent of the consultancy, the project team's activities and proposals for change lacked credibility. Overnight, senior management were confronted with arguments that they could not refute and, quickly, decisions were made and commitments pledged to a broad front of force-wide changes. The key thrust for these changes was to develop a corporate vision and mission which was to be entitled the Force Vision and Statement of Common Purpose and Values.

From the outset, it was recognized that the force would be undertaking a process of change requiring a strong sense of direction provided by solid organization vision, mission and values. To this end, the commissioner and his senior management team attended a series of workshops, facilitated by the consultants, to identify the themes and elements of the Force Vision and Statement of Common Purpose and Values.

The outcome of this workshop was further refined by a team of middle-level managers broadly representative of the myriad of functional areas within the force. The result was a draft document ready for a consultation process designed to underscore force management commitment to the change process in an unprecedented and structured communications approach. This was to be undertaken by way of discussion groups, rather than by using the more traditional paper exercise.

Each member of the force, from chief superintendent down, attended a discussion group run by one of their managers, assisted by a consultation pack and a discussion guide. This was seen as a new approach, designed to involve and commit commanders at all levels to visibly seek genuine feedback from their staff. Over 1,400 such discussion sessions were held.

The results of this consultation were made available to force management, and the commissioner and his management team attended further workshops to consider the feedback and agree on the final version of the statement. At these workshops, the first steps towards developing formal strategic directions for the force were also outlined.

The finalized statement was launched at the force's open day on 7 December 1996, and widespread publicity for the document followed. The process from inception to launch took just over one year. That signalled not the end of the exercise, but completion of the first stage. The next phase was probably the more important: that was the introduction of a strategy to give life to the vision, common purpose and shared values that all had agreed to. This was undertaken through a programme called Living the Values with the intention of preparing senior managers for the change in culture and attitudes that were needed to follow on from the launch of the statement, and the cascading of this message down through the organization to the constable on the beat.

Following on from the strategic workshops held in connection with the Vision and Statement of Common Purpose and Values, the consultants facilitated similar workshops for each of the force's departments with a view to drawing up departmental strategic direction plans. Once all departments had been through this process, the various departmental plans were to be incorporated into the force strategic directions document.

Finally, it is worth clearly stating that it was not intended that the force lift a TQM package from off the shelf; there was no cookbook which told them how to do it. There are plenty of success stories and there are plenty of examples of what not to do. The force will consider adopting only those things which should support, in the commissioner's words, 'our pursuit of excellence in providing a service of quality'.

This story clearly shows how when an enlightened management begins to take the message and intent of a quality programme seriously, it can be spilled down the organization in a structured, consistent and meaningful way that does lead to substantial change.

These were very often sterile, having no relationship to the particular job undertaken and not being reflected in individual performance expectations. Similarly, the 'kick butt and take names', militaristic approach to performance management is not applicable in a more enlightened environment and is particularly foolish in an economic context of full or near-full employment.

Point 7 calls for organizations to be managed along processes rather than up and down functional silos. While many process-based organizations have already achieved this, it is still the case that significant numbers adopt functional specialisms as the basis of organization. In these cases, there remain many hand-offs (breaks within processes) which extend the range of customer–supplier relationships and create opportunities for the buck to be passed. In the process, the consumer (the ultimate customer) is often forgotten. If the organization is process based, this tends not to happen, and communication and teamwork can be encouraged around the process flow since all parties can visualize and share the team objective(s).

Point 8 could be called the elimination round. Here Oakland again reflects the ideas of others. He wishes to see arbitrary goals eliminated; it is useless to call for improvement without supplying the facilities necessary for those goals to be achieved and without a formal basis for evaluation. He wants an end to standards based only on numbers – that is, on volumes. Purely volume-based output measures will always lead to quality problems. As a minimum, it is essential to measure quality performance as well – and to recognize that this may mean a lesser initial output, but that the output received should all be perfect! His third requirement is to eradicate barriers to pride of workmanship. Apart from purely measuring output volume (which is one barrier), this means the design and redesign of jobs as suggested in other parts of the literature to enable the particular worker to have pride in the completion of a meaningful task. Lastly, he calls for reliance on facts, not fiction, proposing costs of quality and level of fire fighting as measures of internal health. The important characteristic here is to recognize measurements that are both meaningful and factual – that is, numbers which cannot be manipulated to present a particular picture. While doctors bury their mistakes, managers frequently reclassify theirs, even to the extent in one factory of making for reject to maintain production efficiency. The particular factory supplied excess or sub-standard output in alternative packaging to a secondary market and repackaged and labelled perfect goods to meet the needs of this secondary market. This was despite the inability of the company concerned to recover more than raw material costs from the purchaser. That secondary purchaser consequently made greater unit profit than the major and highly respected principal customer – while the factory itself lost money.

Stating quite rightly that 'the experts . . . are the people who do the job every day', Oakland calls in point 9 for their constant education and retraining. The dynamics of contemporary business and the rapid changes in the business environment render this absolutely essential. For maximum benefit, such training must be related back to job performance and expectations – that is, it must link to further improvement. This is a particularly strained point in many organizations, especially in times of economic downturn. The first budget items to suffer are normally the training and the research and development budgets!

Finally, with point 10, Oakland calls for a planned, systematic approach to the operational implementation of TQM to realize the vision. Again, this cannot be disagreed with as a platform for improvement. However, such systematization and planning must not preclude capitalizing on spontaneous and unexpected successes. The potential opportunist gain must not be lost through rigid adherence to a particular plan.

To support the implementation process, Oakland predominantly relies on what can be thought of as standard tools for achieving quality such as statistical approaches, quality circles, process analysis and review, and so on. He does, however, enrich his approach by capitalizing on particular developments in the pursuit of quality.

The first of these is Quality Function Deployment (QFD). This is a systematic approach to the design of a product or service around the expressed requirements of the customers. It involves members from across the organization in converting customer requirements to a technical product or service specification. The QFD process is based around seven activities (Box 10.3) and is intended to ensure that the product or service meets the customer requirements first time and every time. Oakland stresses the importance of recognizing the design input of those whose jobs do not include an evident design element.

Second, Oakland stresses the importance of teamwork in his approach and draws extensively on the established literature in this area to explain and elaborate his approach.

This chapter is intended only to provide an introduction to Oakland's approach. Methods, tools and techniques will be elaborated in Part four of this book. This section has introduced Oakland's primary method, which relies heavily on absolute management commitment and leadership of the quality process, supported by a wide selection of tools and techniques.

10.4 SUCCESSES AND FAILURES

The use of Oakland's approach to TQM by thousands of companies speaks volumes for its utility. Quite simply, no programme could achieve such sustained success without substantial benefits being delivered to many customers. The establishment of the European Centre for Total Quality Management and of Oakland Consulting plc further confirm that Oakland's approach adds value to quality practice.

A number of strengths and weaknesses can be identified in Oakland's approach. The strengths are as follows:

- It takes a systematic, methodical approach.
- It takes a process-based view of organizations.

Box 10.3 *John S. Oakland's quality function deployment activities*

Market research

Basic research

Invention

Concept design

Prototype testing

Final product or service testing

After-sales service and troubleshooting

- It capitalizes on developments in quality practice.
- It advocates a participative approach which utilizes ideas from the literature on team working.
- It stresses the importance of management commitment and leadership.

The weaknesses are as follows:

- It ignores many developments in organization theory, especially the systems literature.
- It fails to offer assistance in coercive contexts.
- It justifies quality in terms of developed economies (where the focus is on competition).
- It ignores other aspects of strategy formulation.
- It does not explain how to obtain the commitment from senior management on which the whole process relies.

Turning first to the the strengths, Oakland's systematic and methodical approach provides a straightforward, coherent platform for the quality initiative. Unfortunately, it simply assumes that there is established agreement about the need for quality. Second, the process-based view adheres to current developments in the understanding of how organizations actually function and how effectiveness is improved. Third, the capitalization on current developments in quality practice ensures that 'best practice' is achieved – a fundamental characteristic of quality.

Oakland's emphasis on team working, and in particular his utilization of the literature on effective team working, is to be admired. This shows that he has moved outside the relatively narrow discipline of pure quality to embrace other ideas which support his activities.

The final strength, emphasizing the importance of management commitment, is again fundamental to effective pursuit of quality. It is unfortunate that (as suggested by the weaknesses) he says little about how such commitment can be achieved. While the point has been made before, it is so important that it must be made again. If senior management are not passionately committed to the achievement of quality throughout every aspect of the organization, then it will not happen. Unfortunately, Oakland does not advise on how to achieve this passionate commitment, or on how to overcome the many functional and professional barriers which may obstruct it.

To turn now to the other weaknesses, the failure explicitly to incorporate other aspects of organization theory, and especially to have ignored the value to be derived from a systems-based understanding of organization (together with the associated methodologies), detracts substantially from Oakland's work.

The failure to deal with coercive contexts is common to all quality approaches and is perhaps a little unfair as a criticism. Nonetheless, there are many organizations in the world which are characterized by potentially abusive power relations, and the responsibilities of the management guru or scientist must include attempting to ameliorate such conditions.

Perhaps because Oakland's practice is centred on Europe, the focus of his justification for pursuing quality is, if not entirely Eurocentric, at least based on a perception of the problems and opportunities facing Western organizations in developed economies. These economies are dominated by industrial oligarchies (meaning that there are a small number of major players in each industrial sector). It can be argued that effective competition on strategic issues has almost disappeared and been replaced by a high degree of collaboration, and to some extent a tacit acceptance of established market shares. For example, in the motor industry, there are many interrelationships between manufacturers who promote distinct brands. Thus Volvo (now owned by Ford) made use of Renault (which now owns Nissan) engines; Volkswagen, Seat (owned by Volkswagen) and Ford collaborate in the production of the Galaxy, Sharan and Alhambra – essentially the same vehicle but differently badged and priced. Jaguar and Aston Martin (now both owned by Ford) produce different cars which share the same platform, while the latest model from Jaguar shares its platform with the latest large car from Ford. Globally, the interrelationships become even closer and more confusing.

Developing economies, on the other hand, often experience much lower levels of consumer and producer sophistication, which means that the customers are perhaps less discriminating in their purchasing choices, a factor that lessens the need for Western perceptions of quality. These countries often have much more diverse industrial bases, with a greater proportion of small to medium-sized businesses and less dominance by major players. These two factors taken together generate scope for strategic advantage to be obtained through routes other than quality.

10.5 CRITICAL REVIEW

Overall, the foundation to Oakland's work can be seen in his professional background and practical experience of quality. The approach is sufficiently broadly based for it to be regarded as reflecting a systemic as well as systematic view, but it fails to capitalize on developments in systemic thinking.

Oakland is clearly concerned about management commitment, with his calls for passionate leadership, but the approach falls down in not making a mechanism available by which such passion can be engendered. It may be thought that the fear of competitive failure is enough to stimulate this response, but that is to rely on people running away from something – a negative reaction – rather than running to something – a positive reaction. In the first case, as soon as the stimulus is relaxed – that is, the current danger subsides to a comfortable level – the negative response will cease, and with it the passion for quality. There is clearly a need to develop an ethos where management want quality as a means to a positive end rather than as an alternative to failure, but no tools are made available to support this.

One very positive feature is that the generality of Oakland's overarching methodology renders it potentially useful in the service sector as well as in manufacturing industry. While he says little of the public sector, it is quite clear that the method will also work there, although again the senior management motivation stemming from fear of competition is absent.

To summarize, Oakland's approach is well worth supporting, while recognizing that it relies very heavily on well-established techniques, with all the drawbacks those entail. On the other hand, he has capitalized on recent developments and drawn on at least part of the relevant management literature to support and enhance his work. His practical success speaks for itself.

SUMMARY

This chapter has presented the quality approach of John Oakland through a five-point critical framework. Readers may wish to refer to Oakland's own works *Total Quality Management* (1993) and *Total Organizational Excellence* (1999), to further develop their understanding and knowledge.

QUESTION

Oakland proposes that 'Quality is the only issue for organizational survival.' Discuss this proposal in the light of the current challenges facing organizations.

Chapter 11

Shigeo Shingo

Admit your own mistakes openly, maybe even joyfully.
(Robert Townsend, *Further up the Organization*, 1985)

KEY LEARNING POINTS

Shigeo Shingo's definition of quality: defects in a process.

Key beliefs: defect prevention through eradication of defective processes; human fallibility; 'mechanistic' view of organizations; real-time information processing.

Principal method: Poka-Yoke (zero-defects)

INTRODUCTION

Shigeo Shingo, who died in 1990, is perhaps the least well known in the West of the Japanese quality gurus. Educated as a mechanical engineer, he became a consultant in 1945, subsequently working with a wide variety of companies in many industries. These companies included Toyota, Mitsubishi, Matsushita and Sony. During his later career, he became involved with a large number of Western organizations. Norman Bodek, president of Productivity Incorporated, in the foreword to *The Sayings of Shigeo Shingo* (Shingo, 1987), cited by Bendell (1989: 11), says, 'If I could give a Nobel Prize for exceptional contributions to world economy, prosperity and productivity, I wouldn't have much difficulty selecting a winner – Shigeo Shingo's life work has contributed to the well-being of everyone in the world.'

He is regarded by Gilbert (1992: 24) as 'one of the 20th century's greatest engineers' and he made a number of significant contributions in that area. He wrote fourteen major books, of which several have been translated into English and other European languages.

11.1 PHILOSOPHY

Shingo's early philosophy embraced the 'scientific management' ideas originated by Frederick Taylor in the early part of the twentieth century. Taylor's (1911) approach was based on what is now called the 'economic man' theory of motivation and was briefly reviewed in Chapter 4. This approach was adopted extensively by Shingo, until in his forties he became aware of the methods of statistical quality control. He adopted these methods until in the 1970s he was 'finally released from the spell of statistical quality control methods' (Bendell, 1989: 12). The breakthrough in his thinking arose when he came to believe in defect prevention. This led to his major contribution to the quality debate.

Essentially, Shingo believed that 'statistical methods detect errors too late in the manufacturing process' (Flood, 1993: 28). He suggested that instead of detecting errors, it was better to engage in preventive measures aimed at eliminating error sources. Gilbert (1992: 166) suggests that Shingo meant that we need to change our 'attitude of mind' and 'to organise and then behave in a way' which allows mistake-proofing to happen.

Thus, over time, Shingo effectively rejected the scientific management, 'economic man' theory with all its attendant difficulties, rejected control after the event, and focused on prevention. He became concerned with the total manufacturing process, and Gilbert (1992: 24) cites him as saying that 'he would prefer to be remembered for his promotion of the understanding necessary behind the concepts of looking at the total manufacturing process and the elimination of transportation, storage, lot delays and inspection'. Much of this approach has become embedded in the kanban systems, often called 'just in time'.

Shingo continued to believe in mechanizing the monitoring of error, considering that human assessment was 'inconsistent and prone to error'. He used people to identify underlying causes and produce preventive solutions. In his work, like that of Crosby, we find a clear belief, in a 'zero defects' approach. However, unlike Crosby, whose ideas emphasize worker responsibility, exhortations and slogans, Shingo emphasizes zero defects through good engineering and process investigation and rectification. Bendell (1989: 12) reports that Shingo shared the concern of Deming and Juran that 'posting defect statistics is misguided, and that instead the defective elements in operations that generate a lot of defectives should be hunted down'.

11.2 ASSUMPTIONS

The assumptions about the world that seem to underpin Shingo's approach will now be reviewed.

The first point to note is that, perhaps unsurprisingly, given his mechanical engineering background and training, Shingo can be seen to have adhered to a mechanistic approach to organization throughout his career. From engineering jobs and people in the scientific management approach of his early work, he moved to the quantitative methods of statistical quality control and, finally, to error prevention through good engineering.

The mechanistic view of organization has been challenged by many management theorists and practitioners. It has been criticized for failing to take account of human needs and desires, and for failing to recognize interactions within the organization and between the organization and its environment. Further criticisms have been aimed at the reductionist nature of the approach, which tends to fragment organizations rather than deal with them as wholes. An approach which does not take account of these factors in an increasingly complex and dynamic world must be considered flawed.

The adoption, then abandonment, of statistical methods rests on the assumption that it is possible to develop processes which are error free. While it can be seen that in an engineering context it may be possible to achieve the zero defects objective, it is considered unlikely that the same can be done in other sectors. Food production, as was seen with Chesswood Produce (Vignette 5.1), relies on natural processes which cannot yet be engineered to achieve absolute reliability. While it is possible to improve materials and yields, the processes are still subject to forces which are outside the influence or control of the organization and its people – for example, temperature, humidity, wind, soil condition and crop diseases. Similarly, in the service sector, as previously discussed, there are many variables which cannot be controlled to the extent that Shingo's approach requires.

It has been consistently argued in this book that an appropriate balance of both qualitative and quantitative approaches is most useful. Here Shingo's assumptions must be challenged, because ignoring the human relations aspects of organization and abandoning statistical methods largely restricts the potential applications of his work to the manufacturing sector.

11.3 METHODS

It could be considered that Shingo was the first management thinker and practitioner to engage in what has recently come to be called 're-engineering' (Hammer and Champy, 1993), although the term was used as early as the 1940s in the discipline of operations research. His achievement in reducing hull assembly time from four months to two months at Mitsubishi, and the development of the SMED (Single Minute Exchange of Die) System at Toyota as part of the 'just-in-time' concept were both substantial contributions in their own right.

However, his principal contribution to the quality field is the mistake-proofing concept, Poka-Yoke, 'Defect = 0'. This approach stops the production process whenever a defect occurs, defines the cause and generates action designed to prevent recurrence. Alternatively, 'online' adjustment to the product or process may be made, enabling continuous processes to be managed. For example, in the chemical and steel industries it may be both impractical and expensive to stop a production process.

Poka-Yoke relies on a process of continuously monitoring potential sources of error. Machines used in the process are equipped with feedback instrumentation to carry out this task, as Shingo considered that human personnel are 'fallible' (Bendell, 1989: 12). People are used to trace and resolve the causes of error. Installation of the system is expected to lead over time to a position where all likely recurring errors have been eradicated.

The concept has been adopted to some extent in the food processing industry through the system known as HACCP, (Hazard Analysis Critical Control Points), which has already been outlined. Clearly, it would be unacceptable for even one defective food item to move through a system where its doing so generated risk to health. However, as is regularly seen, even such rigorous systems cannot entirely remove the risks. An example is the *E. coli* food-poisoning outbreak in Scotland during 1996, which led to several deaths.

VIGNETTE 11.1 **CYBERNETIC SYSTEMS**

The idea of Poka-Yoke is similar to the concepts employed in cybernetic systems – that is, systems which in the process of going out of control put themselves back in control again. The simplest and commonest form of cybernetic system is a domestic heating system, which on receipt of feedback information about the air temperature from the thermostat turns the heating system on and off in an attempt to maintain a set temperature. A similar example is the cooling system on an engine, where the thermostat opens and closes to allow or inhibit the flow of cold water circulation, keeping the engine at an optimum operating temperature.

The 'goal' of these systems is a particular temperature. In the case of Poka-Yoke, the goal of the system is zero defects. In each case the goal is determined outside the system, by the house occupier in the case of the heating system or the factory management in the case of a production process.

The concept is now widely employed in industrial control systems for production processes. For example, the baking industry uses a system of this type to control the chamber temperatures in travelling ovens, aiming to ensure that the product is appropriately heated at each stage of the cooking process. The employment of these techniques can reduce or eliminate the need for human monitoring of processes and, as Shingo suggests, enhance reliability.

The advances in information technology and approaches to information management make the application of these techniques much simpler. It is now possible to design and build systems which operate in real time and are capable of both detecting errors and, perhaps more importantly, anticipating errors (on the basis of the information being received) and stopping the line before the error occurs.

A common failure among organizations is not to fully appreciate what it is now possible to achieve in this regard and to stay with outmoded techniques of management. In pursuit of quality, it is useful to adopt proven, reliable techniques but it is essential to embrace those new approaches which have the latent capability to bring about substantial improvement.

11.4 SUCCESSES AND FAILURES

There is no doubt that Shingo's ideas have made a substantial contribution in a variety of areas. The adoption of all or some of his methods by companies throughout the world and his extensive consulting in many countries stand as testament to his success. It does, though, have apparent limitations.

While Gilbert (1992: 166) suggests that the Poka-Yoke concept can be applied equally to administrative procedures and production processes, this is arguable. A production process may well be fully, or extensively, automated, minimizing the opportunity for human or machine error. Administrative and book-keeping procedures, which rely for the most part on the communication and transcription of information, cannot be automated to the same extent; there is, then, scope for error. An error rate of 2 per cent (two keystrokes in one hundred) is regarded as normal for a competent keyboard operator. Human interaction with and intervention in the system is inevitable, and, as Shingo himself said, humans are fallible. A second strand to this is the potential for misinterpretation of data. Language relies on two levels of understanding, the syntactic (signs) and the semantic (meaning). While syntactic understanding can be relatively reliably conveyed, even automated, semantic understanding cannot be guaranteed. It is not therefore possible to build an administrative system which can guarantee that the message, including its meaning, transmitted by one party is received and understood in the same way by the other party.

Flood (1993: 29) lists the main strengths of Shingo's approach:

- It offers on-line, real-time control.
- Poka-Yoke emphasizes effective control systems.

The main weaknesses are the following:

- Source inspection works effectively only in manufacturing processes.
- Shingo says little about people other than that they are fallible.

To take the first of the two strengths, there is little doubt that in a fast-moving and rapidly changing world, online real-time information is not just desirable but essential. However, the feasibility of halting many production processes is questionable.

The use of automated feedback and control mechanisms is a sound starting point for the control of a process in operation and is to be welcomed. However, Shingo says little about the management attitudes towards accountability and responsibility that must go with it. It could be argued that a management unsupportive of this approach would not implement it. Yet a technical system of this sort provides information which an autocratic management could use in a way which might be considered inappropriate: as a stick with which to beat people rather than a tool for improvement. Nonetheless, as Wiener (1948) stated in the early stages of the development of modern cybernetics, there are 'great possibilities for good or evil', and it is up to managers to use the knowledge wisely.

So far as the weaknesses are concerned, the applicability of Shingo's ideas to the service sector has already been questioned. Regarding the attitude to people, it is clear that Shingo's work assumes a willing, co-operative workforce, although he says nothing of how this state can be achieved and maintained. The body of literature concerning this topic which arose during the middle and later years of the last century has not been accounted for.

11.5 CRITICAL REVIEW

There appear to be some consistent themes to Shingo's views, despite the apparent developments in his thinking, from scientific management through statistical quality control to mistake proofing.

He seems to have adhered, in the main, to an 'economic man' view of the people involved in the organization. The wisdom of this view, and his failure to address the body of theoretical and practical knowledge which challenges it, has to be considered a major weakness of his work. While in some Eastern cultures there remains a strong allegiance to collective societary values, notably in Japan, other nations have moved away from this. Many Western countries have seen a significant move towards the pursuit of individual values and objectives, which often translates into the pursuit of individual rather than corporate benefit from work, often reinforced by the style of corporate rewards offered. In a situation where that is the case, the individual may not be willing to contribute in the way that Shingo's work suggests is necessary.

A second clear and consistent theme has been the concentration on good engineering. This is unsurprising given Shingo's background, and his contribution in this area must be considered substantial. However, it does limit the application of his ideas to organizations and processes where the concepts are most readily applied.

The concept of mistake-proofing, by refining and redesigning processes, is of great importance. While it will generally be most easily applicable in the manufacturing sector, there is little doubt that the concept, if not the practice, can be carried across into service organizations. The danger is that it may give rise to additional administrative, auditing and checking procedures, which far from reducing costs and speeding up processes may well serve to increase costs and slow down service. A second danger associated with this is that the procedures may become 'institutionalized', inhibiting or preventing adaptation and learning by the organization. Nonetheless, the underlying emphasis on prevention of error is to be welcomed.

SUMMARY

This chapter has reviewed the major contribution of Shigeo Shingo to the quality movement. Students should refer to Shingo's (1987) own work to develop and enhance their own understanding.

QUESTION

Shingo's approach to measuring quality through technical, automated systems has been criticized for being open to abuse by autocratic managements. Consider how this problem might be overcome while preserving the value of Shingo's ideas.

Genichi Taguchi

All things are numbers.
(Pythagoras)

KEY LEARNING POINTS

Genichi Taguchi's definition of quality: the loss imparted to society from the time a non-quality product is shipped.

Key beliefs: statistical methods; quality as inherent in design; quality is a societal issue.

Principal methods: prototyping method; eight steps of parameter design; quadratic loss function.

INTRODUCTION

Genichi Taguchi trained as a textile engineer prior to his service in the Japanese Navy. He subsequently worked in the Ministry of Public Health and Welfare and the Institute of Statistical Mathematics. In that post, he learned about experimental design techniques and orthogonal arrays. He began his consulting career while working at Nippon Telephone and Telegraph.

His early work in the field of quality was mainly concerned with production processes, but during the 1980s he shifted his focus to product and process design. It was during this period that his ideas began to be adopted in the United States. Logothetis (1992: 17) describes Taguchi's contribution as an 'inspired evolution' in the quality movement by eliminating the need for mass inspection through his process of building quality into the product at the design stage.

Taguchi was awarded the Deming Prize and the Deming award for literature on quality. His best-known works are *Systems of Experimental Design* (Taguchi, 1987), and *Management by Total Results*, which he co-authored.

12.1 PHILOSOPHY

The two founding ideas of Taguchi's quality work are essentially quantitative. First is a belief in statistical methods to identify and eradicate quality problems. The second rests on designing products and processes to build quality in, right from the outset. Logothetis (1992: 13) sees Taguchi's view of quality as a negative, the cost of non-quality – that is, 'the loss imparted to society from the time the product is shipped'. Taguchi's prime concern is with customer satisfaction and with the potential for 'loss of reputation and goodwill' associated with failure to meet customer expectations. Such a failure, he considered, would lead the customer to buy elsewhere in the future, damaging the prospects of the company, its employees and society. He saw that loss occurred not only when a product was outside its specification, but also when it varied from its target value.

Flood (1993: 30) suggests that Taguchi's view 'steps back one further stage on the technical side', pulling back quality management into design. This is achieved through a three-stage prototyping method (Box 12.1). The first stage is concerned with system design reasoning involving both product and process. This is an attempt to develop a basic analytical, materials, process and production framework. This framework is carried forward into the second stage, parameter design. The search at this stage is for the optimal mix of product variation levels and process operating levels, aiming to reduce the sensitivity of the production system to external or internal disturbances. Tolerance design, the third stage, enables the recognition of factors that may significantly affect the variability of the product. Further investment, alternative equipment and materials are then considered as ways to further reduce variability.

Here a clear belief can be seen in identifying and, as far as possible, eradicating potential causes of 'non-quality' at the outset. This ties in with Flood's (1993: 32) view that Taguchi's work perceives quality to be a 'societal rather than organisational issue'. Flood further recognizes that Taguchi's method relies on a number of organizational principles (Box 12.2).

Clearly, Taguchi recognizes organizations as 'open systems', interacting with their environment. The emphasis on communication and control – the systems view – recognizes interdependence between processes, something which he has been criticized for ignoring. Logothetis (1992: 340) considers this unreasonable, and says that 'Taguchi, contrary to common opinion, does recognise interactions – saying: "If one assumes a linear model thinking it correct, then one is a man removed from natural science or reality, and commits the mistake of standing just upon mathematics which is nothing but idealism."'

Summarizing, there appear to be several beliefs running through Taguchi's work. The first is in quantitative methods, providing measurements for control. The second is in the eradication, as far as possible, of causes of failure at the outset. The third is in the societary cost of non-quality. The fourth perhaps reflects the third, and is the systems view of interdependence and interrelationship both within the organization and with its environment.

Box 12.1 *Genichi Taguchi's three-stage prototyping method*

System design

Parameter design

Tolerance design

Box 12.2 *Genichi Taguchi's organizational principles*

Principle 1	Communication
Principle 2	Control
Principle 3	Efficiency
Principle 4	Effectiveness
Principle 5	Efficacy
Principle 6	Emphasis on location and elimination of causes of error
Principle 7	Emphasis on design control
Principle 8	Emphasis on environmental analysis

12.2 ASSUMPTIONS

Assumptions which are considered to underpin Taguchi's approach will now be considered.

The first and quite critical feature is that he seems to assume that quality can always be controlled through improvement in design. While this may be the case for many aspects of manufacturing, its validity in the service sector must be questioned. Similarly, where products exhibit either natural characteristics – as in the case of food – or contain aspects of 'craft' skill – cabinet making, pottery or precious metal work – this may be inappropriate.

A second assumption relates to his attitude to people. Although Taguchi did value their creative input to the design and development process, he appeared not to consider them a significant factor in the production of quality goods. He says little or nothing about people or the process of managing them.

As already mentioned, the work has a clear focus on the manufacturing sector. Nothing is said about how to manage the quality process in service industries.

The next assumption is again quite critical. Taguchi seems to assume that the organization can wait for results – that delays between product conception and production will be acceptable. While these delays are to some extent inevitable, the contemporary market demands are such that they need to be minimized. 'Time to market' has become an absolutely crucial element in success for many organizations. For example, in pharmaceuticals the first in the market with a new treatment becomes the market leader and that firm's position is often then unassailable. The position is similar for information technology, where the most recent innovation tends to act as a key attractor for what the marketing people call 'early adopters' – and the innovator does attract a significant degree of loyalty. It is essential, therefore, if Taguchi's ideas are to be fully implemented, that they are integral to the product development process, not additional, and that the process is designed in such a way that 'time to market' is a key consideration. A conflict may arise between the business need to be fast into the market and the business need to achieve high quality. Adopting the Taguchi method after initial product design must be seen as unacceptable. It is suggested that quality parameters should be as much a part of a basic design brief as timing, markets and prices.

It is easy to see that much of Taguchi's work has been informed by his background in engineering and quantitative methods. What is less obvious is how his 'systems' perspective, with which there is no disagreement, arose. The adoption of a systemic view, while not apparently extending to the management process of the organization, is certainly a step forward from the work of many of his fellow gurus.

12.3 METHODS

The principal tools and techniques espoused by Taguchi centre around the concept of kaizen thinking – that is, continuous improvement. His backward step into the design process helps to ensure a high basic quality standard. Other than the 'quadratic loss function', the other statistical methods are common to many thinkers, and will be reviewed in the appropriate chapter. In this section, concentration will be on the following:

- suggested steps for experimental studies;
- prototyping;
- the quadratic loss function.

The suggested steps (Box 12.3) fall into the 'parameter design' (Logothetis 1992: 306) stage of product development. It is within this process that Taguchi utilizes people. This scientific method is very reminiscent of Deming's 'Plan, Do, Check, Action' cycle. This should perhaps not be surprising, given their common background in statistics.

The first stage is concerned with developing a clear statement of precisely what problem is to be solved. Taguchi considers it of great importance that the experiment should be exactly targeted. The second stage links with the first. It is important to determine what output characteristics are to be studied and optimized through the experimental process, and what measurements are to be taken. It may be necessary to run control experiments in order to validate results.

The third stage is brainstorming. At this point, all the managers and operators related to the product or process are required to come together and determine the controllable and uncontrollable factors affecting the situation. Here the aim is to define an experimental range and suitable factor levels. Logothetis (1992: 306) suggests that Taguchi prefers to consider as many factors (not interactions) as is economically feasible. Whether this represents a sufficient

Box 12.3 *Genichi Taguchi's eight stages of product development*

Stage 1	Define the problem
Stage 2	Determine the objective
Stage 3	Conduct a brainstorming session
Stage 4	Design the experiment
Stage 5	Conduct the experiment
Stage 6	Analyse the data
Stage 7	Interpret the results
Stage 8	Run a confirmatory experiment

involvement by people in the solution development process is debatable. It might be considered that they should be involved at all stages. Nonetheless, their involvement in experiment design, and their contribution of knowledge to the debate, must be considered invaluable. It is normally the case that those who actually perform a task know more about it than anybody else. The opportunity for them to articulate that knowledge in an informal session such as brainstorming is to be welcomed.

The fourth stage is experiment design. At this point, the controllable and uncontrollable (noise) factors are separated for statistical monitoring purposes. This is followed by the fifth stage, the experiment itself.

The sixth stage is to analyse the performance measures recorded, using appropriate statistical methods. This is followed by interpretation of the results, the seventh stage. This aims to identify optimal levels for the control factors which seek to minimize variability and bring the process closest to its target value. Prediction is used at this stage to consider the performance of the process under optimal conditions.

The eighth and final stage is to validate the results so far obtained by running further experiments. Failure to confirm results by further experimentation generates a need to revisit stages 3–8.

This whole process may be regarded as similar to the 'black box' technique used in cybernetics. In that case, altering inputs and monitoring the effect on outputs is used as a device for determining the function of a unit. This technique could be used from a 'macro' perspective in a production or manufacturing facility to determine areas of maximum concern for detailed analysis through Taguchi's methods. Interested readers should refer to the work of Beer (1981) for a more detailed discussion of this approach.

Prototyping is the technique which Taguchi uses to develop what Gilbert (1992: 24) calls the 'up and limping' prototype. This has already been seen in the review of Taguchi's philosophy. The technique consists of three stages. The first, *system design*, is aimed at applying scientific and engineering principles to the development of functional design. It has two elements, product design and process design. The second stage is *parameter design*. This looks at establishing process and machine settings that minimize performance variation. A distinction is made at this stage between controllable and uncontrollable factors (parameters and noise). The specification criterion is for optimization and is usually expressed as monetary loss arising from variation. The third stage is *tolerance design*. This is aimed at minimizing the total sum of product manufacturing and lifetime costs.

The quadratic loss function is Taguchi's principal contribution to the statistical aspects of achieving quality. The point of this calculation is to minimize the cost of a product or service. In this, a particular quality characteristic (x) is identified and a target value (T) set for it. Proximity to the target value is expressed as $(x - T)$. The result of exceeding, or failing to achieve, T is a financial loss to the organization, hence the result must always be positive. This is achieved through squaring the answer, $(x - T)^2$. This result is multiplied by a cost coefficient, c, which puts a cost on failing to meet the target T. A further coefficient, k, representing the minimum loss to society, and with a value always greater than 0, is added. The sum represents the total loss, L, to society. Thus:

$$L = c(x - T)^2 + k$$

139

PROTOTYPING SERVICES

Taguchi's approach to prototyping products can also be applied to the service sector. It is common practice for service organizations to develop new processes or products and test-market them in selected areas, modifying them before a full launch through all outlets. This is a very similar approach to that which should be taken by manufacturing industry – although it often is not! It is much less common practice, though, to prototype other changes, particularly in the way that the organization is run. These changes, which may have much more substantial and long-term impact than a new service, are often developed in secrecy for political reasons and imposed overnight on a surprised workforce.

This is not the only approach to organizational change, and certainly not necessarily the most successful. In 1990, a major retail organization with many outlets decided that its distribution strategy needed to be revised to meet the changing needs of its customers, to enhance the effectiveness of service delivery and reduce costs relative to income. The organization saw the priorities as being in the stated order. The three strands were seen as directly correlated – that is, an improvement in either of the first two would increase income; a consequence of achieving the first two would be the third. Steps were also taken to directly reduce costs by eliminating inefficiency and waste within the organization.

A substantially revised organization was designed, based on 'natural' geographical and business communities. For each such community, there was recognized to be a 'lead' outlet offering a full range of services but specializing in more complex, higher-value activities requiring greater local expertise. The 'subordinate' outlets were focused on the precise needs of their particular community, taking the normal requirements of 99 per cent (approximately ± 3 standard deviations!) of their customers as the benchmark. The relationships with the 1 per cent of exceptional requirements were to be dealt with by staff from the 'lead' outlet.

The principles and broad approach were agreed by the board of the organization and a series of 'pilot' communities were created. The new approach commenced with a prolonged period with one community, where the principles were put into practice for the first time. This was used as a 'learning' situation. The staff of the community were fully involved in the process. While the principles were strictly adhered to, the implementation process was filled with experimentation, reflection, critical review and modification. Once running satisfactorily, the test bed community was visited by representatives from six other communities. These visitors studied what had been achieved, including the mistakes, and with expert facilitation developed solutions appropriate to their own circumstances, providing altogether seven 'up and limping' prototypes.

Once 'tested to destruction' and suitably modified, the revised organization design was rolled out across the organization.

This use of 'live' prototypes, often called beta testing in the case of software products, is an essential part of successfully launching a major innovation. It is simply not possible to test every eventuality or identify every bug until the service is tested on real customers. It may be thought that this requires brave management. This author believes that a management which does not test its services in this way is foolhardy.

This may be viewed, in some respects, as a measure of efficiency and of effective utilization of resources. Of critical importance to its use are the correct selection of criteria and the accurate development of the coefficients c and k. If any of the values selected for the calculation is incorrect, then the whole process becomes useless.

12.4   SUCCESSES AND FAILURES

Like each of the other gurus whose work has been reviewed, Taguchi is accepted as having made a substantial contribution to the field. His books and his consulting indicate the wide acknowledgement of the utility of his approach.

Flood (1993: 32–33), suggests that Taguchi's work has the following strengths:

- It perceives that quality is a design requirement.
- His approach recognizes the systemic impact of quality.
- It is a practical method for engineers.
- It guides effective process control.

Its principal weaknesses are the following:

- Its usefulness is biased towards manufacturing.
- Guidance is not given on management or organizational issues.
- It places quality in the hands of the experts.
- It says nothing about people as social animals.

To look at the strengths, it can again be argued that Taguchi does not go far enough backwards into the design process. Quality parameters are to some extent already determined once the product has moved beyond the initial concept stage, since certain factors such as market and price range will often be decided at that point.

The recognition of the total cost to society of defective products is useful. However, since, as Flood suggests, little account is taken of the people or management process in the organization, the definition of 'total cost' has to be open to question.

That the method is developed for practising engineers, rather than theoretical statisticians, perhaps serves to make it useful. However, the validity of the quadratic loss function should be questioned if each application is not properly understood and underpinned by a validated statistical base.

So far as the weaknesses are concerned, Flood's assessment that the model is of no use where measurement produces no meaningful hard data can be supported. This perhaps limits its usefulness outside the manufacturing sector. That nothing is said about managing people and the organization is also agreed and is considered to be a major drawback to the whole approach.

Taguchi's failure to recognize organizations as social systems contrasts quite sharply with his recognition of quality as a societal issue. There is no explanation in his work for this. He appears to consider the people within the organization as 'machine parts' who will perform whatever function they are allocated to perform. No account is taken of human variability in the measurement of processes. Perhaps he regards this, unsympathetically, as noise!

141

12.5 CRITICAL REVIEW

There can be little doubt that Taguchi's work makes a substantial contribution to the quality movement. That contribution has, however, been focused very narrowly. His engineering and statistical background quite clearly underpins the approaches which he espouses, and this, to some extent, has limited the value of his work. He relies absolutely on quantitative measures of quality, and this makes his approach quite unsuitable for application to the service sector, where quality is often defined by observers at a much more subjective level.

On the other hand, his emphasis on quality of design and the process of prototyping are invaluable, even if perhaps not far-reaching enough. The impact on total (organization) cost of developing quality products and processes must not be underestimated. They will enable substantial reductions, if not eradication, of processes of inspection, rework and reject. Each of these items adds substantially to the operating costs of many organizations, and they often increase directly with the inadequacy of the design and development work.

Taguchi's lack of concern with people and managing organizations must be considered the second major flaw in his approach. He says nothing of how to implement his approaches, which from experience would meet major resistance in many organizations. The necessary reorganization and alteration of corporate structures, the shifts in power, and perhaps the change in budgets associated with his method would all be expected to generate substantial resistance within the organization. Handling this resistance is not addressed.

SUMMARY

The chapter has reviewed the work of Genichi Taguchi. Readers should refer to his original work (Taguchi, 1987) in order to develop their own appreciation of his contribution.

QUESTION

Taguchi believes that quality is a societal, rather than an organizational, issue. Consider whether this is a reasonable belief.

Contemporary thinking

USER GUIDE

Part one of this book showed how quality has become a major organizational issue and placed it in the broader context of early management thinking. In Part two, the work of the quality 'gurus' and its relationship to that thinking was considered. In Part three, the aim is to bring quality thinking up to date by placing it in the context of the contemporary appreciations of management.

Management thinking has developed substantially in the past thirty years, although the dominant literature about quality has not for the most part explicitly embraced the potential benefits emerging from that development. It was shown in Part two that the work of the quality gurus relies principally on the 'machine' view of organization, with some writers moving towards 'human relations' theory but failing to take full advantage of the substantial body of work in that area. For example, Ishikawa emphasizes participation and provides a potentially useful tool for achieving it, but says nothing of the aspects of human behaviour which enable or inhibit meaningful participation. Similarly, the value of holistic or systemic thinking about organizational issues is achieving increasing prominence in other areas of problem solving (for example, Senge's 'Fifth Discipline'), but is largely ignored in the quality literature.

This part of the book explores and explains these holistic approaches to understanding organization. Holistic thinking moves away from treating quality as a technical exercise in improving production performance and product quality to embrace less mechanistic, softer issues of culture, stakeholder relations and organizational politics, as well as offering assistance on the technical aspects. While quality purists might argue, it is believed that from a holistic perspective the pursuit of the traditional narrow interpretation of quality is just one of many strands in the achievement of organizational effectiveness.

Selecting themes to include in this section was very difficult. There are so many books and ideas published each year in the field of management. The works and authors selected have met five criteria. They are (or purport to be):

- systemic;
- contemporary (either recently produced or currently popular);
- practical (they have a well worked out and tested methodology);
- original;
- directly relevant to the pursuit of organizational effectiveness through quality.

These criteria led to the exclusion of specific or extended study of many other significant management thinkers and writers, for example Drucker, Peters, Kanter and Mintzberg. It is not the intention to detract from or deny their substantial contributions to management thinking, and readers are encouraged to study their work. Their exclusion simply means that they did not meet the criteria established for this book.

The chapters in this part are organized along two broad lines. First, they are (more or less) in 'date order' – that is, the earliest ideas are to be found in the earliest chapters. Second, they broadly follow a continuum from 'hard' thinking – how to solve a defined problem – to 'soft' thinking – defining the problem itself. Readers may again work through the chapters in the order presented or 'dip into' the ideas they find most interesting or relevant to their particular interest. The aim of this section is to help the reader identify and understand the various strands of management thought which are currently emerging and to enable informed selection from among those approaches.

Chapter 13

Contingency theory

Sir Roger told them, with the air of a man
who would not give his judgement rashly,
that much might be said on both sides.
(Joseph Addison, *The Spectator* 68,
adapted from Martial, xii, 47)

KEY LEARNING POINTS

Definition of contingency theory: organizational effectiveness is the product of the adequacy of managerial response to five key effectors on the organization: technology, people, goal, size and environment.

Key belief: there is no one best way of structuring an organization.

Contingency and quality: quality is contingent upon the expectations of the customer, not on the products or services offered.

INTRODUCTION

Contingency theory initially arose from the body of work concerning leadership and motivation. The principal proponent of this psychology-based approach is Fiedler (1967), whose work suggested that the best leadership style depended upon the organization's particular set of circumstances. He identified two styles of leadership, 'relationship motivated' and 'task motivated', which were equally valid under different conditions. Relationship-motivated leadership is seen as appropriate when the technical task is relatively easy but the relationships are difficult to manage, task-motivated leadership in the opposing circumstances. There is a 'sliding scale' or continuum of variations between these two extreme positions. Overall, Fiedler's work, unlike that of earlier writers, suggests that there is no 'one best way' of leading or managing.

13.1 CONTINGENCY THEORY AND ORGANIZATION DESIGN

During the 1970s, contingency theory developed from its roots in leadership and motivation theory to became the dominant approach to organization design and management. Theoretically, it reflects some of the development of systems thinking, to be discussed in Chapter 14, but it is based on observation and practice and pre-dates much recent work which has popularized the systems field.

Contingency theory considers the organization systemically as an interacting network of functional elements bound together in pursuit of a common purpose. Each element is essential to the success (that is, the survival, efficiency and effectiveness) of the organization, and the needs of each element must be met within the context of the organization. In other words, an appropriate balance must be struck between the elements. This balance is dynamic, since the environment and the needs of the elements may be continually changing. The nearest analogy is that of riding a bike – its stability relies on its continued dynamism. Like systems thinking, but unlike the classical and human resources theories, contingency theory recognizes that the organization is contained within an environment with which it interacts, both influencing and being influenced by that environment.

Burns and Stalker (1961) proposed that 'organic' organization structures and systems were most relevant to organizations in a dynamic state where conditions and requirements were continually changing. They identified the key variables influencing the structure as the product market and the manufacturing technology. Joan Woodward (1965) and her colleagues studied the relationship between technology and organization design through a survey of manufacturing organizations in south-east Essex in the United Kingdom. Woodward found that there were substantial variations between the organizational characteristics of different firms with notable differences in the number of reportees, the number of levels of management and the formality of communication. Further research showed that a key factor in these differences was not the size of the organization, as was originally assumed, but the technology employed and the production method. This led to the suggestion (Pugh and Hickson, 1989: 16–21) that the 'objectives of a firm . . . determine the kind of technology it uses', and this in turn may be seen as driving the organizational structure – that is, the design of the organization is to some extent 'contingent'.

Jackson (1990) considers that there are five 'strategic contingencies' which affect each other and influence the choice of organization structure. They are:

- goals;
- people;
- technical factors;
- managerial factors;
- size.

The first of these, the goal subsystem, is concerned with the survival of the organization in both the long and the short term – with normative, strategic and operational objectives. These goals need to meet the aspirations of the stakeholders, to match the dynamism of the environment of the organization, which in turn needs to be reflected in the decision-making structure.

146

Contemporary mantras such as 'think global, act local' reflect this demand for appropriate autonomy in goal setting.

Goals should be determined within the organization, although the normative goals (decisions about the nature of the organization) are strongly influenced by the socio-economic context in which the organization exists. All goals need to be thought of as dynamic and evolutionary, sometimes revolutionary, to avoid the danger of a sense of complacency emerging. The goals are driven by a number of aspects. The influence of the environment (socio-economic context) has already been mentioned. The expectations of the managers or controllers of the organization are significant, as are the expectations and needs of the workforce and, increasingly, of the community of shareholders and other stakeholders surrounding the organization.

The people or 'human' subsystem is concerned primarily with the evolving needs of the employees of the organization. These needs must be met if people are to be content within the organization, to be attracted to it and to be fulfilled by their work. It is reasonable to suggest that these needs will vary with the context in which the individuals are employed — that is, the demands of London-based employees may be very different from those in New York, Melbourne or Hong Kong. Essentially, the design of the organization must take account of the needs and capabilities of the staff.

While Jackson draws a boundary which emphasizes differing perspectives for people within the total system as against those outside in the 'environment', it must not be forgotten that the boundary is itself arbitrary, usually reflecting legally established relationships. The work of the 'gurus' and others has shown the notions of 'supplier development', the 'value chain', the 'internal supplier–customer chain' and 'customer feedback' all imply a much closer relationship between the system and its environment — almost to the point that the boundary ceases to exist. Perhaps, as Beer (1979: 94–95) suggests, this creates a 'diffusion' of information within the larger system. The relationships may be seen as symbiotic — meaning that they interact for mutual benefit. Thus while a distinction may be drawn between suppliers, staff and customers, it may be more appropriate to see staff as both *in* and *of* the system — that is, they work within it and are largely loyal to it. Customers and suppliers are *in* but not *of* it. They work *with* or *buy from* the system but do not work for it; their primary loyalty lies elsewhere. They do not necessarily directly share in or benefit from the system's objectives.

The technical subsystem refers to the technology employed by the organization in carrying out its work. We have seen how Woodward discovered that organizations employed different forms of organization according to their size and production technology. She discovered that 'typical' organizational forms had developed within particular industries and that the most successful firms employed these structures. To some extent this may be regarded as a predictable result — the practice now called benchmarking is not new. Although the more formal exchanges which take place today may be more rigorous in their use, there is little doubt that there has always been a fluid movement of ideas between participants in the same industry, particularly when there was high mobility of labour and low job security. Equally, if a particular technology is appropriate to production of a particular product group, it should be no surprise that the organizational forms which succeeds, in terms of manufacturing or creating the product will share many of the same characteristics.

The role of the managerial subsystem is to co-ordinate and enable the activities of the others. Current thinking recognizes that the management of an organization can enable it to respond, through the implementation of strategic choices, to developments in the environment. Thus rather than being at the mercy of the environment, the organization can, through its management decisions, be active in dealing with it. Since the scope for the organization to influence the environment is recognized, the management subsystem as observer can, to some extent, create the environment through its observations and its interference with it.

Jackson (1990) suggests that what he calls the deterministic origins of contingency theory are flawed and that the managerial subsystem is an important determinant of organizational success. This criticism pushes the argument away from the 'mechanistic' view of Woodward – 'technology determines structure' – towards a more organic, interactive view.

The importance of size as a factor in organizational structure was recognized by Pugh and the Aston group in studies (Pugh and Hickson, 1976, Pugh and Hinings, 1976) which considered larger organizations than those studied by Woodward. Their work showed that increasing size reinforces the need for delegation and decentralization of decision making, while simultaneously increasing the need for structured, formal activities. This perhaps can be linked to Fayol's call for an appropriate balance between centralization and decentralization.

While not listed as one of Jackson's key factors, the environment is important to the effectiveness of the organization. Differing environmental demands and constraints require different organizational formats to be employed. Overall, there appears to be a correlation between the level of environmental complexity and turbulence and the requisite level of adaptability or flexibility of an organization. To ensure long-term success – that is, survival – for the organization, it must be capable of responding at an appropriate rate to changes in its environment and, perhaps through marketing and other activities, of influencing the environment in its own favour.

13.2   REITERATION

To summarize, contingency theory views the organization as existing at the confluence of interactions between its goals, people, technology, management and size. These factors, in conjunction with the environmental influences, feed into managers' decisions about the shape of the organization, leading to a particular structure, which in turn pre-controls organizational performance. These ideas are represented in Figure 13.1.

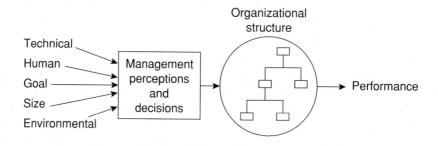

Figure 13.1 *The contingency perspective*
Adapted from Jackson (1990)

13.3 IS QUALITY CONTINGENT?

The question of whether quality is contingent has two distinct dimensions. The first is concerned with quality as an output measure of the organization's performance. The second is concerned with defining quality itself.

So far as the first question is concerned, the answer must be yes. The quality of any product or service is a function of the interaction between all the elements of the system itself and its environment. If any of the inputs, procedures or processes of the organization is flawed, if the demands or influences of the environment are not answered to, or if the expectations of the customers in the environment are not understood, then the product or service may be considered by those customers not to be of sufficient quality. Therefore, achievement of quality must be contingent upon the effectiveness of every part of the system. This perception demands a holistic approach to creating and managing the organization to achieve quality.

Dealing with the second question is much harder, since this is concerned with the definition of 'quality' itself. The 'gurus' reviewed in Part two of this book each offered definitions of quality resting on well-defined, measurable characteristics of a product or service. These are expressed in the form of 'the one best way'. In one form or another, they state that *this is quality* (their various definitions) and *this is how it is achieved* (their different methodologies). It is clear that there are substantial differences between them – for example Deming's statistically based approach; compared with Ishikawa's participative approach, the internal evangelical focus of Crosby's work compared with the societal concerns expressed by Taguchi.

Are they *all* right, or is *none* of them right? *What is quality?* For Crosby, it is 'conformance to requirements'; for Deming and Shingo, it is eradication of error; for Feigenbaum, 'best for customer use and selling price'; for Ishikawa, it is the product, service, management, the company and the people – very near to the contingency view of organization. Juran sees quality as a function of planning, while Taguchi focuses on the cost imparted to society by absence of quality.

It is suggested here that in the contemporary dynamic and turbulent organizational environment, quality cannot be adequately defined in these absolute terms as something fixed and necessarily quantifiable. Perhaps, as Hume (*Essays*, 'Of Tragedy') suggests, quality is like beauty: 'Beauty [or quality] in things exists in the mind which contemplates them.' Perhaps customers experience rather than receive quality of service or product. As each of them has different expectations, they (the customers) continually and individually redefine quality in terms of their past experience and their changing expectations. This means of course that the pursuit of quality, like the hunt for the Loch Ness monster, the American Bigfoot or the Yeti, is doomed to failure because, like the monster, quality is mysterious and ethereal rather than substantial and absolute. Quality, then, *is* contingent, but upon the customer, *not* the organization, its products or services.

This perspective on quality poses a problem for organizations pursuing quality programmes. If quality is not an absolute, then what are they aiming for and how do they know when they have achieved it? The answer seems to be that the quality target is continually shifting and that organizations must pursue 'rightness' or 'appropriateness' in their products or services. Products and services must fulfil the varying purposes for which they are purchased. They, and the processes and procedures by which they are produced, must be error free – within the limits of expectations already created in the customer's mind. Those processes and procedures must minimize cost (land, labour, capital and entrepreneurship – the four factors

149

of production), and, crucially, every aspect and activity of the organization and its management must be focused on doing the right job right.

The key to success in such a scenario rests on communication both within the organization and between the organization and its environment. If internal communication is defective, then staff may do the right job in the wrong way, or the wrong job in the right way. Communication with the environment rests in understanding the expectations of customers (communication into the organization) and creating or modifying the expectations of customers (communication out to the market). If this communication is not effective, then there will be flawed understanding on either (or both) sides, and hence there will not be quality – because however technically good the product or service may be, the expectations of one party from the other will not be met.

VIGNETTE 13.1 **'THAT'S QUALITY!'**

During a seminar on quality in Hong Kong, a student and I went for lunch together, taking an opportunity to discuss his forthcoming project work. The purpose of the lunch was the discussion; eating was incidental, a necessary activity. We found a run-of-the-mill Italian fast food restaurant. The menu was predictable: pasta, pizzas and pollo. The decor was unassuming. The food, served quickly and as ordered, was fully acceptable. The service was surprising: just the right blend of courtesy and friendliness to meet our, admittedly not very high, expectations. We thoroughly enjoyed both our meal and our discussion, paid, walked out into the street, turned to each other and said in unison, 'That's quality!' We had experienced it but could not adequately describe it. The best that can be achieved is to say that it was *all* right on *all* counts.

If asked to nominate a 'quality' restaurant in advance, neither of us would have chosen the chain to which that restaurant belonged. The experience, though, has changed our expectations. If we went there again, would we be disappointed with exactly the same experience?

This story underlines the importance of the customer in defining quality. The food and service no doubt varied to some extent from day to day. Our expectations were low – and the organization as a whole exceeded them – we were then pleased and surprised.

SUMMARY

This chapter has briefly introduced the concept of the contingency view of the world. The emergence and background of contingency theory was explored and its roots in the empirical study of organizations explained. Readers wishing to extend their knowledge should refer directly to the work of the various authors to whom reference has been made.

QUESTION

Consider how the application of contingency theory to the work of Deming or Crosby might enhance the contribution of their approaches to the pursuit of quality.

Chapter 14

Organizations as systems

'Contrariwise,' continued Tweedledee, 'if it was so, it might be; and if it were so, it would be; but as it isn't, it ain't. That's logic.'
(Lewis Carroll, *Through the Looking Glass*)

KEY LEARNING POINTS

Key definition of organizations as systems: the study of organizations and their interactions as wholes, not as an assembly of individual parts.

Key beliefs: the 'system' exhibits behaviour which is not exhibited by any of the parts and has 'emergent' properties which belong to none of those parts individually.

Implications for quality: shift of focus from just the individual parts to embrace the interactions between those parts; recognition that the internal customer chain as creating the organization, quality must be recognized as an emergent property of the system rather than just a technical measure of output.

INTRODUCTION

Contingency theory is seen as systemic. From an organizational as opposed to a psychological perspective, its roots reside in application rather than development of theory – its main tenets being drawn from observation. Thinking about organizations as systems must have strong theoretical foundations if this strand of organization theory is to be more than simply 'best observed practice', which may provide good practice but not best practice. Theory enables the development of general principles upon which rigorous and coherent best practice can be originated. This chapter briefly focuses on the theoretical development of systems thinking and provides the platform for the various approaches outlined in subsequent chapters.

14.1 SYSTEMS THINKING

Systems thinking emerged as a further challenge to the traditional and human relations models and falls within the organic view of organizations. The systems approach is fundamentally different from the reductionist view on which much of modern science rests. The shift in thinking is 'not a gradual evolution, but a discontinuity' (Singleton, 1974: 10–11). A discontinuity in this context means a total change of paradigm – a complete break from traditional, reductionist approaches. While reductionism implies fragmentation – the breaking down and analysis of organizations on a piecemeal basis – systemic thinking implies stepping back from the individual parts and understanding the organization, its behaviours and the interaction of its parts as a whole.

Systemic thinking attempts to deal with organizations as 'wholes' rather than parts, hence the expression 'holistic'. It considers the organization (as with contingency theory) as a complex network of elements and relationships, and recognizes the interaction with the environment in which the organization is contained. Thinking about organizations as 'systems' builds upon the early work of Barnard, Selznick and von Bertalanffy and has become a major, if not yet dominant, approach for management thinkers and practitioners. Practically, thinking systemically has profound implications for organizations, but is not easy to grasp for those educated in a reductionist approach to the world. An explanation of systemic thinking is attempted below.

If we remove the engines from a jet aircraft neither they nor the aircraft, will fly; flight is a product of their interaction and interconnectedness, a synergistic outcome. It is a property which belongs only to the complete aircraft and to none of its parts. Properties such as this are called 'emergent' – they 'emerge' from the interaction of the various system elements. This means that when examining the properties and behaviour of an aircraft, we must look at it in its totality, not just at its components, since the whole may have properties not found in the components. Equally, the parts may have properties not found in the whole. For example, the turbine of a jet engine rotates at high speed while the engine as a whole does not. Similarly, where is the voice in a radio, or the picture in a television? These things are observable outputs of the interactions within such systems and with their environment (the reception of radio or television signals) but cannot be found by reductionist examination or analysis of them.

Ackoff (1981: 18) perhaps offers the most lucid explanation of thinking systemically:

> Suppose we bring one of each of these [types of automobile] . . . into a large garage and then employ a number of outstanding automotive engineers to determine which one has the best carburettor. When they have done so, we record the result and ask them to do the same for engines. We continue this process until we have covered all the parts required for an automobile. Then we ask the engineers to remove and reassemble these parts. Would we obtain the best possible automobile? Of course not. We would not even obtain an automobile because *the parts would not fit together,* Even if they did, *they would not work well together. The performance of a system depends more on how its parts interact than how they act independently of each other.* [Emphasis in the original]

14.2 SYSTEMS THINKING AND ORGANIZATIONS

Parsons and Smelser (1956) attempted to 'elaborate four functional imperatives to be fulfilled for a system, by its sub-systems, if that system is to continue to exist' (Box 14.1). The imperatives they identified are adaptation, goal-attainment, integration and latency (pattern maintenance), and make up the mnemonic AGIL.

Jackson (1990) interprets this somewhat differently, seeing four primary subsystems of an organization – goal, human, technical and managerial, which reflect his contingency theory perspective – as essential prerequisites. He considers that effectiveness and efficiency are attained through the interaction of the subsystems in pursuit of the purpose of the system in its environment.

The goal subsystem is concerned with the purpose of the system and the means of achieving that purpose; the human subsystem deals with the people and their management and motivation; the technical subsystem handles the operations (that is, input – transformation – output); and the managerial subsystem co-ordinates and manages each of the others, balancing the relationships and attending to the environmental interaction.

The systems model adds value to the practice and theory of management in that it demands explicit recognition of the environment and of organizational interactions. The generic system model is of great utility in a descriptive mode, enabling the elaboration of the elements and interactions of the system. However, while this description frequently enables diagnosis of

Box 14.1 *Functional imperatives of a system, according to Parsons and Smelser*

Imperative 1	A = adaptation; the system has to establish relationships between itself and its external environment
Imperative 2	G = goal attainment; goals have to be defined and resources mobilized and managed in pursuit of those goals
Imperative 3	I = integration; the system has to have a means of co-ordinating its efforts
Imperative 4	L = latency (or pattern maintenance); the first three requisites for organizational survival have to be solved with the minimum of strain and tension by ensuring that organizational 'actors' are motivated to act in the appropriate manner

Figure 14.1 *The organization as a system*

faults and failures in the connectivity of the system, it does not offer a prescriptive model based on a projection of an organizational ideal. In terms of weaknesses, the systems model perhaps underplays the essential, purposeful role of the individuals within organizations and the extent to which human interactions can affect outputs unless the context of the discussion fully embraces systemic thinking.

The systems model takes account of the environment and focuses on the generality of survival rather than specific organizational objectives. It does not attempt to quantify the success of an organization, and says little about *how* organizations adapt. The potential for relative autonomy is not explored and little advice is offered in terms of specific remedies for ineffective organizations.

The emphasis in this view is on harmonious internal interaction, whereas conflict and coercion are often present among the human actors. Change is perceived as being environmentally driven, rather than initiated by the organization.

14.3 SYSTEMS THINKING AND QUALITY

The shift from the classical management school of thought to the human relations school represented a change of emphasis within the reductionist paradigm – a shift from a focus on the needs of organizations to a focus on the needs of the individuals and groups within them. The shift in thinking has not been strongly reflected in the quality literature, although the quality gurus do generally recognize in their work the importance of the commitment of all staff to quality initiatives, and some acknowledge the importance of dealing with the totality of the organization. The shift from reductionist to systemic thinking about quality is much more fundamental, involving the acceptance of a new paradigm, a reframing of the entire way in which we think about the world. The impact on thinking about quality is substantial.

When we think systemically about quality, the performance of individual parts of an organization becomes less important; emphasis shifts to their total interacting performance. This means examining not just the performance of functional units such as production, sales, finance, personnel (as would be the case in a reductionist approach), but, crucially, how the performance of those parts is enabled or inhibited by other parts – that is, how they interact to produce goods or services and the impact of change in one part on each of the others.

Conventionally, most quality initiatives focus on the technical performance of production systems, whether for products or services. They examine in detail the characteristics of machines (Shingo), they study the accuracy and reliability of the human and technical inputs to the production system (Deming's special causes of error) and they sometimes look at the internal supplier–customer relationships. Few quality programmes go beyond these technical aspects in any substantial manner.

In a systemic world, the examination needs to step back and consider how each of the parts of the organization interacts with every other part. So, for example, financial objectives, recruitment and training policies and in-bound logistics all impact on production capability and the ability to meet quality targets. Similarly, the sales function and the commitments given to customers by sales personnel are strong determinants of the level of after-sales service which must be provided to meet customer expectations, and of the cost of providing it. These sales commitments also interact with the production elements of the organization, creating demands which need to be met. Overlying all of these aspects are the internal politics of the organization: that is, the ways in which people interact, the coherence or otherwise of their behaviour, the degree of mutuality in their objectives, given that individuals tend to compete for preferment within the organization – and sometimes at its expense.

VIGNETTE 14.1 **A SYSTEMS PROBLEM**

The following story, received from a reliable source in the IT industry, is:

■ reported as true;
■ an illustration of the need to think systemically about problems.

Dialogue between a customer and the Customer Support help desk:

CS:	'Ridge Hall computer assistant, may I help you?'
CUSTOMER:	'Yes, well, I'm having trouble with WordPerfect.'
CS:	'What sort of trouble?'
CUSTOMER:	'Well, I was just typing along, and all of a sudden the words went away.'
CS:	'Went away?'
CUSTOMER:	'They disappeared.'
CS:	'Hmm. So what does your screen look like now?'
CUSTOMER:	'Nothing.'
CS:	'Nothing?'
CUSTOMER:	'It's blank; it won't accept anything when I type.'
CS:	'Are you still in WordPerfect, or did you get out?'
CUSTOMER:	'How do I tell?'
CS:	'Can you see the "C" prompt on the screen?'
CUSTOMER:	'What's a sea-prompt?'
CS:	'Never mind. Can you move the cursor around the screen?'
CUSTOMER:	'There isn't any cursor: I told you, it won't accept anything I type.'
CS:	'Does your monitor have a power indicator?'
CUSTOMER:	'What's a monitor?'
CS:	'It's the thing with a screen on it that looks like a TV. Does it have a little light that tells you when it's on?'
CUSTOMER:	'I don't know.'
CS:	'Well, then look on the back of the monitor and find where the power cord goes into it. Can you see that?'
CUSTOMER:	'... Yes, I think so.'
CS:	'Great. Follow the cord to the plug and tell me if it's plugged into the wall.'
CUSTOMER:	'... Yes. It is.'
CS:	'When you were behind the monitor, did you notice that there were two cables plugged into the back of it, not just one?'
CUSTOMER:	'No.'

CS:	'Well, there are. I need you to look back there again and find the other cable.'
CUSTOMER:	'. . . Okay, here it is.'
CS:	'Follow it for me, and tell me if it's plugged securely into the back of your computer.'
CUSTOMER:	'I can't reach.'
CS:	'Uh huh. Well, can you see if it is?'
CUSTOMER:	'No.'
CS:	'Even if you maybe put your knee on something and lean way over?'
CUSTOMER:	'Oh, it's not because I don't have the right angle – it's because it's dark.'
CS:	'Dark?'
CUSTOMER:	'Yes, the office light is off and the only light I have is coming in from the window.'
CS:	'Well, turn the office light on, then.'
CUSTOMER:	'I can't.'
CS:	'Why not?'
CUSTOMER:	'Because there's a power outage.'
CS:	'A power . . . a power outage? Aha! Okay, we've got it licked now. Do you still have the boxes and manuals and packing stuff your computer came in?'
CUSTOMER:	'Well, yes, I keep them in the closet.'
CS:	'Good! Go get them, unplug your system and pack it up just like it was when you got it. Then take it back to the store you bought it from.'
CUSTOMER:	'Really? Is it that bad?'
CS:	'Yes, I'm afraid it is.'
CUSTOMER:	'Well, all right then, I suppose. What do I tell them?'
CS:	'Tell them you're too stupid to own a computer.'

The point is not that we are too stupid for the organizations in which we work and the technology we use, but that the conventional reductionist mindset leads us to explore only the issue of immediate concern and to ignore the wider issues which a systemic mindset suggests may have implications for the resolution of our particular problem.

Complicating the situation further is the issue of measurement (and the associated rewards and punishments related to performance). It has already been suggested in Chapter 3 that in general, 'we get what we measure', and for many organizations, and the individuals within them, the measurements are narrow, simple and taken in isolation at a single level. Such systems tend to lead to a focus on one aspect of performance at the expense of others. So, for example, if the measurement system (or the boss) emphasizes production efficiency, that is what the management will aim for. In a systemic world, production efficiency cannot be measured in isolation but must be related to the demands of the marketplace, the availability of inputs to the system (land, labour, raw materials) and to the capacity of the organization to provide financial support.

Systemically, quality is not something which can be achieved through enhancing only inde-pendent functional units – however effective they may become individually. Equally, quality cannot be measured in purely technical terms by some inherent and visible characteristics of the product or service such as size, shape, colour or conformance to requirements. Systemically, quality must be recognized as a more or less measurable property of the total organization. It must be inherent in each process and each interaction within the system, and must persist in the organization's dealings with its environment. For example, the products or services of a company may be admired for their apparent quality. However, if the process by which they are made is unnecessarily environmentally damaging or the management system abuses the employees within the organization, then it cannot be considered a quality organization – except by that single output measure of operational performance. In the event that the processes are environmentally damaging or abusive of people, then quality is achieved at some other cost which may not be acceptable at a societal level.

SUMMARY

This chapter has briefly introduced the idea of thinking about organizations as systems and attempted to explain systemic thinking. The implications of systems thinking for quality have been addressed. In subsequent chapters, three different strands of the development of systemic thinking will be explored. Organizational cybernetics stems from the relatively hard, solution-oriented approaches, while soft-systems thinking reflects a more means-oriented approach. Critical systems thinking embraces both of these strands in a systemic inquiry process.

QUESTION

What do you think might be the 'emergent' properties of a university? Why?

Chapter 15

Organizational cybernetics

'I'm not complaining, but There It Is.'
(Eeyore in *Winnie-the-Pooh*, A. A. Milne)

KEY LEARNING POINTS

Key definition of organizational cybernetics: the science of effective organization.

Key beliefs: quality is a product of effectiveness; organizations are extremely complex, exhibit self-regulation, are probabilistic

Tools of cybernetics: the black box technique; feedback; variety engineering; recursion

Cybernetics and quality: descriptive, diagnostic and prescriptive model; offers parallels to mainstream quality thinking; the idea of knowledge workers supports the quality circles approach; distributed power demands management commitment; the cybernetic view supports and enables kaizen.

INTRODUCTION

The science of cybernetics emerged during the 1940s as a part of the systems thinking movement. Norbert Wiener was the founding driver of contemporary cybernetics, working primarily on machine systems. His work has subsequently been developed extensively by others in the modern field of robotics. Wiener's group was interdisciplinary, bringing together mathematicians, biologists, operational researchers and physicists in a ground-breaking approach to developing a unified science for solving complex problems.

Stafford Beer has for nearly forty years led the development of cybernetics in the study of organizations, creating the branch which we now call 'management' or 'organizational' cybernetics. This work extends from the 1950s and is undergoing continued development by Beer and others, including the author and his colleagues. Beer defines cybernetics as the 'science of effective organization' – something from which quality may be considered to result.

This chapter is concerned with the theory and principles of cybernetics and the relationship of the discipline to the achievement of quality in organizations. Organizations are conceived here as societies, composed of people and existing, as proposed in the previous chapter, as the product of their actions, interactions and of the technical artefacts which link and support them. Early work, from which the cybernetic principles were developed, addressed such diverse fields as automation, computing and radar, and built upon earlier discoveries such as Watt's steam engine governor, which are used to illustrate what Jackson (1991) has called 'management cybernetics'.

Organizational cybernetics builds upon and draws ideas from that fundamental work, but 'breaks somewhat with the mechanistic and organismic thinking that typifies management cybernetics' (Jackson, 1991: 103). The distinction is drawn by Jackson on the basis of two differences between the work of Stafford Beer and that of others in this field. First, in *The Heart of Enterprise*, Beer (1979) builds a model of 'any organization' from first principles of cybernetics. Second, he pays significant attention to the role of the observer, whose presence influences the situation observed. If the intellectual insights of Stafford Beer are accepted, it is possible to make use of the principles of cybernetics without relying on analogies between the organization observed and other natural phenomena – although analogies are useful as ways of helping us to order our thoughts about a situation. It can be recognized that the existence and behaviour of the organization studied is, to some degree, a function of the perceptions of the observer.

The role of cybernetics is to help the manager (defined as any person legitimately attempting to command and control an organization) to understand:

- how an organization works (or doesn't work);
- why it works that way;
- what to do to improve it.

This is because 'Cybernetics . . . treats, not things but *ways of behaving*' (Ashby, 1956).

15.1 CYBERNETIC SYSTEMS

The truths of cybernetics are not conditional on their being derived from some other branch of science.

(Ashby, 1956: 1)

This section deals with the major characteristics of systems suitable for the cybernetic approach. Notwithstanding the above quotation from Ross Ashby, a number of the principles have been derived from 'some other branch of science'. It is in taking account of the role of the observer that they reflect the essentially cybernetic operation of those natural systems which have been studied. The principles of cybernetics can be observed operating in nature (e.g. Gell-Mann, Gleick, Lovelock, Hawking, Penrose) and are concerned with 'general laws that govern control processes, whatever the nature of the system under governance' (Jackson, 1991: 92) – and that includes quality systems.

Beer (1959) considers that in order to be a worthwhile subject for the application of the cybernetic approach, the organization is likely to demonstrate three characteristics (Box 15.1). Beer (1959: 12) designates as 'exceedingly complex' any organization which is so complicated

Box 15.1 *Characteristics of cybernetic systems, according to Stafford Beer*

Characteristic 1	Extreme complexity
Characteristic 2	A degree of self-regulation
Characteristic 3	Probabilistic behaviour

that it cannot be described in a precise and detailed fashion. Thus, for example, the wiring loom of a car is, in Beer's terms, 'complex but describable', its design and connectivity can be, and in fact are, recorded. An example of an exceedingly complex organization would perhaps be an interaction between two people in a meeting. This transaction, while apparently simple to observe and record, would, in fact, not be describable. The individual interpretation of words, inflections of speech, degree of eye contact and bodily postures adopted all form a part of the transaction. The recognition of this complexity helps us to understand why managing service quality – which is about human interaction – is so different from managing product quality.

Self-regulation describes the ability of an organization to 'manage' itself towards its purposes or goals while interacting with environmental disturbance. An example is the maintenance of body temperature in humans and warm-blooded animals. The temperature control system behaves in an autonomous manner, needing no active direction or management from the brain – although the brain is where the rules of temperature control are generated.

Probabilism exists where there are elements of the organization whose behaviour is at least partly random. To return to the example of the car wiring loom, it is not only 'complex but describable', but also 'deterministic'. Its behaviour can be known in advance, as any given input to the system, for example operating a switch, will generate a precisely predictable outcome. The outcome of the meeting between two people would be 'probabilistic'. This is because, while the agenda for discussion may be known in advance and a 'most likely' outcome can be predicted, the variables in the meeting, such as mood, posture and experience of the parties, separately and together, make the outcome uncertain.

15.2 TOOLS OF CYBERNETICS

There are three principal cybernetic tools for dealing with these exceedingly complex, self-regulating, probabilistic organizations (Box 15.2).

Complexity is dealt with by the black box technique. Schoderbek et al. (1990: 94) consider that complexity is a property of an organization, which, when examined from a non-quantitative viewpoint, is the product of the interaction of four main aspects: the number of elements, their interactions, their attributes and their degree of organization – a factorial problem.

Box 15.2 *Tools of cybernetics*

Tool 1	The *black box* technique – to address extreme complexity
Tool 2	*Feedback* – to manage self regulation
Tool 3	*Variety engineering* – to handle probabilism

It should be apparent that the interaction of those four 'determinants', because they are factorial rather than linear, can generate what would be seen as an exceedingly complex organization. As such, it does not lend itself to the reductionist analysis of a classical or human relations view, as such an approach would break down the organization and cause the emergent properties to disappear. The organization then examined would be different from that which was initially identified.

The need to study the organization, while interfering minimally with its internal operation, leads to the use of the black box technique. This is a way of gaining knowledge about the operations carried out by an organization without the need to reduce it to its component parts. The black box technique involves manipulating the inputs to an organization and recording the effect on its outputs in order to establish patterns or regularities in its behaviour. As knowledge or understanding of the organization's behaviour is acquired, the manipulations can become more structured. The black box technique is shown diagrammatically in Figure 15.1.

All of us are familiar with and deal with complex black box organizations in our daily lives without ever needing to know or understand how they work (Vignette 15.1). Indeed, the black box technique will never reveal how the transformation process works or how efficient it is.

Managers in organizations, usually unknowingly, perform many tasks using the black box technique. It is not possible to grasp the full complexity of the organizations which are managed. Management is achieved by manipulating the inputs to the organization, recording the outputs, and deducing patterns of response. These patterns can then be used to inform future actions. In order to use the black box technique effectively, it is vital to measure the effect on outputs of changes in input. Unfortunately, most managers, and most of the performance management systems on which they rely, are not integrated in this way. They deny the black box its effectiveness by not recognizing the connectedness of input and output in an appropriate way.

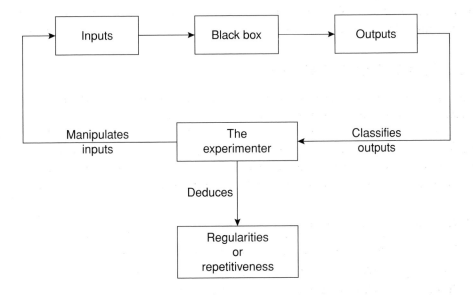

Figure 15.1 The black box technique

VIGNETTE 15.1 **EVERYDAY BLACK BOXES**

- Drivers need not know how an engine works in order to drive a vehicle.
- No understanding of electronics is needed in order to use the computer on which this book is being written.
- Children need know nothing of the internal workings of a video recorder in order to record and view their favourite programmes (something which many adults cannot manage).
- Facsimile machines and photocopiers can be used without understanding exactly how they work.
- Finally, parents learn to manage their children (and children their parents) long before they have a common spoken language with which to communicate and explain their actions. Nobody would propose a reductionist analysis of a baby to 'find out how it works' in order to control it – it is simply managed as a black box.

Feedback is the process which makes self-regulation possible and describes 'circular causal processes' (Clemson, 1984: 22). Self-regulation occurs in both an organization and its environment, and is consequently of major importance. If it is not understood that an exceedingly complex probabilistic organization to some extent regulates itself and how this occurs, then the predictability of the outcomes of managerial actions in relation to that organization is reduced. Self-regulation generates a degree of stability, but if an intervention is undertaken, either in an organization or by an organization in its environment, this stability may be disturbed. If the 'circular causal chains' have not been adequately understood, then the intervention may produce unmanageable instability. The linking of input change and output effect as described in the previous paragraph is what makes feedback systems effective.

The simplest form of feedback occurs when two parts of an organization continuously interact with each other such that the output of one determines the next action of the other. There are two types of this 'first-order' feedback behaviour. In the first, negative feedback or goal-seeking behaviour, the organization will resist disturbances that take it away from its goal. That is to say that the reaction of the one element is to inhibit the change in the other and vice versa. A common example of first-order feedback behaviour is the thermostatic control of a heating or air-conditioning system, the thermostat switching the system on and off in order to maintain a given temperature.

The opposite of negative feedback is positive feedback. In this case, deviation by one element will be amplified rather than reduced by the action of another. These systems, while potentially highly unstable, are also useful. A good example of this is the level of interest acting on a bank account. Positive feedback results in the interest compounding – in effect running away out of control.

A second-order feedback system is capable of choosing between a variety of responses to environmental changes in order to achieve its goal. A third-order system is still more sophisticated. It is capable of changing the goal state itself in response to feedback processes, determining the goal internally as opposed to externally, as in first- and second-order systems. Figure 15.2 shows an example of a closed-loop feedback system.

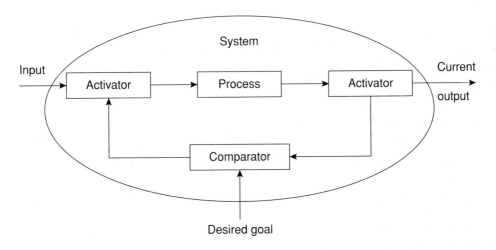

Figure 15.2 *A closed-loop first-order feedback system*

This description of feedback has so far dealt with simple situations. In organizations, the feedback systems may be highly complex, containing large numbers of elements connected in a number of ways and consisting of both positive and negative loops. It may also be the case that at any time the 'sum' of the loops may operate in a positive or negative manner, and in human systems (such as organizations) they need not be physical. Clemson draws from this that: 'there is nothing structural or in the "essence" of the system, about whether the loop is positive or negative'.

Ultimately, systems that include feedback loops are capable of demonstrating exceedingly complex behaviour, and large changes in that behaviour may be brought about by small changes in the direction or extent of internal relationships. There are several key criteria for the design of effective feedback mechanisms (Box 15.3); these will be further elaborated in Chapter 27 when sustainable organization in practice is considered.

Variety is the measure of complexity in an organization – that is, the number of possible states it can exhibit; probabilistic behaviour exists when the behaviour of some of the elements of the organization is considered to be at least partly random. A principal argument of cybernetics is that the mechanisms that are used to manage this complexity must answer to Ashby's 'Law of Requisite Variety', which states that 'only variety can destroy variety'. This means that in order to manage a situation effectively, the management must generate as much variety as is possessed by the operation(s) it seeks to control.

Variety engineering consists of the two prime methods of achieving this control: either reducing the variety of the organization to be controlled (variety reduction), or increasing the variety of the management (variety amplification). In fact, variety can be neither absolutely reduced nor absolutely increased, only managed through appropriate techniques (Box 15.4). This process must be undertaken in a manner which is suitable for the particular organization being managed and should contribute to the achievement of its goals. There are a number of management techniques which are in common use and may be seen as the tools of variety engineering if employed appropriately. These techniques need to be used thoughtfully and with

163

VIGNETTE 15.2 **PSYCHOLOGICAL FEEDBACK**

Given two teams that are roughly evenly matched, if one team plays very well and begins to pull slightly ahead, the other team is stimulated to greater effort and tends to catch up, i.e. the two function as a negative loop in minimising the score difference. However, suppose one team is having a horrible night and gets completely demoralised in the first ten minutes. As the game goes on and they get more and more hopelessly behind they will tend to play less and less well and the better team will relax and everything will go right for them. In this case, the two teams are functioning so that the overall feedback loop is positive in maximising the score difference.

(Clemson, 1984: 23)

Observation of football matches can help us to understand the notion of feedback. Much more explicit (although perhaps equally well hidden) feedback systems are observed in many other fields. The financial markets rise and fall to some, often significant, degree on 'confidence' – the way that traders and investors 'feel' about the prospects of companies rather more than the underlying profit-generating performance of those companies.

The years 1998–2000 saw a massive investment in 'dotcom' enterprises – those established to capitalize on the supposed 'new world' of electronically based organizations – trading in a boundaryless world with none of the usual fixed costs of traditional enterprises. Money from investors was very easy to acquire and all the usual measurements of organizational performance were ignored. The whole market was propelled by confidence.

In 2001, the continued failure of many of the dotcom companies to stop the 'cash burn' and start to generate substantial revenues and profits from their activities led to a complete reversal. Many of these organizations failed; their inability to deliver results ultimately shattered the confidence of investors.

There was never anything inherently good about a dotcom, nor is there now anything inherently bad – but the chances of obtaining new investment in this area are very low indeed. The over-optimism originally shown has now turned into an over-pessimism. Little has changed about the performance of the companies themselves.

Box 15.3 *Design criteria for feedback systems*

Criterion 1	All the elements of the system must be working properly and the communication channels between them must be adequate
Criterion 2	In an organization, responsibility for action (which carries with it accountability) must be clearly allocated
Criterion 3	Controls must be selective
Criterion 4	The control must highlight the necessary action

Box 15.4 *Variety reduction and amplification techniques*

Reduction:

Structural:	delegation (autonomy or decentralization), functionalization or divisionalization
Planning:	establishing objectives and priorities
Operational:	budgeting, management by exception
Rules/policies:	instructions and 'norms' of behaviour

Amplification:

Structural:	team work and groups
Augmentation:	recruit/train experts, employ independent experts
Information management:	management or executive information systems (which may also act as attenuators)

full awareness of their possible consequences, rather than randomly, or politically, as often seems to happen in organizations. Actions or processes that work to reduce the variety faced by managers are known as filters or attenuators, while those which act to increase the variety of the manager are amplifiers.

Recursion is the final topic for this section. In this context recursion refers to the 'organizational and interactional invariance' (Beer, 1981: 72) between levels of an organization. In essence, each level of an organization contains all the levels below it, and is contained in all the levels above it. The organization then exists within a chain of embedded systems. A sample chain is shown in Figure 15.3. In the cybernetic context, the principal elements of structure necessary for decision, information flows and interactions within the organization are perceived as identical at every level. This invariance provides for great ease of understanding of the structure at every level and enables the determination of the relevant autonomy of the system studied. Each level of organization then manages surplus variety from its contained levels and enjoys a degree of freedom in managing variety at its own level constrained by its membership of the next higher level.

15.3   CYBERNETICS AND QUALITY

While the 'systems' and 'contingency' approaches to management progress well beyond the clear limitations of the 'classical' and 'human relations' schools of thought, they each only offer a way of describing organizations. They are descriptive models. However, the ability to describe a situation or problem does little to improve or solve it. The cybernetic model, like these other models, can be used to provide a description of how the organization works, but the work of Beer adds to this the capability to diagnose organizational faults and thence to provide a prescription of changes to enhance the situation. The cybernetic approach, then, through Beer's Viable System Model, can be used to provide a description, diagnosis and prescription for any organization. The application of that model will be revealed in full in Chapter 27.

165

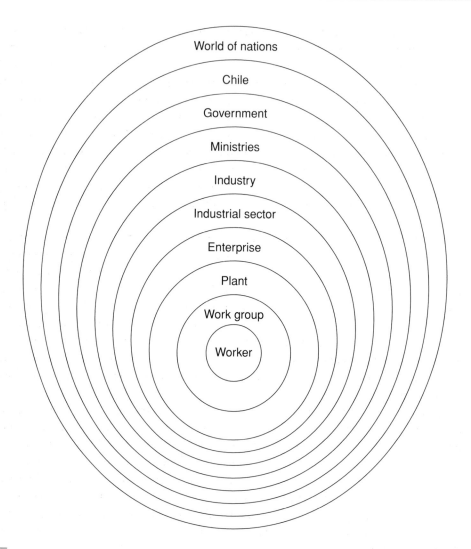

Figure 15.3 *Recursions of a system*

The adoption of cybernetic principles generates several challenges to the established ways of thinking about organizations and achieving quality. First, the cybernetic model of organization relies on appropriate distribution of information. That is to say, information is held at the lowest level in the organization where it is relevant. The design of the information system ensures this and provides the opportunity for local decision making – metaphorically, the equivalent of reflex reactions in the human body. Information received locally may be reacted to locally, provided that reaction is consistent with the needs of the whole organization. Every feedback loop contains a comparator, which implies the capacity for making decisions. The organization provides as much autonomy as is consistent with organizational cohesion. Therefore, the local operation may not undertake activities or engage in reactions which are different from its agreed role or which challenge or threaten the organization, but does have the freedom to react to those matters which are of concern only to itself.

This raises the second issue. If information is distributed, then power is distributed. A common basis of operation in organizations is for power (the right to make decisions) to be relatively highly centralized. Beer, using the expression 'dysfunctional overcentrality', contends that in many organizations, decisions are taken at higher levels than is necessary or desirable for their effective functioning, and raises two points relating to this. First, it is highly inefficient and wasteful of resources. Second, it reduces the adaptability and flexibility of the organization, inhibiting the ability to react to threats and opportunities. In some cases, the result will be the demise of the organization, since failure to respond appropriately and rapidly to a threat may cause 'organizational death' – that is, liquidation, receivership, bankruptcy.

A third issue directly challenges a key assumption which underpins much of early management thinking concerning the abilities of workers. Taylor (1911) provided a prime example of this thinking when he suggested that 'no man suited to the task of handling pig iron is capable of understanding the science that applies to it'. This negative view of the capabilities of workers suggests of course the opposite view of management: as omniscient, god-like creatures of a higher order of intelligence than workers. Whether this view had validity in Taylor's time may be considered open to debate, but its relevance to the contemporary world is highly questionable. The generally higher levels of education now in evidence, coupled with the technology-driven move towards 'knowledge industries', have created a situation where Taylor's view is clearly unacceptable.

This generates a significant difficulty. The adoption of cybernetic principles in the design of organizations demands that those who currently hold power in organizations must release it. Thus the solution to many problems rests in the hands of those least likely to use it. This is a major criticism of cybernetic thinking. In a highly political or coercive situation, the solutions which cybernetics proposes would not be applied. The approach is also criticized for being open to abuse by those with autocratic intentions. It is certainly the case that the concepts and principles underpinning cybernetics may be used in this way. Such applications, though, would be to corrupt the intent of the work of cyberneticians and in the medium to long term would be likely to fail. They would in any event be highly inefficient, demanding a high level of inspection or 'policing' to maintain themselves.

Comparing the cybernetic approach with the various approaches to quality reveals a number of parallels. The cybernetic demand for distributed information, coupled with the devolution of decision making in the organization, reflects the demand in the quality literature for participation and improvement centred on the particular process or workshop. The idea of 'knowledge workers' supports the concept of quality circles – the assumption that the workforce do have the capacity to bring about sustainable, substantial and constructive improvement in quality performance. Cybernetics demands that power be distributed throughout the organization and utilized by those who have the information to make a decision, rather than those whose position on the organization chart suggests that they have power. This in turn reflects the quality call for management commitment. A management which is serious about the pursuit of quality will facilitate and encourage this distribution of power, recognizing that it is both necessary and desirable. If their managerial actions and behaviour do not support their public

167

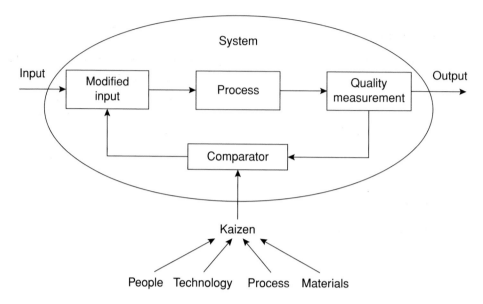

Figure 15.4 *A closed-loop quality feedback system*

calls for improvement, then the psychological feedback loops inherent in any organization will act to inhibit quality performance improvement.

The achievement of quality itself may also be seen as a cybernetic function. Any production process (whether for goods or services) will include a feedback system of the type shown in Figure 15.1. This was a model of any feedback system. In Figure 15.4, the same model is used but this time modified to be explicitly about quality improvement. In this more specific model, it can be seen that the input to a process is modified to reflect some desired quality improvement. The output of the process is measured in some way and the results fed back to a comparator. This compares the actual output with the desired output. The desired output is itself being continually modified by the kaizen process. Results are used to further modify the input to bring the actual output closer to that which is desired. The kaizen process itself consists of a further and similar set of feedback systems dealing with people, technology, processes, materials, and so on. Each time a quality improvement is made in one of those aspects, there is a consequent change in the desired output.

The cybernetic view considers organizations as made up of closely interacting feedback systems. The action of each system is continually modified by the actions, changes and outputs of each of the others. This conception of organization serves to bring the organization 'alive' – it can be imagined as constantly active, engaged in a continual process of self-maintenance and self-improvement, steering itself towards a better future rather than as the static, management-driven and controlled machine of earlier views.

SUMMARY

This chapter has provided a brief overview of the field of organizational cybernetics and its relationship with quality. Many writers (for example, Beckford 1993, 1995; Beckford and Dudley, 1998a, b, 1999; Beer 1959, 1979, 1981, 1985; Dudley 2000; Espejo and Schwaninger 1993) have worked with and sought to develop cybernetic ideas on effective organization. In Chapter 27, these ideas will be applied in practice.

QUESTION

Attempt to describe your class or tutorial sessions in terms of cybernetic processes.

Chapter 16

Soft systems thinking

'It ain't necessarily so.'
(Ira Gershwin and Dubose Heyward, *Porgy and Bess*)

KEY LEARNING POINTS

Key definition of soft systems: the study of problems in human activity systems.

Key beliefs: objectives must be agreed through participation before the study of methods becomes meaningful.

Tools of soft systems: participation, debate, consensus building,

Soft systems and quality: participative approaches can reduce conflict; quality programmes must address hearts as well as minds.

INTRODUCTION

Every venture has a fundamental reliance on human input for control and development, no matter to what extent it is automated and its products or services are believed guaranteed by the excellence of its technical artefacts. If there is an aim to create a quality organization, then it is vital that the people, whether they are relatively unskilled workers or highly qualified experts in a consultancy or research organization, are committed to that aim. This cannot be achieved if they are excluded from the development and decision processes of the organization or its quality programme. They may tolerate the programme or accept it at a superficial level, but they will not take ownership of it, regard it as their own and drive it forward. A programme for quality which is not actively supported at every level in the organization will fail.

16.1 SOFT SYSTEMS EXPLAINED

Organizational cybernetics is often considered, by those not fully familiar with its breadth and depth, as applicable to 'hard' problems: those where the end – the objective – is known and any debate is about means. Soft systems thinking, largely represented in the work of Peter Checkland (1981), proposes the study of human activity systems, those 'soft ill-structured problems of the real world'. Checkland suggests that in 'soft' problems, the identification of the objectives themselves is problematic, and his work focuses on defining a systemic method-ology which helps participants to understand social systems.

The study of 'soft systems' is ends oriented: it is concerned with discovering the purpose of the system. It presumes that the problem of what to do must be solved before the problem of how to do it can be addressed.

Hard systems thinking assumes that the problem to be tackled 'is to select an efficient means of achieving a known and defined end' (Checkland, 1978) – a criticism often levelled at the cybernetic understanding discussed in Chapter 15. Soft systems thinking supposes multiple perceptions of reality. This simply means that reality is not assumed to be the same for every observer. The existence and purpose of the organization are considered to be functions of the observer rather than objective statements of fact. Contrasting with the hard approach, the desired end needs to be defined because only limited agreement about it is believed to exist.

For example, a rainbow exists as a result of the action of light through water droplets suspended in the air, but it can be observed only from the outside and from particular angles. When approached, it disappears; it is a mirage. While we cannot grasp or physically handle a rainbow, we can describe it and understand how it is structured, even though from a different perspective – literally a different angle in this case – the rainbow simply isn't there. Another example is to consider an entity such as the City of Kowloon in Hong Kong. There is only one Kowloon and all parties can agree about its objective existence. However, consideration of Kowloon from vantage points on the eight hills surrounding it would generate different descriptions of that objective existence. Each of the descriptions would be 'right' for the partic-ular observer and viewpoint, but each would describe a different reality.

Similarly, each observer's perception is prejudiced by past experiences, personal desires and expectations. Each observer is unique. This means that even if the same organization is studied from precisely the same physical viewpoint by a variety of people, differing aspects of the organ-ization will be highlighted. Examining Kowloon through a fixed set of binoculars from a hilltop will reveal different sights to different people: an architect may see the buildings, a town plan-ner the roads, an anthropologist the people and an entrepreneur the profit opportunities.

Accepting this very different, 'interpretive' (Burrell and Morgan, 1979) perspective on organizations demands a completely different approach to problem solving and organizational management. The nature and existence of an organization and its purposes can no longer be taken as facts within an established framework; they must be negotiated through a participatory discussion between those observing it. The first step in any problem-solving or improvement process then becomes to develop consensus about the existence and nature of the organization and the problems or issues to be addressed.

The adjective 'soft' does not refer to a characteristic of the system itself but is a function of the perspective taken of the system by those who set themselves up as its problem solvers. It reflects their particular interpretation of how organizational problems should be solved. Thus soft systems thinkers propose that the dominant element in a problem-solving situation is generating agreement among the participants, with this agreement itself leading to improvement in the situation. This is because the generation of agreement will highlight aspects of the organization which do not meet the terms of that agreement and must therefore be modified to fit.

Two well-established methodologies for using soft systems thinking will be explored in Chapter 29.

16.2 TOOLS FOR SOFT SYSTEMS

At a fundamental level, the tools of soft systems may be seen to be cybernetic. That is, effective communication between members of a group may be interpreted as operating through positive and negative feedback loops, comparators of expectations against achievements, and adaptation or modification of attitudes in order to work towards defining goals. The processes by which this takes place, though, make more explicit use of interpersonal action and debate.

For example, in Strategic Assumption Surfacing and Testing (Mason and Mitroff, 1981), there are four phases (Box 16.1). Each of these phases relies heavily on open, effective communication (speaking and listening) between the participants. Phase 1 is concerned with structuring groups on the basis of some common ground. Phase 2 involves the individual groups developing an agreed perspective on the problem. Phase 3 is based on advocacy, with each group presenting its approach and explaining the assumptions which underpin it. Dialectical debate oriented around the underpinning assumptions of the respective arguments follows between the groups. Dialectical debate is debate based on logical argument. At phase 4, the attempt is made to converge the two different views into a consensus view shared by all the participants. Reiteration of the process with additional information is encouraged where consensus cannot be achieved.

It can be seen that this process relies on a number of key characteristics:

- agreement by the participants to open debate;
- a common language – both syntactic and semantic;
- freedom of expression;
- advocacy skills;
- the capacity of the individuals to express themselves, hence freedom from fear;
- sufficient commonality of opinion at the outset for agreement to be a feasible potential outcome.

The tools, then, are the tools of human communication, perhaps best understood and expressed through the science of human psychology. While admirable in theory, some of the characteristics of debate outlined above can be difficult to achieve in practice.

Box 16.1 *Mason and Mitroff's four phases of Strategic Assumption Surfacing and Testing*

Phase 1	Group formation
Phase 2	Assumption surfacing
Phase 3	Dialectical debate
Phase 4	Synthesis

CATHAY PACIFIC: 'SERVICE STRAIGHT FROM THE HEART'

Cathay Pacific Airline launched a programme called 'Service Straight from the Heart' (SSFTH) as a means of developing cultural change within the airline focused on improving customer service. As airline users will know, service is the principal means of differentiating between airlines and is highly influential in customer choice.

Cathay Pacific recognized in early 1995 that the organization and management style of the company needed to create the conditions which would make it possible for SSFTH to be delivered to the customers. A leadership training programme was developed with the purposes of enabling managers to:

- focus on developing a culture supportive to SSFTH;
- understand the company's expectations of its managers;
- understand the impact of personal and organizational styles;
- understand how personal leadership affects service quality;
- experience leadership of high-performance teams;
- identify and plan for the challenges to be faced in delivering enhanced service.

The programme addresses a number of leadership behaviours:

- sharing the strategy and vision;
- supporting others;
- enabling others;
- encouraging others;
- modelling – leading the way.

Crucial in this process of development is the emphasis on enabling the effective participation of staff in decision making. For example, in the section on 'Enabling others', managers are required to involve others in planning, to develop co-operative relationships, to treat others with dignity and respect. Under 'Encouraging others', the programme suggests celebrating achievements, recognition of contributions and sharing successes. These aspects are all expected to have the effect of encouraging and enabling a sense of community and shared purpose within the organization.

Cathay Pacific has expressed within this programme its understanding of the importance of the people within the organization and its recognition of the contribution of those people to its success. By putting people at the heart of its own efforts, it can expect those people to put the customers at the heart of theirs.

The company has enjoyed considerable success with the SSFTH programme and these results are fast becoming measurable where it matters – that is, where the airline serves its customers.

16.3 SOFT SYSTEMS AND QUALITY

The traditional approaches to quality predominantly focus on the technical aspects of quality, paying relatively little attention to the human side. They are 'hard' approaches which assume that the pursuit of quality necessarily leads to improvement. This is, however, to examine quality only from the perspective of the owners or managers of the organization. If quality means less cost and higher profits, then in a profit-oriented world, quality is good for managers and owners. The assumption which underpins those approaches is that 'economic man' will fall in line with the corporate expectations.

However, as has been discussed by numerous writers over the past thirty or so years, the theory that human beings are purely economically motivated does not stand up to practical examination. People work for many different reasons, and while for some, money is a strong, extrinsic motivator, others derive the greater part of their value from the intrinsic value of the work itself. From yet another perspective, it is argued that people work simply because humans are social animals and need both company and work for social and psychological reasons.

If the motivation underpinning an organization's drive for quality is simply economic (as it so often is), then the probable outcomes include reduced numbers of people in the workforce (assuming a stable output) and changes to working practices and the established social mores of the organization. If the management do not appreciate the differing perspectives of the other members of the organizations and accommodate them within their mental models of what is to be achieved, then they will meet varying degrees of resistance to those changes. This resistance will arise from the different interpretations which the individuals put on the organization and its actions.

When resistance to the quality programme is met, the programme will almost certainly fail to fulfil all its stated objectives. Blame will be placed on the 'workers' – 'they failed to make it happen'. The soft systems thinker will immediately recognize that the failure belongs to management because they failed to create the conditions which would have made it possible for the programme to succeed. The management have failed to discover and accommodate the different viewpoints within the organization.

This thinking re-emphasizes the points made in earlier chapters about the need for effective communication and is a reminder of how various gurus have stressed that most of the responsibility for quality lies with the management.

SUMMARY

This chapter has introduced the concept of 'soft systems'. In this view, organizations are not products of objective reality but products of the interpretations put on them by their members. The different approach to solving organizational problems necessitated by this view was introduced and the implications for the pursuit of quality discussed. Readers wishing to expand their knowledge of soft systems should consider the work of Checkland (1981), Mason and Mitroff (1981) and Checkland and Scholes (1990).

QUESTION

When do *you* use 'soft' approaches to problem solving in your day-to-day life? Why do you use them?

Critical systems thinking

. . . to transcend their alterable, historical and essentially ideological limitations.
(John C. Oliga, 1988)

KEY LEARNING POINTS

Critical systems thinking (CST) has three goals: complementarism, sociological awareness, emancipation.

Key belief: management problem-solving has become divided among pragmatists, isolationists and imperialists.

Total Systems Intervention (the meta-methodology of CST) has seven principles:

- Complexity demands sophisticated approaches.
- Metaphors add value by aiding thinking.
- Metaphors link to problem-solving approaches.
- Each method has strengths and weaknesses.
- Problem solving must be systemic and iterative.
- Participation and engagement of actors is essential.

CST and quality:

- CST rejects the idea of 'one best way'.
- All approaches and gurus are both right and wrong.
- Beware of imposing an alternative value set.
- LST encourages reflection and choice.

INTRODUCTION

Critical systems thinking (CST) which began to emerge in the late 1970s and early 1980s, is founded on the pursuit of three goals: 'complementarism', 'sociological awareness' and 'emancipation'.

Complementarism recognizes that different situations lend themselves to different problem-solving approaches. CST proposes that the most appropriate methodology should be applied to a problem and that this *must* be done with full understanding and respect for the theoretical underpinnings of the approach.

Sociological awareness is simply a commitment to the understanding that the nature and culture of societies is different between varying organizations and nations, and alters over time, hence the choice of methodology must be guided by the acceptability of a particular approach in a given context. In the absence of such contextual awareness, any approach is likely to fail. It is essential that the conditions demanded by a methodology or way of working are met. Thus it might be of limited value to apply a very 'hard' methodology in a very liberal environment – for example, a creative organization. Similarly, it might be inappropriate to apply a very 'soft' approach in a prison camp or a dictatorship since the approach would be doomed to failure by the power relations within the system studied.

Emancipation and human well-being are cornerstones of the critical systems approach and act to support the development of human potential and freedom from externally imposed constraints. Theoretical support for this aspect is drawn from the work of Habermas (cited by Flood and Jackson, 1991), who suggested that the two fundamental conditions underpinning the 'socio-cultural' form of life are 'work' and 'interaction'. Work is goal oriented and enables improvement in material things, generating a 'technical interest' in control. Interaction is a 'practical interest' concerned with the development of understanding between people. A further, and major, concern is with the way in which power is, and has been, exercised in forming social arrangements. Awareness of the power of individuals or groups in a given organizational context frequently disrupts the free flow of discussion, inhibiting the potential for genuine debate.

It should be clear that taking these three strands of thought together creates the potential for management problem solving through all available and theoretically substantiated routes, thus enabling technical, practical and emancipatory interests to be fully served.

17.1   TOTAL SYSTEMS INTERVENTION

Flood and Jackson (1991) suggest that the world of management problem solving and systems thinking has divided itself along three principal routes: pragmatism, isolationism and imperialism.

The first of these concentrates on practical solutions – what works for the manager or consultant – and it might be argued that the varying approaches of the quality gurus fall into this category. Concern has been expressed that solutions developed without the appropriate theoretical underpinnings are somewhat sterile, as we cannot learn from them (since they apply only in the given situation) and because it seems that such solutions lead to distortion or abuse, such as 'simply serving the powerful'. It is also observed that without the ability to move from the particular to the general, there is no management science which can usefully be passed on to future generations of managers.

Isolationism, on the other hand, suggests that only one method, based on only a single rationality, is appropriate in *all* circumstances – in other words, it fits the problem to the solution, rather than the solution to the problem.

The dangers of 'imperialism' are also highlighted. Imperialism occurs when alternative methodologies are subsumed into the preferred theoretical position of the user. This must cause concern when, as was seen in Part two of this book, each different approach is based on a particular set of assumptions about the world. The results postulated by the approach can be achieved only if that set of assumptions is recognized, respected and adhered to by the user and the prevailing organizational conditions allow the approach to flourish.

For example, in Chapter 15, the application of organizational cybernetics required substantial devolution of the power to make decisions within an organization to achieve maximum benefit. Such devolution forms part of the philosophy of the approach. It is undeniable that the understanding of organizational interactions derived from the cybernetic approach can be used, at the 'tool' or 'method' level, to achieve greater centralization of power. There is nothing inherently devolutionary about cybernetic interactions. However, to use the tools in a centralizing manner is a denial of the founding philosophy and negates the power of the approach – rendering sterile its objective of improving the total efficiency and effectiveness of the subject organization.

Taking action on this theoretical work and connecting it with the work of Jackson and Keys (1984) on the development of a 'system of systems methodologies', Flood and Jackson (1991) have developed a meta-method for problem solving which enables the informed use of each systems methodology in its most appropriate context. This approach is called Total Systems Intervention (TSI).

17.2 PRINCIPLES OF TOTAL SYSTEMS INTERVENTION

The practice of TSI in the quality context will be considered in Chapter 26. In this chapter, we are concerned with its principles and philosophy. There are seven underpinning principles to TSI (Box 17.1). Let us consider them briefly in turn and reflect on their relevance.

To take the first, it is certainly the case that the many extremely large organizations of today are very complicated and that the complexity of their problems is beyond what could have been envisaged by the management writers of the earlier parts of the twentieth century.

But what of small organizations – those which make up the bulk of the world's economies? A significant proportion of the world's businesses are classified as 'small to medium' (as defined in the United Kingdom by the Companies Act 1985, the criteria are annual turnover below £5.75 million and fewer than 250 employees). These are generally owner-managed, independent organizations with minimal influence on pricing within their industry or sector. In these cases, it might be thought that lesser tools would be adequate. However, it seems to be the case that the problems of these organizations are in many ways *more* complex than those of their larger brethren. On the economic side, the smaller business is seeking to maintain viability in a marketplace dominated by large organizations which have significant advantages in cost and in economic information, increasing the challenge to the small player. In human terms, the intimacy of small organizations may be considered to lead to an increase in the relevance of people management and relationship issues, where people are often personal friends, not

Box 17.1 *Flood and Jackson's seven principles of Total Systems Intervention (TSI)*

Principle 1	Organizations are too complicated to understand using any single management 'model' and their problems too complex to tackle with a 'quick fix'
Principle 2	Organizations, their strategies and the difficulties they face should be investigated using a range of systems metaphors
Principle 3	Systems metaphors which seem appropriate for highlighting organizational strategies and problems can be linked to appropriate systems methodologies to guide intervention
Principle 4	Different systems metaphors and methodologies can be used in a complementary way to address different aspects of organizations and the difficulties they face
Principle 5	It is possible to appreciate the strengths and weaknesses of different systems methodologies and to relate each to organizational and business concerns
Principle 6	TSI sets out a systemic circle of inquiry with iteration back and forth between the three phases
Principle 7	Facilitators, clients and others are engaged at all stages of the TSI process

simply reference numbers on a payroll. In management terms, the small business is again at a disadvantage. Small businesses are relatively unattractive to many managers because they often cannot, or do not, offer the same level of either monetary or non-monetary reward (extrinsic rewards) as the larger organizations – although the intrinsic rewards arising from the work itself are often greater. They are not well placed to attract staff of the highest calibre, and frequently lack the resources to properly educate and train those whom they do attract.

Complexity is not necessarily a function of the size of the organization. It may be seen as a product of dynamism (the frequency of interaction), the number of elements (the number of relevant subsystems within the organization studied) and the necessary rate of change of the organization and its environment – factors which may be considered to be more predominant in small organizations than in larger ones.

The second principle, use of systems metaphors, is useful because it enables individuals to generate high-level descriptions of their circumstances without the need for great elaboration or reductionist analysis. The 'meaning' conveyed by descriptions such as 'prison', 'brain', 'culture' is normally relatively clear to the listener since there exists a common understanding of the word. The use of metaphor provides a systemic language which can be easily shared. A good source for further exploration of the use of metaphors in this context is Morgan (1986).

The third principle follows from the second. The image generated by a particular metaphor is linked to a group of methodologies. The methodologies so identified are considered applicable to organizations which display the 'metaphorical' characteristics. The assumptions about the world which underpin the methodology match the behaviour of the actors within the organization. Thus a 'prison' is suggestive of a coercive environment with a relatively low level of interaction between the stakeholders: one group is dominated by the other. The methodology proposed for this situation is Critical Systems Heuristics, which will be introduced in Chapter 29.

VIGNETTE 17.1 **BUSINESS BANKING: SIZE DOESN'T MATTER**

In the late 1980s a major high street bank reviewed the way in which it managed its relationships with business customers – those whose accounts were not held purely for personal purposes. This review led to the development of a wholly new operating structure based on the division of customers according to their industry rather than the traditional alphabetic division. It was felt that in this way the bankers could develop higher levels of industry-focused expertise and understanding, generating in turn higher levels of customer service and lower levels of risk.

This new form of division created difficulties of its own. It was no longer considered adequate to simply lump customers together and shuffle their problems up and down the hierarchy, as had traditionally been done. If 'relationships' were to be the basis of satisfying customers, it was essential that the customer-facing staff must be able to deal with the majority of the particular customer's problems and needs.

Traditionally, the organization had assumed that size (particularly borrowing requirements), complexity and risk were positively correlated: the bigger the amount borrowed, the greater the complexity and risk associated with the account. It was suggested by the staff that this assumption might be flawed and that an alternative division based on complexity of requirements and difficulty of control should be considered. The staff involved undertook the task of dividing the relationships into industry sectors, at the same time allocating a complexity code (which would determine the seniority of the member of staff who subsequently managed the relationship) according to their knowledge and experience of the customer. It emerged that many of the largest accounts (as measured either by turnover or by borrowing requirements) were the simplest to manage – being categorized as 'simple' by the staff. Their requirements were simple to understand and relatively unchanging, and the sophistication of the customer matched the needs of the organization. In contrast, many much smaller accounts were designated 'very complex'. These smaller businesses often had rapidly changing requirements (because of rapid growth, or the unexpected demands and opportunities facing small businesses) and had less financially sophisticated staff, requiring a greater degree of more sophisticated support from the bank.

The fourth principle addresses the issue of 'complementarity', which has already been adequately elaborated at the outset of this chapter.

The fifth principle is of particular importance. It acknowledges that any given methodology has both strengths and weaknesses, meaning that there are situations for which it is useful and situations for which it is not. This specifically addresses the issues of isolationism and imperialism raised in the previous section. No craftworker uses only a single tool for the completion of all their tasks. They select, from the range of tools available, one which is appropriate for the task in hand. Management scientists should be no different.

The sixth principle reflects the dynamic nature of contemporary organizations. TSI is proposed as setting out a 'systemic circle of inquiry', with iteration back and forth. This issue is perhaps understated in much of the literature. A key assumption which underpins much of management thinking is that problems can be solved. Beer (1981) prefers to think that, through the application of organizational cybernetics, rather than being solved, problems can be dissolved. While there is truth in both of these positions, the author tends to the view that rather than problems being solved, situations can be managed. While any particular and discrete management problem may have a definable solution, the overall problem of managing can never be complete. The continual changes both within the system of interest and in its environment ensure that effective management is a non-stop activity.

Thus it may be helpful to think of TSI as a systemic meta-model for managing, rather than as a meta-methodology for problem solving. Taking this view, it is easier to understand that the process may be simultaneously at different stages for different problems, and that more than one metaphor may be employed simultaneously to describe a given organizational situation.

The final principle addresses the issue of emancipation, again raised in the previous section. TSI requires that all relevant parties should be involved throughout the process. There is much scope for debate and consideration about how to make such participation meaningful under certain circumstances – particularly where coercion exists.

17.3 THREE PHASES OF TOTAL SYSTEMS INTERVENTION

TSI consists of three phases of work: *creativity*, *choice* and *implementation*.

The first phase, creativity, asks questions in two modes: which metaphor best describes the current situation (the 'is' mode) and which best describes the desired situation (the 'ought' mode). A third approach to the inquiry is to consider which metaphors help to explain the difficulties and areas of concern. Metaphors suggested by Flood and Jackson view the organization as a 'machine', 'organism', 'brain', 'culture', 'team', 'coalition' and 'prison'. This list is by no means exhaustive, and any other metaphor may be used by the participants. What is essential, however, is that the description can be linked to one of the systems approaches.

Encouraging participants to go beyond the metaphors suggested by Flood and Jackson may encourage more creative thinking about the situation. In one case, that of a large Hong Kong-based corporation, the metaphor used was 'elephant' – slow-moving, lacking in colour (no flair), deliberate but instinctive rather than reflective. This perhaps suggests a mechanistic view with organismic overtones – a rather more complex description which captured the essence of the situation for the participants. The result of this phase is a choice of a dominant metaphor which is used to guide the selection of methodology or methodologies in the next phase. It is legitimate to use 'dependent' or subordinate metaphors to capture areas of secondary concern.

The choice phase utilizes Jackson and Keys's (1984) 'system of systems methodologies' (SOSM) (Figure 17.1) to provide a framework for choosing between approaches. The SOSM typology offers 'guidelines' to assist the participants in making their choices. It sorts methodologies according to two dimensions: the relative complexity of the system studied and the relative plurality of views of the participants.

A 'simple' system will have few elements, a low level of interaction, a high degree of determinacy and will be highly organized and highly regulated. It will be relatively static and closed to environmental influence. A 'complex' system will have a large number of elements in

	Unitary	Pluralist	Coercive
Simple	Operations Research Systems Analysis Systems Engineering Systems Dynamics	Social Systems Design Strategic Assumption Surfacing and Testing	Critical Systems Heuristics
Complex	Viable System Diagnosis General Systems Theory Socio-technical Systems Thinking Contingency Theory	Interactive Planning Soft Systems Methodology	?

Figure 17.1 *The system of systems methodologies*
Adapted from Flood and Jackson (1991)

highly dynamic interaction. It will exhibit probabilistic behaviour and a lower level of apparent organization, and will be evolutionary.

Unitary, pluralist and coercive refer to the relationships between the participants in the system. A unitary view suggests common interests, values and beliefs between the participants, with general agreement about ends and means, and actions matching objectives. In a pluralist situation, the participants have a basic common interest but divergent values and beliefs. They can compromise on ends and means and will also act in line with agreed objectives. In a coercive situation, there is no common interest; values and beliefs are in conflict, compromise is not possible and some parties may be coerced by others.

TSI interventionists must select a methodology or methodologies (albeit one of their own choice or design not included in the SOSM) in order to move to the next phase, implementation. The framework of the SOSM should enable the users to select a methodology which reflects the characteristics of the situation studied.

Implementation rests in the coherent application of the chosen methodology to the situation in accordance with its own theoretical assumptions but constrained by the recognition of those secondary characteristics highlighted during the choice phase. Thus the approach to the methodology must be modified or 'tempered' to ensure that the use is suitable. Flood and Jackson (1991: 15–22) provide an example of the use of TSI in the quality context.

17.4 CRITICAL REVIEW

TSI, although it appears complex, serves to simplify and perhaps demystify choice among systems methodologies while also enabling coherent understanding and debate in a common language about the characteristics of a situation. It provides a framework for the exploration of issues of concern to an organization and for the 'dominant' issues to be highlighted.

While the SOSM framework may appear to be almost reductionist in its approach, this is too literal a view. Flood and Jackson (1991) acknowledge this in their own critique and refer to the framework as offering 'ideal-type' proposals. In any given situation, the practitioner must exercise professional judgement in choice of methodology and recognize that most situations have a significant degree of 'grey' in their make-up, rather than the simple 'black and white' so often sought by clients and apparently suggested by the SOSM. This area is one which demands sophisticated knowledge and understanding by the user (and may account for some of the inadequate uses of the TSI process).

In terms of use, TSI adds much of value to its users, provided that they are prepared to deal with the uncertainty and complexity which rigorous application of the technique may provide. For those who perceive all of an organization's problems as simple and trivial, the method is of little value since they have decided, before the start of the exploration, what the problem is and how it may be solved.

While the theoretical foundations of TSI appear fairly sound, there are two principal limitations. The first is that the approach is so complex in use that for managers without the appropriate background knowledge it may be difficult. For maximum benefit it requires expert facilitation. This limitation may lead managers to avoid the approach, preferring something simpler and more straightforward. The second opens the whole model to the potential for abuse of power for which other models have already been criticized. In this context, the facilitators are the powerful and may divert the model to their own ends.

17.5 CRITICAL SYSTEMS THINKING AND QUALITY

CST has great relevance to the quality movement (and to the content of this book, which reflects that thinking). Simply, CST rejects the idea that there is 'one best way' of solving any problem (whether or not a problem of quality), proposing instead that each method has potential utility in organizational contexts which reflect the theoretical assumptions that underpin the approach and in which human freedom and well-being are respected.

In the quality context, this suggests that, far from any one quality guru being absolutely right and the others absolutely wrong, they are all right *and* all wrong. Similarly, the various strands of thinking being introduced in this part of the book are equally right and wrong, depending upon the circumstances in which their use is attempted.

For example, in a certain situation the statistically based approach espoused by Deming may be most appropriate, while in another the participative approach preferred by Ishikawa may have greater utility. Equally, at a higher level of intervention, both of those approaches may be rejected in favour of a systems-based approach which embraces the whole system of interest in the pursuit of quality.

A word of caution is appropriate at this juncture, at the risk of offending some readers. It is not only quality methodologies and ways of thinking about the world that have different value in different contexts. These differences also apply to the words which we choose to use and the concepts which we attempt to apply. Thus such concepts as freedom of choice, participation and emancipation have different meanings and value in different contexts. These ideas are essentially products of Western thinking, reflecting primarily what philosophers consider important in societies which are relatively complex in both the economic and the social senses.

183

They are aimed at furthering the interests of those parts of societies already supposed capable of exercising substantial political and economic choices and accustomed, even if for relatively short periods of history, to making those choices. Such parts of societies may be thought of as enjoying significant psychological maturity.

Other societies operate under different sets of opportunities, demands and constraints; they may be considered less psychologically mature. Thus while in a mature society the idea of participation in process design and improvement may be wholly applicable, in some contexts the members of the society may not be wholly familiar with the concept of a job. Consequently, they may require a totally different (although not dictatorial) management approach, one perhaps placing greater emphasis on the parental role of the manager. This difference in approach does not apply solely to emerging or developing economies but also to those parts of Western economies which have suffered high levels of unemployment over many years, for example the steel, coal-mining and shipbuilding regions of most Western economies. In these regions, there are significant numbers of people to whom the concept of a job is wholly unfamiliar since work has been unavailable there, in some cases for two or more generations. This might be thought of, in part, as a product of the failure of employers and employees to embrace changes in management thinking and practice which might have enabled organizational survival. CST enables the thoughtful manager to recognize and reflect upon these aspects of the circumstances in which he or she works and to choose quality implementation methods accordingly.

17.6 TOTAL QUALITY MANAGEMENT THROUGH TOTAL SYSTEMS INTERVENTION

In 1993, Flood undertook the task of exploring Total Quality Management (TQM) through the ideas of critical systems thinking, seeking to establish a sound platform for the theory and practice of the former. His findings are encapsulated in the book *Beyond TQM* (1993).

He defines quality as follows: 'Quality means meeting customers' (agreed) requirements, formal and informal, at lowest cost, first time every time.' Flood sees ten principles (Box 17.2) emerging from this definition. These are to some extent a distillation and synthesis of the work of the gurus already explored in Part two of this book.

The first principle, the call for agreed requirements, implies a need for a high degree of communication both within the organization and with the customers in its environment. The demand for agreement implies that the communication must be focused on discussion rather than discourse – it must be a two-way process of finding out and informing, rather than a matter of giving orders. For it to be effective, there must be understanding and voluntary consensus.

The second principle, 'first time, every time', reflects Crosby's call for zero defects. The clear implication is that there is no benefit to be gained from failing to meet customer requirements and that achieving quality is a matter of consistency. Third is the belief that quality improvement will reduce waste and total costs. The important issue here is the positive nature of the statement. Note that Flood uses the unconditional word 'will', not may, could or should. This is of great importance as a belief, since many quality improvement programmes, initially at least, produce solutions which seem to have the opposite effect, increasing costs and waste

Box 17.2 *Robert Flood's ten principles of Total Quality Management*

Principle 1	There must be agreed requirements, for both internal and external customers
Principle 2	Customers' requirements must be met first time and every time
Principle 3	Quality improvement will reduce waste and total costs
Principle 4	There must be a focus on the prevention of problems, rather than an acceptance of coping in a fire-fighting manner
Principle 5	Quality improvement can result only from planned management action
Principle 6	Every job must add value
Principle 7	Everybody must be involved, from all levels and across all functions
Principle 8	There must be an emphasis on measurement to help to assess and to meet requirements and objectives
Principle 9	A culture of continuous improvement must be established (continuous includes the desirability of dramatic leaps forward as well as steady improvement)
Principle 10	An emphasis should be placed on promoting creativity

in the short term while new techniques or processes are learned and embedded. Often, managements not fully committed draw back from the changes in response to this negative short-term effect and hence fail to achieve any of the expected benefits.

The fourth principle, 'focus on prevention', again reflects ideas of the mainstream gurus and is fundamental to achievement of quality. If the previous principle is to hold good, then clearly the process of achieving quality has to start with error prevention, since as soon as an error occurs, extra cost is incurred, whether in rectification, rework or after-sales support. As Crosby suggests, 'It is always cheaper to do it right first time.' This links neatly to the fifth principle, planned management action.

Planning is at the root of success in all manner of activities in life. Planning implies intent, which in turn implies commitment to a particular course of events. All too often, managements attempt to deal with some form of operational organizational crisis (usually a cost-based crisis) by trying to achieve 'quick hits' through an instant TQM programme. This is sure to fail since the focus is wrong. The banner headline may read 'quality' but the sub-text reads 'save money' and, since the latter is much easier to understand and measure, that will become the focus of the exercise. Some money may be saved in the short term, but what is almost certain is that greater quality will not be achieved. A commitment to quality improvement is a long-term commitment and planning is the key to success.

The sixth principle, 'every job must add value', is perhaps a recognition of the extent to which organizational processes are characterized by jobs and tasks which do not add value, being either unnecessary or obstructive to the process. An interesting point to note is that this 'every' does not apply just to production-focused jobs but to every job in the organization – from the board downwards. This again links to the seventh principle: the involvement of 'everybody' – all levels and all functions. This takes the responsibility for quality away from the quality assurance or inspection department and places it firmly in the hands of those responsible for actually doing the job.

185

VIGNETTE 17.2 **ENSURING FAILURE IN QUALITY IMPLEMENTATION**

In late 1996, a food manufacturer decided, within the context of its overall quality improvement programme, to investigate the poor performance of an established food factory. The plant had been built some ten years previously but had never achieved the levels of productivity and profitability expected.

The investigation was undertaken by a team dispatched from the head office, who proceeded to undertake a thorough review of all activities at the plant. Their findings were extensive, showing poor utilization of equipment and labour, inadequate maintenance, poor record keeping (of production, quality, waste and yield) and abuse of the shift system by some employees. Findings were presented to the local manager, together with a well worked out performance improvement plan.

The manager demanded 'instant' improvements – a focus on the simple operational matters requiring attention – in order to reduce current-year budget deficits. The team from head office argued for a systematic fundamental overhaul of processes and procedures, designed to achieve sustainable improvement over time.

No agreement was reached, and eventually the team from head office was banned from the premises by the manager. The dispute was referred to the lowest-level manager with reporting lines to both parties. To date the problem has not been solved.

There are several mistakes evident in this process:

■ The problem-solving team was imposed on the factory rather than being invited in (implying that while the problem belonged to the factory, the solution belonged to head office).

■ A 'them and us' situation was guaranteed by the exclusion from the process of any members of the factory staff.

■ No 'agreed requirements' were developed between the 'customer' (factory manager) and the 'supplier' (head office team).

■ No educational process was undertaken – that is, no sharing of knowledge by either party.

■ Not everybody was involved.

■ The protagonists allowed themselves to be distracted into a 'tribal war' rather than focusing on the particular problem faced.

The eighth principle – emphasis on measurement – is taken not as a call for reliance on purely statistical methods but as a recognition that without some form of measurement there is no effective basis for evaluation of performance. The importance of effective, integrated measurement systems was explored in Chapter 15, 'Organizational cybernetics'.

The ninth and tenth principles can be taken together: calls for continuous improvement and the promotion of creativity. The first of these relies on the second. Flood specifically recognizes in the ninth principle that continuous improvement should include 'dramatic leaps as well as steady improvement'. In this case we can argue with word choice and suggest that

Figure 17.2 *Continual and continuous change*

'continual' improvement implies a more dynamic frame of reference for these 'dramatic leaps' than 'continuous', with its implications of incremental behaviour. Figure 17.2 attempts to high-light the difference that may be perceived between continual and continuous improvement.

Quality, then, is considered by Flood to be a function of effective communication between the organization and its customers. This communication clarifies expectations and is supported by consistent effort from all those within the organization to meet those expectations. This necessitates meaningful measurement and a creative approach to continual improvement.

17.7 ASSUMPTIONS

Flood's assumptions about the world in the quality context will now be explored.

First, it can be seen that Flood assumes a willingness on the part of organizations to commu-nicate and negotiate with their customers. This suggests recognition of equality of power between the supplier and customer. In practice, such equality of power is rare; normally, one party or the other assumes a dominant role in the relationship. When power is unequal – that is, one party is reliant on the other for its continued existence or financial well-being – it is unlikely that equality will be maintained in negotiations about quality. For example, it is often the case in the motor industry that component or sub-assembly manufacturers rely on orders from a single manufacturer for the majority of their business. This means that the buyer can dictate quality standards and prices. Similar behaviour is seen in the food industry, where the major supermarket groups exercise enormous power over their suppliers. The banking and telecom-munications industries often demonstrate similar characteristics in relation to their customers.

Second, Flood's approach assumes a willingness within an organization to distribute power among the members – since this is the clear implication of involving 'everybody, at all levels and across all functions'. Again, the relative lack of power held by many employees and their vulnerability to loss of employment in many contexts makes it more likely that managers will

187

behave autocratically, dictating how things will be. This will not lead to full commitment and co-operation – which Flood requires – but does more accurately reflect the power relations in many contemporary organizations. This assumption is also implicit in the ninth principle: the culture of continuous improvement. It suggests again effective sharing of power within the organization.

Flood's third assumption is that it is possible to be 'right first time, every time'. While in the manufacturing context this is not at all an unreasonable expectation, in the service and public sectors it is arguably extremely difficult. The technical aspects of any transaction are of course no more difficult to get right than the technical aspects of a physical product. Where the service and public sectors will always have difficulty is at the customer–organization inter-face. While the technical aspects of any particular transaction are constant, each transaction is unique since it depends upon the mood and expectations of the particular customer and of the member of staff at the particular point in time. There are, then, three variables within any given transaction which are largely beyond the scope of the organization to control. It is inevitable that there will be an occasional mismatch between expectations and delivery.

The final assumption in Flood's work which distinguishes it from that of others is the wholehearted embrace of the systemic approach. This comes through in his recognition of both external and internal customers and in the use of the word 'every' in relation to meeting expec-tations, to jobs adding value and to the involvement of all levels and all functions. He does not preclude the involvement of customers in this – although he does not specifically require it.

Overall, Flood's principles rely on a systemic world in which people behave as if they are in partnership. Power is distributed, with those having the information making the decisions, and collaboration rather than competition as the keynote of success. This is a rather different world from the one which many people experience each day.

Other aspects of Flood's approach will be examined in later chapters. The practice of TQM through TSI will be considered in Chapter 26. This section has simply outlined the overall process he proposes.

17.8 SUCCESSES AND FAILURES

It is too early to make properly informed judgements about the success or failure of this approach as, unlike the approaches reviewed in Part two, it has not had the benefit of extended development and empirical study. It is reasonable, though, to attempt some preliminary eval-uation of this work. Its probable strengths are the following:

- It attempts to be truly holistic.
- It is systematic, methodical and iterative.
- It embraces much of value from the established approaches, overcoming some weaknesses previously recognized.
- It is rooted in a substantial appreciation of management and organization theory.

Perceived weaknesses include the following:

- The theory and practice of TSI is not yet accepted as part of mainstream management theory.

- TSI is regarded by many practitioners as too complex in itself.
- There is a lack of widely reported case studies in the literature.
- Substantial empirical development has been principally undertaken by Flood himself.
- As with the other approaches already considered, the approach is of limited value in a truly coercive context.

Let us look first at the strengths. The truly holistic view stems from the meta-methodological, complementarist framework of TSI which underpins the approach and tries to avoid the isolationist, pragmatist and imperialist criticisms made of other methods. The systematic, methodical and iterative process provides a heuristic aspect which reflects the Deming or Shewhart cycle of learning. The embrace of established approaches recognizes that there are strengths in them and supports them with a broader conceptual framework, increasing their potential utility. Finally, the appreciation of management and organization theory recognizes that quality is only one aspect of organizational effectiveness and opens the pursuit of quality to the importation of ideas from other frames of reference within the total knowledge set.

With regard to the weaknesses, the lack of acceptance of TSI among mainstream theorists is not necessarily a fault of the approach itself but a function of the different paradigms within which people are educated and work, and the complexity of the world itself. Unfortunately, contemporary problems cannot always be addressed through simple techniques. It could in fact be argued that many of the failures of problem-solving approaches rest on their simplicity; they are perhaps inadequate for the problems which they attempt to address.

The lack of available case studies and empirical development are functions of the time which has been available for such development. While the work of many others has been under development for forty years or more, Flood's has been in the public domain only for eight.

The final weakness – limited value in truly coercive contexts – is common to all the quality methodologies reviewed (and indeed to other problem-solving approaches). This weakness is one which no adequate methodology exists to address. For many practical purposes, this may be regarded as relatively unimportant. Power relations in most organizations are distorted to some degree, but in most contexts there are practical limits. If the organization becomes too oppressive, the people will leave; thus the power of those in charge is finite. Employees in many contexts do have choices.

There are situations in fully developed as well as developing countries where a considerable degree of practical oppression does exist, where the employees do not have effective choices. This might occur in communities which have experienced high unemployment or where there is a single dominant employer. In these situations, it must be hoped that the effective pursuit of organizational survival and quality will ultimately force those in power to adopt a less dominant position and engage the willing co-operation of the workforce by recognizing that quality cannot be achieved without it.

17.9 CRITICAL REVIEW

Overall, Flood's adherence to the concept of a complementarist approach to organization, and to problem solving, opens a new holistic avenue for the pursuit of the quality ideal. He precludes no ideas which are theoretically substantiated, requiring only that they be used in full understanding of the principles and world-views which underpin them.

The principal tenets of various strands of quality management are subsumed into his approach, thus ensuring the use of participation, the value of appropriate measurement, the informed use of a wide range of tools and the coherence generated by a deeper level of understanding. The approach overall, then, offers a considerably enhanced perception of the 'quality problem'.

The generality of the approach would appear to render it directly relevant to both manufacturing and service industries, although it will suffer many of the same shortcomings as the dominant approaches when dealing with the very soft aspects of organizational behaviour. For example, it may be possible to specify what words should be used in any given transaction – and this is often done. What cannot be specified is the sincerity with which the words are spoken, and most certainly not the response of the particular customer to each utterance. The sincerity conveyed is probably more important to the customer than the exact form of words. Sincerity can be attained only when the staff member truly believes in what he or she is saying. No methodology exists which can guarantee such belief, although, as we shall see, approaches do exist (Chapters 28 and 29) which make it possible.

Pending further reported and substantial empirical work using Flood's approach by a broader range of practitioners, the conclusion must be that it appears to have potential to enhance the implementation of quality programmes. This has yet to be proven.

SUMMARY

This chapter has introduced critical systems thinking and the use of the Total Systems Intervention methodology in a quality context. Readers wishing to extend their knowledge should consider the various works by Jackson (1991), Flood and Jackson (1991) and Flood (1993) to develop and enhance their understanding.

QUESTION

What difficulties might be encountered in attempting to adopt a TSI-based approach to quality management?

Chapter 18

Business Process Re-engineering

Ideas are good for a limited time – not forever.
(Robert Townsend, *Further up the Organisation*, 1985)

KEY LEARNING POINTS

Definition of Business Process Re-engineering: radical reinvention of organizations on process lines.

Key characteristics: pragmatic and empirical, not theoretically based; systemic; exploits developments in technology.

Central themes: discontinuity; radical change; cybernetic understanding; complexity theory; chaos theory.

Key drivers: economic, social, environmental.

Method: the Business System Diamond; process analysis; job and structure review; management and measurement systems; values and beliefs.

BPR and quality are complementary.

INTRODUCTION

Business Process Re-engineering (BPR) emerged as a formal business practice in the United States during the 1980s and early 1990s, although the term had been used in the discipline of operations research as early as the 1940s. In its 1990s incarnation, it is an essentially pragmatic approach that resulted from observation and evaluation of the efforts of several companies to reinvent themselves. It can perhaps be most usefully thought of as a form of business strategy focused on gaining competitive advantage rather than as a theoretically rooted approach to management problem solving. Michael Hammer and James Champy (1993) formalized and crystallized the approach, which is characterized as systemic and capitalizes on many established problem-solving methodologies and techniques.

18.1 WHAT IS BUSINESS PROCESS RE-ENGINEERING?

BPR challenges many of the assumptions which underpin the way organizations have been run for the past two centuries. First, it rejects the idea of reductionism – the fragmentation and breaking down of organizations into the simplest tasks – preferring the systemic recognition of flows of interconnected activities with a common purpose. Second, it encourages organizations to capitalize on substantial developments made in technology, particularly those of the 1990s. The role of IT as an enabler of the radical redesign of organizations is emphasized – although it is stressed that using IT is not the point of BPR. Third, BPR enables organizations to take advantage of the more highly developed education, skills and capabilities of the staff they employ. People are treated within BPR as McGregor's (1960) capable 'theory Y' individuals rather than as lazy, incompetent 'theory X' machine parts.

BPR embraces many of the developments in management thinking that have arisen in the recent past, particularly those concerned with the management of human resources. Ideas such as empowerment are fundamental to the BPR-oriented company.

18.2 DISCONTINUITY, CHAOS AND COMPLEXITY

Central to the BPR process is one key idea: that of 'discontinuous thinking', a notion raised by Hammer and Champy, but earlier given prominence by Handy in *The Age of Unreason* (1990a). Discontinuous thinking and the idea of 'discontinuity' demand some explanation.

The Western world relies on continuous thinking, largely derived from scientific thinking. It is an approach to development which is best thought of as incremental – that is, an apparently seamless, flowing approach. This has served extremely well and retains immense value in certain areas. It is reflected in the continuous improvement (kaizen) approach to quality adopted successfully by many companies throughout the world. However, it is suggested that this approach is inadequate to solve the problems currently besetting organizations. Readers will recall Handy's view cited in Chapter 3.

The call for discontinuous change may be seen as 'special pleading' by management gurus and consultants seeking for a 'new' product to sell – perhaps just another form of organizational snake oil, a solution in search of a problem. After all, it does represent the opportunity for major projects and large fees! This, though, would be an extremely cynical view and would ignore the substantial theoretical support which can now be drawn upon in this area from the 'hard' sciences, particularly biology and quantum physics. That Hammer, Champy and other writers in this area have not drawn on these sources does not negate the value of their work; it merely reflects different backgrounds and knowledge bases. It is fair to say, though, that their work would be substantially enhanced by the explicit recognition and use of these ideas. As suggested by Flood and Jackson (1991), if there is no underpinning science in the work of management gurus, they have nothing to rely on but experience and nothing to pass on to subsequent generations but stories.

The mathematically substantiated science of organizational cybernetics (which in its application to organizations has already been discussed in Chapter 15) is concerned with the control of dynamic systems – those which are changing or evolving. This science has, in its contemporary interpretation, been evolving since the 1940s. It demands of organizations that they become discontinuous in the way they operate, embracing a whole new philosophy of management and decision making and distributing power in ways previously almost unheard of. Early development of this work involved mathematicians, biologists, physicists and engineers. As has already been shown, this work has reached its most developed and useful form through the writings of Stafford Beer.

More recently, developments of this work in the hands of physicists, biologists and others have proven (by scientific methods) that discontinuities may be considered as natural phenomena. Catastrophe theory (a branch of mathematics) is cited as the original identifier of the 'butterfly effect' in which a butterfly beating its wings in one part of the world may generate a thunderstorm in another – the potentially massive consequences of a relatively minor disturbance or perturbation in a dynamic system.

Complexity theory (Waldrop, 1992) has shown how in dynamic systems equilibrium emerges from apparently random or chaotic behaviour and how indescribably complex systems can be studied and their behaviour understood. These systems again can be disturbed from their stable states by minor perturbations, and then, changing discontinuously for a period, settle into a new point of stability. The studies of complexity identify that patterns of behaviour emerge in what at first sight appear to be randomly oscillating systems.

Chaos theory (Gleick, 1987) – which some might argue is not significantly different from complexity theory – has shown how systems evolve apparently chaotically, while on closer examination order can be discerned in movements about a representative point in phase space. Often, system behaviour is almost repeated in a kind of spiral dynamics forming orbits around a fixed point. The orbit may never be quite the same twice but the fulcrum (or turning point) of the orbit remains the same. Again, minor disturbances can cause major effects.

These developments reflect much of the earlier thinking in the systems and cybernetics paradigms and are given great credence by the contemporary facility to model such systems on computers, which allow us to observe the consequences graphically for the first time. Early studies, which did not have this advantage, relied upon the mathematical knowledge of the reader for their proof.

Grasping the concept that discontinuity is as natural as continuity (if not more so), while discomfiting to many, must ultimately be seen as reassuring – since many discontinuities are met in life. The task of management is to drive and control the discontinuity, ensuring that it leads to survival of the organization. The ultimate alternative is the discontinuity that is called death, or, in the case of organizations, liquidation and bankruptcy. Discontinuity is sure to arise within organizational systems, but its consequences are a matter for management choice.

18.3 WHAT DRIVES BUSINESS PROCESS RE-ENGINEERING?

Hammer and Champy (1993: 1) suggest that the alternative to BPR is for 'corporate America to close its doors and go out of business'. The comment is related to the behaviour of organizations for many years, which when faced with increasing costs at home and competition from abroad have chosen, in effect, to export jobs rather than products – an argument already adequately explored in Chapter 1. The same imperatives which drive the quality movement should drive BPR.

Thus a key impetus for BPR is the imperative of economic survival for mature organizations and nations. While the focus of Hammer and Champy's work is the United States, the arguments apply equally well to the United Kingdom and elsewhere in Europe, and to certain Asian economies. The message is to stop exporting jobs and start reinventing the way we perform work in order to match the lower costs of manufacturing elsewhere.

It must be recognized at this stage that the imperative does not simply apply to the manufacturing sector but also to service industries and the public sector. The export of 'information processing'-based tasks, supported by the explosive developments in the capabilities and use of information technology, is already exporting jobs.

Resistance to BPR and inhibition of its application in both the public and the commercial sectors of the economy arises from the same sources. The focus of both tends to be short term, a product of government financial systems and commercial employment contracts. So long as there are profits (or an adequate budget) today, there is no need for action to be taken. Even where the need can be identified by those in power, they often lack the will or commitment to take action since the consequences will not be felt during their own incumbency.

18.4 WHAT DOES BUSINESS PROCESS RE-ENGINEERING MEAN?

Hammer and Champy define BPR as 'the fundamental rethinking and radical redesign of business processes to achieve dramatic improvements in critical, contemporary measures of performance, such as cost, quality, service and speed'. They comment that most established organizations have grown up with, and still adhere to, outmoded, traditional methods of work which are now relatively inefficient and often ineffective. These methods have often led to convoluted, complex ways of dealing with activities, with many steps, checks and balances. These are, in many cases, rendered redundant by the development of both production and information technology, by the universal spread of education and by our current understanding concerning the needs and capabilities of people. Added to this should be the exponential growth in our understanding of the systemic nature of the world and the sophisticated methodologies and tools which have been developed in order for us to manage our organizations more competently. Let us now examine the key words (Box 18.1) in the definition.

Key word 1, 'fundamental', is a clear call for the organization to examine itself at the most basic level. Hammer and Champy suggest the question 'Why do we do what we do?' Perhaps we should go further and ask the question 'What do we do?' This second question demands

Box 18.1 *Hammer and Champy's key words for Business Process Re-engineering*

Key word 1	Fundamental
Key word 2	Radical
Key word 3	Dramatic
Key word 4	Processes
Key word 5	Performance

that the participants focus on the purpose that they perceive for the organization – that is, a redefinition of the organization's goal – without which any improvement, however radical, may actually become trivial or banal. It is important that the organization focus on doing the right thing to the best of its ability – not on doing the wrong thing better!

For Hammer and Champy, key word 2, 'radical', means 'not making superficial changes or fiddling with what is already in place, but throwing away the old'. Ackoff (1981) offered, within the rigorous process of Interactive Planning, the process stage of 'idealized redesign'. This asks the question, put quite simply by Ackoff, 'If you were designing the organization today, what would it look like?' This implies *not* working from established processes and procedures but designing the organization from scratch on a clean sheet of paper. In impact, it is much the same as zero-based budgeting, since it forces a fundamental re-appraisal of every activity within the organization.

Key word 3, 'dramatic', implies that BPR does not seek to achieve marginal or incremental improvement in performance, the normal 5–10 per cent. For companies with that scale of problem (if they are sure of it), the process of BPR may be too powerful. Rather, the focus is on companies which want, or need, to achieve much more substantial performance improvements. Personal experience shows that through effective BPR, practice improvements of 35–50 per cent are achievable. Within certain processes, up to 70 per cent is claimed. It is suggested that every company should undertake a study of its processes to determine what level of improvement might be available. Simply being at or near best in class, which seems to satisfy Hammer and Champy, is not enough. If you are the best, but another organization finds a way of being better still, then you will face the re-engineering challenge anyway. Far better to undertake this activity while ahead of the pack and profitable than while running behind, trying to catch up.

Processes, key word 4, are best defined as the 'value chain' or 'cost chain' running through the organization and linking its inputs to its outputs. A process is the series of revenue-generating or cost-incurring steps involved in any activity. Certain industries, for example chemical and oil producers, are inherently process focused at an operational level. Processes describe the enchained patterns of activity of the organization. Many other organizations are broken down into functional departments with 'baronial' (Jay, 1987) responsibilities for parts or subset activities. Those involved often have limited awareness that they form part of the overall chain, and sometimes no idea what value or cost they generate for the organization. They are narrowly focused on a particular task with no knowledge or interest of what this contributes to fulfilling the purpose of the organization or the needs of its customers. Readers will realize the relevance to quality in this aspect when recalling Deming's contribution to the quality movement in his recognition of internal 'supplier–customer' relationships.

Key word 5, 'performance', while not highlighted by Hammer and Champy, is a very significant word. Performance does not necessarily mean profit – although this is the common interpretation. Rather, it should be taken to mean the fulfilment of the purposes of the organization and the effective utilization of resources.

BPR, then, relies on several unconventional ideas. First is an orientation of the organization towards its processes rather than its fragmented activities – an orientation becoming more common. Second, it requires the drive and ambition to make far-reaching and 'dramatic' improvements. Third is what Hammer and Champy call 'rule-breaking', a willingness to challenge the conventions of the organization. Last is the creative use of information technology. This means using it to enable genuine improvements in performance rather than to set in electronic tablets of stone the established ways of working.

Added to these should be the concepts of bravery and determination, so often absent from corporate life. For, as Machiavelli wrote in 1513 in *The Prince*,

> It must be considered that there is nothing more difficult to carry out, nor more doubtful of success, nor more dangerous to handle, than to initiate a new order of things. For the reformer has enemies in all those who profit by the old order, and only lukewarm defenders in all those who would profit by the new order, this luke-warmness arising partly from their fear of their adversaries, who have the laws in their favour: and partly from the incredulity of mankind, who do not truly believe in anything new until they have had actual experience of it. Thus it arises that on every opportunity for attacking the reformer, his opponents do so with the zeal of partisans, the others only defend him half-heartedly, so that between them he runs in great danger.

Prior to concluding this section, it is worth noting what is *not* meant by BPR. For Hammer and Champy, what it does not mean is downsizing, rightsizing, restructuring, automating or any other management activity which may or may not be necessary or desirable. These things should happen anyway, and of course may result from re-engineering, but that is not the purpose of the BPR process.

If that is how the organization interprets re-engineering, then two things are certain. First, that the process will fail (as do over 50 per cent of so-called re-engineering projects) – that is, the management commitment and understanding needed to really make it work will be absent. Second, that the organization will grow back all the parts reduced in size since no fundamental change in its basis of operation will have occurred. The problem will simply be deferred rather than solved, dissolved or resolved.

18.5 THE BUSINESS PROCESS RE-ENGINEERING PROCESS

The process of undertaking BPR draws on a wide variety of tools, approaches and under-standing. Many of these have been or will be elaborated within this text – for example, statistical methods, communication issues, problem-solving tools, process-mapping tools and the use of information technology.

In this brief section, the focus of attention will be on the overall process, called the 'Business System Diamond'. This is presented in Figure 18.1.

Adopting a process-based approach to organization implies first identifying what the key processes (value-adding connected activities) of the organization are. These in turn control the number, nature and content of jobs, which leads us towards the definition of structure. From the new expectations concerning desirable outputs (the results of processes) and the activities of employees, it is possible to define the management and measurements systems necessary for performance (and it should always be remembered that the tendency is for those charac-teristics which are measured to be delivered). Finally, with the other linkages in place, the values and beliefs of the members of the organization will be modified.

Figure 18.1 *The business system diamond*

It can easily be seen how each stage in the diamond drives the next. The diamond also suggests an iterative process – the organization having successfully re-engineered, its culture should be supportive of aspirations to further development. This may be interpreted as a call back towards continuous improvement.

197

18.6 BUSINESS PROCESS RE-ENGINEERING AND QUALITY

There is some ongoing debate as to whether BPR replaces or subsumes the pursuit of quality, or quality subsumes BPR. This debate is sterile. The pursuit of quality is about 'rightness' in all the actions and interactions of an organization, both internally and externally. The greater part of the quality methods and tools are incremental in their impact and lead the organization towards the kaizen philosophy of continuous improvement. This implies linear, progressive change in the organization. BPR is about embracing the hidden potential for change by recognizing that incremental change only improves what is already done, while BPR may fundamentally change what is done. If a procedure or part of a process is redundant, in the sense that it adds no value to a product or service, improvement in its efficiency is a false gain. While efficiency improvement reduces the amount of waste, the procedure still remains as a cost in the system. The adoption of BPR techniques in process analysis can help to overcome this problem, eradicating procedures rather than improving them. BPR and quality are complementary, not competitive.

Perhaps somewhat perversely, and as with the strategic process outlined in Chapter 2, it is vital that the BPR process itself exhibit appropriate quality characteristics. If the BPR process is flawed, then the outcome will also be flawed.

SUMMARY

This chapter has introduced the concept of Business Process Re-engineering and placed it in the context of theoretical developments in recent years. The links to systemic approaches based on cybernetics, complexity science and chaos theory were explored. In the latter part of the chapter, BPR was defined and its key process explained. While this chapter draws heavily on the pioneers of BPR (Hammer and Champy, 1993), readers may wish to extend their knowledge by considering the work by Johansson et al. (1993), and by moving beyond this narrow focus to consider the work of systems thinkers in depth.

QUESTION

What barriers would you expect to meet in designing and implementing a Business Process Re-engineering programme?

Chapter 19

Organizational learning

Education makes a people easy to lead, but difficult to drive;
easy to govern but impossible to enslave.
(Lord Brougham, 1778–1868)

KEY LEARNING POINTS

Organizational learning

The organization must be structured to:

- interact with the present more efficiently;
- monitor and anticipate the future;
- manage the interaction of the two.

Organizational learning is *not* about data mining and knowledge management, but about structural and behavioural adaptation.

Senge's learning organization

Key definition: a learning organization is one engaged in an iterative, circular process of evolution.

The seven disabilities:

- 'I am my position';
- 'the enemy is out there';
- the illusion of taking charge;
- the fixation on events;
- the parable of the boiling frog;
- the delusion of learning from experience;
- the myth of the management team.

The five disciplines: systems thinking, personal mastery, mental models, shared vision, team learning.

Organizational learning means adaptation of individual and collective behaviour.

Learning implies quality implies learning.

INTRODUCTION

The chapters on Critical Systems Thinking and Business Process Re-engineering have both espoused iterative processes which should lead to the continuing evolution, and perhaps revolution, of the organization. This chapter introduces early ideas about adaptation and learning based on Ashby's *Design for a Brain* (1952) before considering the specific work of Peter Senge (1990), author of the best-known current text in this area. Senge's *Fifth Discipline*, identifies five principles for learning and seven learning disabilities which inhibit the development of truly successful organizations. Flood (1999) revisited this theme in *Rethinking the Fifth Discipline* to bring to the field a deeper and more robust appreciation of the breadth and power of systemic thinking applied to the notion of learning. The present book cannot provide a fully comprehensive review of the literature in this field. This has grown substantially in recent years, and readers should refer to Morgan's *Images of Organisation* and Pettigrew and Fenton's *Innovation* to further develop their understanding.

Learning itself is a cycle of planning, experimentation, reflection and consolidation, which the PDCA cycle and EPDCA cycle from Deming and Oakland reflect. A learning organization needs to be capable of employing these cycles systemically throughout the organization, both horizontally and vertically. This means it must be embedded in the organization's structure and behaviour.

19.1 ORGANIZATIONAL LEARNING

Organizational learning is commonly associated with issues of data mining and knowledge management (physical retention of documented records) in an organization. The precept is that in knowledge-based economies, such information constitutes an asset of the organization and that it should be managed in the same ways as other assets. This has given rise to growth in document management systems, data-mining technologies and the creation of more substantial organizational archives. All of this rather misses the point. Organizational learning is not so much about the storage and retrieval of data as about organizational structures which adapt to changes in their environment. This adaptation must occur at least at the same rate as the environment demands such change. Changes in behaviour of the people must also happen such that they actively support and encourage adaptation rather than inhibit it.

Lessons can be drawn from the work of evolutionists such as Darwin which help us to understand that in a persistently evolving environment those species which survive are those which are best adapted to their environment over time. Those characteristics of a species which enable its survival in any one time period may ultimately lead to its failure when the environment changes. Thus there is a conflict. To maximize opportunities for survival in the present requires characteristics which meet the demands of the present environment. To maximize opportunities for survival in the long term necessitates characteristics which cannot even be known about, but which the species or entity must be capable of evolving if it is to survive – and this capability must, to some extent, detract from the closeness of fit to the current environment. This conflict applies at least as much to organizations as it does to living species. In fact, it may be argued that the organizational case is stronger because, in general, the organizational economic ecology changes faster than that of the world in general.

Drawing on Ashby (1952), for an organization to resolve this conflict, it has to do three things simultaneously – and at various levels of organization. It must:

- be increasingly efficient in its interaction with the marketplace, persistently pursuing faster, cleaner and cheaper means of delivering present products and services to present markets;
- scan the organizational environment, searching for new opportunities, considering the closeness of fit to the market and reflecting on past performance to create future products and services for future markets;
- conduct a meaningful dialogue internally which enables the organizational objectives stimulated by considerations for the future to be translated into the organizational reality of the future.

In essence, the organization is attempting to move smoothly to ensure a continuous fit between its product and service offerings and the changing demands of the customers. Such an approach means that the organization must structurally separate, either literally or in the behaviour of its employees, the roles which are necessary to enable this evolutionary, adaptive behaviour by the organization to occur. Commonly, organizations are oriented around current products, services and markets. Little or no attention is paid to the future, and consequently the organization is hit with unexpected events for which it has carried out no preparation. The demands of operating today's business nearly always override the necessity of creating tomorrow's, and the organization dies – most often by being absorbed by another.

Organizations do not exist (except in the sense of a legal entity) other than through the interactions of their members. They are socially constructed devices assembled to achieve a common aim, and ultimately cannot learn except through their members. The collective memory of an organization is best described through its culture – that is, the ways of thinking and behaving which are common to its members. Organizational learning is not, then, about the addition of data to a corporate memory (although such memories are capable of being created) but about change in the behaviour of the organization through structural change and adaptation of the individual and collective behaviour of its members. Offered in Figure 19.1 is the author's cybernetic interpretation of how such adaptation might take place. This is explained as follows. Members of the company, through their interactions with the environment, come to question the way in which things are done (questioning), through comparison of their real-world experience with the organization's model of 'self ' (their model of the organization and its environment). They conceive potential solutions to the defined problem (conceptualization) and design an experiment to test their hypothesis (experimentation). The results of the experiment are fed back to them and the organizational model is modified according to their new experience (consolidation). They proceed to manage the organization in accordance with the modified model. Learning fails to take place when the last of these steps, consolidation, does not occur. Alert readers will have noticed the direct comparison which can be drawn here with other learning approaches such as the Deming cycle (Plan, Do, Check Action), Ishikawa's quality circles (which focus on problem solving) and Taguchi's prototyping methodology. Questioning, conceptualization, experimentation and consolidation are drawn from Handy (1985).

The structure for an adaptive organization has been considered in theory here and extensively in Chapter 15, 'Organizational cybernetics'; the practice will be assessed in Chapter 27, 'Sustainable organization'.

201

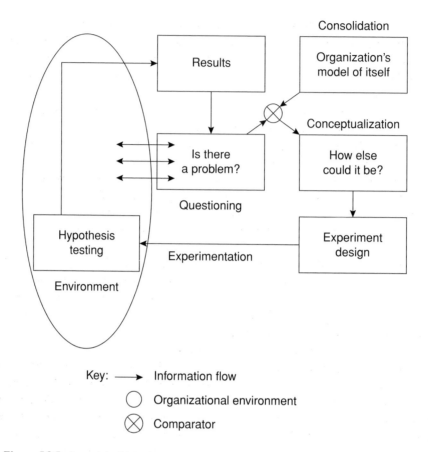

Key: ———→ Information flow

○ Organizational environment

⊗ Comparator

Figure 19.1 *A model of learning*

19.2 SENGE'S LEARNING ORGANIZATION

A 'learning organization' is defined simply by Senge (1990: 3) as one where 'people continually expand their capacity to create the results they truly desire, where new and extensive patterns of thinking are nurtured, where collective aspiration is set free, and where people are continually learning how to learn together'. The idea is supported in other parts of the literature. Beer (1979, 1981, 1985) writes about adaptive, ultra-stable systems – organizations which are capable of reacting to situations and conditions not envisaged when they were designed. Ackoff 's (1981) work and that of Checkland (1981) both call for participation, exploration and critical reflection – essential activities for learning. The critical systems work of Flood, Jackson and others can also be called upon to support this view, with its calls for complementarism (requiring understanding of different theories and methodologies), sociological awareness (different cultures) and emancipation (the growth and development of human freedom). A recent work in this area comes from Flood and Romm (1996), in which they elaborate an approach to 'triple-loop learning'. Senge also draws widely on the literature in organization theory and business practice to support his work.

Looking at Senge's definition (Box 19.1), there are a number of key words and phrases. First, learning organizations are clearly focused on people. However, this focus is not in the sense of the mainstream human resource literature which aims to satisfy human needs and wants, but in an approach centred on developing human potential – which will in turn lead to those same satisfactions.

Second, 'continually' implies a commitment to an ongoing process, a further move away from the static thinking which dominated earlier management science.

Third, 'create the results' suggests that the people's abilities enable them to control and create the future of organizations. This reflects the thinking of Ackoff and others. It must be acknowledged, though, that limits exist to the potential control exerted by organizations, these limits being enforced by the actions of others in a competitive world.

Fourth, 'new patterns of thinking' reinforces the points made earlier in the book. While one should not necessarily reject all the old thinking, the new should be capitalized on where appropriate.

Finally, there is 'collective aspiration/learning together'. Here Senge appears to object to much of the development of Western society in recent years. This has seen a move away from collective, shared values and hopes towards a rather more selfish world in which the individual considers her- or himself supreme. This is perhaps reflected in life in such areas as divorce rates, executive compensation packages, the increasing trend towards litigation over relatively minor matters and the drift away from religiously based societies towards a more secular approach.

The issue of learning is given real prominence when the leaders of large industrial organizations take it seriously. Senge quotes Arie De Geus, then head of planning for Royal Dutch Shell: 'The ability to learn faster than your competitors may be the only sustainable competitive advantage.' The American business guru Tom Peters makes the comment, 'There is a surplus of everything.' This is taken to mean that there is more capacity in the world to create goods and services than exists to consume them. This can only generate further competitive pressure, driving down prices and margins and consequently profits. It is not simply about learning to work 'smarter' to do better, but to survive.

19.3 THE LEARNING DISABILITIES

Senge (1990) suggests that even the 'excellent' companies may be performing at only a mediocre level (reflecting again some of the thinking behind BPR). He proposes that the ways we design and manage our organizations and the narrow, convergent ways we are taught to think and to interact create 'fundamental learning disabilities' (Box 19.2).

Box 19.1 *Key words and phrases concerning the learning organization, according to Peter Senge*

Key word 1	People
Key word 2	Continually
Key word 3	Create the results
Key word 4	New patterns of thinking
Key word 5	Collective aspiration/learning together

VIGNETTE 19.1 **LEARNING STIMULATES LEARNING**

Berkshire Young Musicians Trust is a highly successful music education organization. The public face of the trust is its highly successful bands, which compete in music festivals at United Kingdom national level and regularly tour internationally, entertaining audiences in many countries. These competitive successes and international tours are seen by the head teacher as a bonus rather than being the real work of the trust. He sees the real work and achievement as the opportunity given to every child within the Berkshire community, regardless of ability, to take part in musical activities and succeed to their own best level.

The philosophy adopted is that 'every child can grow through music, every child should be given the chance.'

The successes of the trust are attained through a number of factors such as enthusiastic staff, a large core of young musicians and exciting, stimulating music and projects. To enable these to come about, the trust operates on a highly devolved structure, with day-to-day decision making delegated as far as possible. Because the work of the trust stands or falls by its teachers, they aim to recruit the best and retain them. Performance is monitored through a system of curricular heads led by the Head of Education. Monitoring includes observation of lessons and assessment of problems as well as sharing of opportunities and experience.

The known strengths and weaknesses of the staff are seen as the basis for the development of training programmes designed to capitalize on the strengths and overcome the weaknesses. The opportunity is taken to use outside speakers when appropriate and bring fresh ideas and experiences into the organization.

Staff are encouraged to find new and creative ways of stimulating the learning of their pupils, rather than simply regurgitating the lessons they themselves received as young musicians. Many members of staff write and arrange music specifically for their groups. They are passionate about music and aim to achieve the best possible results.

The only selection criterion applied to pupils wishing to study with the trust is their desire and expressed interest in their instrument. In discussion, the head revealed how recent research into the effects of learning music showed that this stimulated other learning by the child. Three groups of students were studied. Those in the first group received music instruction, the second computer instruction; the third received no extra tuition. While the second and third groups demonstrated no change in their performance, the group receiving music instruction showed a 30 per cent improvement. The conclusion (however preliminary) is that learning music stimulates other learning.

The phrase 'I am my position' argues that we become what we do for a job. The classic example of this is first meetings or parties when we introduce ourselves and are almost always asked, 'What do you do?' Our response – 'I am a . . .' – defines us as being our work.

'The enemy is out there' reflects our human tendency to place blame or guilt elsewhere, rather than to acknowledge the faults in ourselves. This tendency has been recorded in literature since at least biblical times. Commenting on the illusion of taking charge, Senge (1990) suggests that when we think we are being 'proactive', very often we are just being differently

Box 19.2 *The learning disabilities, according to Peter Senge*

Disability 1	'I am my position'
Disability 2	'The enemy is out there'
Disability 3	The illusion of taking charge
Disability 4	The fixation on events
Disability 5	The parable of the boiling frog
Disability 6	The delusion of learning from experience
Disability 7	The myth of the management team

reactive. He proposes that 'true pro-activeness comes from seeing how we contribute to our own problems'.

Our reductionist views of the world, the tendency to analyse scientifically, leads us to a simple 'cause–effect' view of the world, hence the fixation on events rather than processes and interactions. This events-oriented view has already been challenged with the recognition of the systems-based approach. Senge suggests in this area that our focus on events prevents us from seeing the patterns in gradual processes which tell us much about what is actually happening.

The parable of the boiling frog was fully rehearsed in Chapter 3. It is the recognition of the need for discontinuous change and, perhaps, learning to be uncomfortable with continuity in a non-linear world (chaos! complexity!).

At the simple, individual level, if we reflect on our actions and their consequences, then we learn. Unfortunately, we do not always learn from experience as, particularly in organizations, these consequences cannot be known in this way. They may well extend across organizational boundaries and have impacts for future time which we cannot be in a position to assess. Beer's Viable System Model (VSM) starts to address this point, with its emphasis on information management. The VSM calls for an internal model of the organization within the development function and for abandonment of the traditional functional silos or stovepipes of management.

Suggesting that management teams are often little more than gentlemanly turf wars, Senge (following Beer and others) talks about the 'myth' of the management team. He recognizes that appearances are often more important to people within organizations than reality. Consequently, the management team is often not a team at all, particularly when under pressure. Each member is fighting to defend his or her own credibility and position in adversity. Thus we end with what Argyris (cited by Senge, 1990) calls 'skilled incompetence': 'teams full of people who are incredibly proficient at keeping themselves from learning'.

All readers will be familiar with these issues within their organizations. Senge requires that the familiarity is made within ourselves – a much more difficult task.

19.4   THE FIVE DISCIPLINES

Senge (1990) proposes that in order to overcome our difficulties with organizations and learning we must adopt five disciplines – that is, become disciples of five beliefs (Box 19.3).

205

Box 19.3 *Senge's five disciplines for overcoming an organization's learning difficulties*

Discipline 1	Systems thinking
Discipline 2	Personal mastery
Discipline 3	Mental models
Discipline 4	Shared vision
Discipline 5	Team learning

Readers will by now be familiar with the ideas of systems thinking. Senge's work draws heavily on the theories and practice of Systems Dynamics developed by Jay Forrester. Flood and Jackson (1991) offer a full critique of that approach. Here it is sufficient to say that the work studies the behaviour of non-linear dynamic systems.

Personal mastery refers to the discipline of personal growth and personal learning. It demands of the individual an open-minded, inquiring approach leading to them creating their own future. Taking into account here the critical systems commitment to 'sociological aware-ness', it can be suggested that the extent to which personal mastery is achievable will be a product of the capabilities and the cultural and educational background of the individual.

Mental models are formed because it is clearly impossible to know in finite detail all there is to know – our minds carry only models of reality. These are necessarily abstractions from the full richness of the reality and, as Beer (1985) suggests, are 'neither true nor false but more or less useful'. Problems arise when the models are significantly flawed, which is often the case, or when it is forgotten that they are simply models and they become perceived as the reality. In these cases, reliance on them is certain to be equally flawed. Senge (1990) suggests that learning to unfreeze and regenerate our mental models of the world is critical.

Shared vision is the call for all stakeholders in the organization to have a common (or unitary) view of what the organization is and what is to be achieved. Senge suggests that when there is shared vision, the desire is for the same things for everyone. To achieve this, the vision cannot be 'handed down from the mountain' like the Ten Commandments, as is so often the case, but must be built from the ground. This calls for the sort of participative approaches espoused by Checkland (soft systems methodology: 1981), Ackoff (Interactive Planning: 1981), Beer (Syntegration: 1994) and Ulrich (Critical Systems Heuristics: 1983).

Team learning does not easily occur but is driven by a number of key characteristics. Senge (1990) suggests that the team members must have first embraced the other four disciplines already described. The first key characteristic is alignment (the shared vision); the team can accomplish little unless there is a commitment to the same outcomes. Second is the need to think and consider 'insightfully' [sic] about complex issues. Third is the need for co-ordinated action. Here Senge refers to championship sports teams and jazz ensembles enjoined in 'oper-ational trust'. Finally, there is recognition of the need for the team's effectiveness to be spilled over into other connected (and usually) subordinate teams. This final point reflects the concept of recursion from the systems literature.

Holding all of these insights together is one, so far unstated, requirement. That is the need for effective communication, both vertically and horizontally throughout the organization.

206

Effective communication requires a subtlety of approach often absent from daily dialogues. It means effective listening as well as effective speaking. It sometimes requires discussion and at other times dialogue. It does not mean the generation of conflict or the adopting, as is so often the case, of rooted, entrenched positions, nor reliance on dogma or ideology. These ways of 'communicating' lead more often to breakdown and obfuscation or unsatisfactory compromise, which conflict with the other disciplines.

19.5 QUALITY AND LEARNING

This brief section seems now almost redundant. The whole basis of the pursuit of quality rests in the idea of learning – that is, in finding ways of carrying out activities so that the outputs of an organization more nearly match the requirements of its customers. If the same mistakes are repeated, then clearly no learning is occurring and no quality improvement is being attained. The kaizen philosophy demands improvement in all processes all of the time. Learning is implicit in this. It can, then, be argued that any organization successfully pursuing quality is also learning, and any organization pursuing learning is also improving quality. The two words imply each other in the organizational context, the organization needs to be structured in a way which makes this possible.

SUMMARY

This chapter has given a brief introduction to the idea of organizational learning and the 'learning organization' according to Senge. Readers should refer to the works suggested in this chapter to further develop their understanding and knowledge.

QUESTION

Compare and contrast the learning models of the quality gurus with that outlined in this chapter.

Part four

Methods, tools and techniques

USER GUIDE

In the first three parts of this book, a substantial platform has been developed for thinking about quality theory and the dominant methods. This platform has been derived from management theory and the extended practice of the quality gurus.

Part four builds upon this theoretical platform by examining methods for implementing quality. The methods explored range from general techniques such as process analysis, used in many management problem-solving activities, to those specifically focused on quality such as ISO 9000, the value and limitations of statistical techniques, and quality circles. Equally, both reductionist techniques and systemic methodologies are included, each having value in particular contexts. The part concludes with an afterword on the implementation of quality programmes.

209

Specific changes have been made to this part of the book from the first edition. Chapter 21 has been completely revised to address a range of quality management systems, including ISO 9000:2000, the Business Excellence Model and ISO 14000. Chapter 22, 'Understanding statistical methods', has been revised in response to readers' comments to focus on critical evaluation of statistical arguments rather than on the techniques themselves. Chapters 27 and 28 now focus on the creation of sustainable, learning organizations and the application of Skills-Based Quality Management. This has been done to provide insights into a methodology for dealing effectively with issues of service as opposed to manufacturing quality – something not adequately addressed in the rest of the literature. Chapter 29 brings together the issues of stakeholder participation, examining the notion of the internal and external stakeholders and considering methods in which stakeholder views can be used to drive the development of the organization.

Like Parts one, two and three, Part four can be used in two ways. It can provide a straight-forward critical introduction to those tools for achieving quality which are derived from the various theories already explained. For those with a practical focus, the section provides a comprehensive tool kit enabling the pursuit of a quality initiative in a way that is both practically informed and theoretically sound.

Process analysis

Wherever there is an end, it is for this that the previous things are done, one after the other.
(Aristotle, *Physics*: II: 8)

KEY LEARNING POINTS

Key definition of process analysis: the mapping, analysis and critical examination of processes.

Key belief: it is vital to appreciate whole processes, not just functional parts.

Examination techniques: process charting, process analysis, critical examination, method development.

Development techniques: brainstorming, analogies, morphological analysis, attributes, convergent and divergent thinking.

INTRODUCTION

This chapter introduces techniques associated with the identification and mapping of processes. Process mapping is a fundamental starting point for any quality initiative, since it is vital to understand the whole of a process (or processes) if the use of other quantitative or qualitative tools is to become meaningful. Process definition and mapping helps to identify the processes and the location of particular quality problems. It is followed by process analysis and critical examination, which are focused on generating improvements.

Since the first edition of this book was published, the idea of process-based management has attained far greater currency having been adopted by the International Organization for Standardization as the basis of the substantially revised ISO 9000:2000 family of standards. Certification to the standard now demands that the organization adopt a process-based view of its operations, its interactions with suppliers and customers, and of its own internal management. None of this changes the core content of this chapter; it simply serves to underline its importance.

20.1 DEFINING PROCESSES

Defining processes in an established manufacturing environment is a straightforward activity; the process is largely defined by the flow of manufacturing. In a service environment, it is often more difficult, since processes are often not recognized as such, their elements being linked across separate functional areas. For example, in a bank, processing a customer's cheque may involve the signature of an official for authorization of payment, a cashier, a computer input operator and a filing clerk. Each of these individuals may work in a different department (functional silo) within the bank, and the process may be subject to a number of variations and subroutines, dependent upon circumstances. For this reason, fragmentation of processes has traditionally been the most frequently used approach to process study and design. For an organization serious about achieving quality, it is vital to move beyond this fragmented approach to something more coherent. Process definition is vital in this regard.

A process chart is valuable in providing an overall picture of a connected set of actions by recording, in sequence, each of the operations and activities. These operations and activities are recorded regardless of who does them or where they are performed. Functional boundaries within the organization are ignored for mapping purposes.

Process charting can be carried out at a number of nested levels or recursions. At the first level, the 'Total Process' records the process from start to finish, with a minimum of detail and identifies where exceptions and subroutines occur. The second level, 'Process Operation' or 'Task', details the specific actions taken at each stage (including the exceptions and subroutines), while a third level, 'Process Detail' or 'Procedure', studies detail potentially down to the level of individual hand movements (a work study level of analysis). For many purposes, especially where a skills-based approach (see Chapter 28) is used, capturing information at the Total and Operational levels is sufficient. Figure 20.1 shows how the three levels are linked.

The process charts are developed by identifying particular operations and linking them together along with any inspections, audits or delays. The process may be defined in either a vertical or horizontal flow, whichever is more convenient, and, for clarity and economy of effort, ASME symbols are used to indicate each stage. The ASME symbols, with some additions, are shown in Figure 20.2.

For tracking and reference purposes, it is common practice to give each process a unique name or identifier and to number the sequence of actions. The process charts provide a record of the operation at various levels of detail and provide the basis for later process analysis and critical examination. They also provide a basis for deciding what should be measured and at which point. Such charts may usefully be overlaid on a scale plan or topographical diagram of the building layout, indicating paths of movement. This can prove helpful in eradicating delays and identifying why and where quality problems occur – for example, storage of temperature-sensitive materials in an unprotected area. An example of a completed 'Total Process' chart overlaid on a building plan is provided in Figure 20.3. This chart represents the receipt, preparation and dispatch of a purchase order. The order is received by a storeman, who prepares a

Figure 20.1 *Nested or 'recursive' process levels*

Figure 20.2 *ASME symbols*

STORES   BUYER'S OFFICE   GENERAL OFFICE   ACCOUNTS DEPARTMENT

Figure 20.3 *A total process chart*

request form, creates a folder and passes the folder to the typist (that is three operations). The typist types the order and passes it to the checker who checks the typed order against the request form and, if everything is correct, passes the order to a progress clerk. The progress clerk passes the forms to the relevant buyer for signature, who signs them and passes them back. The progress clerk then passes the order to the supplier, passes one copy of the order to the Accounts Department and holds the other in the buyer's file. This undoubtedly cumbersome process is a real example found in a UK factory in the early 1990s and is, in this author's experience, while obviously inefficient, not unusually bad.

It is reasonable to suggest that many, if not most, long-established organizations have not yet fully exploited the potential for process re-engineering enabled by innovative approaches to process management and contemporary information technology. An intervention completed by the author in late 2001 provided an example where data captured electronically in the first instance from a system outside the organization was subsequently typed and retyped at least five times within the organization – a hugely inefficient process.

20.2 PROCESS ANALYSIS AND CRITICAL EXAMINATION

Once a process has been defined, it can be analysed. Of particular concern in the quality management context is the recognition of where error or failure does or may occur in the process. This enables a focus to be maintained on those aspects of the process most in need of improvement or redevelopment. It also provides cues for key measurement points at which statistical process control techniques may be most usefully employed.

The purpose of analysing the process at the outset is to eliminate unnecessary or irrelevant activities and to identify the 'triggers' which start other processes and subroutines. The critical

VIGNETTE 20.1 **COOKING THE BOOKS**

A productivity and quality study was undertaken in a commercial bakery. This bakery, a subsidiary of a major public company, supplies cakes and other products to various supermarket chains. A map of the finishing process was created as the first step in the study; this was to act as a guide to understanding the process and as the basis for both quality and productivity measurement. The process was as shown in Figure 20.4. This map shows what will appear at first a simple and efficient process, but it is important to remember that it has been prepared at the 'total process' level. Other, more detailed maps were prepared at lower levels. For example, the operation 'Decorate' at the next level down subdivided into between five and seven sub-processes depending on the particular product being made. Each of those sub-processes again contained subroutines directly related to the product. The company had never prepared such a map before. The map was used as a basis for evaluating the scale of the 'quality problem', which had been estimated by them as a 10 per cent reject rate. Discussion revealed that this rate was arrived at on the basis of the volume difference between the number of cakes entering the 'Cut' process and the number completing the 'Pack' process. There was no measure of intra-process rejects or rework. The inspection process 'Inspect 1' was not even recognized by the management, or the supervisors undertaking it, as an inspection. Simple observation of the various process operations was enough to indicate major quality problems within the process. When numbers were recorded, the actual reject rate – that is, the proportion of cakes recycling through various stages of the process, in particular 'Decorate' – was found to be 35 per cent – a figure which did not vary substantially between differing products and thousands of individual items throughout the evaluation. Subsequent further studies confirmed the accuracy of the numbers.

This process map proved vital in three respects. First, it provided the management with a clear picture of how the production line actually operated, as opposed to how they believed it to operate – it helped them to modify their mental models. Second, it enabled the quantification of a problem which they had only vaguely suspected. Third, by examining the reject rate at different stages in the process, it enabled sharp focus to be brought on the key problem area: the process 'Decorate'.

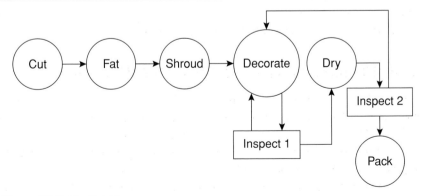

Figure 20.4 The finishing process

examination should reveal the reasons for each activity and enable the compilation of a systematic and prioritized list of potential enhancements.

The benefit gained from critical examination is influenced by the attitude of mind of the analyst. The final result will depend upon the skill with which the process is recorded. Attention must be paid to the following points:

- Actions should be recorded as factually as possible.
- Preconceived notions and ideas should be abandoned.
- All aspects of the process should be challenged and verified.
- Hasty judgements must be avoided.
- Small details must be recorded at the appropriate level of analysis; these may be more important than the major items.
- Hunches and 'bright ideas' should be set aside until the recording is complete.
- New methods should not be considered until the undesirable or quality problem-causing attributes of the existing method have been exposed.

In the context of work study, it is common to classify each of the activities into one of three groups: 'Make Ready', 'Do' and 'Put Away'. This refinement is probably inappropriate in the quality context since the primary issue of concern is not productivity (although processes with quality built in are normally more productive than those without).

Similarly, there is debate as to whether the productive or non-productive parts of the process should be examined first – the former tending to lead to more rapid productivity improvements. In the quality context, the concern is with identifying where error and failure occur, and a systematic approach should be taken – following the process from the start. This is because errors made in early parts of the process may be driving failure at later stages. It is important, therefore, to eliminate these prior causes. Measurement of performance and error at key points of the process may be desirable as a means of identifying where failure occurs and in what proportions. The information so derived can be used to help in prioritizing work.

The examination of the identified process can be carried out through a two-stage sequence of questions which adopt the pattern shown in Box 20.1.

In present-day organizations, it is useful to ask similar 'means' questions about the machines and technology used to support the process. That is: what machines are used? Are they suitable for the task? Are they reliable? Do their outputs match or exceed the task requirements? – and so on. Taken together, these questions enable the analyst to determine precisely what the existing process is, to question it and to identify its flaws. The movement towards quality is begun by proposing alternatives and highlighting failures. Properly supported by valid statistical techniques, this 'is–ought' approach is useful.

A final issue to address in this context is process labelling. What the process is called may have a significant influence on how it is treated by both management and staff. For example, while building an ISO 9001:2000 quality management system for a Hong Kong organization, a process called 'Customer Complaints' was identified. The volume of complaints was very high relative to the total number of customers, and each was responded to effectively. However, complaints were regarded as an interruption of or intrusion into the 'real work' of the business. Because the volume was so high, it was anticipated that some difficulties might

Box 20.1 *Process analysis: critical examination procedure*

Primary questions	Secondary questions
Purpose	
What is done?	What else might be done?
Why is it done?	What should be done?
Place	
Where is it done?	Where else might it be done?
Why is it done there?	Where should it be done?
Sequence	
When is it done?	When might it be done?
Why is it done then?	When should it be done?
Person	
Who does it?	Who else might do it?
Why do they do it?	Who should do it?
Means	
How is it done?	How else might it be done?
Why is it done like that?	How should it be done?

arise with the certification process. It was therefore decided to examine this area in greater detail. The examination revealed that what the organization called 'Customer Complaints' were actually requests for maintenance and repair work on the various premises managed by the organization and were, in reality, 'Requests for Service' – that is, they were, for the most part, reports of minor building defects in need of attention: blown light bulbs, dripping taps, failed door locks. All these were matters which the organization could not know about without advice from the customer.

It was therefore decided to retitle the 'Customer Complaints' process the 'Requests for Service' process. A complaint was deemed to arise where the same fault was reported more than once – that is, the organization had failed to respond. The impact was to change the attitude of the tenants – because they perceived that the organization had created a better communication facility for them – and to change the attitude of the staff to dealing with 'Requests for Service'. The number of genuine complaints fell substantially.

20.3 METHOD DEVELOPMENT

Method development covers a range of techniques which can be used to identify alternatives to the established process and ways of overcoming quality problems. It relies on creative thinking about the situation, which in turn requires an open and inquiring mind. A lateral approach is useful, which attempts to find fresh angles from which to view the process. Determination to succeed is important, as is an acceptance that all ideas can, at the outset, be treated as equally valid, even though they may appear remote from the problem. Creative thinking is supported by a variety of techniques. Readers might wish to refer to the works of Edward de Bono for further inspiration.

217

Brainstorming is a method of enabling groups of individuals, normally between 4 and 12 in number (as for quality circles!), to generate ideas for problem solving. The process is relatively simple. The group leader outlines the problem and answers any questions submitted by the members. Thereafter, the group generate ideas, which are recorded without comment or judgement on flip charts, whiteboards, or sometimes on Post-it stickers. After about half an hour (or when the ideas dry up), the ideas are evaluated by the group. Those offering most apparent value are subject to further evaluation and, where appropriate, experimentation and development. Note that it is vital for the leader of a brainstorming session to be experienced in problem solving and able to create and maintain enthusiasm among the group members.

Analogies are also useful. An analogy is an agreement or commonality in certain characteristics between things which are otherwise different. To use analogies is to apply alternative knowledge and experience to a problem. The problem solvers consider items which are different but possess attributes similar to those of the problem under consideration. This approach encourages cross-fertilization of ideas from people of different professional backgrounds and disciplines. There are three types of analogy which are particularly useful:

- Functional: What else does what this process does?
- Simple: What does this process look like?
- Natural: How is this done in nature?

This last is a particularly helpful approach, since natural systems tend towards self-organization (see Chapter 14), effectiveness (if not always apparent short-term efficiency) and evolution. A particular example of the use of a natural analogy is the invention of artificial fibre. The realization by Robert Hooke in 1664 that the process of silk spinning by silkworms could be emulated by humans enabled Louis Schwabe, in 1842, to create a machine for making artificial filaments by forcing liquid through fine holes. This technique is used today in the manufacture of rayon.

Morphological analysis is a systematic method of creating possible lists of logical combinations of variables already known to solve a problem. It enables the range of possible solution spaces to be matched and a 'most reliable' method to be chosen. One example of this could be solving a delivery problem to a customer's premises as follows:

- Method: post, courier, in-house delivery system
- Speed: JIT, same day, overnight, non-critical
- Packaging: crushproof, airtight, palletized, unimportant

The possible number of logical combinations of variables is $3 \times 4 \times 4$, so there are forty-eight possible solutions to the delivery problem, given that each combination of variables is feasible. In reality, some, such as post and same day, are 'illegal' solutions – that is to say, they will not work. Once the range of possible solutions has been defined, quality and other criteria can be applied to identify those which meet expectations and requirements.

Listing and combining attributes is another way of highlighting potential for improvement in a process. This technique requires the creation of a list of the attributes that the process must possess in order to fulfil the requirements – such as zero defects. Changes to the process are then proposed which enable these attributes to be attained.

Heuristic analysis fits within the context of kaizen quality thinking. The heuristic method is to generate changes to the process, apply them and review the results. The results are then used as the platform for testing further changes, and so on in an iterative cycle. This is similar to the PDCA cycle proposed by Deming, and to the ideas of organizational learning outlined in Chapter 19. Heuristic improvement should never stop, but to be effective must be used in a systematic rather than random manner. The principal disadvantage of the heuristic method lies in its incremental nature. A heuristic approach may never generate the sort of radical, discontinuous (or step) change in a process that may be provoked by the use of other methods.

Convergent and divergent thinking are also useful approaches. Convergent thinking occurs when the analyst(s) attempt(s) to separate the essential items of the process from the incidental. In this way, the aim is to focus on the most important issues, reminiscent of Juran's 'vital few and useful many'. Divergent thinking is the opposite, and occurs when the analyst(s) expand(s) the problem to take account of other information that is not central to the defined process.

The initial task of identifying the 'Total Process' suggested at the outset of this chapter may be seen as a representation of convergent thinking, while the second- and third-level analyses (Process Operation and Process Detail) represent divergent thinking. A further level of divergent thinking may be seen in expanding the 'Total Process' chart (Figure 20.1) to encompass other interdependent processes.

SUMMARY

This chapter has introduced process mapping and critical examination as a fundamental technique for the pursuit of quality. This provides a platform for the other techniques which will be explored in subsequent chapters. Process analysis techniques can be further studied through books concerned with organization methods, operational research and business process re-engineering.

QUESTION

Use the techniques outlined in this chapter to map, critically examine and redesign a process in your university (for example, the book management process in the library).

Chapter 21

Quality management systems

. . . to mistake the epiphenomena of the system . . . for the system itself.
(Stafford Beer, *Diagnosing the System for Organisations*, 1985)

KEY LEARNING POINTS

Key definitions of quality management systems: the ISO 9000 series is the internationally accepted standard for quality management systems; the ISO 14000 series is the internationally accepted standard for environmental management systems.

Quality management system: a formal record of an organization's method of managing the quality of its products or services. It needs a systematic, ordered approach, leading to third-party certification of the system, not the quality.

Purpose: provides a basis for measuring and monitoring quality performance.

The Business Excellence Model: framework of performance criteria for the achievement of the European Quality Award. Suitable for organizations already certified to ISO 9000. It considers nine criteria:

- leadership;
- policy and strategy;
- people;
- resources;
- processes;
- customer results;
- people results;
- societal results;
- business results.

INTRODUCTION

This chapter is concerned with effective quality management systems (QMSs), of which the ISO 9000:2000 family represents the currently established global standard – that is, the one most commonly adopted. Without adherence to a QMS, it is impossible for the organization to know and record how well (or badly) it is performing. However, there are many quality management systems in existence which do not conform to the ISO 9000 standard.

This chapter will not provide a full guide to the development and implementation of a QMS. That task is beyond the intended scope of the book and better left to a dedicated work, of which there are several (for example, Hoyle, 1994; Gilbert, 1994; Waller *et al.*, 1993; McGoldrick, 1994), although these are focused on the 1994 rather than the 2000 version of the standard. There are several authoritative books due to be published on the revised standard, including one from Hoyle. What this chapter does seek to achieve is a broad understanding of the nature and purpose of a QMS, its utility and limitations. A specific interpretation of the ISO 9000:2000 series is provided.

21.1 WHAT IS ISO 9000?

ISO 9000 is one of a series of quality management systems standards developed over a long period of time, beginning with quality standards in the defence industry. For example, NATO began developing quality standards in the late 1940s to enable a degree of harmonization between co-operating military forces. These standards were consolidated and revised in DefStans (Defence Standards) 05–08, 05–21, 05–24 and 05–28 between 1951 and 1973. Dominant systems in the civil world include BS 5750 (the British standard) and EN 29000 (the European standard), as well as unique local systems which have been developed in several countries and industries, such as QS 9000 in the motor industry. However, ISO 9000 (Box 21.1) is generally accepted as the standard for quality systems practice in most countries.

A QMS constitutes a formal record of an organization's method of managing the quality of its products or services. It enables the organization to demonstrate to itself, its customers and, importantly, to an independent certification body that it has established an effective system for managing the quality of its products or services. Meeting the accreditation standards permits the organization to claim quality certification for its products and services and to advertise the fact. This is seen as an important factor by many organizations, and there is a trend in certain areas, notably the public sector and parts of the construction industry, particularly in South-East Asia, to deal only with quality-accredited organizations. A QMS will also assist the organization in attempting to formalize its operations and attain consistency of outputs.

Box 21.1 *The ISO 9000:2000 series of standards*

BS EN ISO 9000:2000	Fundamentals and vocabulary
BS EN ISO 9001:2000	Quality management system requirements
BS EN ISO 9004:2000	Guidelines for performance improvements

The ISO 9000 standards are comprehensive in their coverage, ranging from product or service development to after-sales service. However, they have tended to have a clear bias towards the manufacturing sector. That is, after all, where the process started and where greatest use continues to be made of the standards. The ISO 9000:2000 family of standards, launched at the end of 2000, attempts to harmonize all the standards and remove the manufacturing bias.

21.2 ISO 9000:2000 INTERPRETED

The revision to the ISO 9000 family of standards was adopted in late 2000. This was a much more substantial revision than that of 1994. Overall:

■ The 1994 family of standards (ISO 9001, 9002, 9003, 9004) was consolidated into a single standard ISO 9001:2000 with a new ISO 9004:2000 providing a set of guidelines for continuous improvement.
■ The standard has a substantially increased customer focus.
■ An attempt has been made to reduce the manufacturing bias.
■ The scope has been widened to include more management elements.

All the core requirements of the 1994 version of ISO 9001 continue to be present, but the new standard restructures these (and other elements) under four headings:

■ management responsibility;
■ resource management;
■ process management;
■ measurement and analysis, improvement.

The aim of these changes is to encourage organizations to think about their management processes and react to the changing demands placed upon them. Management responsibility is extended to include a specific responsibility for ensuring continuous improvement and benchmarking (relying on ISO 9004:2000 for guidance) and for management review. There is a much greater emphasis on supplier relationships, customer satisfaction, market and competitor analysis, and on the development of improvement opportunities.

Resource management is extended to focus very clearly on human resource management – especially the match of the skills of the individual to the requirements of the task. A major shift in emphasis here enables the organization to rely extensively on the skills-based approach and consequently to minimize the extent of procedural documentation required to support the system. Issues such as health and safety, the environment and financial management as part of the overall well-being of the enterprise are also given prominence.

Particular issues in this respect will be to consider the means by which the quality policy message is conveyed to employees and subcontractors, and to ensure that all employees understand their contribution to quality. The standard expects the organization to be able to demonstrate that every employee will be provided with the opportunity to realize her or his full potential and contribution to the organization. This perhaps reflects aspects of the IIP

(Investors in People) expectations and the Business Excellence Model, which will be briefly reviewed later in the chapter.

The shift towards process management reflects the shift in managerial thinking in recent years. Within this area, there is a requirement for appropriate risk analysis, recognition of the interactions between departments and functions (the internal customer chain), capability to respond to changing customer expectations, formal and documented review of capabilities, and a focus on the delivery and post-delivery activity. It is no longer adequate for an organization to be able to demonstrate that 'we made it right'; it also has to be able to demonstrate that it was delivered 'right' and serviced 'right'. Rather than a focus on the physical aspects of product quality, the shift is towards the customer's total experience of dealing with the organization – perhaps reflecting the thinking of Taguchi and Feigenbaum.

Measurement and analysis simply requires that an appropriate performance measurement system is in place. This captures the adherence (or otherwise) of the product or service to the standards specified. This in turn enables audit of the product or service delivered and monitoring of customer satisfaction and of competitor and market performance, and demonstrates continuous improvement. For certification under ISO 9000:2000, it's what you do with it that counts!

21.3 ISO 9000:2000 – THE LIMITATIONS

It is undeniable that the revised standard is a major step forward from the 1994 revision. It explicitly recognizes the process-oriented nature of many organizations, attempts to address the manufacturing bias and pays particular attention to the 'people' issues within organizations – recognizing perhaps that this is an area in which many quality initiatives fail.

It does, however, have a number of limitations:

- Notwithstanding the process orientation, it continues to reflect a 'static' interpretation of organization. It deals with 'what', not 'how'.
- It does not explicitly address the issue of business or organizational benefit.
- The process orientation is to be welcomed, but not enough emphasis has been placed on developing the 'special processes'. The focus on people (especially in the service sector) as the heart of quality is still significantly underplayed.
- It retains the potential limitations of bureaucracy, disuse and disrepute associated with the previous standard.

As organizations are working to make the transition from the old to the new standard, it is becoming more and more apparent that there are limitations of real understanding of organization and skills management (on both their part and that of their external auditors). This will inhibit the achievement of the full potential benefits of the changed standard. The potential advantages offered can be eradicated if the designers of quality management systems continue to work with the same procedure-focused, mechanistic and bureaucratic mindset that has so often been employed in the past.

A compliant QMS based on the traditional 'paper record' and 'checklist' approach will clearly, and very rapidly, become a bureaucratic nightmare, with ever more people required simply to maintain the system – let alone collate, analyse, interpret and synthesize data in such a way that they can be used as a springboard for performance improvement. In the service sector in particular, the variability in requirements of individual customers would be impossible to track properly. Chapter 28 will address this particular issue.

21.4 HOW IS A QUALITY MANAGEMENT SYSTEM CONSTRUCTED?

Construction of a QMS relies upon the use of the ISO 9000 series to provide guidelines and instructions, adherence to which ensures that the system will meet certification standards. As with every aspect of quality, the development of an effective QMS relies on a systematic approach.

Kanji and Asher (1996) propose a thirteen-step programme (Box 21.2) of actions. Step 1, commitment to the quality management approach, has already been met on several occasions. This commitment is fundamental to any aspect of achieving quality. Unfortunately, managers find it far easier to commit themselves to a QMS than they do to commit themselves to quality. If you have the latter commitment, then that implies commitment to the QMS. If you only have commitment to the QMS, then you have a system which will not only fail to assist the drive for quality, but will enable the manager to decide precisely whom to blame (other than her- or himself) for that failure. It will become an instrument of the penal system rather than a guide for the successful pursuit of quality. An effective QMS can be created only within the context of a fully supported quality programme.

Step 2, defining the scope of activities to be included, seems to be a little short-sighted. If an organization is to be effective in its quality drive, then every part of it must fall within the

---

Box 21.2 *Kanji and Asher's thirteen steps to a quality management system (QMS)*

Step 1	Obtain management understanding of, and commitment to, the quality management approach
Step 2	Define the scope of the activities to be included in the QMS
Step 3	Define the organizational structure and responsibilities of those within the scope of the QMS
Step 4	Audit the existing systems and procedures against the requirements of the standard
Step 5	Develop a plan to write the necessary procedures
Step 6	Train sufficient personnel to write their own procedures
Step 7	Draft and edit the procedures and gain agreement to them
Step 8	Compile a draft quality manual
Step 9	Implement the system on a trial basis
Step 10	Train internal auditors to carry out audits of the system and its operation
Step 11	Revise the operation of the system in the light of the results of audits and other information
Step 12	Apply for registration (sometimes called third-party approval) from an accredited body
Step 13	Maintain the system by internal audit, using it as an opportunity to improve

QMS. There will certainly be a need to assess priorities for inclusion in the QMS – production before personnel and the canteen, perhaps – but the ultimate aim should be an all-inclusive system. This system may even extend to link with those of suppliers where appropriate.

Step 3, defining the organizational structure and responsibilities, while necessary, carries the danger of inhibiting necessary organizational change. While it is vital that the appropriate organizational structure is in use and that responsibilities are clearly defined, it is essential to realize that the correct organizational form is, or may be, a rapidly changing element. The dynamism and fluidity of the organizational environment demand this. It must be the case, therefore, that the organizational structure and responsibilities define the organization of the QMS – not the other way around.

The fourth, fifth, sixth and seventh steps, audit of current systems and procedures and development of new procedures, are fundamental to the achievement of the QMS. It may be preferable, however, to place the sixth element in fourth place and extend the training element such that operational staff are trained to audit and review their own processes as well as develop the appropriate documentation. No one knows a job better than the people who do it. Step 8, compiling the draft quality procedures manual, is a product of the four steps which precede it. A warning is necessary here. The revised standard demands only a very limited set of compulsory procedures. To minimize the bureaucracy associated with the QMS, organizations should reflect on how many additional procedures they really need to ensure consistency of operation. Wherever possible, the reliance should be on active skills management rather than on procedural adherence.

Step 9 reflects Taguchi's 'up and limping prototype'. The proposed system must be tested in action and validated or modified against empirical data. This step links naturally to step 10. Training of internal auditors is vital, and again should draw on the experience and knowledge of those who actually carry out the operations of the organization. Use of the staff in this way, and proper training of them in the correct meaning of effective audit outputs – helpfulness, guidance and assistance to improvement – rather than oppressive policing, is likely to lead to highly productive outcomes. These generate the modifications demanded by the eleventh step as an output of the audit process.

The twelfth step, accreditation of the QMS, should happen almost naturally. Within the context of the overall quality programme, accreditation should be a by-product. The application and registration should be easy to come by, if the organization genuinely has quality and has taken the development of the QMS seriously.

The final step reflects the demand for continuous improvement, not only in the core activities of the organization but in everything that it does.

It must always be remembered that the purpose of the QMS is not accreditation to a particular standard, but improvement in the quality of output of the products and services of the organization. It has been observed that many more organizations have accredited QMS systems than generate quality products and services. It is perfectly possible to develop and implement a QMS with absolutely no improvement to quality whatsoever.

Conventionally, a QMS will require three core sets of information. The first will be a statement of the quality policy of the organization. This may form the first part of the quality manual. The second set is the procedures which will be adopted to fulfil that policy. The third set is the task instructions which set out how each activity should be performed. With the increasing trend towards process-oriented structures, it is useful to give serious consideration to documenting the procedures along process lines, rather than on the traditional functional basis. Similarly, task instructions can be minimized where skills are used as the basis of quality.

To support these three sets of information, the organization will also require a record system to provide the evidence that the quality procedures are being adhered to. This record system should be as simple and straightforward as possible but should also be proofed against corruption and fraudulent completion as far as possible. If the data are not accurate, then they are less than helpful. Accuracy will decline with complexity, volume of data and difficulty of collection. Wherever possible, data should be recorded automatically.

21.5   ISO 14000

The ISO 14000 series of standards for environmental management systems was launched in 1996 in response to rising awareness of damage to the environment and the need for a common set of standards which could be adopted by any organization. The standards provide guidelines on the elements that an environmental management system should have and on the supporting technologies. The standards prescribe what should be done by an organization, but not how it should be done.

VIGNETTE 21.1   **BEAT THE SYSTEM**

It is common today for service-based organizations, particularly those which operate buildings open to the public, to install quality management systems for the public-facing areas, particularly rest rooms. They aim to ensure that these facilities are checked, serviced and cleaned on a regular basis, usually hourly. To make it easier to monitor that this servicing has been carried out, timed ticksheets are placed in each rest room for the cleaner to initial on each visit.

Imagine a cleaner, or even a small team of cleaners, in a twenty-storey building, expected to check and service the restrooms on each floor every hour. Not only is this level of service probably unnecessary, but in many cases, with low levels of staffing, it is impossible. Nonetheless, the ticksheets are initialled every hour. The QMS is working – or is it?

As one who regularly works in such buildings, I take an interest in these things. It is far from uncommon (particularly at a weekend when the management are not about) to find that by 9 p.m. on a Friday, the tick sheet for the weekend has been completed through to 7 a.m. on Monday. By Saturday afternoon the soap has run out; by Sunday morning (at the latest) there are no paper towels. The rest can be left to the imagination. The QMS is not working – although the records show that it is.

Such deceptions are commonplace throughout the world – this is by no means an exclusively British, European, Asian or American problem. They occur everywhere in nice buildings and bad ones, in 'quality' organizations and in 'non-quality' organizations. The organization may have an accredited QMS, but what it doesn't have is quality – somebody, somewhere, just does not care.

ISO 14001 and ISO 14004 provide the specifications and general guidelines for the series and allow it to fulfil business needs, for any organization, from general guidance to self-assessment and registration. Achievement of the standards is claimed to lead to genuine business benefit, with companies claiming process performance improvement, cost reductions, reduced pollution, legislative compliance and enhanced public image.

ISO 14000 has much in common with ISO 9000 and can capitalize on systems and procedures already established. It extends from the ISO 9000 criteria of meeting customer requirements to capture regulatory and mandatory environmental requirements. While ISO 14000 is established on a voluntary basis, there are indications that some countries may enshrine the standards in environmental legislation.

21.6 THE BUSINESS EXCELLENCE MODEL

While this chapter has focused on the ISO standards, there are other approaches to the management of quality which, though perhaps not carrying the same global authority, have delivered significant value to their adopters.

Revised in the year 2000, the Business Excellence Model (BEM) is sponsored by the European Foundation for Quality Management. This model is developed from the belief that contented customers, satisfied staff and positive societal impact can be achieved only through effective leadership. Leadership in turn steers both organizational policy and strategy in relation to organizational processes and human resource actions. Taken together, this integrated approach is considered to drive the organization towards excellence in business.

While the model refers to business, the BEM has been widely adopted in the public sector in the United Kingdom under the 'Service First' approach, itself the successor to the Management Charter initiative. This programme operates under the auspices of the Cabinet Office's, Performance and Innovation Unit.

Using the BEM the organization assesses itself against nine performance criteria (Box 21.3) divided into two sets: 'enablers' – those aspects of the organization which provide the foundation for excellent performance – and 'results' – the impact of those enablers on staff, customers, society at large, and ultimately on business performance.

Box 21.3 *The Business Excellence Model: criteria*

Leadership

Policy and strategy

People

Partnerships and resources

Processes

Customer results

People results

Society results

Key performance results

'Leadership' considers how effectively those who manage the organization act in relation to the drive for excellence. 'Policy and strategy' examines how those aspects of the organization are oriented towards the achievement of total quality and how it goes about delivering them. 'People management', in concert with the revised requirements of ISO 9001:2000, explicitly recognizes that quality is ultimately delivered by people, to people, through people. It is a major factor in achievement of the award. 'People management' considers how the organization works to realize the capabilities of its employees in driving improvement.

'Resources' (or *resource management* in the ISO language) is focused on the effective use and maintenance of the organization's physical assets (buildings, finance, information, technology, suppliers and materials). 'Processes' is concerned with the design, development, production, delivery and service processes which add value to the organization. The BEM examines how these processes are identified and managed to achieve improvement.

Results criteria focus on people, customer and societal satisfaction with the organization and on the business results. This category attempts to compare the organization's actual achievements with its internal standards, with its competitors' performance and with those organizations considered to be the best in the organization's market. Results are generally presented quantitatively using time-series graphical representation – charts!

'People satisfaction' attempts to determine the degree of satisfaction of staff in terms of how the employees feel about the organization in relation to issues such as morale, terms and conditions of employment, management behaviours, development, the work environment and participation in the quality programme. Objective measures include issues such as staff turnover, development activity, absenteeism and numbers involved in suggestion schemes and improvement programmes.

'Customer satisfaction' considers the response of customers to the goods and services provided. Again the results are split between customer perceptions of performance on delivery, reliability, service levels, complaints, warranty and accessibility of staff, and objective measures based on error and rejection rates, actual delivery performance, numbers of complaints and warranty claims, and, significantly, numbers of repeat customers.

'The impact on society' examines many of the issues which would be considered under ISO 14000, such as environmental impact, impact on quality of life, preservation of resources, and internal measures of resource utilization efficiency. Again the model looks at both external perceptions – how well the organization represents itself to its community – and objective internal measures of employment, recycling, waste reduction, pollution and complaints.

Finally, the BEM addresses the 'business results' – the success or otherwise of the organization in meeting the expectations of its financial stakeholders and in meeting business objectives. This section consider objective aspects of business performance focused on the range of measures traditionally associated with business success. These include statutory accounting information (profit and loss, margins, sales, net worth), cash flows, share prices and ratings, dividends, productivity and returns on investments. Other aspects may include market share, performance of suppliers, error rates, process performance and cycle times.

While the basic process of using the BEM is primarily an internal matter, companies can pursue the European Quality Award (EQA). The process leading to the award engages external assessors in evaluating the performance of the company against the award criteria – and in competition with other organizations also pursuing the programme.

228

Overall, the BEM is suitable for companies which have already made significant progress towards excellence in all aspects of their operations. Frankly, it is unattainable to those organizations which have not already been pursuing meaningful quality initiatives for some time. It can be thought that the EQA is a target to work towards for organizations which have already achieved the ISO standard.

The key limitation of the BEM is that it relies rather heavily on perceptions rather than on ongoing objective measures. It has been found by some organizations to be cumbersome and bureaucratic in use (especially in the public sector), and its reliance on self-assessment leaves creative managers free to evaluate their performance (at least initially) at a lower level than is actually being achieved, enabling them to demonstrate improvement at the next evaluation – without changing anything. While this criticism may seem unfair (and is necessarily difficult to prove), it is undoubtedly the case that the strategy is frequently employed.

The second major criticism relates to the lack of real dynamism in the model itself. Considered as a foundation for a management system, the BEM framework has the potential to represent a network of interrelated enablers and results, and could be used, with appropriately objective performance measurement, to drive a dynamic business model in which the impacts of change on other areas could be usefully assessed before being made, rather than reflected upon after the event.

21.7 CRITICAL REVIEW

The ISO 9000 series is well accepted as the standard for quality management systems around the globe. It is comprehensive and has enjoyed substantial development over many years. However, as has been recognized in the inception of the ISO 14000 series, the scope of ISO 9000 is restricted to quality standards which are essential but not sufficient for contemporary organizations.

An effective QMS is a vital part of any quality programme; without it there is no basis for properly measuring and monitoring quality performance. It must not, though, be allowed to become an end in itself (as is so often the case). The QMS will inform the organization how well or badly it is doing against the standards which it has set itself, nothing more. Unless action is continually taken to improve standards and performance, the measurement activity is sterile. This is the purpose of the ISO 9004:2000 *Guidelines for Continuous Improvement*. Continued certification to the ISO 9001:2000 standard now requires that the organization demonstrate improvement over time.

Documentation and procedures for the QMS should ideally be developed by the staff who actually carry out the tasks. Monitoring systems should be accurate and robust, and generate accurate meaningful data.

Overall, a well-designed QMS, within the context of a coherent quality programme, should generate significant benefits for the organization. Failure to heed the cautions outlined will render the activity useless.

The BEM provides a higher-level framework to which already ISO-certified organizations should aspire to drive their continuous improvement. The lack of objectivity in measurement and failure to explicitly recognize the dynamic interrelationships between the enabler and results criteria inhibit full value being achieved from the model.

229

SUMMARY

This chapter has presented a brief overview of the core elements of a quality management system and the ISO 9000 series. The ISO 14000 series and the Business Excellence Model were also introduced. A QMS has been shown to be a relatively simple aspect of the overall quality initiative, which may explain its popularity. Limitations of a QMS have been highlighted. Readers should refer to specific texts on ISO 9000 and ISO 14000 to further develop their knowledge. A good text for examining the range of quality standards and award schemes is *Assessing Business Excellence*, (Porter and Tanner, 1998).

QUESTION

Identify the strengths and weaknesses of an ISO 9000 standard quality management system. Consider how this system may be used to improve quality performance.

Understanding statistical methods

'What is truth?' asked Pontius Pilate. 'It ain't statistics,' said a voice in the crowd.
(Darrell Huff, *How to Lie with Statistics*, 1973)

KEY LEARNING POINTS

Statistics and statistical methods must be used intelligently and thoughtfully.

Statistics tell you what has already happened – they tell you nothing of why;

Providers of statistics are always trying to demonstrate a point – How have the statistics been presented to reinforce that point and hide others?

Statistics can be deliberately or accidentally misleading. What are the assumptions that underpin the figures presented to you?

INTRODUCTION

This chapter considers the utility and application of statistical tools for quality management. It does not attempt to explore each of the individual techniques – that has been left to the specialist texts by authors such as Logothetis (1992) – but rather it seeks to explore their limitations and some of the games that are often played with them.

22.1 STATISTICAL METHODS

Statistical methods offer techniques for measuring and evaluating performance and performance improvement on a sampling basis. However, they also offer the greatest scope for fooling both others and yourself. They must be used properly, intelligently and with full understanding of their accuracy and implications.

Statistics are frequently used to support decision making – and support is their proper role. They should not become the only factor used in making a decision. There are a number of reasons for this. First, they may not be accurate. Even where machine counted, measures of volume, throughput, and so on can often generate misleading numbers. When people are involved in the counting process, a degree of error is almost inevitable. Try counting sheep in a field or fish in a pond; the difficulty of counting is similar to that of counting finished products on a production line or service events in a retail outlet. Similarly, however accurate the actual numbers, if some critical process event has been overlooked (for example, the 'within process' recycling in the bakery example in Chapter 20), the measurements, and the statistics derived from them, will be wrong.

Second, statistics represent probabilities, not actualities – remember the number of 'averages' used in the calculation of standard deviation – particularly where batch or sample sizes

VIGNETTE 22.1 **LOOKING BEHIND THE NUMBERS**

A major retail organization developed a staff productivity system for each of its various outlets. The system used output activity volumes to derive recommended staffing levels for each outlet. Procedures and processes within each outlet were standardized, but the system was individually tuned to allow for physical peculiarities of different buildings, for example working on multiple floors, and for the size of the particular outlet, which sometimes required variations to procedures.

Despite the accommodation of these individual differences and the adjustment of staff numbers to reflect workload variations, it was found that certain outlets were under constant pressure, with high levels of overtime. The managers of these outlets were placed under pressure by the senior management to bring their costs under control and match the productivity of the 'better' outlets. After some time, it was found that there was no significant improvement in most of these cases; the complaints about pressure and the high levels of overtime continued.

Eventually, short investigations were authorized in the problem outlets, focused on improving their productivity. Three drivers of the problems were identified:

- mismanagement of resources;
- inexperienced, untrained staff;
- high levels of business development activity.

The first driver was expected; after all, one purpose of the system was to assist managers in maximizing the utilization of resources. The second driver represented a major problem. The system assumed an 'average' level of competence and experience among the staff, whereas, in that fast-growing organization, the real 'average' was a lot lower, owing to high levels of staff turnover and continuing recruitment. Finally, the system recorded only 'successful' business development activity – that is, activity which led to a measured output. Any unsuccessful business development activity was excluded. The effect of this was that those outlets which tried hardest to develop new business were 'punished' by the inadequacies of the system.

vary. The answers given for these calculations are 'more or less' accurate – never precise. Third, since the calculations are to some degree 'wrong', pure reliance on them is bound to generate some degree of mismatch to reality, often leading to complaints and witch-hunts.

Fourth, understanding how the numbers are driven is much more important than the numbers themselves. Pure reliance on the statistics leads to a focus on improving the statistics rather than improving the process which supports them. It is frequently observed that in a failing or struggling company the focus is put on reducing costs. Company-wide cuts are imposed – for example, 10 per cent of head count or 10 per cent of wage costs. While in the short term this might address the specific problem of immediate cash flow, it usually does nothing for the medium- to long-term future of the company. Blanket reductions in staff not supported by changes in the volume of work simply lead to increased stress on those remaining (leading to higher levels of sickness), removal of key performers or simply to increased overtime for those remaining (which can actually increase costs). Problems with the organization may anyway be related to pricing, competition, market behaviour, delivery problems, or a whole host of other factors which the managers have failed to identify.

As it is with money, so it is with quality. A short-term hard-nosed push for quality is a recurring feature of organizations. However, unless changes are developed for the processes of production, the common causes of failure are simply overridden. As soon as the pressure is released, the system will revert to its previous behaviour. A further phenomenon is called 'squeezing the snake', or 'corset' management. In this case a quality problem is identified at a particular stage of a process through a statistical quality control mechanism. Managerial pressure is applied to that point and performance improvement is generated, the quality problem reduces. What is not realized until much later is that the problem has not disappeared; it has simply been moved, either back up the process by constricting the inputs to the problem area, or further down the process by widening the exit point (usually by varying the criteria for quality).

22.2 COMMON STATISTICAL ERRORS

A headline in the UK press proclaimed that 'Women are safer drivers than men!' This headline generated much debate in the press, on radio and television, with many men incensed by the claim (their manliness insulted) and many women and men responding to the headline by citing examples of poor driving by the other sex.

The whole debate was highly entertaining but built on an entirely false premise. The headline created for the original newspaper article had one intention: to sell more newspapers. In the newspaper tradition of 'never let the truth get in the way of a good story', the journalist involved had distilled a useful headline, with strong emotional impact, from a probably rather dull report. The research had been undertaken by the insurance industry in relation to claims experience among British insurers. What the research actually established was quite simple: women, on average, make less frequent insurance claims than men, and, again on average, the size of their claims is smaller.

The research findings themselves can be accepted – they are probably matters of fact. They do not, though, establish the superiority of either female or male drivers. So what is established?

233

- The average claim by women drivers, on policies held in their own names, is smaller than the average claim by male drivers.
- The average frequency of claims in respect of those policies is lower for women drivers than for men.

These statements have everything to do with the claims experience of the companies participating in the research relative to female and male policyholders. They say nothing of substance concerning the safety or otherwise of either sex behind the wheel of a car and, because claims are made by the policyholder, they cannot differentiate between a wide number of aspects of the claims experience. For example:

- the number of claims made by female policyholders whose cars were, at the time of the damage, being driven by men;
- the number of claims made by male policyholders whose cars, at the time of the damage, were being driven by women;
- the number of vehicle repairs carried out for which no claim is made;
- the number of accidents for which no repair is carried out;
- the difference in claims between high-mileage drivers and low-mileage drivers – that is, the average miles driven per claim made, a measure perhaps of relative safety;
- the relative value and cost of repair of vehicles driven by either sex;
- the context in which accidents take place – that is, urban, rural or motorway;
- the speed of vehicles when accidents occur;
- the meaning, in context, of *average*.

One other key factor underpins this headline: what did the journalist mean by 'better'? It can be seen that the headline has been used for the purposes of the journalist while the research on which it was based was almost certainly carried out for an entirely different purpose. The headline, though probably not the research itself, was meaningless in statistical terms.

It is vital when developing and applying statistical techniques that the claims made as a result of quantitative analysis are not subverted to other ends. Some common errors arise as follows:

- *Faulty data-collection.* A common error is to rely on statistics for which the raw data have been collected in an unreliable manner. A good example of this is the measurement of footfall on the pathway outside a shop or fast food outlet. Footfall (the number of people passing by) is generally regarded as a good guide to the likely number of customers for an outlet in the location. However, even with the best of intentions and concerted effort, the count of passers-by will have some degree of inaccuracy, simply because the method of measurement is unreliable. Often, such numbers are compiled from the 'best estimates of those who know' – in other words, an entirely subjective measurement. When these subjective measurements are summed, aggregated, averaged and otherwise manipulated, they give results with a degree of accuracy which is entirely spurious. If the base data are no better than a subjective estimate, then neither is the end result – however well it has been manipulated!
- *Sampling error.* On every occasion where a sample (as opposed to an entire population) is used, the opportunity exists for either accidental or deliberate bias to be introduced to

the survey. The sample must be sufficiently large and properly selected for any meaningful data to be derived from it.

■ *Missing numbers.* Tying in with sampling error is failure to provide (either deliberately or accidentally) the key figures which validate (or otherwise) the statistic. If the population is 1 million and the sample size is 10, then a statistic which claims that '100 per cent of respondents agreed with our findings' is meaningless unless the sample size and confidence factor are also quoted. In this case, the confidence in the accuracy of the answer would be low!

■ *Taking the wrong average.* There are three different types of average: the mean, the median and the mode. These are in turn the arithmetic average (total divided by number), the middle one and the most frequently occurring. It is important to know which average is being used in each context and what it really tells you. That is, for what purpose is the statistic being quoted.

■ *Spurious correlations.* It is often found that there is some apparent correlation between the incidence of two events or happenings and that somebody, somewhere states that because they appear to correlate, then one must be the cause of the other. This causal chain view of the world has already been challenged in Part three of this book. When a correlation is proposed, it is vital to understand why the proposer suggests it and to examine the evidence for and against the proposal – particularly to consider what other factors might explain the coincidence of the events. For example, creative people such as musicians, artists or writers are also often seen as heavy drinkers or users of narcotic drugs. There is a positive correlation between artistry and substance abuse. Does one cause the other? Could I be a great artist if I were to drink more? Could I drink more if I were a great artist? A third factor must be allowed to intrude. That third factor is personality. Perhaps an individual who challenges convention in one area of his or her life will also challenge convention in others; the causal link is not artistry and substance abuse but arises through personality. It is necessary to challenge the assumptions which underpin the causal link view of events.

■ *Misleading presentation.* Many statistics are reported graphically. Graphical portrayals of a situation are often easier for people to understand than the raw numbers derived from surveys and samples. However, they also make it easier either deliberately or inadvertently to misrepresent the real situation. For example, 'an increase in the rate of decline' can be represented as an upward path – if it is the rate of decline which is being reported! The words tell the truth: things are getting worse; but the picture, with its upward-sloping line, suggests the opposite. Similarly, a slow rate of growth in something can be presented as fast by the simple device of shortening the horizontal axis relative to the vertical axis on a graph.

It is important always to know:

■ Where did the statistics come from?
■ How big was the sample size?
■ How representative of the total population was the sample?
■ What average(s) have been used – and for what purpose?

- What point was the presenter of the statistics trying to prove?
- What counter-evidence was found – and perhaps not presented
- What assumptions underpin the points being made?

SUMMARY

Good, accurate statistics are vital for performance measurement, but they cannot replace competent, informed management. Good – that is, accurate, well founded and reliable – statistics can tell the manager much about what is happening within the processes of an organization. That is the limit of their usefulness. The statistics say nothing about *why* the reported events occur – which is much more important. Statistics are simply a statement of the characteristics and events the managers have chosen to record. Demanding an improvement in the statistics – as managers often do – will ensure they get just that! The processes, products or services of the organization will not change at all. Managers need to look behind the reported numbers and consider the deeper aspects of the organization. Aspects to consider might include the quality and amount of supervision, the reliability and accuracy of equipment, the feelings and attitudes of the staff, the expectations of the customers (many complaints are, after all, the result of a mismatch between the customers' expectations – created through marketing – and the reality of the product or service – as produced by the organization).

Readers are reminded to develop their understanding further through the use of a good text on statistics.

QUESTION

Is statistical process control a valid means of understanding process performance?

Chapter 23

Benchmarking

. . . a disinterested endeavour to learn and propagate the best that is known and
thought . . .
(Matthew Arnold on criticism)

KEY LEARNING POINTS

Key definition of benchmarking: the practice of formal comparison of processes and systems
with those of other organizations as the basis for improvement.

Key technique: identify key characteristics; identify partners; design data collection
methodology; select tools; implement changes.

Critique: demands humility, willingness to learn; risk; only match, not exceed competitor
performance, hence danger of levelling, not competing.

INTRODUCTION

That an organization is meeting the perceived requirements of its existing customers is insufficient to ensure long-term success in today's highly competitive environment. If some other
organization is providing, in the perception of the customers, better products or services, then,
over time, there is likely to be a drift of customers towards that higher-quality supplier.

Equally, when commencing a quality programme, it is inadequate to define improvement
relative only to existing internal performance and measurements. It is vital to define quality
and improvement in terms of the customer's requirements and in terms of the 'best' competing
products. The foundation for quality improvement, then, is knowing how good or bad one set
of products and services are when compared to others in the same marketplace, particularly
in relation to customer perception. The 'fact' that one product or service is technically better
than another (as might be argued for the Macintosh and Sun computer operating systems when
compared with that from Microsoft) is not enough. Microsoft, through more effective interaction with customers, has achieved the dominant market position. It is creating the foundation

for quality improvement – across all aspects of the product or service – which benchmarking helps to establish. One particular benchmark now being used by many organizations is the ISO 9000 series (see Chapter 21), which provides the standard for quality management systems and is thought by some to create competitive advantage.

Benchmarking, also now often called 'best practice' – and reinterpreted and broadened for the UK public sector as Best Value – is used by large and small organizations throughout the world to help them understand their own performance against the best that they can measure. This enables them to develop more profitably and grow their businesses.

23.1   WHAT IS BENCHMARKING?

Benchmarking is a process of comparison between the performance characteristics of separate, often competing, organizations intended to enable each participant to improve its own performance in the marketplace.

The objective of benchmarking is to obtain a clearer understanding of competitors' success factors and of customers' requirements. This understanding, particularly of customers, will lead to reduced complaints, a sharper focus on customer needs and higher levels of customer satisfaction. Discovering process improvements will assist in reducing the costs associated with rework, rectification, waste and other quality problems.

Benchmarking will also enable innovations (of either process or product) to spread more rapidly through an industry and across industries where appropriate – for example, in supply or distribution logistics, where many problems are similar regardless of the industry.

Benchmarking involves a number of simple steps. The first establishes what, from the customer's perspective, makes the difference between one supplier of a product or service and another – for example, why one is considered adequate and another excellent. It is important to remember that the customer's perception – not the actual, technical quality of the product or service – is what matters. The second step is setting standards according to the best practice found – in other words, regarding best practice as the 'benchmark' for the organization's performance. The third step is to determine by what means the benchmark organization achieves those standards – which will always look challenging from the benchmarker's perspective. The final step is utilizing the capabilities of the staff to meet and, if possible, exceed the standards observed.

It is important to understand at this stage that what is important is not the industry but the core characteristics of the product, service or activity. While it may be ideal to benchmark one airline against another, this may be difficult for reasons of competition, politics or law (for example, where such behaviour may be regarded as anti-competitive or likely to lead to cartel pricing). On the other hand, it is perfectly reasonable to compare an airline's marketing or logistics function with those of a newspaper or a bread bakery since the products share a significant characteristic: nobody buys yesterday's bread or newspaper, and no one can occupy an airline seat once the flight has left. A similarly useful comparison can be drawn between customer and enquiry handling in a bank and that at an airline counter or in a department store. The core process may be the same, even though the particular questions may be very different.

Benchmarking provides a rigorous framework through which the benefits outlined above can be obtained. It enables a disciplined, demanding assessment of performance in areas which are crucial to the particular organization. It also enables avoidance of the errors and mistakes already made by others, thus preventing further reinvention of the wheel.

Two major limitations on performance improvement can be usefully addressed through benchmarking. First is the limitation to knowledge, which so often affects organizational performance. The experience and knowledge which most people have of a process or product are gathered in a particular environment. Unless those people have the opportunity of advanced training, perhaps through a business school, or some form of collaboration, they are largely closed off from developments which could improve their process. Thus they become content with the way things are – because they know of nothing different or better. The story of Fletcher Challenge Steel in China (Vignette 9.1) perhaps reinforces this point.

Second, the syndrome known as NIH – Not Invented Here – can be overcome through benchmarking. NIH is a typical response by many organizations and employees to proposed changes to improve performance. It is often accompanied by remarks such as 'that may work all right in xxxx but it just wouldn't apply here', frequently supported by 'because we're unique', 'our circumstances are different' or 'our customers don't expect . . .' or some similar excuse. The truth is that NIH is a defensive ploy intended to inhibit the disruption to established patterns and habits of work, and the effort that is often associated with a change programme. If the employees who will be affected by a change are involved in its design through the benchmarking programme, then they will be much less likely to resist the change and more likely to develop unique aspects which will 'make it work here'.

Overall, benchmarking first requires senior management commitment, particularly to supporting actions arising from the exploration. Second, it requires staff to be trained and guided in the process to ensure that maximum benefit is obtained. Finally, it requires allocation of part of the relevant employees time to enable it to be carried out.

23.2 HOW IS BENCHMARKING DONE?

There are only five steps (Box 23.1) to a benchmarking process, regardless of the size of companies involved, although larger companies may indulge in greater amounts of data gathering than smaller ones and may have to be conscious of issues surrounding anti-competitive or monopolistic behaviour.

Step 1, appraising and identifying which characteristics to benchmark, can be achieved through Pareto analysis. While it is possible to benchmark every characteristic of a process which can be measured, the return to the company from doing so will vary substantially. Remembering Juran's comment on 'the vital few, the useful many', we can try to determine at the outset

Box 23.1 *Five steps in benchmarking*

Step 1	Identifying what characteristics to benchmark
Step 2	Identifying benchmarking partners
Step 3	Designing the data-gathering methodology
Step 4	Selecting analytical tools
Step 5	Implementing changes

which activities the company needs to excel in to succeed in its particular business, bearing in mind that in the context of quality this should be expressed in terms of the customer's requirements. A substantial improvement in a process which delivers no benefit to customers will not necessarily and directly improve the company's competitive position, although it may generate improvement in profit performance which may be of great importance. Quality benchmarks might include aspects such as reliability, longevity, consistency, accuracy, levels of in-process rework or rectification, service intervals, after-sales response, and so on. Factors which affect profitability – and which may enable more effective competition through reductions in prices – include reductions in rework, working stocks, inventory levels, and relationships between factors such as sales dollars (or other currency) per employee, enquiry to sale conversion rates, space utilization and, increasingly, the effectiveness in use of management information systems.

The selection criteria for projects should be based on delivery of maximum benefit to the customer rather than on matters which might be considered as exciting or interesting to a particular professional group. Approaches based on the latter view often lead to major disappointment. For example, since the mid-1980s, many organizations have invested heavily in continually upgrading computer systems from the 286-chip technology of the late 1980s to the fast 1.8-GHz processors of 2001. While the dramatic increase in processing speeds has undoubtedly been delivered (technically the machines work much faster than they used to), little genuine business benefit has been delivered to the users (most people type at the same speed they always did!), and much procedural inefficiency continues to surround the uses to which the computers are put. The processor speed is not of overriding importance so long as the response time of the machine is always equal to or faster than that of the operator. In terms of the customer, he or she generally has little interest in the speed of the machinery in use but a great deal in the accuracy of output of the process – an area where little evident progress has been made, with many organizations still blaming 'the computer' for errors. It does not really need repeating that it is people that make mistakes, not machines!

Characteristics to be benchmarked should be, first, those which are of genuine concern to the customer, and second, those which are of material importance to the organization. Other areas for benchmarking include those where the organization knows that it is experiencing a problem in relation either to its customers or to its competitors. Issues might include staff training and development, recruitment and turnover, and raw material and other input costs.

The second step is deciding which other organizations to benchmark with. In the case of a very large, perhaps divisionalized operation, it may be perfectly reasonable to start by internal benchmarking, for example comparing the distribution logistics processes of two factories. If this is not possible, then it is necessary to look outside the organization for benchmarking partners. These may be domestic or overseas. A starting point is to ask the customers whom they regard as the best in your particular business; after all, it is the customers that you are trying to satisfy. Doing so will also help to identify those characteristics of performance which the customers regard as important.

Other sources include the press, trade and industry associations, industry expert consultants or academics. Overseas, the various trade commissions, embassies and state departments should be able to provide useful leads. For example, in Hong Kong the Productivity Council could help, while in the United Kingdom there are a number of organizations focused on benchmarking practice and co-operation.

There are four key issues to address in selecting benchmarking partners. First, do the companies have some knowledge of each other? For example, is there a customer–supplier relationship already? Second, is the experience of the proposed partner directly relevant to our needs? Third, is it as good as its reputation suggests? It is quite normal for a company's reputation to outlast the quality of its goods or services; equally, some companies with established 'bad' reputations may have made substantial performance improvements. For example, in the 1970s the Fiat company developed a reputation for building cars which rusted very quickly and very badly. This has not been the case for many years, yet the reputation still surrounds their products despite the evidence on the roads that the reputation is unfair.

Finally, and as mentioned before, is the exchange of information with this partner permissible? Apart from any legislation concerning anti-competitive behaviour, organizations also need to be aware of limitations on the transfer of technology to and from certain countries and for certain purposes. These general cautions need to be supported by appropriate legal advice and of course the application of common sense.

Designing the data-gathering methodology moves beyond the basics of ensuring that any statistical methods are rigorously applied and the results meaningful, to the real issue of how physically to obtain the information. The first and most readily available sources are in the public domain – for example, company annual reports, press articles, trade association journals and libraries, academic studies (where these have been undertaken and published), and from the various bodies and consultancies which specialize in enabling benchmarking. While direct competitors will normally exchange data only through a third party, such as a trade association, some may be amenable to a direct contact – particularly if the company approaching them is able to offer comparable assistance to them on another issue. For example, you may swap information on staff retention and development programmes for information on distribution logistics. As long as each party perceives there to be a fair exchange (in terms of problems solved), the volume of data will probably not be an obstruction. What is vital at this stage is that the data necessary to enable the benchmarking to be carried out are identified right at the outset. Nothing is worse than having to return to the partner for more information, nothing is more unhelpful than designing improvements based on incomplete or inaccurate information. The services of a statistician and other suitably qualified professionals should be used to support the data-gathering process – for example, consultants (either internal or external) with expertise in process mapping and analysis, and so on.

The fourth step reflects the similar stage in process review already elaborated in Chapter 20. The key difference is that rather than seeking general improvement, the search in the benchmarking exercise is for specific differences between processes which give one organization a significant performance margin over the other. This recognition of the performance gap is the basis for improvement, although it is always necessary to recognize that what works for one company in one set of circumstances will not necessarily work for another in a different set.

The fifth and final step is the implementing of changes. Technically this is quite straightforward. New performance standards need to be set, based on the improvement scope identified. The lowest level of management with an overview of the whole process affected, appropriately supported, needs to take direct responsibility for implementing the changes. Additional resources must be provided to support the changes if required. For example, overtime working may be necessary to create a window enabling the absorption of disruption associated with a particular change. This might occur in a dispatch unit, where a redesign of the storage layout could demand that a significant amount of space be created in the short term. Finally, a performance-monitoring programme must be implemented to make progress visible.

Benchmarking, like quality improvement, is never complete. It is a continuing process, and although the incremental gains from the first exercise are likely to be the largest, the process should be continued to ensure that the organization always reflects best practice in the particular area.

23.3 CRITICAL REVIEW

Benchmarking is essentially an exercise in organizational humility. It demands that rather than being complacent about how good an organization is, those carrying out the exercise respect the idea that there may be others in the industry who carry out a particular process more effectively. Effective means cheaper, quicker and more closely meeting customer expectations. The organization then has to set out to learn from those higher performers.

Technically, as has been shown, benchmarking is not a difficult process. Each of the five steps is relatively straightforward, and overall it amounts, first, to emulating the best, and second, trying to improve on their performance. As any author will tell you, it is far harder to write an original book than to prepare a review or critique of another's.

The risk with benchmarking is that the organization aspires only to be as good as the rest – and sets its sights accordingly. This means it simply copies others' practices without adapting them to the particular and unique set of circumstances in which it operates. Relying on such a model (a model is simply a representation of reality), the organization will never achieve the levels of performance of the organization copied. This is because the model does not reveal everything about the organization or its circumstances, only those characteristics which the modeller thought important.

The second problem with straight copying is of course that no competitive advantage is gained. The process simply levels the playing field further, reducing diversity in the market and thereby reducing effective consumer choice. If there is no measurable difference between products or services, then purchasers will make their choices on other criteria such as convenience, accessibility or taste (fashion), the last of which is extremely fickle.

Benchmarking is a potentially valuable technique for quickly lifting the performance of an organization. However, the establishing of benchmarks must be used as the platform for significant improvement over the best, if it is genuinely to improve the competitive position of the organization rather than simply keep it in the game.

BENCHMARKING FOR SURVIVAL: DERWENTSIDE DISTRICT COUNCIL

The Technical Services Department of Derwentside District Council in the United Kingdom proceeded to certification under BS 5750 (subsequently ISO 9001) in June 1994. This successful conclusion was reached after a long and arduous process which started with a preliminary feasibility study and report submitted in September 1990. Commitment to the strategy ebbed and flowed over time, dependent upon conflicting work priorities. However, the process was completed well in advance of the main target, and achieved within budget.

The main motivation for applying quality management techniques was the prospect of competing in the future with private sector organizations under the rules of compulsory competitive tendering for professional services. The key element to the success of the initiative was to change the ethos of the organization through the drive and commitment of senior managers. The strategy was adopted on the perception that service quality aspects of the tender evaluation process would be most easily demonstrated through reference to a third-party-approved quality management system.

In addition to enabling competition with the private sector organizations, two other advantages were realized. First, the image of the department within the council was improved. Second, the QMS provided a useful vehicle to support other necessary changes. Greatest benefit was derived where existing systems were inadequate or non-existent – particularly as it was in these areas that most resistance was encountered.

The system has been successfully in operation for three years and is now deemed 'mature' by the external assessors. The department believes that it has also given it an advantage in pursuing the Best Value proposals made by the government.

Benchmarking its services against external standards has clearly served Derwentside District Council well.

SUMMARY

This chapter has briefly introduced the idea of benchmarking as a platform for performance improvement within the context of a quality programme. The major steps in a benchmarking process were considered and a critical review provided.

QUESTION

What measures of performance would you use to select benchmarking partners?

Chapter 24

Supplier development

Why beholdest thou the mote that is in thy brother's eye, but considerest not the beam that is in thine own eye?
(Matthew 7:3)

KEY LEARNING POINTS

Key definition of supplier development: buyers working co-operatively with suppliers to improve quality throughout the value chain.

Key technique: commitment; carry out audit and evaluation; define changes; develop agreement; form teams; define precise objectives; implement them.

Critique: benefits through streamlining, cost reductions, enhanced productivity, drawbacks from vulnerability of suppliers, unbalanced power within the value chain, potential to reduce choice and variety.

INTRODUCTION

The issue of supplier development is not one which has traditionally been well explored in the quality literature, although there has been recent substantial development in the area, particularly following the integration of supplier relationships with the revised ISO 9001:2000 standard. A useful text is Kenneth Lysons's *Purchasing and Supply Chain Management*, which provides a broad grounding in this area.

Suppliers of both materials and services are critical to the achievement of quality. The quality of material inputs to a manufacturing process are strong determinants of the quality of output. Similarly, the quality of bought-in services, such as distribution and logistics, accounting, information technology support and building or machine maintenance, affects either the production process or the interface with the customer – for example, through deliveries or invoicing. Clearly, a part of being a quality organization is ensuring that the external factors affecting the input and output ends of the internal processes meet the requisite quality standard.

24.1 WHAT IS SUPPLIER DEVELOPMENT?

Supplier development is best thought of as a business policy espoused by a company which is serious about achieving quality. It involves a commitment by that company to set and attain internal quality standards which meet the requirements of its customers, and to support its suppliers in enabling them to meet those same requirements.

Traditionally, companies wishing to exercise a degree of control of the upstream or downstream elements of the value chain have followed the route of vertical integration, either through development of their own services or through acquisition. However, these traditional routes have usually proven less than fully successful. The company loses the focus on its core business, often operating the other parts of the business less successfully and at greater cost than specialists, so that instead of excelling at one task it becomes mediocre at many. Equally, it is frequently the case that overall profitability is adversely affected. Supplier development moves away from this strategy, recognizing its inherent difficulties and limitations, and respecting the expertise and knowledge specific to the fulfilment of a particular need.

Supplier development requires that the company change its posture in relation to its suppliers. Traditionally, the buyer–supplier relationship is adversarial, each party seeking to maximize its own benefit from the relationship. Supplier development requires that this relationship become co-operative or collaborative, such that buyer and supplier work together to maximize their mutual interests. Forming the new relationship demands a change in buying processes. The placing of orders based on lowest price and sealed tenders has to cease, with a change to open exchange of information and negotiations based on a willingness to achieve an equitable outcome for both parties. For example, the need of each party to generate an adequate return on its efforts must be respected.

A move towards using a single supplier is also advocated by some writers, including Deming (1986: 35–40). This policy has both advantages and drawbacks. Positively, utilizing a single source of supply should ensure greater reliability of inputs in terms of consistency, lack of variability (that is, closer adherence to standards) and the potential for continually improving standards and reduced paperwork. From the supplier's perspective, it is perhaps assured of a particular level of order, potentially higher-order values, greater certainty in its business planning and longer production runs with bigger batch sizes (with reductions in down-time and set-up time, which in both cases increases productivity), more reliable payment and availability of additional expertise (from their customer).

However, there are drawbacks; the buying organization may close itself off to other options, reducing the opportunity for speculative or spot purchases of materials (which meet requirements), and may reduce its leverage in price negotiations with the supplier, particularly when supplier power is high (Porter, 1980). The organization becomes vulnerable to changes in strategy, tactics or performance by its supplier. This is particularly important when the product or service purchased is critical to the process. An example of this would be when distribution is contracted out to a dedicated haulage firm, which then, for reasons unrelated to the particular contract, experiences financial or other difficulties such as a strike or limitation on the

245

availability of vehicles. From the supplier's perspective, becoming the sole source of supply to a particular organization may involve the dedication of a significant proportion of its resources to fulfilling that order. In this case, it in turn may become vulnerable to any difficulties experienced by its customer or any change of product or strategy on the customer's part. For example, if the buyer ceases to produce a particular product, or suffers from extensive competition, leading to falling volumes, the fortunes of the supplier are similarly affected. This is a particular issue for small businesses acting as specialist suppliers to large organizations. The maintenance of the relationship and the volume of resources required to maintain the supply can swamp the small company.

The foregoing comments are general considerations which must be addressed before any sole supplier relationship is agreed. It may be that both parties feel that the advantages outweigh the disadvantages and associated risks in the particular case and choose to proceed. On the other hand, one or the other may find that the relationship would make it especially vulnerable, in which case it should instead seek alternative arrangements.

Clearly, there is a significant degree of risk to a supplier if the agreement with a buyer constitutes a significant proportion of the total business and limits, for whatever reason, the supplier's ability to undertake business with other parties. That said, there is also significant potential advantage to the buying organization in successfully pursuing the strategy of supplier development, particularly in the creation of a long-term and stable relationship.

24.2 HOW IS SUPPLIER DEVELOPMENT UNDERTAKEN?

The decision to pursue a policy of supplier development can reasonably be undertaken only by an organization already fully committed to quality and which recognizes that improved input quality is necessary to support its implementation programme. To pursue this policy when the organization is not already achieving high standards may well be seen by the supplier as an attempt to shift the blame for quality failure. Such an approach is unlikely to be well received.

Supplier development takes place in seven stages (Box 24.1). The first stage is, like the first stage in a quality programme, crucial. If the senior management are not committed to the process and its outcomes (including the need to provide short-term financial support and to commit workforce resources to the strategy), it will fail.

Box 24.1 *Seven stages of supplier development*

Stage 1	Make a commitment (at senior management level) to supplier development
Stage 2	Audit and evaluate internal standards
Stage 3	Define and quantify the desirable or necessary changes
Stage 4	Develop agreement with identified suppliers
Stage 5	Form joint teams and develop a training programme (if necessary)
Stage 6	Teams define precise objectives, deliverables and timescale
Stage 7	Implement changes and monitor impacts

The second stage is to audit and evaluate the processes in which the supplier's inputs are used, to ensure that these meet the current internal expectations. Similarly, the inputs themselves must be formally evaluated. If a process is failing because of internal factors, then no amount of supplier development will cure it. Similarly, if suppliers are to be approached to improve their performance, it is vital that the buyer can precisely demonstrate the need by showing the impact on the buyer's own output.

Stage 3 is for the buying organization to determine what standards it expects its suppliers to achieve and, consequently, what changes are necessary and which desirable. It is important to discriminate between those aspects which are essential to acceptable performance – that is, meeting requirements – and those which would be beneficial in the longer term but are not currently essential. This stage, taken together with stage 2, defines the gap between the current

VIGNETTE 24.1 **CO-OPERATION OR COMPETITION?**

As the public face of the food industry, the large supermarket chains adopt what might be regarded as supplier development strategies. They are committed to continuously enhancing the quality (by their measures) of the foodstuffs they sell, and make use of this commitment in their advertising.

These organizations work closely with their suppliers through the buying process, evaluating not just the goods themselves, but the factories, farms and delivery systems. They agree exacting standards with the suppliers for all aspects of the product and reserve the right to refuse deliveries which do not meet those standards. Pricing is a difficult issue in this area, with strong competition between the supermarket chains and consequent pressure on suppliers to reduce costs.

They do not always, however, adhere to the supplier development strategy outlined in this chapter. While the first three phases are usually completed, thereafter the process often breaks down. The agreement is often rather one-sided. The buying power of the supermarket chains, coupled to the fragmentation of the food production industry, with its many competing small suppliers, tends to make those suppliers vulnerable to pressure. Similarly, stages 5, 6 and 7 are usually forgone, with the supermarkets expecting the supplier to conform to the new standards and to bear the cost of so doing – and it has been widely reported in the press that they sometimes require the supplier to contribute financially to the allocation of shelf space in the supermarket itself. While in the short term this appears beneficial to end-consumers, there is a danger in the longer term that the number of suppliers will be significantly reduced. In this circumstance, choice and variety will fall and prices will rise, reflecting the greater strength of those suppliers in their relationships with the supermarkets.

The idea of 'partnership' between buyers and suppliers, which supplier development strategies imply, would probably be most beneficial to all parties in the long run. Variety would be maintained, prices would be relatively stable as a result of continuing competition, and food quality would continually improve. This beneficial outcome can be achieved only under co-operative rather than combative conditions.

performance of the supplier and the necessary performance. This defines the initial scope for the supplier development strategy and provides a basis for measuring subsequent performance improvement.

The first three stages simply prepare the ground for approaching suppliers. The buying organization is now equipped with the information necessary to engage in meaningful discussions. Stage 4 is the development of agreement with the identified suppliers. Clearly, if the suppliers are not willing to join in with the programme, then nothing is lost, since the organization is fully prepared to approach alternative sources with a clear idea of its expectations. The supplying organization must be prepared to make the same commitment to improving performance as the buying organization. The basis of moving forwards should be a written agreement setting out the aims and objectives of the programme and the benefits to be delivered.

Stage 5 is the formation of joint problem-solving teams tasked with pursuing the various benefits. These should take the form of quality circles and may require training or development input in order to function effectively. Ideally, these teams should include representatives of all relevant functions in the two organizations. For example, a team made up exclusively of product buyers and sales staff would not be effective, since they are likely to have only limited knowledge of the problems in use of the particular product or service. Operational staff must be regarded as fundamental to such a team, which should have the authority to draw on other resources when appropriate – for example, accounting staff (for costings), statisticians (for the development of process control measurement), and so on.

Stage 6 is the implementation phase, when the designated teams should initially define precise objectives, tasks and timescales in the light of the current performance gap. Implementation itself should more or less follow the pattern of quality circle operation, using the same quality tools and techniques.

Finally, stage 7 is concerned with implementing any changes arising, and monitoring the impacts against the expected benefits. It may be that for very large organizations a supervisory or steering board is required to oversee the implementation programme (particularly if a part of the strategy is to transfer the learning which takes place to other parts of the respective operations). For smaller organizations, this should not be necessary.

Like most other aspects of a quality programme, supplier development can never be considered complete. It is an ongoing, iterative process which aims to continually improve performance for the benefit of both parties.

24.3 CRITIQUE OF SUPPLIER DEVELOPMENT

There is clearly significant benefit to be gained by organizations working together to improve performance. They can streamline processes, reduce costs, enhance productivity and more adequately satisfy their customers' expectations. The drawbacks to this strategy principally surround the issue of vulnerability of either the supplier or buyer through dependence on a single source. This vulnerability relates to financial leverage and to the risks of failure to supply.

To be successful, a supplier development strategy relies upon absolute commitment by both parties to making the arrangement work and a willingness and intent to act in the utmost good faith at all times.

SUMMARY

This chapter has briefly introduced the concept of supplier development as part of the overall quality strategy. The issue has received insufficient attention in the quality literature, and the ideas expressed here provide a basic outline only.

QUESTION

Consider the food industry example just provided. Suggest ways in which a more equitable balance of power could be achieved.

Chapter 25

Qualitative methods

Success nourished them; they seemed to be able, and so they were able.
(Virgil, *Aeneid*, II, V.231)

KEY LEARNING POINTS

Key idea concerning qualitative methods: while quantitative approaches are vital, these measure only what is apparently happening; qualitative approaches are focused on changing what happens.

Key approaches: quality circles; job design: natural work units, task combination, vertical loading, task feedback, self-managed work teams, organization structure.

INTRODUCTION

The aim of this chapter is to review a selection of the non-quantitative methods for achieving quality and consider how they may be used. Readers will recall the overall methodologies of the gurus from Part two; in this chapter, specific tools are considered.

25.1 QUALITY CIRCLES

Quality circles are usually considered to be the brainchild of Dr Kaoru Ishikawa but have been adopted in a variety of forms by many companies throughout the world. The circles exist (Box 25.1) to identify and solve quality problems associated with a particular activity or interest group within the organization.

The aims of using quality circles are to improve and develop the organization, to show respect for people and enhance their satisfaction in the job, and to stretch them to their potential. Each circle is made up of between four and twelve workers led by a supervisor or manager. The focus of attention is on problems within their own area, although problems imported from

---

Box 25.1 *Aims of quality circles*

To improve and develop the enterprise

To respect human relations and build job satisfaction

To stretch human potential and capabilities

---

a prior process should also be recognized. These become the responsibility of the supervisor or manager to address.

The effectiveness of quality circles depends upon a number of key factors. Prime among these is support from senior and operational management. If these levels obstruct or inhibit the effort, even passively, then the initiative will fail. Similarly, participation by the workers must be voluntary, and both they and the leaders must be trained in appropriate techniques.

It is usually suggested that circle members have a common work background. This may be seen as perhaps inhibiting the development of solutions to problems that cross process or functional boundaries. It is certainly the case that a problem within a particular area may be solved by a circle drawing its membership from within that area. This approach, though, will not necessarily help with problems which cross internal boundaries, and it denies the use of interdisciplinary teams. Interdisciplinary working has been found to be extremely helpful in the field of operational research and is continuing to gain popularity in many other areas. The principal benefit of a 'common background' circle is that the membership will not feel that a solution has been imposed by an outside, uninterested body. A sense of 'ownership' in solutions is generally recognized as a powerful means of overcoming resistance to change.

The orientation of the quality circle is towards solutions. It is very easy for them to become enmeshed in complaints about the organization and its management. This may be made manifest in moaning about other parts of the process, or fruitless comparisons of working conditions, pay rates and other issues which are not central to the purpose of the circle.

Organization of the circle should be a matter of normal good practice for meetings – that is, a specific (but limited) time should be set aside, an agenda circulated and invitations to attend issued to all members, plus managers/supervisors at least as a matter of courtesy. It is recommended that the leadership of the circle be rotated on a regular basis and that hierarchy in the circle be avoided. Apart from its benefit to active participation in the circle, this provides the opportunity for every member to try the role of manager, even if in a very limited sense. It may also be regarded as good training practice and an opportunity for a manager to see how individual workers might cope with more responsible and supervisory positions.

It is generally considered important that the efforts of the participants should be recognized, although debate continues about this aspect. One school of thought suggests that a participant in a quality circle is only fulfilling his or her responsibility to an employer by showing how improvement can be achieved. If satisfaction and increased job security are achieved through this, then the effort brings its own reward. The other school of thought believes that an employee is paid to carry out a specific task and that extra responsibility should carry extra reward.

Any recognition or reward aspect needs to be related to the culture of the organization and its geographical location. Decisions need to be made on the basis of the socio-cultural context

251

of the particular organization. This means that what may be appropriate in Hong Kong or Singapore may be wholly inappropriate in Tokyo or London.

Quality circles do not stand on their own as an approach to TQM; they must be supported by other initiatives. One important weakness in this respect is the lack of a quality circle hierarchy for working across organizational boundaries and at higher levels in the organization. This means that interactions cannot be recognized and appropriately addressed within this conventional approach.

25.2   JOB DESIGN

Job design covers a range of issues associated with obtaining improvement in quality through enhanced job performance. It involves recognizing that, to a large extent, jobs have historically not been designed; more often they have been initially described and subsequently allowed to evolve. Redesign may have been undertaken in the pursuit of greater efficiency and error reduction, including the application of work study and organization and methods techniques, but this will have often served to fragment tasks into smaller parts. Frequently, managers do not actually know how any given employee does in fact use the working day. Decisions about particular tasks have often been made without understanding the whole process or the purpose to be served. This section proposes a variety of approaches which help to address the problems so caused, including dissatisfaction, fragmentation and ineffectiveness.

Often, organizations are not systematically organized, and work is allocated on the basis of current workload and/or past experience. In this way, work appears to move randomly around the organization. Consequently, little sense of ownership or responsibility for particular aspects of the work is engendered among the workforce. On that basis of allocation, the work has little or no meaning or value to them.

Creating natural work units (Box 25.2) means adopting a different approach whereby logical (or natural) groupings of work are created and allocated to individuals or teams, each accepting total responsibility for the work allocated. If the employees can identify with the work, there is a greater opportunity for them to take ownership and pride in accomplishment. A sense of ownership of the task and pride in its completion will often lead to improved quality through the sense of responsibility of the individual.

Natural or logical groupings of tasks may be developed along a number of dimensions, depending on what is to be achieved (Box 25.2).

It is of course necessary to maintain an equal work-loading in the creation of these work units. This may mean either allocating more staff to an area with a particularly heavy workload, or creating vertical or horizontal subdivisions of the work. Such subdivisions can be achieved by cross-matching categories – for example, matching a geographical area with an industrial sector or by delimiting authority for taking action. An example is the use of lending authorities in banks, which are often split both horizontally and vertically. For example, a lending officer may be able to authorize loans up to £250,000 in a particular market segment, while another lending officer can authorize loans from £250,001 to £1,000,000 in the same sector.

Jobs have often been broken down into tasks (and even subtasks) so that in order to create a complete product or service, a team of five or six people is needed. In the service industries in particular, these people may be in separate areas or departments. Such an arrangement is

Box 25.2 *Natural work units*

Geographical	Each worker is assigned work arising from a particular location, for example a country, county or district
Organizational	Each worker may be allocated work according to its divisional or departmental source
Alphabetical	Customer processing work may be divided according to alphabetical groupings, for example A–D, E–K, L–R, S–Z
Numerical	Work in a supply depot may be allocated to clerks according to bin locations or part numbers
Customer	Work may be allocated according to customer size or type. For example, some banks have divided customers into four principal sectors – large corporate, small business, high-net-worth individuals, mass-market – and these divisions are reflected in their allocation of work
Industry sector	Each employee specializes in servicing customers, or making products in particular market segments – for example, engineering, property, education, medical

apparently highly efficient (in the sense of Adam Smith) since the individuals become highly adept at the particular task. However, simple, repetitive tasks often provide little or no challenge and hence provoke little interest from the employee. This lack of interest leads to dissatisfaction, falling productivity, increased error rates and absenteeism, and, often, increased labour turnover – this last item leading to increased recruitment and training costs. This approach rests heavily on the work of Frederick Taylor (1911), and may be considered at least partly responsible for some of the problems of industrial relations seen in Western countries throughout the twentieth century.

Recombining tasks into complete jobs can help to counter this source of dissatisfaction, allowing the employee a sense of pride and achievement in what is created. Using task combination, the employee is given the chance to manage his or her work, rather than being simply required to repeat the same simple task again and again.

To implement this approach, it is necessary to have a comprehensive understanding of the work process. This can be obtained through the use of the process charting techniques discussed in Chapter 20. Analysis will need to be undertaken at the Process Operation or Process Detail level. An alternative is to involve the affected staff in the redesign. They already know the process and, from experience, they normally have a good understanding of how changes and improvements can be achieved.

Perhaps the most famous, and certainly the most extreme, example of this is Volvo in Sweden. Volvo redesigned a whole car factory, abandoned the production line approach and created a factory where teams built complete cars. Within this set-up, each team member employed a range of expertise to complete the task. This may be contrasted with a conventional, production line approach where each worker carries out only a single task on each vehicle.

Another example is the operation of post rooms in large organizations. A common sequence of work might be as follows:

1   Clerk 1 accepts and seals outbound parcel.
2   Clerk 2 weighs the parcel.
3   Clerk 3 affixes stamps.
4   Clerk 4 records the parcel in the postage book.
5   Clerk 5 sorts and stacks the parcel for dispatch.

It is clear that this fragmented process could be reorganized into a single task completed by one individual, rather than a team of five, or, where volume of activity demands it, the five team members would each carry out the entire process in relation to individual streams of work. Equally, it may be considered that other problems are inherent in the current fragmentation. For example, can each clerk perform the tasks currently carried out by the others? It might easily be the case that the post room ceases to function when one clerk is missing, not because of workload, but because only that one clerk has the necessary knowledge for the completion of a portion of the task.

There are a whole range of possible issues to emerge from the knitwear case profiled in Vignette 25.1, not least those of control and power in the organization. For the current purpose, it is enough to recognize that the fragmentation of the dispatch process created a major weakness in the organization and, regardless of whether or not the control issue was resolved, the process depended upon the presence of every member of the dispatch team, surely an undesirable state of affairs.

In most organizations, the worker works, while the supervisor or manager, at least notionally, carries out the tasks of planning, organizing, controlling and co-ordinating. Conventionally, tasks, performance standards, time frames and objectives are set by the management for their subordinates with little or no consultation. This can mean that the workers feel no obligation to achieve those targets, which they consider as belonging to the management rather than themselves.

VIGNETTE 25.1   **THE KNITWEAR FACTORY**

While it may sound farcical to suggest that a process may cease because of the absence of one person, I experienced a directly similar situation in a knitwear factory. This factory, in the Birmingham area of England, contracted out embroidery work to a range of specialist organizations. Batches of pullovers were dispatched on a daily basis to these organizations for completion of embroidery – they were in mid-process at the subject factory – needing to be returned for labelling and packing.

The dispatch process was not unlike the post room example, with one exception: Clerk 4 also selected an embroiderer from the approved range and recorded, in a notebook, the dispatch address. It emerged that this was the organization's only record of the allocation of embroidery work. The notebook was supplied by the clerk concerned and was kept by her 'so that I ensure a fair allocation of work'. During her absences on sick leave and annual holiday, no embroidery work was dispatched since the other clerks did not know where to send it! This of course brought the finishing process to a halt, not just for the factory concerned but also for the subcontractors. The factory management were totally unaware of this situation.

Vertical loading consists of allowing responsibility to descend through the organization so that workers are allowed a degree of freedom in setting their own standards, thereby accepting a degree of responsibility for their achievements. Equally, degrees of latitude in decision making can be increased, empowering the employee to solve problems and take appropriate action.

Using the vertical loading approach can enable the reduction or removal of some control and checking activity, the assignment of more demanding tasks and increased levels of authority among the workforce. This, if properly handled, should lead to a virtuous circle of improvement at the lower levels and should enable managers to concentrate more effectively on the issues which really matter about their own work. Successful use of vertical loading depends upon three key characteristics among the workforce. They must be willing to accept the additional responsibility; they must have the appropriate ability and level of training; and their competence must be commensurate with the need of the task (Box 25.3).

It is the responsibility of management to ensure that these conditions are met and to provide appropriate training where necessary. Management must also ensure that scope is provided for the empowered staff to become accustomed to their freedoms and to learn to use them wisely. It is almost inevitable that at the outset, mistakes and errors will occur while staff learn to apply skills of decision and judgement which were previously the exclusive preserve of the management. Mistakes must be accepted at the initial stage as part of the learning process, and management must avoid the temptation to withdraw the freedoms and retake direct control while the employees learn to work with the new-found freedoms.

Decision making is based on information. Very often, employees exist in what might also be considered an information vacuum. They are unaware of performance standards (or even whether they exist), receive a performance appraisal once a year (or once every two years in many public sector organizations), and gain no specific current information on how well, or badly, they are performing their particular task. Frequently, where appraisal systems do exist, they are used as instruments of blame and punishment rather than enablers of improvement.

In these circumstances, the employees will set their own standards, either explicitly in conjunction with each other, or more commonly on an individual basis – doing what they think is best for them. Nature abhors a vacuum, and in the absence of information from management, the workforce will create their own, which may or may not be in line with management expectations. To correct this, task feedback information must be provided, and to be effective must be driven by the process itself, must be as near 'real-time' as possible, must be provided continuously and must be meaningful to the recipient (Box 25.4). Failure to meet any of these conditions will render the information useless.

The word 'feedback' is one of the most commonly abused in the English language. In this book, it means information drawn from the output side of a process which is compared with

Box 25.3 *Key requirement for vertical loading*

A willingness to accept responsibility

Ability which matches the increased requirements

A level of training commensurate with the new responsibilities

Box 25.4 *Characteristics of task feedback information*

Driven by the process itself

Real-time (or as near as possible)

Continuous

Meaningful (it must be in the recipient's language)

a target, the comparison being used as the basis for adjusting the input to the process. Given the power of contemporary information technology, none of these requirements is difficult to achieve. However, the most frequent difficulties arise with the last requirement. What constitutes meaningful information for a manager may be very different from what constitutes meaningful information for the worker affected. For instance, a manager may wish to work with reports expressed in terms of profit and loss – that is, with monetary measurements of performance. For the worker in the service department of a car dealership, monetary measures may be meaningless. He or she may measure performance in terms of the number of vehicles serviced or the level of utilization of servicing bays. It is useless, then, to provide information to these individuals on profit or loss, since those data cannot be used by them for control and self-management purposes. It is more useful and more effective to use information technology to provide information to each recipient which is meaningful in his or her own terms.

The idea of the self-managed work team is essentially an extension of vertical loading. While an overall task is set, the team are free to organize themselves towards its achievement, either having no supervisor or appointing their own from within the team, often on a rotational basis. In extreme cases, the self-managed work team will take responsibility for organizing holiday schedules and other activities which have traditionally been regarded as the exclusive province of management. The team will have the freedom and responsibility to devise improvements and changes within a process, and will often have ways of communicating successes and failures to other teams. This idea has been adopted in both the manufacturing and the service sectors, and by companies as diverse as General Motors and Texas Instruments.

Semco, a Brazilian company, has taken the concept of self-management to real extremes. Workers set their own hours, managers set their own salaries, the majority of the workforce are allowed to vote on corporate-level decisions. Such an approach would appear to many to be a recipe for disaster, yet at the time it was studied, Semco was one of Brazil's fastest-growing companies and had a net profit margin of 10 per cent. Its products included marine pumps, digital scanners, commercial dishwashers, truck filters and all kinds of mixing equipment; a range of products with considerable complexity. Semco is regularly named as the best company in Brazil to work for and receives 300 applications for every job – none of which is advertised! Interested readers may wish to study this case further in *Maverick!* (Semler, 1993) and *Organisational Fitness* (Espejo and Schwaninger, 1993).

25.3 ORGANIZATION STRUCTURE

The issue of organization structure will be further explored in Chapter 27. In this section, only the role and position of the quality function will be briefly examined.

A normal position for the quality control or quality assurance manager in many organizations is as a direct reportee of the production manager. This often serves to institutionalize the potential conflict between the two and allows the production manager the final decision. Such an approach enables the production manager to override quality decisions in the pursuit of some other interest – for example, shipping a full order, regardless of quality, to satisfy the customer in the short term. It also enables the manipulation of other data such as those concerning productivity, labour utilization and even reject/rework levels.

It is vital that the quality assurance function enjoy complete independence from the production function in order that effective inspection and audit become possible. In a company which has fully adopted the quality ethic, this becomes a much less significant issue, since quality ideas will be embedded in the workforce and quality standards will be clearly defined and recognized. In these circumstances, the quality decisions, to a large extent, may make themselves. There will be limited scope for arbitrary decisions.

A key factor in creating an organization for quality is the recognition of processes and the consequent realization that each part of a process has customers, either internal or external. A company which uses these processes as the cornerstone of the way in which it is organized, and sets its quality criteria in recognition of the needs of customers, will become an organization for quality.

SUMMARY

The aim of this chapter was to move away from quantitative methods and consider a selection of the qualitative, human-centred approaches which help in the development of a quality organization.

The use of quality circles, job design tools and organization design approaches was considered. Each of these must be used intelligently and thoughtfully, and within the context of an overall, systemically based quality programme. In isolation, none will achieve very much.

QUESTION

Consider the way in which tasks are undertaken in a fast food restaurant near you. How could the tasks be redesigned to increase job satisfaction? What do you think would be the effect on the organization?

Total Quality Management through Total Systems Intervention

TQM is common sense.
(Robert Flood, *Beyond TQM*, 1993)

KEY LEARNING POINTS

Key idea: if Total Quality Management is to be genuinely total, then it must use a methodology which embraces all potential methods

Key approaches: Total Quality Management within Total Systems Intervention within Total Quality Management; Flood's implementation programme.

Critique: is Total Systems Intervention systemic or reductionist?; added value through ideas of a dynamic, iterative process; formally structured quality councils.

INTRODUCTION

Each of the methods introduced so far is rooted in a reductionist approach to quality, isolating and dealing with particular aspects of problems which in truth are organization-wide. They do not deal with whole organizations but with parts and sub-parts, with processes and operations.

This chapter starts to introduce systems methods in the context of quality – approaches that attempt to deal with the organization and with quality holistically, particularly with the concept of Total Quality Management. First, Total Quality Management (TQM) through Total Systems Intervention (TSI) will be considered.

26.1 TOTAL QUALITY MANAGEMENT THROUGH TOTAL SYSTEMS INTERVENTION IN THEORY

Readers will recall that TSI (Chapter 17) is designed as a meta-methodological process intended to enable participants in an organizational situation to highlight the continually changing issues that are of dominant concern to them in the organization. This is achieved through the creative use of metaphors which enable them to capture particular characteristics of that situation and highlight dominant issues.

TQM through TSI becomes relevant when the dominant issue of concern in the organization is with the pursuit of quality. This concern emerges from the 'creativity' phase of TSI. Flood (1993) proposes that a TQM programme can be derived through the same basic framework used by the TSI process, as shown graphically in Figure 26.1. This shows that when 'quality' is dominant in the TSI process, the same three phases of creativity, choice and implementation can be used to select and implement tools for achieving quality. The figure shows how the logical framework of TSI supports the application of TQM in the holistic context of all of the problems of the organization. This will lead to better-informed use of the range of tools and methodologies available for implementing quality, and in turn leads back to the further use of TSI to address other issues within the organization. The process is iterative both through TSI and through TQM, reflecting the idea of continuation, which is vital to TQM.

26.2 TOTAL QUALITY MANAGEMENT THROUGH TOTAL SYSTEMS INTERVENTION IN PRACTICE

It is important to appreciate that TQM through TSI is appropriate only when, within the TSI process, quality emerges as the dominant issue of concern. TQM is not proposed as 'the one best way'. If within TSI the dominant concern is with quality, then, it is suggested that the TSI approach to TQM should be pursued. In this context, the tools of quality may be used in a complementary manner to the systems approaches. How might this occur?

An issue, or series of issues, is identified by the management group of an organization as giving cause for concern. The decision is made to address these issues using the process of TSI.

Figure 26.1 *Total Quality Management within Total Systems Intervention within Total Quality Management*

The problem context is defined and debated and its characteristics elaborated. Driven by both internal factors (perhaps rework and rectification costs) and external factors (maybe falling sales and customer complaints), the primary issue of concern to the organization emerges as 'quality'.

The group recognize (having already used the TSI process) that any one approach to quality will highlight and address particular aspects of the quality problem but not all of them. They therefore seek to adopt a complementarist approach. They re-enter the TSI process in the context of TQM, seeking to identify, within the whole quality problem, those characteristics which are dominant, which in turn leads them to a choice of primary quality implementation methodology. That is not to say that the organization simply adopts an approach based on the work of a particular guru, rather that one approach, say statistical process control (SPC), is recognized as desirable as a first step, perhaps because there is no quality or performance measurement system in place. SPC is then implemented. This provides a platform for formally evaluating quality performance. Once quality performance is known, what was a secondary concern – for example, solving quality problems – can be addressed through other techniques – perhaps by the use of quality circles.

The process is continuous: the satisfactory resolution of one issue does not mean that the whole quality problem is solved, it simply means that the organization has moved a step closer to being effective. As each gain is achieved and consolidated, so the primary issue continually changes, bringing the organization one step closer to the goal of zero defects or whatever other quality objective it has set itself.

Inevitably, during the course of the TSI/TQM process, other issues not identified at the outset emerge and become dominant. It is essential therefore that the process of TSI is observed and that the three phases of creativity, choice and implementation are kept open to fresh innovation and new problems.

Adopting this approach to achieving quality places the emphasis of choice on the participants within the organization rather than leaving it, as is so often the case, to choices imposed by those outside, such as consultants. This means that any solutions suggested should be closely aligned to the preferences of those within the organization, since they are developing them. This approach dramatically increases the chances of success since the solutions are owned by those working with them.

In essence, the way of managing for quality through TSI has no end because it is an iterative process. In a dynamic, changing world there will always be newly emergent problems to solve or new messes to manage, and the validity of the process remains constant even though the particular methodology in use may be ever-changing.

26.3 FLOOD'S TOTAL QUALITY MANAGEMENT METHODOLOGY

Flood (1993) proposes an overall TQM implementation programme within which he proposes the use of TQM through TSI as already outlined. This implementation programme is essentially straightforward and includes eleven steps (Box 26.1).

The first step in this process addresses the requirement for quality to be taken not in isolation but within the context of a coherent understanding of management theory and practice. This approach reflects the concern that quality should be taken not as an end in itself but as

Box 26.1 *Robert Flood's eleven steps to Total Quality Management*

Step 1	Develop an understanding of organizational design and organizational behaviour
Step 2	Set up a steering committee
Step 3	Set the organizational mission
Step 4	Set up the next layers of quality councils
Step 5	Design or choose educational modules
Step 6	Set local missions
Step 7	Undertake customer analysis
Step 8	Choose projects for implementation
Step 9	Choose tools for implementation
Step 10	Implement educational modules and communicate details of the project(s)
Step 11	Implement projects

part of the overall management of an organization and that the vast body of established management knowledge should be drawn on to support and enhance the quality process.

Step 2, the establishment of a steering committee or 'executive council', is a recognition of the need for quality to belong not to an individual but to the whole organization. The composition of the committee should adequately represent the functions and responsibilities through the organization so that 'everybody is involved'. The responsibilities of the committee are to establish the quality mission, to guide and monitor the implementation process, to select and enable quality education programmes in the organization, and to establish lower-level councils with specific responsibilities (either functional or organizational).

Steps 3, 4 and 5 are the primary responsibilities of the steering committee already outlined. For step 3, setting the organizational mission, Flood (1993: 148) suggests six questions (Box 26.2) which need to be addressed to focus the attention of the organization on its purposes. These questions are intended to focus the attention of the participants on what they want to achieve, leading to the formulation of a crisp statement of purpose for the organization. The questions, while useful, are essentially internally focused. To be systemic in defining the organization's purposes, it is essential that outwardly focused questions are asked, especially questions concerned with the expectations of customers and other stakeholders in the

Box 26.2 *Robert Flood's questions to help an organization define its mission*

What do we think we do?

Are we doing what we think we do?

Why are we doing it?

Are we doing the right thing?

What else could we do?

What would be the benefit of doing something else?

enterprise. The literature on corporate strategy provides more rigorous and fully developed tools for dealing with this issue.

The selection of councils at the next and subsequent levels (step 4 in Box 26.1) will reflect the way in which the organization is oriented. Selection should be based on the most appropriate format. For example, an organization based in a single location may orient itself around products, processes, functions, or according to the tenets of some specific organizational paradigm such as cybernetics. A multi-outlet or geographically diverse organization may first choose to use its geographical locations at the next level below that of steering committee and then to orient itself around some other criterion at lower levels. The essential rule is to ask what will serve the needs of the organization best.

Step 5 reflects the need to enhance understanding of quality throughout the organization. If consistency of approach to quality is to be achieved, then a consistent approach to training will be needed to support it. The particular approach chosen will reflect the paradigm of those on the steering committee but must recognize the differing needs of other participants.

The sixth step is for each local council to establish a local mission. Again using the list of questions, they can orient the local approach within the framework of corporate thinking. It is essential that unity of approach be maintained. The local mission must always fit within this unity and complement the corporate view. If it does not, then the initiative will fail. It is therefore essential that a protocol exists which will enable meaningful debate between the levels.

Customer analysis is step 7. This should be a relatively simple phase consisting of identifying who the customers are, determining (and agreeing) their requirements, evaluating performance against those requirements, identifying where improvements can be made and defining improvement projects. The more difficult task is that of refining broad proposals so that they are converted into meaningful, appropriately prioritized and achievable tasks – identification of necessary resources, supporting measurement of the critical success factors and making clear allocation of responsibility for their completion. A mechanism must also exist (step 8) to enable comparative analysis of competing projects (even between local councils) where resources available to support the programme are limited. Ideas from Juran and others can be drawn upon at this stage.

Flood suggests that step 9, the choosing of tools, should be guided by the complementarist framework of TSI, which is considered to provide an informed guide to methodology choice. Step 10 is implementation itself. Full and detailed planning of this phase is essential to ensure maximum effectiveness and efficiency – that is, no duplicated efforts, no gaps and appropriate scheduling, since timing is of great importance to gathering meaningful information.

The responsibility of the steering committee at this stage is to oversee and co-ordinate the whole implementation programme, monitoring progress, ensuring that information is appropriately shared and reporting successes and failures. The steering committee may be viewed as the mechanism of organizational learning.

26.4 CRITICAL REVIEW

A critical review of TSI has already been provided in Chapter 17. It is therefore necessary to reflect only on the additional aspects, particularly those derived from Flood's methodology.

VIGNETTE 26.1 **SALES PERFORMANCE REVIEW**

A company decided to review the performance and standards of its sales force prior to recruiting additional staff to support a major business development thrust. The review had two purposes:

- to establish a best practice model;
- to develop an idealized staff profile to guide recruitment.

The recruitment drive was to commence in September, the decision to undertake the review having been taken in late June.

The basis of the study was for external consultants to interview and observe the behaviour of the established sales staff, to compare their observations with the results achieved by those staff and to identify which characteristics were of greatest importance.

Unfortunately, the study was undertaken in late July and August. It was difficult to obtain appointments with the staff since many were taking annual leave during that period. At the same time, the staff were finding it difficult to make their own appointments since many of their target customers were also taking leave, and hence it was difficult to observe the staff working. To add to the problems, initial discussions highlighted concerns over the way in which performance was measured and the accuracy of the results. When these concerns were discussed with the senior management, it transpired that they shared the same concerns.

The review proceeded: many useful discoveries were made and a best practice model was developed, notwithstanding the uncertainty surrounding the accuracy of performance measurement. At the final review meeting with the client company, it transpired that its management had already recruited nearly half of the additional staff while the review was still in progress. A number of these recruits did not match the newly established profile.

This was a case of poor implementation of a good idea.

The theoretical platform supporting TSI can, and no doubt will, be debated extensively. There are essentially two camps of protagonists. The first consider that TSI is a major step towards reunifying systems approaches which have become fragmented and non-systemic. The other suggests that the TSI process is itself reductionist, further fragmenting the systems discipline and reinforcing the barriers between differing schools of systemic thought, particularly through the 'system of systems methodologies'.

Regardless of this debate, there is substantial value in the idea of TQM through TSI as a dynamic, iterative process. The continual engagement of all three phases of TSI brings home the understanding that the pursuit of TQM (through whatever means) is not a function of a single decision or a single act, but an ongoing search for ever higher standards. The conventional approaches cover this point with their calls for reiteration at the completion of the particular methodology chosen, but the TSI approach emphasizes that this can and should happen throughout and within the process, not simply when it is completed. All too often, detailed decisions are made by senior management in an organization, with authority for action delegated to lower-level staff. The decision makers, believing themselves to have discharged their responsibility in the matter, move on to the next issue. The TSI process demands that senior management are continually aware of and involved in the change process and refocus it when the situation so demands. Whether or not the organization chooses to use the TSI process, it should embrace the idea of continual awareness and review of the situation and the methods being applied.

The implementation methodology proposed by Flood is in many ways a refinement and consolidation of the approaches espoused by others, and could be applied to almost any change process. However, in the context of TQM it adds value in two areas.

First, it demands that those responsible for the organization develop a full appreciation of the theory and practice of organizational design and behaviour. While admitting (as a management scientist) to a bias in this regard, it is certainly the case that while many managers have undergone extensive training and education in their particular discipline, their understanding of how organizations behave is often limited. Since quality is to be regarded as an emergent property of the behaviour of the organization in its totality, the behaviour of that organization must be fully understood. The failure of many quality programmes may perhaps be attributed to management inadequacies in this area.

The second significant contribution is the requirement for the establishment of formal quality councils at lower levels in the organization. This approach helps to ensure the devolution of decision-making power in respect of quality, while at the same time making responsibilities and accountabilities clear to all the participants. The idea of such devolution has already been met, but not in this formalized, structured manner.

SUMMARY

This chapter has focused on the use of Total Systems Intervention as a guiding process for the pursuit of Total Quality Management both in theory and in practice. Flood's programme for implementing TQM was reviewed and its particular strengths highlighted. Readers may wish to refer to the original works of Flood (1993) and Flood and Jackson (1991) to further enhance their knowledge and understanding.

QUESTION

What problems might you encounter in establishing a hierarchy of quality councils? How would you structure them to ensure that interactions between units were adequately catered for?

Chapter 27

Sustainable organization

. . . because the instability feeds upon itself; and the catastrophic collapse . . . is an inevitable output of the system.
(Stafford Beer, *Designing Freedom*, 1974)

KEY LEARNING POINTS

Key definition of an effective organization: a system is viable when it is capable of survival in a given environment and capable of learning and adaptation to changes in that environment.

Principles: observer-defined systems; systems thinking; black boxes; self-regulation; requisite variety.

Three modes: descriptive, diagnostic, prescriptive.

Three phases: purpose, identification, diagnosis.

Critique: general applicability; environmental interaction; observer definition; difficulty of use; threat to established power bases; static not dynamic goals.

INTRODUCTION

The essence of organizational effectiveness is viability: the capacity of an organization to sustain its existence in a changing environment. The keys to sustainability are learning and adaptation. The theory of the cybernetic approach which underpins viability was explored in Chapter 15, and approaches to adaptation and learning were explored in Chapter 19. In this chapter, Stafford Beer's 'Viable System Model' will be examined as a practical, contemporary tool for the design of an effective, sustainable organization. Effectiveness – the achievement of organizational purpose – drives the perception of quality. An organization which is not effective in the long term will not generate quality products or services. Ultimately, organizational effectiveness (the capacity for adaptation) subsumes the concept of quality, rendering it redundant.

27.1   THE VIABLE SYSTEM MODEL IN THEORY

The Viable System Model (VSM) was developed by Stafford Beer from the principles of organizational cybernetics, which is concerned with steering organizations into their future. Organizational cybernetics is the science of effective organization.

An organization is considered to be viable when it is capable of survival in a given environment and capable of learning and adaptation to changes in that environment. To achieve this ultra-stable state, the process of its management must have five functions – implementation, co-ordination, control, planning and policy – which taken together constitute the viable system.

The model enables multiple interpretations of any organizational situation to be developed, all according to the same principles, but focused on the different purposes imputed to the organization by its various observers. Through this modelling process, dialogue and debate is generated, from which an agreed organizational purpose can be derived and a most useful approach developed.

The approach to cybernetics espoused by Beer rests on five principles. First, Beer pays great attention to the role of the observer in defining a system, its purpose(s) and its design. Managers must recognize that they, and any experts they employ, choose what defines the organization. This guarantees them freedom in those definitions but means that they must accept responsibility for the outcomes.

Second is the recognition of the systems principle: that any system has emergent properties that are possessed by none of its parts, and that each part has properties not possessed by the whole. Managers must therefore seek to deal with the whole organization or system of interest, not just the parts. Practically, in the quality context, the definition of the organization may be extended beyond its legal boundaries to incorporate suppliers, and in certain circumstances distributors of the product or service and customers. This approach reflects the demands of the ISO 9000:2000 standards and enables supplier development strategies to be coherent with the quality strategy of the organization itself.

Third is the 'black box' principle. This assumes that no complex system can be known completely but that managers can learn to control the system by manipulating inputs and monitoring the effect on outputs. This can be done without entering the 'black box'. This assumption should be contrasted with the traditional approaches to management, which call for detailed analysis and description of the organization at every level from a pseudo-omniscient manager at the peak of an organizational hierarchy.

Fourth is the principle of self-regulation. This recognizes that a complex system may be expected to exhibit a degree of self-regulation arising through feedback loops within itself and between it and its environment. This tendency of complex systems to self-organize is of great benefit to managers, provided it is recognized and actively encouraged.

The final principle is known as the 'law of requisite variety'. Elucidated by Ross Ashby, this states that to be effective, the variety of the controller (the management function) must be equal to that which is controlled (the organization). Variety, in cybernetics, is a measure of the number of possible states of a system. An example of this is provided in Box 27.1. Readers should bear these principles in mind when studying the next section of this chapter.

▦ **Box 27.1** *Measuring variety in a system*

Four possible states of a working traffic light (in the United Kingdom)

Red	Stop
Red and Amber	Prepare to go;
Green	Go
Amber	Stop, unless stopping would cause an accident

To control this device, the traffic light regulator must be able to recognize and generate any of those four states. If it cannot do so, it will be ineffective.

27.2 THE VIABLE SYSTEM MODEL: CONCEPTION AND CONSTRUCTION

The VSM is an observer-dependent, general model of any organization. It is concerned with mechanisms of adaptation, communication and control. It consists of a set of five subsystems, each of equal importance to the viability or effectivness of the organization. These subsystems are richly interconnected by a network of information loops in continuous operation. The whole system is capable of learning – that is, of adaptation. The five subsystems are implementation, co-ordination, control, planning and policy, as already mentioned.

Implementation is what the organization does, the products or services which it creates. The co-ordination and control mechanisms ensure cohesion of the organization, yet at the same time allow for the grant of maximum appropriate autonomy to the implementation parts. This tends to maximize the use of the self-regulating tendencies and enable the resolution of problems as near to source as possible. This is considered to generate two outcomes, each of which has clear relevance to the pursuit of a quality approach. First, it leads to greater motivation at more junior levels in the organization – a vital aspect of achieving quality. Second, it frees higher management to concentrate on the issues which are of greatest relevance to them.

The planning function enables the organization to interact with its environment, both influencing and being influenced. This function helps, for example, to ensure that changing customer requirements are known to the organization – a vital part of the quality process. The policy function is responsible for the whole organization, creating and sustaining its identity and arbitrating between demands for change and stability. It is the policy function which determines whether or not the venture will be organized for quality.

As a starting point, it is useful to consider the organization as embedded in an environment. The organization consists of two parts: Operations and Management (see Figure 27.1). The boundaries between these three elements should be thought of as permeable membranes, open to flows of information. These membranes permit the continuous communication which is necessary between the elements. Diagrammatic conventions demand that these normally be shown as discrete information channels, as will be done in subsequent diagrams.

This particular representation is of limited practical use. It provides a general conception rather than a detailed understanding. Figure 27.2 demonstrates the next step in building the

267 ▦

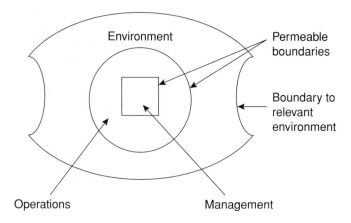

Figure 27.1 *The organization in its environment*

VSM by separating the three elements and showing the communication channels. Each of the communication channels is used either to amplify or attenuate variety. That is, the variety of the environment is absorbed by the organization and its management, and the operational and managerial variety are amplified into the environment. The standard strategies by which these interactions are achieved were reviewed in Chapter 15.

Figure 27.2 provides an overview of an entire organization interacting with its environment. Most organizations will consist of a set of operational and management units embedded in a total organization – for example, the divisions of a multinational company, the branches of a bank or the production lines within a factory. These units, taken together, constitute the implementation part of the organization – those parts which fulfil the purposes of the organization. Each must have the capability to be viable, within the constraints imposed on it by virtue of its membership of the containing organization. Equally, within each unit will be found further, lower-level units, each of which again must be viable. The lowest-level unit for practical purposes is the individual worker. This 'nesting' effect is called recursion and constitutes a special form of hierarchy built on organizational logic rather than power.

A chain of recursively embedded viable systems is presented in Figure 27.3. Each oblong box encapsulates a complete recursion.

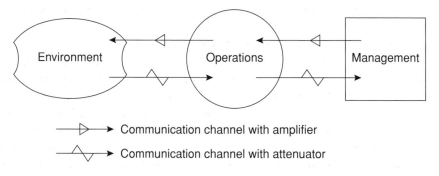

Figure 27.2 *The environment, operations and management separated*

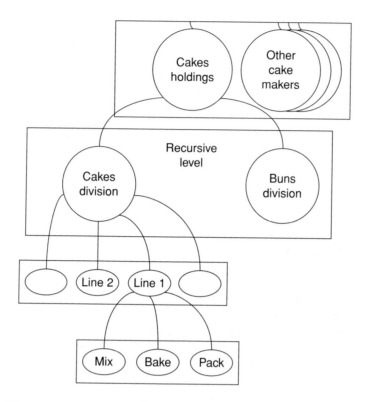

Figure 27.3 *A chain of recursively embedded viable systems (for a bakery)*

Figure 27.4 shows all of the operational elements of a company at the same level of recursion – for example, the divisions of the company. As stated, this set constitutes the implementation function of the organization, the parts which carry out the purpose(s) of the organization. The communication channels are simplified in this presentation. The figure shows that for each division, there is some degree of overlap between the environments. This could represent shared customers, physical overlap between geographical marketing areas or competition for customers whose requirements could be satisfied by either of two or more product ranges from the same company. For example, for a computer manufacturer, the overlap might represent customers whose requirements could be satisfied by either a large PC network or a mid-range system.

Conflict arising between the divisions could cause problems and inefficiency both within the organization and in its dealings with the customers. It is necessary therefore to create a co-ordinating mechanism to deal with sources of oscillation or conflict. It would be possible to achieve this through a higher-level edict – a set of rules or policies handed down by senior management. Such an approach, however, would have two principal effects. First, every exception to the policy would need to be sanctioned at the highest level. This would increase the volume of communication and potentially overload the senior management with relatively trivial decision making. Second, the degree of freedom which the individual elements enjoy would be severely constrained. This would reduce flexibility at the operating level, inhibit the

269

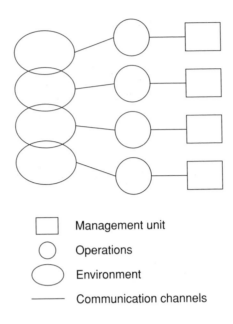

Management unit

Operations

Environment

Communication channels

Figure 27.4 *A set of implementation elements*

development of kaizen, and fail to utilize fully the self-regulating properties of the organiza-tion. A final effect is that the organization would come to be seen as oppressive, since individuals would perceive themselves to have limited freedom of choice and action.

The co-ordinating mechanism, then, needs to exist as a service to the operating elements and to be perceived by them as an aid rather than an obstruction. Prime examples of co-ordination are progress chasers/production controllers in factories, the creation of a timetable in an educational institution, and the allocation of service bays in a car dealership or telling windows in a bank. Each of these devices serves the implementation function, preserving the perception and practice of freedom and reducing the need for routine decision making at the higher levels. Figure 27.5 presents the organization with the co-ordinating mechanism in place. A second feature included in this diagram is the links between the operational elements. These represent the informal communication which always occurs between stages in a process, or divisions of an organization. In the quality context, they may perhaps be regarded as repre-senting the internal supplier–customer relationships.

The next stage in the process of management is control. This is the regulation of the ongoing activities of the organization. Control is concerned with the allocation of resources to the oper-ational elements, with accountability for those resources and with adherence to corporate and statutory regulations. It achieves this through two principal processes: resource bargaining and auditing. Resource bargaining is the process of budgeting for resources which is carried out in all organizations. The VSM requires this to be carried out on a negotiated basis. The control functions and the operational elements should engage in meaningful discussions about what resources are required and what objectives are to be achieved with them. The resource bargaining process should encompass all the resources utilized and objectives set: money, staff, equipment, profitability, quality standards, and so on.

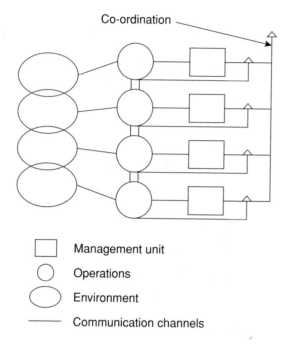

Co-ordination

Management unit

Operations

Environment

Communication channels

Figure 27.5 *Operational elements with co-ordination and interaction*

The control function is made up of the various departments involved in regulatory activity. It would include units such as administration, personnel, production management, perhaps the general or divisional manager's office, and quality assurance.

Audit is a sporadic intervention by each of the control departments in the operational elements. It serves to increase their knowledge and understanding of how those functions are performing. It is essential that these audits be sporadic; if they are not, then they will lose their effect.

The control function being in place, the organization may now be considered to be self-regulating. It will be able to function effectively, carrying out its allotted tasks. Parallels may be drawn between this and devices such as heating/air conditioning systems which are self-regulating against a target temperature in the same way. Figure 27.6 presents the model at this stage.

An organization which is simply self-regulating will not be viable in the longer term, since it cannot respond to environmental changes. Neither will it be capable of generating contin-uous improvement, since it has no facility for development. This brings us to the next stage in the management process: planning.

Planning covers all the research and development activity of the organization. It may be concerned with market research and marketing activity, product development, financial plan-ning, staff training and development, and most certainly is the root of quality planning. The planning functions interact with the emergent environment of the organization, considering possible courses of action either for adapting the organization to the environment or, where appropriate, for influencing the environment towards the organization. The planning and

VIGNETTE 27.1 **INEFFECTIVE AUDIT**

Stories of ineffective audit are commonplace; examples are reported regularly on television and in newspapers. In recent years, action has been taken against some major accountancy firms because their annual audits have failed to reveal major errors or flaws in accounting systems.

Other, less public examples are equally frequent. In the United Kingdom, the Ministry of Transport (MOT) roadworthiness test is applied to vehicles on a twelve-monthly basis. Thus the certificate states only that the vehicle was roadworthy on the day tested, yet a further test is not required for twelve months. The vehicle user has a legal obligation to maintain the vehicle in roadworthy condition at all times, and the police and Vehicle Inspection Agency inspectors have the legal right to inspect a vehicle at any time. However, in relation to the number of vehicles on the road, such inspections are relatively rare, particularly for private cars. Motorists therefore ensure that on the annual test day their vehicle reaches the appropriate standard, but since the likelihood of inspection between tests is so small, many budget-conscious motorists pay no attention to that aspect until the vehicle is again due for testing. This probably means that there are a significant number of vehicles in daily use which are not roadworthy.

The benefit of the audit function to road safety is lost in its regularity. The system is designed to be ineffective.

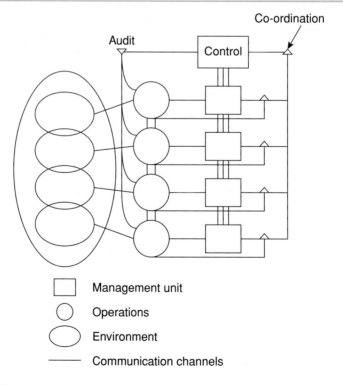

Figure 27.6 *The self-regulating organization*

272

control functions also interact with each other, continual renegotiating the resource allocations and objectives of the organization.

This process of negotiation will almost inevitably lead at times to conflict and dispute, the control functions wishing to maintain the status quo, while the development functions wish to promote change. The conversation between them will be monitored by the last management function, policy, which will arbitrate between them according to the ethos of the organization.

The ethos is the set of values and beliefs that underpin the philosophy of the venture. Without this policy function, the planning–control debate can enter unmanageable oscillations, neither having the power to override the other. In this respect, policy may be considered to be fulfilling an equivalent function to that of co-ordination at the implementation level. There is, however, one significant difference. The policy function through its activities represents the entire organization to the outside world and is the formal link to the next higher level of organization.

The complete Viable System Model is represented in figure 27.7.

The responsibility of the policy function for representing the identity of the organization to the outside world has been stated. At this stage, the model can be linked back to the prior

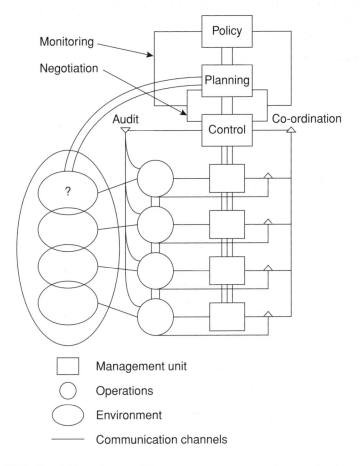

Management unit

Operations

Environment

Communication channels

Figure 27.7 The viable system model

writings on quality, with the consistent demands from all writers for top management commitment. It is clear that without this commitment, the quality initiative will fail, and such commitment demands changes in both the words and the actions of the senior management. If our organizations are as closely linked as is suggested by the Viable System Model (and from experience they seem to be so), then the actions and behaviour of the policy-making group will soon come to affect the behaviour of those in the rest of the organization. If they are serious about quality, then this message will filter through very rapidly; if they are not, that message will move just as fast. Through the cybernetic model, the justification for senior management commitment to quality is realized because they transmit vital messages throughout the organization and to the environment: the customers and suppliers of the organization.

The model of an effective organization is complete, and an organization constructed in accordance with this framework will be viable, but there remain three major points to be made at this stage. First, the communication channels must be in continuous operation; and second, they must be capable of carrying more information in a given time than the transmitting system is capable of generating. This ensures that information is not lost or distorted in the system. Similarly, it is important to remember that every time information crosses a boundary, it must be converted into the 'language' of the receiving system. For example, a message concerning volumes or types of individual transistors or capacitors may have no meaning for a receiving department whose 'currency' is expressed in financial terms, or in units representing aggregations of components such as computers or keyboards.

An organization designed in accordance with these design principles does not look like the conventional hierarchy, but more like Figure 27.8. In this figure, the operational parts of the organization are focused on the present market. The management are considering the wider

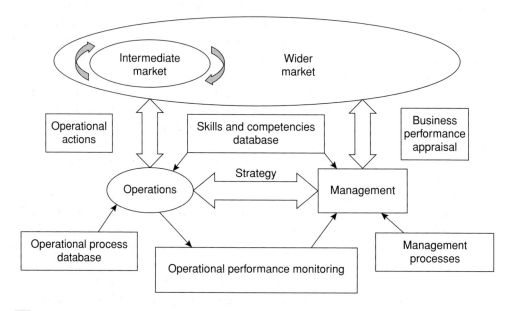

Figure 27.8 The ultra-stable organization
Adapted from Ashby (1952)

market – other present and potential future opportunities. Strategy joins the two together, representing the continual dialogue between the corporate and the operational managers. In order to provide adequate information to all managers for effective management, the corporate managers continually review the interaction with the environment in terms of business performance appraisal. The operational managers use the performance monitoring system to consider current performance in relation to characteristics such as efficiency, productivity and speed. Information arising from that system is also provided to the corporate managers for inclusion in the business performance appraisal. The operational processes, management processes, and skills and competencies records provide the standing information necessary to support management decision making.

An organization designed along these lines will be viable.

It is perfectly legitimate to use this approach to examine specifically only a single aspect of the organization. It is possible, and often useful, to model purely the quality management function. Such an approach ensures that the effectiveness of the quality programme is understood at all levels in the organization. It may be found that while the senior management have implemented a quality programme, this has purely been done at the operations level and no changes have been made in other parts of the organization to support it. For example, control may be focusing purely on volume as an output measure and ignoring the quality issue. Development may be focused on the demand for new products and ignoring customer calls for better quality of existing products.

27.3 CRITICAL REVIEW

The VSM can be, and has been, applied to organizations of all sizes and types from one-man businesses to entire nation-states. It has a general applicability and utility which exceed those of other organizational models. The model fully embraces the interaction between the organization and the environment in which it is embedded, and caters for the definition of the organization and its purposes by its stakeholders.

The model is criticized for being difficult to use in practice, but although the methodology appears lengthy and complex, it can be very rapid in use. The standard modelling format generates great economy. On one occasion, the author undertook a brief diagnosis of the problems of an insurance company subsidiary. Rather than the standard diagrams, individual milk, marmalade and butter portion containers were used to construct the model. The process took only thirty minutes and revealed to the management group a major flaw in the design of their organization.

The model is also criticized for focusing on static rather than dynamic goals, although this criticism rather misses the point of the model. Similarly, it is argued that the model can lead to and support autocratic management behaviour. This argument is easier to sustain, but the principles of the model call for appropriate levels of autonomy, and if this is not granted, the organization will not be viable. The major barrier to its use is the necessity of devolving power within the organization; this requirement frequently generates resistance from those already in power.

In the field of quality systems, the model has been used by Flood (1993) to deal with the structural elements of the organization, while Beckford and Dudley (1998a, b, 1999) and Dudley (2000) have used it as the basis of a complete approach to skills-based quality management.

SUMMARY

This chapter has introduced the Viable System Model, shown its relevance to quality management and demonstrated how the model may be used. Readers should refer to the work of Beer (1979, 1981, 1985), Beckford (1993) and Dudley (2000) to further develop their understanding.

QUESTION

Use the VSM to study your university or college. Diagnose its faults according to the cybernetic principles and recommend improvements.

Chapter 28

Skills-Based Quality Management

No matter how long the procedure it never quite reaches the customer.
(Beckford and Dudley, 1999)

KEY LEARNING POINTS

Services are different from manufacturing.

Skills-Based Quality Management (SBQM) recognizes that:

- management and development of professional skills is the key to service quality;
- procedures can never substitute for human interaction and judgement.

Skills are acceptable as the foundation of an ISO 9000:2000 quality management system.

SBQM:

- has been tested in a variety of sectors;
- is in need of further development.

INTRODUCTION

The content of this chapter was originally the basis for an international series of seminars aimed at introducing a fundamentally different approach to quality management for the service and professional sectors. The ideas were subsequently developed into a paperless quality management system using the structure outlined in Chapter 27.

28.1 THE SERVICE QUALITY PROBLEM

In a manner which parallels past experience in manufacturing, recent years have brought about increasing pressure on the service sector to address the quality issue. However, this drive to improve quality, which has not been overwhelmingly successful in the manufacturing sector, seems to have been even less so in the provision of services. There are two basic reasons for this. First, quality has been described in this text, and widely in the literature, as conformance to specification or fitness for purpose or use. Quality is, then, often equated with standardization. Hence the level of quality is perceived as the inverse measure of deviation from a specification, rather than the warm rosy glow of the experience of a good thing. Second, in service quality there is often no tangible product resulting. Service, and therefore service quality, is an emergent property of the process of its provision.

The interaction of these points has perhaps driven the proliferation of unusable paper-based 'quality systems' for the control of service quality. The attempt to capture the richness of service provision in flow chart format makes them so large and complex as to be unintelligible. The fact is that no system which is internally consistent can completely capture all the complexity of the organization, and hence such models are incapable of achieving the purpose for which they were designed. These quality management systems are, by their own definition, of poor quality. What is needed is a rethinking of quality and quality management appropriate to the service sector. This rethinking is developed in Figure 28.1.

28.2   WHAT IS SKILLS-BASED QUALITY MANAGEMENT?

The essence of Skills-Based Quality Management (SBQM) is simple. The professions in particular and the service sector in general rely for service quality on the professionalism and judgement of the individual employee or partner. Not everything can be proceduralized and, in the service sector, the customer often falls through the gap between alternative procedure outcomes. The only way to solve the problem of quality in the service sector is to employ trained, educated staff and grant them the freedom necessary to do the job.

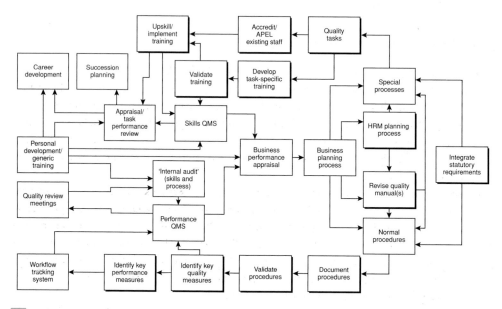

Figure 28.1 *The Skills-Based Quality Management System. APEL = accreditation of prior experience and learning; HRM = human resource management (see Glossary)*

SBQM is an approach to the construction of an effective and manageable quality management system (QMS) based on the development and recording of the skill base of a service organization.

- 'Effective' means that the QMS provide the information necessary for the maintenance and improvement of service quality.
- 'Manageable' means, quite simply, small.

The philosophy underlying the approach stems from the definition of 'professional' and the fundamental belief that the complexities of service provision and the improvement of its quality cannot be modelled in a once and for all manner in the style of the industrial model of quality control. The traditional, documented, procedure-based approach to quality management is guaranteed to fail in the service sector.

In order to be effective, any system designed to maintain professional service quality must not only explicitly recognize the nature of professionalism, but provide robustness in practice and embed it in a structure both sensitive to new data and intelligent enough to learn. In addition, it must be small and unintrusive enough to be willingly used. To achieve this, it must be transparent to those who use it and manage it. Such a system necessarily involves the planning, intelligence gathering, human resources and operational levels of the organization in an integrated whole. The alternative is to continue to create the systems which have, in so many service organizations, fallen into disrepute and disuse.

Given the capabilities of contemporary information technology, it is only sensible that the method outlined takes advantage of this. However, this choice of technological platform for the approach is a convenience rather than a necessity; the concepts are independent of the choice of information media.

28.3 THE OVERALL STRUCTURE

SBQM is based in a wider model of organization rooted in the viable systems approach outlined in Chapter 27. Figure 28.1 illustrates those parts of the organization that relate directly to quality.

The process of quality provision is the result of a set of highly interconnected sub-processes, and it is important to note that many of these continue to be susceptible to traditional performance monitoring and control methods. The model is made more robust by this and by their utilization in an intelligent manner. This element of the model is represented by the flows in the lower half of the diagram.

When the links to the environment available through the business planning process are activated, the whole model represented by the diagram provides the ability for the organization to learn from its experience, changing its behaviours and its value sets over time in relation to environmental (market) and internal needs. The diagram is a simplification of a highly complex process containing many circular and self-referential sub-processes. Unfortunately, managers all too often argue for the simple: 'Give me simple propositions, simple charts and simple answers.' Unfortunately, these do not work.

The idea of using skills to assure quality is not new (consider the medieval craft guilds), even among the quality community. Section 6 of the ISO 9001:2000 standard explicitly deals with the effective management of skills – and this was also possible under the 'special processes' clause of the 1994 standard, though the potential of this was usually ignored by quality experts and auditors. The distinguishing factor of the SBQM approach is that it explicitly uses skills as the basis of quality, with the organizational processes being captured at a higher, less detailed level. This means that task and procedure descriptions are minimized or even done away with in many situations.

The quality of the outputs in this approach is assured through the determination of the abilities and competence needed to deliver the service, a process known as 'qualification'. Once a process is 'qualified', formal quality assurance is achieved by ensuring that only those operators whose skills match those needed for the special process are permitted to work on it. This, though embryonic and static, is the beginning of a skills-based QMS.

The traditional attraction of process control is based on the premise that the better you control the process, the less error, and the less error, the higher the quality. As service is a process, the less error in the process, the higher the provision of service quality. How can this be achieved?

All services are 'special processes' in the sense of ISO 9000:1994. Fundamental process control can be achieved by recognizing and treating them as such. A further chapter – or even whole book – could be written on the interpretation of 'control'; it is not the purpose of this text to explore it. Readers should be aware that in this instance, control refers to creating a situation where the individual can be self-controlled because he or she shares the objectives of the organization and has the skills necessary to complete the task and the autonomy required to adapt service delivery to the needs of the individual customer.

Services are delivered by people. Therefore, process control in the context of service provision is the control of the behaviour of the people providing the service. Appropriate behaviour, assuming the absence of malice, is behaviour which is likely to achieve the purpose of the service being provided. This is assured by ensuring that the provider of the service has the skills, knowledge and competence deemed to be necessary to the provision of the service.

Services are also delivered to people. People (especially clients, patients, passengers, customers) vary, therefore no two service provision events are ever the same. Even assuming an impossible situation, such that the education of the service providers ensures that they are consistent in approach, there will be as many variations on a single service as there are recipients. This is why the complexities of service provision arise. It is the potential variety of the situations that arise in service provision which, of necessity, defeats the traditional process engineering approach to quality management. It is not possible to model all possible situations in advance, therefore it is not possible to specify all activities and solutions in advance. It is not, then, possible to chart the process fully in advance – even with charts a mile long – and it is the very attempt that creates the bureaucracy.

In contrast to machines, people are extremely good at dealing with complexity. However, this ability to deal with complex situations and make sensible decisions in the absence of complete data becomes prominent only when the people involved have become skilled, educated or trained for the task at hand.

Utilizing this human ability to deal with complexity has two distinct advantages over the traditional 'chart, measure and count' approach in the assurance of quality in service provision. The first is that it significantly reduces the amount of paper necessary to the operation of the

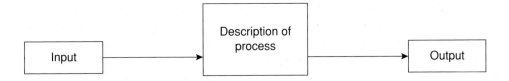

Figure 28.2 *Diagrammatic representation of a process*

system. Quality-relevant procedures can be stated in a descriptive form, as in Figure 28.2. The ideal situation in this model is:

- Input: client with problem.
- Process: negotiate solution to problem.
- Output: client without problem.

    While it must be accepted that this ideal will be difficult to achieve in some cases, complicating the documentation of the process to be undertaken will not make it any less difficult. Indeed, the production of rigid procedure charts (which, as has been argued, cannot entirely capture any situation) may give a false impression of the operation of the process, and may very well remove the things that would allow a solution to be reached – negotiation, informed choice and compromise – creating a 'jobsworth' mentality. The second advantage to be gained runs in parallel with the first. By ensuring that individual service providers have the skills necessary to carry out the tasks they have been set, it is possible to devolve responsibility.

    Because professionals draw on a shared body of core knowledge (see Figure 28.3) in their decision-making processes, it is possible to predict the range of solutions professionally available to the front-line providers with a degree of accuracy. Doing so standardizes the outcomes at the level of 'client-perceived quality' without the necessity of standardizing the potential solutions available to non-standard clients.

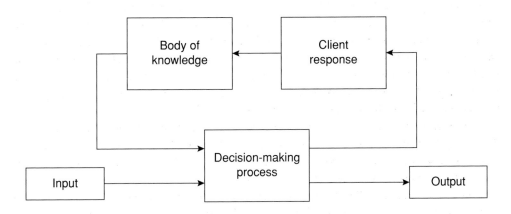

Figure 28.3 *Applying skills*

The professionalism implicit in this model allows the quality of the outputs of the organization to be 'process controlled' rather than 'post-delivery inspected' (see Figure 28.4), which is meaningless in the service context as it can only ever be complaint management. This is because the evaluation of the service provided using a mechanistic process is possible only after the event, rather than as an integral part of it. By defining the skills necessary to the fulfilment of the task:

- The complexity of the procedural system necessary for its control is reduced, process definition is transformed into a statement of professional competence (less paper).
- The level of managerial and supervisory intervention is reduced; tasks become owned by the front-line provider (less overhead cost).
- The level of perceived autonomy at the individual level is increased and greater personal responsibility is taken for the delivery of quality (lower degree of alienation from task).
- The process becomes more flexible; the potential for client perception of quality is increased (fewer complaints).

28.4 THE MODEL FOR A SKILLS-BASED QUALITY MANAGEMENT SYSTEM

In its purest form, the creation of a skills-based QMS is very simple:

- Identify the tasks to be undertaken.
- Identify the skills necessary to undertake the tasks.
- Ensure that only those people who have these skills undertake the task.

In practice, however, each of the three stages will contain sub-tasks and require ongoing operational validation. Identification of the tasks to be undertaken is, effectively, a mapping of those processes that are vital to service provision. Outcomes of this stage of the approach should be:

- identified key tasks;
- identification of those tasks that can be reduced to flow diagrams;

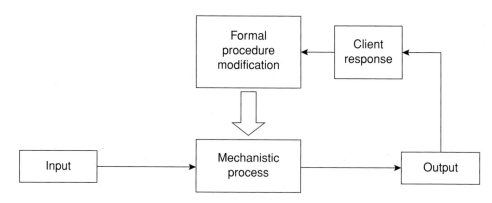

Figure 28.4 *Applying procedures*

■ statement and general description of those tasks that cannot be reduced to flow diagrams;

■ identification of those tasks which are routine or frequently repeated and thus susceptible to standard performance measures.

The selection of key tasks tends to be a negotiation process between the QMS designers and the users. It is advantageous to keep an open mind regarding the perception of what is and is not a key process; decisions made at this stage can return to haunt the intervention later on.

Selection of the processes for inclusion on the skills-based side of the design process is based on a heuristic relating to the complexity of the charting necessary to map the process. If it is possible to achieve significant reduction of complexity through the acceptance of some minimal level of skill on the part of the operator, it can be assumed that there are also significant operational efficiency gains to be made by using a skills-based approach to the quality assurance of the process (see Figures 28.2 and 28.3).

The demands of the quality management model presented in Figure 28.1 are satisfied by the outcomes of this stage of the approach through the production of:

■ documentation of those processes that can be represented as linear flows, including control points and performance measures (Figure 28.5);

■ generic description of those processes that cannot be represented as linear flows but are 'routine', including control points and performance measures (Figure 28.6);

■ a statement of those processes that cannot be represented as linear flows and are 'non-routine'.

With the operational elements of the model defined (in the case of the linear processes) or described (in the case of non-linear processes) and performance measures stated, it is possible to move on to skills definition. Note that Figures 28.5 and 28.6 assume that the processes themselves are fixed. For the most part, linear processes are input controlled and routine skills-based processes are activity controlled.

The skills used in an organization are categorized into three types:

■ generic;
■ role specific;
■ professional.

Figure 28.5 *Performance management*

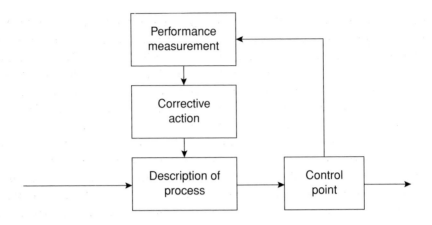

Figure 28.6 *Performance improvement*

Each of these skill types, and their level of development and importance to the operation of the organization, have an impact on the type of QMS appropriate and the potential success of the skills-based approach. This categorization, shown in Figure 28.7, indicates a model of the interrelationships between the varying skills available in a service organization. It also provides a basis for deciding the extent to which a planned education and development programme can be used to enhance performance and, therefore, the type of QMS appropriate to support it.

Generic	Role	Professional
MBA	Specific masters and research programmes	Memberships and professional recognition
NVQ level 5	Knowledge-based quality management	
4	Skills-based quality management system	Product assurance and development
3	Procedure-based quality management	

←————————————————— Records —————————————————→

Feeds ————————————————→   ←———————————————— Feeds

Figure 28.7 *The hierarchy of skills*

284

In practice, the effective professional service organization will rely on a balanced utilization of all three skill types. Each organisation shares the common characteristic that, as the operations of the organization move towards a dependence on skills typical of the upper half of the diagram, it will become increasingly difficult to control quality using the more traditional charting approach. A quality management system which aims to support the improvement of the performance of the organization will focus on role performance. Hence the skills baseline in any organization is the ability necessary to follow the process flow charts.

However, as the organization moves away from the baseline, to the 'non-linear but routine' tasks, the skill necessary to absorb the complexity generated moves onto the lower end, and to the left, of the scale. Such skill levels are consistent with the ability to operate competently within the established processes. This competence within processes is reflected throughout the left-hand side of the diagram. As the operator becomes more skilled, the imperative changes from the achievement of objectives to the setting of these objectives.

Tasks in this category might be typified by such roles as telesales or help-desk operation. They are susceptible to performance measures such as 'how many?', 'how often?', 'how long?' or 'how accurate?'. The human operators are trained to deal with the procedural aspects of the task and have some limited discretion to deal with 'non-standard' occurrences. As the individual moves up this scale, he or she contributes to the organization through his or her management or administrative skills.

To the right of the scale, the emphasis is very different: it is on the consideration of what the processes can or should be. Professional knowledge brings with it the capacity for critical reasoning around the structures through which the service is provided, and forms the basis of the non-linear, non-routine skill set. At this end of the scale, the imperative is not 'What are the objectives?', but 'What are suitable indicators by which to measure the objectives?'

It is not possible to set commercial performance indicators for professional skills, as the focus of these skills is based on the integrity of the professional discipline. The professional contributes to performance through the appropriate application (and in some cases extension) of the body of professional knowledge to the furtherance of organizational objectives. To a large extent, the only performance indicator applicable to the professional is the performance of the core product in the market.

Choice of skill type (i.e. generic, role-specific, professional) should be based on the contribution to the process and will provide (in conjunction with the appraisal process and personal career ambitions) indicators as to the appropriate development strategy for individual role incumbents.

At this point, it should be possible to assign 'qualifications' or skills lists to the roles identified. The lists should also identify those qualifications where possession is a legal requirement. Ensuring the skills-to-task link has two main elements:

- skills assessment;
- records management.

The 'skills possessed' assessment section of the link comprises the appraisal process of the organization. Operational service quality can then be assured through the creation of an auditable documentation system which demonstrates that the skill sets of operators at least meet the skill set necessary to carry out the specified task.

The idea is that organizations possess a body of skills held by their personnel and a set of skills needed which have been identified through role analysis. It is relatively simple to construct a relational database to carry out this task and to extend its utility to the creation of personal development plans, pre-selection for internal promotions and the generation of job specifications for recruitment purposes. At its simplest, the database need comprise no more than two tables, each containing a set of triples.

The adoption of this approach to quality management has a clear impact on the role of the human resources department in a large organization. It becomes very clearly the focus of a strategic operation whose role is to ensure that the individual and aggregate skill set of the employees is at least equivalent to the needs of the organization all the time. This approach has implications for training, recruitment, promotion and retention policies – but is the key to consistent service quality. Strategic human resource development, as a sub-set of the wider strategic function, forms the link between current and future performance by managing the skills base of the organization.

28.5 REVIEW OF SKILLS-BASED QUALITY MANAGEMENT

For an organization to maximize its gain from investment in ISO 9000 certification, the QMS itself must have the lightest possible negative impact on the organization while generating the maximum business value. That is, it should not be cumbersome or bureaucratic, and must generate more organizational benefit than it does cost. In particular, it must directly act to enhance rather than inhibit the performance of the organization in every respect. Experience suggests that most fail to achieve this.

The SBQM approach differs from traditional systems in a number of ways. First, it is based on a dynamic, learning model of the organization, driven by events within the process and linking directly to business planning, staff performance and staff development processes. It learns at two levels. First, it promotes learning by individuals – the improvement in skills and competencies. Second, it stimulates learning at the organizational level, adapting itself on the basis of recorded experience and enabling informed, structured adaptation of the organization. The second key difference is that the approach directly supports the business or organizational needs – it is driven by business performance appraisal and planning, operational processes and active skills management, and feeds the outputs directly back into them.

The SBQM represents a major challenge to the dominant methods of addressing the problem of quality. It has significant benefit in a service environment as well as providing new insights to manufacturing management quality programmes. While the approach has been developed, and certified to ISO 9000:2000, and applied in a number of sectors – chemicals manufacturing, healthcare, chemicals research and property management – it undoubtedly requires further development and refinement.

SUMMARY

This chapter has given insight to a wholly new approach to quality management focused especially on the service sector. Readers should refer to the work of Beckford and Dudley (1998a, 1999, 2001) and Dudley (2000) to extend and develop their knowledge.

QUESTION

Outline the benefits and drawbacks of adopting a skills-based approach to quality.

Stakeholder participation

Hierarchy is endemic to the human experience of social system. And yet it seems never to suffice as an organising principle.
Stafford Beer, *Beyond Dispute*, 1994

KEY LEARNING POINTS

Key definition of soft systems methodology: an approach based on the belief that solving complex problems relies on the innate subjective views of the participants in a situation.

Principle: engage participants in the organization in changing its operation; improve commitment to outcomes; purposes must be defined before means can be decided.

Method: seven-stage process of inquiry – finding out, rich picture, root definitions, redesign, real-world comparison, debate and decision, taking action.

Critique: best with small numbers; brings 'order' to a debate; caters for diverse opinions; no desired or ideal-type outcome other than consensus.

Key definition of Interactive Planning: participants' values and ideals must be paramount in the planning process.

Principle: plan or be planned for; ends must be agreed before means can be decided.

Method: five-stage process: formulating the mess, ends planning, means planning, resource planning, design of implementation and control.

Critique: outcomes bounded by expectations and knowledge of participants; multi-level participation; structure enables mass participation; potential for strategic perspective; means oriented; no 'ideal' solutions.

Definition of Critical Systems Heuristics (CSH): an emancipatory systems approach for developing true consensus.

Principles: purposefulness; systems; morality; guarantors.

Method: CSH methodology of stakeholder participation, dialectical debate

Critique: useful only where the powerful permit debate, overt coercion stops the process; may enable barriers to quality to be identified; develops understanding; no ideal-type solutions.

INTRODUCTION

It is impossible in this book to do full justice to the vast literature now surrounding the idea of stakeholder participation and the plethora of approaches to it. There is no doubt that the full and proper engagement of all parties interested in or affected by an organization's activities will influence it dramatically, nor that the direct engagement of employees, suppliers and customers is critical to the survival of the organization.

There was an argument that coverage of the topic should be greatly extended in this new edition – the alternative being that it should be dropped. I have chosen instead to compress the original chapters on this subject into one, to highlight the extent of the research being undertaken and to recommend to those readers who have a particular interest in the area that they explore the dedicated literature.

Chapters 27 and 28 have considered the structure of sustainable organization and the approach through which the talents and skills of the employees can be actively managed to meet the needs of the organization. In this chapter, three methodologies for enabling active engagement in the organizational dialogue are reviewed.

The methods, tools and techniques so far examined in this book have one prime common theme: they are all designed to improve the quality performance of the organizations in which they are used. Similarly, they all rely on an assumption that what is good for the organization is good for society and for the individual workers. Nowhere in this set of tools is this assumption either exposed or investigated. The focus is on practical issues of what to do and how best to do it; the question of whether or not it should be done is simply not asked.

Recognition of the desirability of employee participation in decision making goes back at least to the beginnings of the human relations school of management thinking and has been a constant theme in subsequent work by many authors. This need is also made evident in the work of the established quality gurus. Crosby's entire approach is built around participation, while Ishikawa's quality circles emphasize his view of the need to interlink statistical and participative methods to achieve quality. From the work undertaken so far, it is undeniable that active participation in the quality process by all the actors within the organization will help to procure success in the pursuit of quality. The perennial difficulty is how to make that participation truly meaningful in organizations which are frequently characterized by internal power struggles and dominated by small power groups.

This chapter introduces three systems methodologies, each of which is designed to enable meaningful participation. They are Checkland's Soft Systems Methodology (SSM), Ackoff's Interactive Planning (IP) and Critical Systems Heuristics. All are operational methodologies, the first two based on soft systems thinking, the last on critical systems thinking.

Flood (1993) suggests that when 'freedom by debate' (enabled through SSM or IP) fails, 'people become emprisoned'. They become trapped in a way of thinking or a set of assumptions about the world which represent other people's interests rather than their own. They may be subject to practical constraints which, either by accident or design, lead them to conform to the expectations of a more powerful individual or group. People are trapped either by the limits of their own knowledge and understanding or by the structure of the society and organizations in which they exist. A means is necessary through which those affected by a change or process can work with the powerful group to review the assumptions and consequences of the change. The process for addressing these problems is called Critical Systems Heuristics.

While the idea of stakeholders is one which has much currency in political science and sociology it has only recently become used in the language of management. In the context of this book, a stakeholder is defined as anyone (or group) with a legitimate interest in the behaviour of a system, including those who are involved in it, those affected by it (whether involved in it or not) and those affecting it.

29.1 SOFT SYSTEMS METHODOLOGY

29.1.1 Principles and conception

SSM (Checkland, 1981) rests on the assumption that the resolution of complex problems (of which achieving quality may be considered one) relies on the innate subjective views of the participants in the situation. SSM has been developed for use in ill-structured situations where there is an absence of clarity in the definition of the problem and no agreement as to what action is required to solve it. SSM enables a variety of viewpoints to be elaborated and evaluated by a group of problem solvers, allowing them to make informed choices about the future. It is considered that by exploring the various viewpoints in an open forum and evaluating their strengths and limitations, an approach can be generated to which all participants will commit themselves. Solutions generated through the seven-stage process of inquiry which constitutes SSM will normally lead to changes in three dimensions: in attitudes, structure and procedures. It is considered that as many people as possible should be involved in the SSM process, and it does not have to be driven by 'experts'; it can be used by managers as part of everyday working practice.

29.1.2 Methodology

As already stated, SSM consists of a seven-stage process (Box 29.1) and should be used in an iterative manner. Although the description in this chapter starts at stage 1, any other starting point would generate an equally valid result. The methodology is pursued by the members of the organization, although it may be facilitated by a 'problem solver' – often a consultant.

The first two stages take place in what is called the 'real world' – that is, they are based on the experience and knowledge of the participants, of how things are to them. Stage 1 consists of exploring the problem situation and gathering information about it through observation by evaluating formal data (such as company records) and via interviews. Stage 2 is often an entertaining stage and is usually expressed in the form of a cartoon called a 'rich picture'. This consists of creating a representation of the problem situation as it is experienced by the participants. Stages 1 and 2 taken together lead the participants to define a number of themes

Box 29.1 *Peter Checkland's seven stages of soft systems methodology*

Stage 1	Finding out
Stage 2	Rich picture
Stage 3	Root definitions
Stage 4	Redesign
Stage 5	Real-world comparison
Stage 6	Debate and decision
Stage 7	Taking action

or systems which they need to examine. These can usefully be thought of as processes within the overall organization studied.

Stages 3 and 4 are abstract processes designed to explore how things could (and arguably should) be, as opposed to how they are, as perceived by the actors. They are concerned with what Ackoff (1981) calls 'idealized design'. Stage 3 develops concise statements about the purpose of the various systems or processes, called 'root definitions'. The 'root definition' presents an ideal view of what the relevant system 'ought' to achieve and is refined through the use of six principal elements (Box 29.2) and six key questions (Box 29.3). Stage 4 uses the validated root definitions to redesign the activities (the transformation process), aiming to overcome the limitations of current transformations. The 'conceptual model' developed identifies the minimum set of activities necessary to ensure that the transformation achieves its purpose. The set of activities is ordered into a process based on how the activities would occur

Box 29.2 *Six principal elements of a soft system*

Element 1	Customers: those who gain by or suffer from the activity
Element 2	Actors: those who perform the activity
Element 3	Transformation: the action itself
Element 4)	World-view: the perspectives on the situation which validates the action
Element 5	Owners: those who can stop the activity (often the management)
Element 6	Environment: external constraints upon the system behaviour

Box 29.3 *Six questions to help refine the 'root definitions' of a system*

Question 1	What is required?
Question 2	Why is it required?
Question 3	Who will do it?
Question 4	Who will benefit?
Question 5	Who will be hurt or damaged?
Question 6	What external factors constrain the activity?

in the 'real world' – this ensures that carts are not put before horses! It may be necessary to define sub-sets of activities which naturally group together, perhaps under the headings of operations, control, co-ordination, and so on (rather like the VSM model seen in Chapter 27).

The aim of stage 5 is to compare the models constructed with the real-world understanding of the group members. This enables them to highlight possible changes in the actual situation to bring it closer to the systemic ideal now developed. Devices for forming a comparison might include highlighting areas of difference, generating and ranking (for evaluation) options, and generating projections of possible futures (in the style of the scenario planning technique used by Royal Dutch Shell).

At stage 6, the comparisons drawn in the previous stage provide the basis for discussion and debate among the participants. This should lead to the selection of culturally feasible

VIGNETTE 29.1 **EXPLOITING INTERNAL MODELS**

The chief executive of a large organization was pleased with the progress which it had made under his leadership but had an uneasy feeling about the future. He invited a consultant to 'Come and have a look, tell me if you think anything is wrong.'

The consultant, with limited knowledge of the organization and equally limited knowledge of the country and its culture, was faced on the first day of the project with a room full of senior managers from the organization. None of the participants, including the consultant, really knew why they were there. The chief executive had been very economical in giving out information. Introducing the consultant and saying, 'I don't really know why he's here, or whether he will do us any good', the chief executive announced his departure on a business trip – extending for the duration of the consultant's visit.

The consultant chose to make a partial use of SSM at this point. This choice had several purposes:

- It would enable the development of a relationship between himself and the senior managers.
- It would facilitate the development of his understanding of the organization.
- It would engage the senior managers in a participative dialogue, involving them immediately in the problem-solving process – the immediate problem being that of defining the problem to be solved!

Introducing himself and explaining his background provided the mechanism by which the participants could be drawn into the discussion. Questions and their answers were used to draw comparisons between the consultant's 'real-world' experience of organizations (his mental model) and the 'real world' of the participants (their various mental models).

Within thirty minutes of the start of the process, open and frank exchanges of views were occurring between the managers. The consultant was reduced to the role of referee. The problem of identifying the problem had begun.

changes in the actual situation – that is, changes which are systemically desirable and are considered achievable within the culture of the particular organization. There are few, if any, absolute rights or wrongs at this stage. The point of the exercise is more the process itself (for generating mutual understanding and appreciation) than the outcomes – although unless these lead to practical and beneficial changes in the organization, the exercise may be seen as somewhat sterile. The final outcome should be a set of changes to which all parties are willing to commit themselves.

The final stage of the process, stage 7, is 'taking action' – that is, implementing within the real-world situation the changes that have been proposed. These may affect any part of the totality of the organization studied – that is, its structure (organization design, job design), attitudes (the culture and values) and procedures (the actual operations of the organization). The total process is shown diagrammatically in Figure 29.1.

29.1.3 Critical review

While SSM does not preclude the inclusion of large numbers of people in the process, the approach is often recognized as working best with relatively small numbers. The methodology offers no specific help in using SSM in a situation where there are large numbers and where some degree of 'order' needs to be brought into the inquiry process, say in a factory employing two thousand workers, or in a total organization which might employ hundreds of thousands of staff in a distributed network of offices and factories. A more apparently useful approach for such organizations is Ackoff's Interactive Planning (IP) (Ackoff, 1981), which will be discussed in the next section. This approach adheres to the participative and subjective views recognized in SSM but provides a structured method for involving all the people in the organization in the process of creating its future.

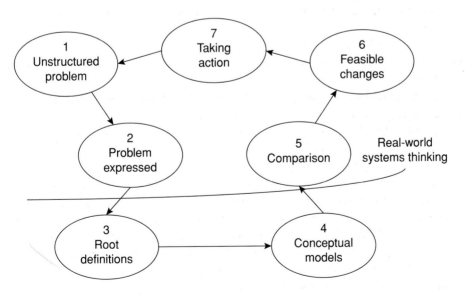

Figure 29.1 Soft systems methodology

SSM has great strength in its capacity to bring together groups with diverse opinions and offer them a structured process through which those opinions can be debated. However, it does not offer any form of desired, or ideal-type, outcome. It does not suggest any principles to which an ideal solution should adhere, other than the forming of a consensus view. The solutions proposed therefore will ameliorate the concerns of those participating in the process but not necessarily others who, either willingly or not, are excluded from the process. Neither will it necessarily adhere to any specific organizational, cultural or procedural principles which might be thought desirable. Unless these things are already present within the 'weltanschauung' of the participants or introduced at the problem definition stage, there is no scope for them to be considered.

29.2 INTERACTIVE PLANNING

29.2.1 Principles and conception

Ackoff holds the view that a planning methodology is required which enables people to plan for themselves, rather than be planned for by others. He sees such a methodology as enabling the participants to make their own values and ideals paramount in the planning process. This lets participants express their own view of 'reality' rather than having the reality of others forced upon them, and it necessitates wide participation in the creation of the future of organizations. Reflecting ideas already met in other approaches, IP recognizes three sets of interests in the organization: those of the organization itself as a purposeful, viable entity; the interests of the wider community (environment) in which it exists; and the interests of the individuals who work within it.

Interactivist planners take into account the past, present and predictions about the future as inputs to a planning process aimed at creating their future and the mechanisms by which it can be achieved. They work with their conception of the ideal future for the organization.

IP rests on the three principles of participation, continuity and holism. The participative principle is that all stakeholders should participate in the stages of the planning process. Ackoff, like Checkland, suggests that the process of planning is more important than the plan which is produced, since it is the process which enables individual contributions to be made and it enhances understanding of the whole organization by those involved with it.

The principle of continuity recognizes that values and ideals of the stakeholders change over time and that further problems and new possibilities emerge during the implementation of any plans. For Ackoff, this means that the plans must be adapted to meet these changes such that they continually reflect the current circumstances; perhaps they should be considered as for ever in final draft form! This idea reflects the notion of 'learning' examined in Chapter 19 and the organizational proposals made in Chapter 27.

The last principle is that of holism – that is, systemic thinking. This suggests that planning should be simultaneously and interdependently carried out for the entire organization (or at least, as many parts and levels as is possible). The notion of holistic or systemic thinking has already been explored in Chapter 14.

To enable the participative principle of Interactive Planning to be practised, Ackoff proposes a particular form of planning organization. This form is seen as embedding the planning process as an integral part of the organization. In this design, the organization is divided into planning boards. The heads of units within the organization are members of boards at three levels: their own, the one above and the ones below. In this respect, they act similarly to and may be characterized as like Likert's 'linking pins', or perhaps as the 'policy' function in the Viable System Model which links recursive levels. At the highest level, external stakeholders are represented on the board, while at the lowest level all the workers are members of their unit board. This organization could usefully be used as a design for linking the activities of quality circles within an organization.

Although it is apparently time-consuming, with some managers belonging to as many as ten boards, the organization is considered to derive major benefit through improved communication, co-ordination and integration of ideas. Morale is also improved. The organization of IP is represented diagrammatically in Figure 29.2. It can clearly be seen that this structure does not replace the existing hierarchy, but interleaves with it. It is a hierarchy of planning rather than control. This generates possibilities of communication and debate which the power hierarchy itself tends to inhibit. It is particularly noteworthy that the approach explicitly incorporates the views of external stakeholders, who might, for example, include local government representatives, community leaders, suppliers and perhaps customers or consumers of

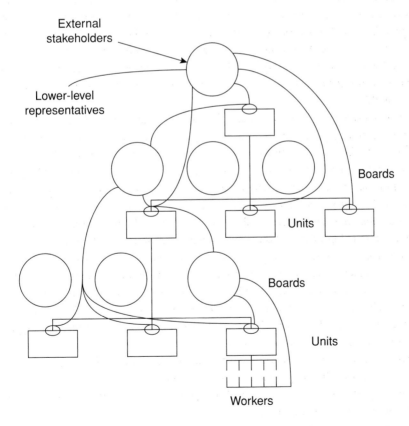

Figure 29.2 *Organizational design for Interactive Planning*
Adapted from Ackoff (1981)

the product or service. This has evident implications for organizations pursuing quality programmes. For example, where a supplier development strategy is being pursued, suppliers can be linked into the planning process of the organization. Similarly, customer feedback becomes truly meaningful when the customers form a part of the organization.

29.2.2 Methodology

The methodology for IP includes five steps (Box 29.4). Holding to the systemic requirements of the approach, the process may be run in any order and the whole should be regarded as an iterative process, with plans, as already suggested, being always in the latest 'draft' form.

Formulating the mess (step 1) consists of a SWOT-type analysis intended to highlight the strengths, weaknesses, opportunities and threats faced by the organization. Ackoff proposes that a useful device is to work out the 'future the organization is currently in'. This is a scenario representing the future of the organization if nothing is done about its internal situation and the environment continues to develop along the lines anticipated. Ackoff suggests that this requires three types of study (Box 29.5). A synthesis of the three sets of results is considered as a reference scenario of the current 'mess'.

Ends planning (step 2) seeks to specify the future the organization wants. It begins with idealised redesign: a vision of the sort of organization the stakeholders would create if they were free to do so. This involves selecting a mission, specifying the attributes of the design, and designing the organization. Normally, two versions of this redesign are created, one constrained by the existing wider system, the other unconstrained. The difference between these two idealized organizations indicates to what extent the organization must address its efforts towards modifying its environment during the planning process.

Idealized redesign is a creative process and as such permits only two constraints. First, the design must be technologically feasible – that is, it must not rely on a potential future invention or breakthrough. Second, it must be operationally viable – that is, it must be capable of functioning if created.

Box 29.4 *Russell Ackoff's five steps of Interactive Planning*

Step 1   Formulating the mess

Step 2   Ends planning

Step 3   Means planning

Step 4   Resource planning

Step 5   Design of implementation and control

Box 29.5 *Three methods of 'formulating the mess' (Russell Ackoff)*

Systems analysis – which will detail the organization, how it works and its environment

Obstruction analysis – which will unearth the obstacles to corporate development

Reference projections – which predict future performance by extrapolating current performance in the given environment

Flood and Jackson (1991: 151) suggest that the design should answer to the criteria of the best 'ideal-seeking system' that the stockholders can imagine. From this point, it is clear that the organization designed must be capable of learning and adaptation. Ackoff's outline design for such a system requires it to be capable of:

- observation: to recognize opportunities and threats;
- decision making: enabling a response to those opportunities and threats;
- implementation: actually doing something;
- control: performance monitoring and self-correction;
- communication: the acquisition, generation and dissemination of information.

The alert reader will by now have identified some similarities in ideas between IP and other approaches already discussed such as the VSM with its requirement for implementation, co-ordination, control, development and policy – the five functions of management. It must be stated that there are some fundamental differences in the theories underpinning the approaches.

Means planning (step 3) is the term used for the process of generating the 'hows' to support the 'whats' of the first two steps. It is concerned with making operational the changes considered necessary by those involved. Alternative 'hows' should be generated, perhaps using some of the techniques outlined in earlier chapters of this book and comparisons made to find the most effective.

Resource planning (step 4) looks at the requirements for materials, supplies, energy and services – all of the inputs to the organization – as well as at facilities and equipment, personnel and money. For every aspect, it is necessary to determine what changes need to be made in order to support the idealized redesign. This stage is very similar to the internal business audit in a strategic review process as it attempts to assess the capabilities of the organization and its personnel.

Implementation and control (step 5) is concerned with ensuring that the decisions made are carried out. This involves the allocation of tasks and the monitoring of their completion. The outcomes of implementation should be fed back into the planning process such that necessary modifications and further changes can be made.

29.2.3 Critical review

IP shares with SSM the criticism that its outcomes are bounded by the knowledge and expectations of the participants in the process. For quality to be addressed as an issue, it must be highlighted at the outset as part of the formulation of the mess. Similarly, at the implementation phase, the need for knowledge of quality theory and practice must be recognized.

While IP and quality circles appear to have much in common, they are differentiated in two ways. First, quality circles operate only at a single level within the organization, whereas IP links all levels. Second, quality circles are focused on purely localized operational problems whereas IP, used properly, has the scope to capture strategic perspectives from the lowest levels of the organization. Quality circles may be thought of as a problem-solving technique, IP as a way of managing the organization.

Like SSM, IP is oriented towards defining the problem. It is focused on providing a methodology for generating solutions. It does not offer any guidance as to what those solutions should be, demanding only that they are derived in an emancipatory manner.

297

29.3 CRITICAL SYSTEMS HEURISTICS

29.3.1 Principles and conception

The work of Werner Ulrich – *Critical Heuristics of Social Planning* (1983) – broke new ground in systems thinking by setting out an emancipatory systems approach. This approach enables critical reflection upon the means and goals attained through hard systems thinking and the nature of consensus achieved through soft systems thinking.

The approach is intended to reveal the normative aspects of a proposal: the underlying value assumptions, consequences and side effects for those affected by planning. Ulrich suggests that whereas the dominant tools of systems thinking consider the means or ends in problem solving, there is a need to consider 'whether' – that is, to ask what 'ought to be done'. This is seen as enabling freedom of choice to create better social systems and leads to the development of procedures whereby those who are subject to the consequences of designs can challenge the rationality of the planners.

Ulrich's approach is considered to offer a method for proceeding in coercive situations, those where the powerful in society can impose their views on others. It is suggested that Critical Systems Heuristics (CSH) enables the true interests and motivations underlying proposals to be revealed and that plans must be supported by all stakeholders if they are to be considered rational.

By 'Critical Systems Heuristics', Ulrich is considered to mean the following:

- Critical: an approach which explores the assumptions underpinning a particular approach (in much the way this book has explored the work of the quality gurus);
- Systems: the network of elements and interactions to be studied;
- Heuristics: the iterative search process for developing a solution free from the bias of the planners (reflecting Ackoff's 'plan or be planned for').

The last part of this definition is suggestive of an 'ideal'-seeking process which maintains the assumptions and presuppositions at the forefront of the process of inquiry. They must be constantly open to question and debate.

Ulrich establishes a basic distinction between those 'involved' in a planning decision and those 'affected' but not involved, and creates a framework of twelve critically heuristic categories around this, together with three (Flood and Jackson, 1991: 201–202) 'quasi-transcendental ideas': systems, morality and guarantors. CSH rests on four principles (Box 29.6) which incorporate these three ideas together with a concept of purposefulness.

Box 29.6 *Werner Ulrich's four principles of Critical Systems Heuristics*

Principle 1	Purposefulness
Principle 2	Systems
Principle 3	Morality
Principle 4	Guarantor

298

Purposefulness requires that the ability to determine purpose should be spread throughout the system. The system should generate and disseminate knowledge relevant to purposes thus enabling debate. All plans should be critically examined in respect of their normative content.

The systems principle provides a critical standard against which understanding of the world (assumptions) can be measured. The moral principle requires system designers to continually seek to improve the total human condition through their designs. The guarantor principle recognizes that there can be no absolute guarantees of improvement. This principle requires that system designers seek opinions from a wide range of experts and from various stakeholder groups in creating proposals and that these proposals should be agreed by both those involved and those affected.

Essentially, Ulrich's approach may be considered as an endeavour, in a relatively practical way, to ensure the meaningful participation in social systems design by all those who are members of, or interact with, that system.

29.3.2 Methodology

The methodology of CSH consists in essence of two parts. In the first part, twelve questions are employed in two modes: 'is' and 'ought'. The first use, in the 'is' mode, is intended to reveal how the interests of four groups relevant to the system are served. These groups are the client, the decision taker, the designer(s) (those involved) and the witness(es) (those affected but not involved). The questions explore the value (normative) basis of the design by considering the basis of power and the basis of the design's legitimacy. The second use is in the 'ought' mode, examining whose interests perhaps should be served by the system. The questions are shown in Box 29.7.

Question 1 is concerned with defining who belongs to the group whose purposes (interests and values) are served, as distinct from those who do not benefit but may have to bear the costs or other disadvantages of a particular system design. Question 2 seeks to evaluate what is achieved as opposed to what the planners claim will be achieved. Question 3 considers the measurement of success in terms of what is actually achieved.

Question 4 seeks to establish who can actually change the measure of success by asking in whose terms success is measured. Question 5 tries to determine the resources necessary and constraints to be overcome to enable successful planning and implementation of the system.

Question 6 is concerned with defining the boundaries of the system, by attempting to determine which aspects fall within the system to be managed and which fall outside. Question 7 is concerned with identifying those who are undertaking the planning, while question 8 tries to differentiate between the expertise being offered and that which is desirable to develop a solution – questioning the legitimacy of their involvement. Question 9 seeks to establish how the promises made can be fulfilled, while question 10 seeks to establish who will be affected by the operation of the system but is not involved in it – and therefore has no direct influence on its operation.

Question 11 follows this by requiring the inclusion of representations from the 'affected but not involved' so that their views may be taken into account. Question 12 brings reflection upon the assumptions about the world which underpin the proposals being made. For example, in the quality context, question 12 might cause the participants to consider whether

Box 29.7 *Twelve questions for Critical Systems Heuristics in the 'is' and '(ought to be)' modes*

Question 1	Who is (*ought to be*) the actual client of the design of the system?
Question 2	What is (*ought to be*) the actual purpose of the system's design?
Question 3	What is (*ought to be*) the in-built measure of success?
Question 4	Who is (*ought to be*) actually the decision taker?
Question 5	What resources and constraints are really (*ought to be*) controlled by the decision taker?
Question 6	What resources and constraints are *not* (*ought not to be*) controlled by the decision taker?
Question 7	Who is (*ought to be*) actually involved as planner?
Question 8	Who is (*ought to be*) involved as expert?
Question 9	Where do the involved see the guarantee that their planning will be successful? (*Who ought to be the guarantor of success?*)
Question 10	Who among the involved witnesses represents the concerns of the affected? (*Who ought to get involved?*)
Question 11	Are the affected given an opportunity to emancipate themselves from the experts? (*To what extent ought the affected be able to escape the influence of the experts?*)
Question 12	What world-view is (*ought to be*) underlying the design of the system?

quality improvement was necessarily a good thing or whether it was simply a function of a particular set of assumptions and expectations about the world.

The gap between the two sets of answers is the basis for the second part of the methodology, the 'polemical employment of boundary judgements' – more commonly, the adoption by those engaged in the process of the standpoint of 'devil's advocate'. The objective of this dialectical debate is to force the system designers (the 'problem solvers'), through the process of debate, to demonstrate the validity of the boundaries to the system (the parameters under which it would operate and the expectations from it) which they have selected. Thus, rather than those 'affected but not involved' having to prove that their alternative views are correct, the planners must prove the superiority of the original boundaries.

The affected are able to demonstrate through this process that:

- The planners have employed boundary judgements in creating their proposals and calculating effects.
- The experts are not able through their expertise to prove, or justify, their own position, or alternatively to falsify those of their critics.
- Experts (planners) who are unable to justify their proposals on the basis of their 'knowledge' are employing dogmatically or cynically held positions and hence disqualify themselves from the debate.

The employment of this polemical process is considered to generate an equality of position between the parties, enabling 'reasonable dialogue'.

Through the process of exploration and debate outlined, it is considered that system design can be explored and modified to better meet the needs of those both involved and affected.

29.3.3 Critical review

The process of CSH is, of course, only useful where all parties are willing to contribute to the process and to make adaptations based upon the findings. Where overt coercion exists (in other words, the circumstances in which this approach is most fully justified), it may be considered unlikely that the powerful would willingly engage in debate with the weak. They are more likely simply to use their power to overrule.

The approach is most useful in the pursuit of quality at the outset of a TQM programme. Considered use of CSH at this stage may enable the revelation of barriers to the quality movement by enabling both the involved and the affected to highlight hopes and fears which usually remain unexpressed. It is these hopes and fears, the 'hidden agendas' of the participants, that often prove fatal to the quality initiative. For example, a management might recognize the need for improved quality in order for their organization to continue to compete and survive, but also recognize that this may generate threats to their own positions as well as that of the workforce – they are involved and affected. The workforce itself may also consider threats to be present – to job security, to accepted and accustomed working practices, indeed to a whole way of organizational life. The CSH approach should enable all these fears and hopes to be expressed through the questioning and debating process, enabling them to be accounted for in the system design, and granting the experts insights which they would not otherwise have. Equally, the affected, but not initially involved, will be better able to understand the motivation and rationale of the management.

One of the most beneficial effects may be the need which the process generates for 'self-reflection' by the powerful. The debating device will force them to express their understandings and, in so doing, to justify them to themselves. If they cannot do this, then they may well change their approach.

As with other 'soft systems'-based methodologies, the use of CSH does not lead to any specific problem solution. It will not generate a new organization chart or a different way of working. What it will do is enable the rationale behind any particular solution derived from another methodology to be justified in terms of the people affected.

SUMMARY

This chapter has reviewed three methodologies for participation in the creation of a quality organization. The need for an emancipatory approach to be taken to quality has been intro- duced — creating freedom of thought and action for all. The second part of the chapter introduced the theory and practice of Critical Systems Heuristics. Readers should refer to the work of Checkland (1981), Ackoff (1981) and Ulrich (1983, 1987) to further develop their understanding of this complex and demanding approach.

QUESTION

Compare the three methodologies outlined in this chapter. Under what circumstances would you use each? What particular difficulties might you experience with the use of Critical Systems Heuristics?

Chapter 30

Implementing quality programmes

'Suit the action to the word, the word to the action.'
(Shakespeare, *Hamlet* III, ii)

KEY LEARNING POINTS

Key idea concerning the implementation of quality programmes: quality projects *must* be holistic.

Methods: variety of techniques: Gantt charts, critical path analysis, project management from within the group(s) affected; ongoing control and adaptation of programmes.

Critique: tools must be used thoughtfully and systemically; recognize links between projects; managers must behave as they expect others to behave.

INTRODUCTION

It is necessary, but not sufficient, that those pursuing quality management should be competent in the use of the wide variety of quality-specific tools and methods available. It is also essential that those tools should be used in the context of a well-organized and overarching project methodology. A fragmented or partial approach will only generate partial quality management! It should be acknowledged that although implementing quality is a continuous activity and must become an embedded part of the management process of the organization, initiating a quality programme depends upon a successful first project.

The basic approaches of the quality gurus were outlined in Part two of this book, from Crosby's 'fourteen steps for quality improvement', through Deming's 'seven-point action plan', to Feigenbaum's 'four steps to Total Quality Control' and Ishikawa's 'Company-Wide Quality Control'. Each of these suffers from the limitation that it is designed to achieve those things which the particular guru finds important, and neglects other aspects of the process. Flood's (1993) holistic process attempts to overcome this difficulty by commencing the TQM initiative with an educational programme and encouraging eclectic use of all of the ideas of quality – in context and fully justified. Flood's process was outlined in Chapter 26. A thoughtful manager can work from the sets of principles for achieving quality outlined in this book, select appropriate tools and develop a quality programme which will work in his or her organization. To provide a further general TQM methodology would be redundant, so this chapter will examine some general issues of project management, implementation and control.

30.1 PROJECT MANAGEMENT

This section assumes that the quality process has been commenced using some of the tools already outlined and that what is required is to implement the projects. Project implementation consists of three sets of activities (Box 30.1).

Implementation is a dynamic, iterative process which continually steers a project towards its goal – a goal which may itself change during the life of the project. In a large-scale project, it is quite likely that the 'target' will move during its lifetime. For example, the benchmark against which original objectives were set may change, a new technology may move from the research laboratories into the mainstream, or the customer base of the organization may change substantially, all leading to a revision of plans.

Before commencing any project, it is vital that the project managers consider the major tasks to be completed, the order in which they should be undertaken, the resources required and the availability of 'float' or 'slippage' time within the project. They also need to take account of any constraints upon the project such as the availability of working capital, the effect of seasonal weather changes and the delivery commitments given to the client(s).

A small project with a limited number of variables and activities can be undertaken with a minimum use of the formal tools of project management. Larger projects, including TQM initiatives, should draw on these tools to support the process and ensure that the best results are obtained.

There are a number of approaches available for project planning. One of the oldest, and probably best known, is the Gantt chart. This device breaks the project down into its constituent parts and these are scheduled against the time frame of the project. Progress is indicated by use of shading. While useful – the Gantt chart is very simple – it does not take account of interdependency between separate elements and ignores 'slippage' or 'float' time. During the life of the project, it can be difficult to maintain awareness of activities which are behind schedule and whether the project can be completed on time. An example Gantt chart is provided in Figure 30.1.

The technique of network analysis (or critical path analysis) provides a more comprehensive system for planning and controlling large projects. Unlike Gantt charts, it recognizes

Box 30.1 *Three sets of activities that go to make up project implementation*

Planning

Implementation

Control

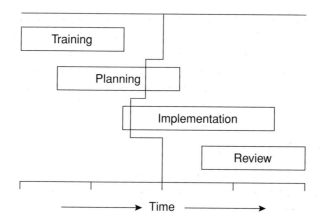

Figure 30.1 *A Gantt chart*

interdependency and highlights those events in the project which are critical – that is, those on which other events depend. Critical aspects are those which if not achieved on time will delay or prevent completion of the project, and managing these is vital in the programming of resources and in the minimization of project costs. The network process consists of two stages: preparing the network (Box 30.2) and analysing the network.

In the quality context, shortening of the project time may be desirable in order to meet the requirements of a key customer, or to establish a quality margin against a competitor whose activities constitute a threat. Major benefits are derived simply from the construction of the network since this forces the planners to consider every aspect in detail well in advance of implementation. This process should lead to improvement in the plan, provided a 'critical' stance is taken.

Each activity is represented within the network diagram by an arrow with a circle at each end. A letter is used to denote the activity, and numbers are used within the circles to denote events. Some activities within a project will be dependent on the completion of a prior activity, while

Box 30.2 *Critical path analysis*

Preparing a network
Define the scope and purpose of the project as a whole

Identify the various activities

Determine the logical relationships between activities and events (the start or end of individual activities) and construct the network diagram

Determine for each activity the probable duration, resources required and any restrictions, for example a starting date, or daytime working only

Analysing the network
Analyse the network to discover which jobs are critical in determining completion time

Determine whether or not it is economically feasible (or desirable for other reasons) to shorten the completion time others will be able to occur simultaneously. Where activities are carried out simultaneously, dummy events are introduced simply to resolve the logical difficulty of having separate activities defined by the same pair of events. Figure 30.2 provides a simple example. In this case, activity P can be carried out simultaneously with Q and R, but Q must be completed before R can commence. Activity S can be carried out simultaneously with Q and again must be completed before R begins. A dummy event T is introduced to enable the separation of the Q and S lines. Line lengths are of no significance; duration is given by the number below the line.

The 'critical path' is the route through the network which occupies the minimum time passing through all the critical points. In the case given, the route would be 1, 2, 3, 4, giving a duration of 13 minutes, since S must be completed before R is started. Activities R and S in this example are the critical activities, since delays affect the entire project, whereas P and Q are non-critical. They could be delayed by 6 minutes and 4 minutes respectively without affecting the overall time. This permissible delay time is called the total float.

The network provides a 'time budget' for the project (and may even be used to develop the financial budget if cost and time are directly related). As with any budget, it should be updated during the course of the project to incorporate 'actual' values achieved, and the balance of the project should be modified and replanned accordingly. Software packages are now available which will conduct and support network analysis.

A large project, one in which there are many variables or one with a long time line, would benefit from the construction of a dynamic project model. This involves developing the critical path analysis in a form which allows the modelling and simulation of events within the project in response to real events happening, ultimately a project plan which rewrites itself in response to ongoing events. The benefit of developing such an approach is that it allows the manager to simulate and evaluate a range of alternative strategies and resource allocation approaches in order to optimize the whole project. It also enables the easy assessment of the impact of changes and other, perhaps unforeseen events. Such models can be constructed easily within standard spreadsheet packages.

30.2 IMPLEMENTATION STRATEGIES

Implementation (through whichever set of methods and tools) can be achieved in two primary ways: expert-owned – a programme driven by a consultant or quality specialist; and self-owned – a programme owned and driven by the staff but supported by consultants or specialists.

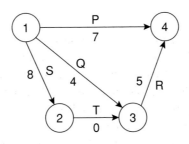

Figure 30.2 Example of a network

Expert-owned programmes are most common and commence with the appointment of a project manager and implementation team. Normally, such a team will take full responsibility for the project, identifying and making appropriate changes and handing over the new system or approach to the subject staff on a 'turnkey' basis. This team will deal with training, debugging new systems and procedures, and ironing out any difficulties before handing over the project.

Such an approach has significant advantages in certain circumstances, such as in 'greenfield' situations where there are no established methods or preconceived ideas. It can be very rapid (and consequently cost-effective) in the short term. The approach can take advantage of functional specialisms that would perhaps otherwise be unobtainable or very expensive. Its primary disadvantage, and particularly so in an established situation, is that it places ownership of the new methods in the hands of the project team rather than the affected staff. Success or failure is allocated by both management and staff to the project team and it is usually the case that barriers or objections to change are not eradicated but by-passed – those affected are over-ruled. This in turn may slow or inhibit the process of change and generates the possibility of reversion to previous approaches, in effect negating the work done.

The self-owned approach is both more sustainable and more effective. It involves appointing a project manager from within the affected group and supporting him or her with functional specialists as necessary, while using members of the working staff as the implementation team. They can then generate the changes for their area themselves, promoting ownership and acceptance of the changes and avoiding the difficulty of imposed change.

The role of the functional specialists then becomes to support the initiatives of the staff, rather than to take those initiatives themselves. This approach combines the high expertise of the functional specialists with the grassroots knowledge of the staff in the organization to produce solutions acceptable to all sides. The principal apparent disadvantage of this approach is that it can take longer to achieve the desired changes. This extra time, which perhaps bears an additional cost, must be balanced against the greater likelihood of creating accepted, sustainable change.

A further advantage of this approach is that the staff involved will learn from the functional specialists and thus enhance their own knowledge and understanding. While difficult to measure, this is a substantial benefit, as it establishes a 'change orientation' among the staff, and they come to recognize what is and is not possible from a new perspective. It also embeds the notion of learning in the organization. Experience of working in both implementation styles leads the writer to suggest that the second of these methods is to be preferred.

30.3 CONTROL

Control rests in a constant monitoring of project progress with information 'fed back' from the project used as the basis for comparison with expectations (usually derived from the Gantt chart or network). The results of the comparison are used as the basis for altering the inputs to the project, or perhaps changing the objectives, with consequent replanning of resource allocation. Readers will recognize this as a cybernetic process and that the Viable Systems architecture can be used to support the approach.

Altering the inputs to a project might include increasing or decreasing the level of resources used, enhancing the level of expertise employed when a particularly difficult problem has emerged, or bringing in new resources or expertise to deal with unexpected events or obstructions. Deming's PDCA cycle at the 'Check' stage, for example, would be expected to highlight difficulties or unexpected results from experiments, which would lead to redetermination of other changes which were themselves consequent upon the experimental change. Such unexpected results should be regarded not as failures, as is so often the case, but as part of the process of learning associated with an evolutionary activity. Experiments which do not produce the expected results are as valuable as those which do. Knowing how *not* to do something is at least as important as knowing how to do it. Used intelligently, this information enables further failures or continuation of a failing method to be avoided.

Equally, an unexpected success is a further opportunity for learning. It may be a conceptual or practical breakthrough which makes some future step in the process of change redundant, or a new opportunity arising as a result of the change. It is important that the control system can recognize these aspects and take advantage of them.

It is quite common in managing change programmes to persist for long periods with a particular experiment or trial and meet nothing but resistance from the workforce. This can, quite suddenly, be overcome, and it is important that the breakthrough moment is recognized and the advantage gained capitalized upon. Such a breakthrough in one area commonly creates the opportunity for breakthroughs in others.

Changing of project objectives becomes possible when the progress made indicates that the original objectives cannot be achieved (for whatever reason) or have become inappropriate, or objectives originally thought unattainable have become accessible owing to unexpected breakthroughs or progress. Frequently, those involved in the project will be criticized for setting objectives incorrectly, or for making 'mistakes'. It is a sign of good management that the need to change objectives has been realized and that action is proposed. This is a fundamental part of most quality approaches: a constant seeking of higher goals and higher achievements.

30.4 CRITICAL REVIEW

It is not possible to give other than a brief overview of the implementation of a quality programme in a text such as this. There are myriad techniques for project management available and in use, most of which will contribute value.

The overall pattern of planning, implementation and control applies just as much to the writing of this book or to undertaking a journey as it does to completing a quality programme. Nonetheless, the techniques identified are considered of great value in helping to understand the total implementation process, and they can be used at every level within the organization. For example, a Gantt chart could be prepared for the whole quality initiative and used as the driver for all the lower-level (recursive) quality initiatives. Hence, if Flood's programme were being used, each quality council would employ its own Gantt chart and these would be derived from and linked with each other. If the plans are not integrated in this way, then inevitably some aspect of the programme will fall through the gap. The important point is to use these tools thoughtfully, exploring how much they can help the organization rather than deriding them for how little they achieve on their own.

MANAGEMENT AND KEYBOARDS

A large institution employed staff who strongly resisted the introduction of PCs and an electronic mail system. They were accustomed to armies of PAs and typists producing all work requiring keyboard skills.

A key part of a service quality initiative for the organization involved shortening the timescale for responses to written enquiries (both internal and external), and it was recognized that this could be achieved by removing steps from the production chain – that is, encouraging staff to produce their own mail. It had also been demonstrated that this could be more cost-efficient up to quite senior management levels, could lead to a reduction in numbers employed and save significant quantities of paper.

Resistance was organization-wide. The staff would not accept the idea, and the IT experts could not confirm the cost–benefit case using their own costing model. The breakthrough arose when the directors were persuaded to allow a pilot study to be undertaken in one location where the general manager was open to the innovation.

In what could be seen as a coercive move, a wide area network was installed and staff were told that they were to receive these machines – not that they had to use them. In addition to e-mail facilities, the machines were equipped with spreadsheet and database packages which supported the 'non-correspondence' activities of the staff. They were trained to use the facilities, having accepted already that these would improve their performance and being able to measure the advantage to themselves of such a system. They soon 'discovered' the e-mail facility and started using it because they found that it enabled them to perform various tasks much more quickly. Within a month, the staff were typing the bulk of their own correspondence, the previous objections having been forgotten. They recognized, for themselves, the benefits of the system through acceptance of what had been originally a subsidiary use.

Once these staff acknowledged the benefits, resistance throughout the organization crumbled, and there was a sustained clamour of demand from many other locations for the same facilities. The IT department's personnel were able to prove the cost–benefit case (since they were able to amend their model to reflect a new reality), and indeed claimed credit for the whole operation, creating a model system for themselves within their own department!

This breakthrough in acceptance of one change created the possibility of other changes, previously equally strongly resisted, being accepted right across the organization. These changes affected job descriptions, management roles, staff numbers employed and a whole range of systems and procedures, all of which could be redesigned to support the quality initiative.

SUMMARY

This chapter has briefly introduced the overall process of quality implementation and shown how the three phases of planning, implementation and control can be managed.

QUESTION

Study the quality programme of one of the gurus featured in this text. Decide which activities you think fit into the three phases of planning, implementation and control. What additional steps would you add to these programmes to enhance them?

Afterword

Whatsoever is done rightly, however humble, is noble.
(Henry Royce)

Management commitment is the single most critical issue in the pursuit of quality. Without it, the programme will fail – as so many do.

Each of the writers on quality mentioned in this book mentions the need for this commitment – normally listing it as the first step in the programme. None, however, is very specific about how it can be obtained. The reasons given for pursuing quality are most often negative: to avoid failure, to reduce costs, to avoid defeat by overseas competition. While these are all conveniently measurable, they are also all inherently short term. They cause management to focus on the, often financial, return from pursuing quality – and quality consultants equally often package their programmes in terms of the direct cost–benefit case, reinforcing the approach. In terms of Maslow's hierarchy of needs (1970), quality programmes focused on avoidance are addressing basic organizational needs of physiology and safety.

These objectives are all in themselves worthwhile. It is important to achieve all of them. However, once they are achieved – in terms of the initial cost–benefit case – the focus of the organization may well, and often does, move on to some other short-term objective such as increasing market share or improving margins. The pressure for quality will subside in the face of increased emphasis on some other objective. Quality, in the absolute sense, can never be achieved. There will always be scope for further improvement, and once the pressure for improvement is released, the organization will tend to slide backwards towards a lower level of achievement.

In the context of an effective organization (one which is to be sustainable or viable in the long term), quality is not an objective, it is a given. The essence of effectiveness and survival for the organization rests in 'rightness': being perceived as providing a quality product or service. This 'rightness' arises from an attitude of mind which obtains satisfaction from doing the job correctly, for no other reason than that is the way the job should be done. This attitude most frequently comes out as a sense of caring: the sense that it matters to the individual whether or not the job is done correctly, not for the benefit of the measurement system or for the purposes of statistical process control, but just because it is right. This parallels Maslow's idea of self-actualization: to be all that one can be.

311

This attitude is most often met in those who work in the service sector, especially 'caring' professions: doctors and nurses, vicars, priests and rabbis. Similar behaviour can be observed in the tradition of the guild craftsmen, whether butchers or buttonmakers, whose only 'benchmark' or measure of quality performance may be against themselves: Are they pleased with what they have done? Is it the best that they could do?

It is met, though more rarely, in those pursuing other occupations. This attitude is met in unexpected places; it is remarked upon. It does delight the customer and may exceed their expectations.

Throughout this text, the concentration has been upon quality as an exercise in technical correctness – that reflects the literature on which it is based. However, 'caring' reflects the other aspect of quality: its aesthetic. Management must focus on pursuing quality not just for its short-term extrinsic benefit but for the intrinsic worth in attaining quality of product or service. They must truly believe in and pursue quality for its own sake.

Glossary of terms and abbreviations

AGIL   Adaptation, Goal, Integration, Latency – being the four functional imperatives considered necessary by Parsons and Smelser if a system is to continue to exist.

APEL   Accreditation of Prior Experience and Learning – a term used in relation to the award of certain qualifications, such as the National Vocational Qualifications in the UK, which take account of practice and experience, similar to apprenticeship-based qualification.

aphorism   A short, clever saying expressing a general truth.

benchmarking   Formal comparison of the processes and standards of one organization against those of another, with the aim of performance improvement.

black box   A technique for studying the behaviour of complex systems, used where the system to be studied is so complex as to be impossible to analyse or where an attempt at such analysis would destroy the phenomenon to be studied.

BS5750   British Standard quality management system (now subsumed into ISO 9000).

Business Process Re-engineering (BPR)   A process-oriented organizational performance discipline intended to transform the organization.

Business Systems Diamond   A meta-methodology for Business Process Re-engineering (BPR) linking the four key phases in the overall process of BPR.

Call-centre   A centralized telephone enquiry office designed to deal with high volumes of essentially similar telephone calls, e.g. telephone sales, account enquiry and complaint handling.

comfort zone   An accustomed way of behaving and working, drawn from the literature on psychology. The expression describes the method and style with which each individual is most at ease.

complementarism   An approach to problem solving in which choice and use of methodology is guided by the characteristics of the situation and understanding of the theory underpinning the method.

cowpath   A process that has evolved naturally to satisfy an objective but which, while effective, is not efficient.

CSH   Critical Systems Heuristics, an emancipatory approach to problem solving developed by Werner Ulrich and designed to ensure that those affected by plans have informed freedom of choice.

CST   Critical Systems Thinking, a technique that involves approaching problem solving by recognizing that the selection of tools should be dependent on the nature and culture of the organization studied and that any solution should work to improve human well-being and enable the development of human potential.

culture   The set of values and beliefs which guide behaviour in an organization or nation and define its identity.

deterministic/determinism   A deterministic system is one in which the outcome of any process or action can be known in advance – that is, it is designed to function in a particular and specific way and will always do so.

direct costs of quality   The visible costs of quality failure – for example, warranty and after-sales service work.

emergent properties   Behaviour which is exhibited by a whole system but by none of its parts.

empirical   Refers to knowledge derived from practice or observation, not theory.

EN 29000   European Standard quality management system (now subsumed into ISO 9000).

feedback   Communication enabling self-regulation, explicitly the use of the output of a system to modify its inputs in such a way as to bring the output nearer to a desired goal or state.

GDP per capita   The total amount of income generated by a nation through economic activity divided by its population.

guru   Originally a Hindu spiritual teacher now often used to refer to leaders in a discipline.

HACCP   Hazard Analysis Critical Control Points a food production management system which assures that critical criteria of temperature or duration are met to guarantee safety.

heuristic   A process of trial and error or test and evaluation applied to a process in order to derive a solution.

holism/holistic   The attempt to deal with organizations or systems as wholes rather than sets of parts.

HRM   Human Resource Management – the contemporary approach to managing people, which assumes that people are a strategic asset of the organization whose value can be maximized by investment in their development.

IIP   Investors in People, a UK government-supported standard for corporate training programmes. Organizations with programmes that conform to the standard are awarded the IIP status and are recognized for excellence in training.

invisible costs of quality   Consequential and hidden costs of quality failure such as customers who do not purchase again or service and maintenance costs which are carried by a separate part of the organization.

IP   Interactive Planning, Ackoff's approach to organizational development through the involvement of all employees in a series of linked planning boards.

ISO 9000   International Organization for Standardization guidelines for a quality management system.

ISO 14000   International Organization for Standardization guidelines for an environmental management system.

just-in-time (JIT)   A system of supply which delivers parts to a production process when they are required, obviating the need to hold stocks and thereby minimizing waste.

kaizen   A Japanese belief system oriented towards continuous improvement in *all* aspects of life.

kanban   The operating system to support just-in-time, consisting of a system of signals indicating needs.

mechanistic   Refers to a view of organizations which suggests that they and their staff can be organized to behave like machines.

meta   Of a higher logical order.

methodology   A systematic set of methods for studying issues and problems or a process for achieving a specified objective.

NIH   Not invented here – an attitude representing a barrier to change, a common response to initiatives generated in one department or organization for application in another.

normative   Concerned with defining ethics, morals and social standards.

organismic/organic   A view of organizations as being like organisms.

organizational cybernetics   The science of effective organization developed by Stafford Beer and expressed through the Viable System Model.

paradigm   A personal framework of thought or system of beliefs.

PDCA cycle   Plan, Do, Check, Action – a systematic continuous improvement cycle developed by Deming from the Shewhart cycle and extended to EPDCA by Oakland.

Poka-Yoke   defect = 0; a process standard developed by Shigeo Shingo for manufacturing processes in which the operation is stopped when a defect is detected and the process rectified before restarting.

probabilism/probabilistic   Behaviour, on the part of a system, which cannot be precisely predicted but which shows tendencies to behave in a particular way.

process   All the successive operations required to complete a task.

QA   Quality Assurance – methods for assuring quality by prior action.

QC   Quality control – methods for ensuring quality by *post hoc* inspection.

QFD   Quality function deployment – a systematic method developed by Oakland for designing a product or service around the expressed requirements of the customer.

QMS   Quality management system.

quality circle/(QC/QCC)   A problem-solving team for quality issues.

recursion   Structural invariance at different levels of an organization.

reductionism   A way of studying organizations through fragmentation and analysis.

replacement cycle   The time period between repeated purchases of a good or service.

rework   The fixing or repairing of defective finished goods before dispatch.

SBQM   Skills-Based Quality Management – a means of seeking to achieve quality, particularly in the service sector, based on the recording and developing of the skills of those who work for an organization.

self-regulation   The ability of a system to manage itself towards achievement of a goal.

slipping clutch syndrome   An effect on productivity and quality sometimes found when a production system is placed under pressure. As volume increases, so the rate of failure increases at an equivalent or greater rate.

SMED   Single-minute exchange of die – a fast-change process for machine tools developed by Shingo for Toyota to reduce delays in product changeovers on a production line.

soft systems   The study of organizations as human activity systems.

SOSM   The system of systems methodologies developed by Jackson and Keys to enable the selection of problem-solving methodologies appropriate to the relationships within a system and its complexity.

SSM   Soft Systems Methodology, developed by Checkland as a participative approach to problem solving.

stakeholder   A person, or another organization, affected by or involved with a particular organization.

Statistical Process Control (SPC)   A quantitative system for monitoring process performance and maintaining variability of the process within appropriate limits.

Statistical Quality Control (SQC)   A quantitative system for monitoring quality performance.

supplier development   A business strategy of co-operation between buyer and supplier to jointly improve quality.

syntegration   A process and structure for guaranteeing democracy in any problem-solving process.

systemic   Refers to an approach that deals with whole systems and the interactions of their elements and the environment.

total cost   The lifetime cost of purchasing, using and maintaining a product.

Total Quality Control   Feigenbaum's approach to quality and management.

TQM   Total Quality Management.

TSI   Total Systems Intervention – developed by Flood and Jackson as an iterative meta-method for solving organizational problems.

variety engineering   Techniques for managing probabilism by reducing the variety of the environment or increasing that of the organization.

VSD   Viable System Diagnosis – a methodology for using the Viable System Model which compares the organization with an idealized representation leading to action to close the gaps.

VSM   Viable System Model – developed by Stafford Beer as an idealized representation of an organization capable of survival and adaptation. The core model for organizational cybernetics.

zero defects   a quality target focusing on error-free production.

Further reading

Throughout this book, reference has been made to a wide selection of sources which have been found informative and interesting in the attempt to understand the role of quality in the wider context of management thinking, organization theory and emergent social issues. Following is a list of texts which will help the reader to explore further the themes and issues raised in this book.

Beer, S. (1959) *Cybernetics and Management*, Wiley, New York. Beer exposes in detail how an approach to organizations rooted in cybernetics can be applied to revolutionize management thinking.

Beer, S. (1974) *Designing Freedom*, Wiley, Chichester, UK. Beer discusses the impact of conventional management thinking on the development of society and suggests ways in which the apparent threats to freedom can be overcome. This book is Beer's most lucid attempt to elaborate his philosophy.

Crosby, P. (1979) *Quality Is Free*, Mentor, New York. Crosby introduces his quality approach in a highly readable, accessible text.

Deming, W. E. (1986) *Out of the Crisis*, MIT Center for Advanced Engineering, Cambridge, Mass. Deming elaborates his fears for the future of American industry and proposes solutions based on his quality thinking and practice.

Feigenbaum, A. V. (1986) *Total Quality Control*, McGraw-Hill, New York. This text provides a full explanation of Feigenbaum's approach to managing for quality.

Flood, R. L. (1993) *Beyond TQM*, Wiley, Chichester, UK. Flood develops his holistic approach to Total Quality Management, drawing on his background in systems science. The book is readily accessible to non-specialists in systems and quality.

Galbraith, J. (1974) *The New Industrial State*, Penguin, Harmondsworth, UK. Galbraith develops an argument about the power of big corporations in the future economy of the world.

Hannagan, T. J. (1986) *Mastering Statistics*, 2nd edition, Macmillan Education, Basingstoke, UK. Hannagan provides an introduction to the development and use of a wide variety of statistical techniques.

Hoff, B. (1994) *The Tao of Pooh and the Te of Piglet*, Methuen, London. Hoff provides an insight to Western systems thinking through a reinterpretation of elements of Chinese philosophy.

Hoyle, D. (1994) *ISO 9000 Quality Systems Handbook*, Butterworth-Heinemann, Oxford. Hoyle provides an easy-to-follow guide to developing and installing a quality management system.

Huczynski, A. and Buchanan, D. (1991) *Organisational Behaviour*, 2nd edition, Prentice-Hall International (UK) Ltd, Hemel Hempstead. This text provides a substantial and reader-friendly guide to the principal strands of management thinking which dominate contemporary organizations.

Huff, D. (1973) *How to Lie with Statistics*, Pelican, Harmondsworth, UK. Huff explores in an entertaining but ruthlessly critical manner the ways in which poor understanding of statistics is used to manipulate decision making.

Ishikawa, K. (1986) *Guide to Quality Control*, 2nd edition, Asian Productivity Organisation, Tokyo. This book, based upon Ishikawa's practical work, was originally developed as a guide for the work of quality circle members.

Juran, J. M. (1988) *Juran on Planning for Quality*, Free Press, New York. This substantial and detailed text provides the most useful guide to Juran's thinking and his approach to achieving quality.

Kanji, G. P. and Asher, M. (1996) *100 Methods for Total Quality Management*, Sage, London. The authors provide an easy-to-follow, simple 'how to' guide covering the major activities in a Total Quality Management programme.

Logothetis, N. (1992) *Managing for Total Quality*, Prentice-Hall International, London. Logothetis provides a guide to the statistically based methods for achieving quality.

Lovelock, J. (1979) *Gaia: A New Look at Life on Earth*, Oxford University Press, Oxford. Lovelock explains the development of his theory of the environment. Appreciation of this perspective helps in understanding the environmental imperative for the pursuit of quality.

Oakland, J. S. (1993) *Total Quality Management*, 2nd edition, Butterworth-Heinemann, Oxford. A readable and well-structured book in which Oakland elaborates in detail his programme for attaining quality.

Ormerod, P. (1994) *The Death of Economics*, Faber and Faber, London. Ormerod explores the assumptions which underpin much of currently dominant economic theory, highlighting the weaknesses and flaws which he perceives.

Pirsig, R. M. (1974) *Zen and the Art of Motorcycle Maintenance: An Inquiry into Values*, Black Swan Edition, Arrow Books, London. Presented as an account of a man's journey with his son, the book reflects a process of inquiry into two strands of quality thinking: the technical and aesthetic.

Shingo, S. (1987) *The Sayings of Shigeo Shingo: Key Strategies for Plant Improvement*, (trans. A. P. Dillon, Productivity Press, Portland, Oreg., 1987): Shingo's message is expressed through his many mottoes for achieving quality.

Stickland, F. (1998) *The Dynamics of Change*, Routledge, London. Based on his doctoral research, this is a book that offers fascinating insights into the processes of organizational change through analogies with the natural world.

Taguchi, G. (1987) *Systems of Experimental Design*, vols 1 and 2, Unipub/Kraus, International Publications, New York. Taguchi's own guide to his process for developing quality within the product and the production process.

Waldrop, S. (1992) *Complexity*, Simon and Schuster, New York. Waldrop reports the development of complexity theory, giving insight to thinking about organizations as non-linear dynamic systems.

Warboys, B. C., Kawalek, P., Robertson, I. and Greenwood, R. M. (1999) *Business Information Systems: A Process Approach*, McGraw Hill, New York. Very useful for understanding how to build information systems to support and reflect process orientation in organizations.

References

Ackoff, R. L. (1981) *Creating the Corporate Future*, Wiley, New York.

Ashby, W. R. (1952) *Design for a Brain*, Chapman and Hall, London.

Ashby, W. R. (1956) *An Introduction to Cybernetics*, Chapman and Hall, London.

Bank, J. (1992) *The Essence of Total Quality Management*, Prentice-Hall International, London.

Beckford, J. (1993) 'The viable system model: a more adequate tool for practising management?', Ph.D. thesis, University of Hull.

Beckford, J. (1995) 'Towards a participative methodology for the viable systems model', *Systemist*, 17 (3).

Beckford, J. and Dudley, P. (1998a) 'That's not very big, is it?', *Management Issues in Social Care* 5 (4).

Beckford, J. and Dudley, P. (1998b) 'Size isn't everything', *Management Issues in Social Care* 6 (1).

Beckford, J. and Dudley, P. (1999) 'It's what you do with it that counts', *Management Issues in Social Care* 6 (3).

Beer, S. (1959) *Cybernetics and Management*, Wiley, New York.

Beer, S. (1979) *The Heart of Enterprise*, Wiley, Chichester, UK.

Beer, S. (1981) *Brain of the Firm*, 2nd edition, Wiley, Chichester, UK.

Beer, S. (1985) *Diagnosing the System for Organisations*, Wiley, Chichester, UK.

Beer, S. (1994) *Beyond Dispute: The Invention of Team Syntegrity*, Wiley, Chichester, UK.

Bendell, T. (1989) *The Quality Gurus: What Can They Do for Your Company?*, Department of Trade and Industry, London, and Services Ltd, Nottingham.

Burns, T. and Stalker G. M. (1961) *The Management of Innovation*, Tavistock, London.

Burrell, G. and Morgan, G. (1979) *Sociological Paradigms and Organisational Analysis*, Heinemann, London.

Carroll, L. (1866) *Alice's Adventures in Wonderland*, Macmillan, London.

Checkland, P. B. (1978) 'The origins and nature of "hard" systems thinking', *Journal of Applied Systems Analysis*, 5 (2): 99.

Checkland, P. B. (1981) *Systems Thinking, Systems Practice*, Wiley, Chichester, UK.

Checkland, P. and Scholes, J. (1990) *Soft Systems Methodology in Action*, Wiley, Chichester, UK.

Clemson, B. (1984) *Cybernetics: A New Management Tool*, Abacus, Tunbridge Wells, UK.

Clutterbuck, D. and Crainer, S. (1990) *Makers of Management: Men and Women Who Changed the Business World*, Macmillan, London.

Crosby, P. (1979) *Quality Is Free*, Mentor, New York.

de Bono, E. (1970) *Lateral Thinking: A Text-Book of Creativity*, Spain Press, London.

Deming, W. E. (1982) *Quality, Productivity and Competitive Position*, MIT Press, Cambridge, Mass.

Deming, W. E. (1986) *Out of the Crisis*, MIT Center for Advanced Engineering Study, Cambridge, Mass.

Dudley, P. (2000) ' "Quality management or management quality?": An adaptive model of organization as the basis of organizational learning and quality provision', Ph.D. thesis, University of Hull.

Espejo, R. and Schwaninger, M. (1993) *Organisational Fitness: Corporate Effectiveness through Management Cybernetics* Campus Verlag, Frankfurt and New York.

Fayol, H. (1916) *Administration industrielle et générale*, SRL Dunod, Paris *General and Industrial Management*, (trans. Constance Storrs, Pitman, London, 1949).

Feigenbaum, A. V. (1986) *Total Quality Control*, McGraw-Hill, New York.

Fiedler, F. E. (1967) *A Theory of Leadership Effectiveness*, McGraw-Hill, New York.

Flood, R. L. (1993) *Beyond TQM*, Wiley, Chichester, UK.

Flood, R. L. (1999) *Rethinking the Fifth Discipline*, Routledge, London.

Flood, R. L. and Carson, E. R. (1988) *Dealing with Complexity*, Plenum, New York.

Flood, R. L. and Jackson, M. C. (1991) *Creative Problem Solving,* Wiley, Chichester, UK.

Flood, R. L. and Romm, N. R. A. (1996) *Diversity Management: Triple Loop Learning*, Wiley, Chichester, UK.

Galbraith, J. (1974) *The New Industrial State*, Penguin, Harmondsworth, UK.

Gilbert, J. (1992) *How to Eat an Elephant: A Slice-by-Slice Guide to Total Quality Management*, Tudor, London.

Gilbert, M. (1994) *Understanding Quality Management Standards*, Institute of Management, London.

Gleick, J. (1987) *Chaos*, Heinemann, London.

Hammer, M. and Champy, J. (1993) *Business Process Reengineering,* Nicholas Brealey, London.

Handy, C. (1985) *Understanding Organisations*, 3rd edition, Penguin, London.

Handy, C. (1990a) *The Age of Unreason*, Arrow, London.

Handy, C. (1990b) *Inside Organisations*, BBC Books, London.

Heller, R. (1989) *The Making of Managers*, Penguin, London.

Herzberg, F., Mausner, B. and Snyderman, B. B. (1959) *The Motivation to Work*, 2nd edition, Wiley, New York.

hofstede, g. (1980) 'Motivation, leadership and organization: do American theories apply abroad?', *Organizational Dynamics*, Summer, 42–63.

Hoyle, D. (1994) *ISO 9000 Quality Systems Handbook*, Butterworth-Heinemann, Oxford.

Huczynski, A. and Buchanan, D. (1991) *Organizational Behaviour*, 2nd edition, Prentice-Hall International (UK), Hemel Hempstead.

Ishikawa, K. (1985) *What Is Total Quality Control? The Japanese Way*, Prentice-Hall, London.

Ishikawa, K. (1986) *Guide to Quality Control*, 2nd edition, Asian Productivity Organisation, Tokyo.

Jackson, M. C. (1990) *Organisation Design and Behaviour: An MBA Manual*, University of Hull.

Jackson, M. C. (1991) *Systems Methodology for the Management Sciences*, Wiley, Chichester, UK.

Jackson, M. C. and Keys, P. (1984) 'Towards a system of systems methodologies', *Journal of the Operational Research Society* 35: 473–86.

Jay, A. (1987) *Management and Machiavelli*, revised edition. Hutchinson Business, London.

Johansson, H. J, McHugh, P., Pendelbury, A. J. and Wheeler, W. A. III (1993) *Business Process Reengineering*, Wiley, Chichester, UK.

Johnson, G. and Scholes, K. (1993) *Exploring Corporate Strategy*, 3rd edition, Prentice-Hall, Hemel Hempstead, UK.

Juran, J. (1988) *Juran on Planning for Quality*, Free Press, New York.

Kanji, G. K. and Asher, M. (1996) *100 Methods for Total Quality Management*, Sage, London.

Logothetis, N. (1992) *Managing for Total Quality*, Prentice-Hall International, London.

Lovelock, J. (1979) *Gaia: A New Look at Life on Earth*, Oxford University Press, Oxford.

Lovelock, J. (1988) *The Ages of Gaia*, Oxford University Press, Oxford.

Lovelock, J. (1991) *Gaia: The Practical Science of Planetary Medicine*, Gaia Books, London.

Lovelock, J. (2001) *Homage to Gaia: The Life of an Independent Scientist*, Oxford: Oxford University Press, 5th edition.

Lynn, J. and Jay, A. (1982) *Yes Minister*, BBC Books, London.

Lysons, K. (2000) *Purchasing and Supply Chain Management*, Englewood Cliffs, NJ: Prentice-Hall.

McGoldrick, G. (1994) *The Complete Quality Manual*, Longman, London.

McGregor, D. (1960) *The Human Side of Enterprise*, McGraw-Hill, New York.

Machiavelli, N. (1513) *The Prince*, trans. G. Bull (1961) Penguin, Harmondsworth.

Maslow, A. (1970) *Motivation and Personality*, 2nd edition, Harper and Row, New York.

Mason, R. O. and Mitroff, I. I. (1981) *Challenging Strategic Planning Assumptions*, Wiley, New York.

Mayo, E. (1949) *The Social Problems of an Industrial Civilisation*, Routledge and Kegan Paul, London.

Morgan, G. (1986) *Images of Organisation*, Sage, London.

Oakland, J. (1993) *Total Quality Management*, 2nd edition, Butterworth-Heinemann, Oxford.

Oakland, J. (1999) *Total Organizational Excellence: Achieving World-Class Performance*, Butterworth-Heinemann, Oxford.

Oliga, J. (1988) 'Methodological foundations of systems methodologies', in R. L. Flood and M. C. Jackson (eds) (1991) *Critical Systems Thinking: Directed Readings*, Wiley, Chichester, UK.

321

Parsons, T. and Smelser, N. J. (1956) *Economy and Society*, Routledge and Kegan Paul, London.

Peters, T. J. and Waterman, R. H. (1982) *In Search of Excellence*, HarperCollins, New York.

Pettigrew, A. and Fenton, E. (eds) (2000) *The Innovating Organization*, Sage, London.

Porter, L. and Tanner, S. (1996) *Assessing Business Excellence,* Butterworth-Heinemann, Oxford.

Porter, M., (1980) *Competitive Strategy: Techniques for Analysing Industries and Competitors*, Free Press, New York.

Porter, M. (1996) 'What is strategy?', *Harvard Business Review*, November–December, 61–78.

Pugh, D. S. (1990) *Organisation Theory*, 3rd edition, Penguin, London.

Pugh, D. S. and Hickson, D. J. (1976) *Organisational Structure in Its Context: The Aston Programme 1*, Saxon House, Aldershot, UK. (Fourth edition 1989.)

Pugh, D. and Hinings, C. R. (eds) (1976) *Organizational Structure – Extensions and Replications: The Aston Programme II*, Gower, Aldershot, UK.

Schoderbek, P. P., Schoderbek, C. G. and Kefalas, A. G. (1990) *Management Systems: Conceptual Considerations*, 4th edition, Business Publications, Dallas.

Semler, R. (1993) *Maverick!*, Arrow, London.

Senge, P. M. (1990) *The Fifth Discipline*, Century Business, London.

Shingo, S. (1987) *The Sayings of Shigeo Shingo*, trans. A. P. Dillon, Productivity Press, Portland, Oreg.

Singleton, W. T. (1974) *Man–Machine Systems*, Penguin, Harmondsworth, UK.

Taguchi, G. (1987) *Systems of Experimental Design*, vols 1 and 2, Unipub/Kraus International Publications, New York.

Taylor, F. (1911) *The Principles of Scientific Management*, Plimpton Press, Norwood, NJ.

Townsend, R. (1985) *Further up the Organisation*, Michael Joseph, London.

Trist, E. A. and Bamforth, K. W. (1951) 'Some social and psychological consequences of the Longwall method of coal-getting', in D. S. Pugh (ed.) *Organisation Theory: Selected Readings*, 3rd edition, 1990, Penguin, London.

Ulrich, W. (1983) *Critical Heuristics of Social Planning*, Haupt, Berne.

Ulrich, W. (1987) 'Critical heuristics of social systems design', *European Journal of Operational Research* 31: 276–283.

Waldrop, S. (1992) *Complexity*, Simon and Schuster, New York.

Waller, J., Allen, D. and Burns, A. (1993) *The Quality Management Manual*, Kogan Page, London.

Weber, M. (1924) 'Legitimate authority and bureaucracy', in D. S. Pugh (ed.) *Organisation Theory: Selected Readings*, 3rd edition, 1990, Penguin, London.

Wiener, N. (1948) *Cybernetics, or Control and Communication in the Animal and the Machine*, MIT Press, Cambridge, Mass.

Woodward, J. (1965) *Industrial Organization: Theory and Practice*, Oxford University Press, London.

Index